FLORIDA STATE
UNIVERSITY LIBRARIES

JAN 10 1997

TALLAHASSEE, FLORIDA

COLLECTED PAPERS

PHAENOMENOLOGICA
SERIES FOUNDED BY H.L. VAN BREDA AND PUBLISHED UNDER THE AUSPICES OF THE HUSSERL-ARCHIVES

136

A. SCHUTZ

COLLECTED PAPERS

Editorial Board: Director: R. Bernet (Husserl-Archief, Leuven) Secretary: J. Taminiaux (Centre d' études phénoménologiques, Louvain-la-Neuve) Members: S. IJsseling (Husserl-Archief, Leuven), H. Leonardy (Centre d' études phénoménologiques, Louvain-la-Neuve), U. Melle (Husserl-Archief, Leuven), B. Stevens (Centre d' études phénoménologiques, Louvain-la-Neuve) Advisory Board: R. Bernasconi (Memphis State University), D. Carr (Emory University, Atlanta), E.S. Casey (State University of New York at Stony Brook), R. Cobb-Stevens (Boston College), J.F. Courtine (Archives-Husserl, Paris), F. Dastur (Université de Paris XX), K. Düsing (Husserl-Archiv, Köln), J. Hart (Indiana University, Bloomington), K. Held (Bergische Universität Wuppertal), D. Janicaud (Université de Nice), K.E. Kaehler (Husserl-Archiv, Köln), D. Lohmar (Husserl-Archiv, Köln), W.R. McKenna (Miami University, Oxford, USA), J.N. Mohanty (Temple University, Philadelphia), E.W. Orth (Universität Trier), B. Rang (Husserl-Archief Freiburg i.Br.), K. Schuhmann (University of Utrecht), C. Sini (Università degli Studi di Milano), R. Sokolowski (Catholic University of America, Washington D.C.), E. Ströker (Universität Köln), B. Waldenfels (Ruhr-Universität, Bochum)

Alfred Schutz

Collected Papers

Volume IV

Edited with preface and notes
by
Helmut Wagner and George Psathas
In collaboration with Fred Kersten

KLUWER ACADEMIC PUBLISHERS
DORDRECHT / BOSTON / LONDON

A C.I.P. Catalogue record for this book is available from the Library of Congress.

H
61
S44
v. 4

ISBN 0-7923-3760-3

Published by Kluwer Academic Publishers
P.O. Box 17, 3300 AA Dordrecht, The Netherlands.

Kluwer Academic Publishers incorporates
the publishing programmes of
D. Reidel, Martinus Nijhoff, Dr W. Junk and MTP Press.

Sold and distributed in the U.S.A. and Canada
by Kluwer Academic Publishers,
101 Philip Drive, Norwell, MA 02061, U.S.A.

In all other countries, sold and distributed
by Kluwer Academic Publishers Group
P.O. Box 322, 3300 AH Dordrecht, The Netherlands.

printed on acid-free paper

All Rights Reserved
© 1996 Kluwer Academic Publishers
No part of the material protected by this copyright notice may be reproduced or
utilized in any form or by any means, electronic or mechanical,
including photocopying, recording or by any information storage and
retrieval system, without written permission from the copyright owners.

Printed in The Netherlands

ALFRED SCHUTZ

Table of Contents

B
STUDIES IN THE METHODOLOGY OF SOCIAL THEORY

Foreword

In November 1982 Mrs Schutz and I first discussed the possibility of publishing this sequel to her husband's *Collected Papers*. Helmut Wagner brought this project to life. I remember them both with respect and gratitude and regret that neither of them can now see the final result in print.

I should like to thank those whose efforts have ensured that the work was completed: Lester Embree, Claire Wagner-Kimball, Evelyn Lang and Samuel IJsseling and especially George Psathas and Fred Kersten.

Alexander Schimmelpenninck,
Publisher

Editor's Preface

Dorion Cairns (or was it Aristotle?) once said that the worst fate that can befall a teacher is to have his work posthumously edited by his students. Uncertain whether this is necessarily true, I have nonetheless borne it in mind while editing the manuscripts of Alfred Schutz and, at times, editing the editing of the original editor, Helmut Wagner. Indeed, it must be said at the outset that this book is as much the book of Alfred Schutz as of Helmut Wagner.

The first three volumes of Schutz's *Collected Papers* were published between 1962–1966 by Martinus Nijhoff in The Netherlands. Some twenty years later the publisher agreed to publish one or more volumes, the actual content and editing of which were entrusted to Helmut Wagner by Ilse Schutz.[1] By the time of his death in 1989 Wagner had assembled a fourth volume containing 39 items in various stages of editorial completion. The selection had its foundation in Wagner's *Alfred Schutz: An Intellectual Biography*, a short version of which had been published by the University of Chicago Press in 1983. The items included were manuscripts and publications of Schutz during his last fifteen years in Europe in addition to manuscripts, lectures and in a few cases letters written by Schutz after 1939 during his stay in the United States. Although the contents of this fourth volume of *Collected Papers* differ greatly from that of the first three volumes, there is a continuity intended by Wagner and which is perhaps best indicated by the volume-title provided by Wagner: "Complementary Studies of the Problem of Social Reality, of Sociological Theory and of Phenomenological Philosophy."

Before his death Wagner had consulted with his friend and colleague at Boston University, George Psathas, about the contents and editing of this volume. After Wagner's death, Psathas worked on the manuscript of Volume IV until 1992 when it was turned over to me for completion. In many respects, arriving on the scene this late created new, and compounded old, editorial problems, the resolution of which further delayed publication of the volume. To indicate what was involved, as well as to give an idea in advance of the nature of the contents of the fourth volume, it is

[1]For a list of the unpublished papers of Alfred Schutz now in the Beinecke Library at Yale University, and a bibliography of published writings by and about Alfred Schutz, see Manuel Martín Algarra, *Materiales para el Estudio de Alfred Schutz* (Servicio de Publicaciones de la Universidad de Navarra, 1991).

best to refer to a surviving draft of Wagner's introduction to the whole volume followed by brief discussion of the final shape now taken by the volume.

The central organization of this volume followed that of the thematic divisions of the first three volumes: the Problem of Social Reality, with its subdivisions of "On the Methodology of the Social Sciences" and "Phenomenology of the Social Sciences"; Studies in Social Theory, subdivided into "Pure Theory" and "Applied Theory"; and Phenomenological Philosophy. These thematic divisions, as Wagner notes, covered the various areas Schutz wished to consider starting with his "plan for life" of 1924 and continued to the last months of Schutz's life.[2] Moreover, they enabled Schutz himself to establish the organization and contents of the first three volumes of *Collected Papers* by the end of 1958. With one exception, Wagner was able to fit, with some variation, the contents of Volume IV into the systematic scheme of the first three volumes. The one exception is best described by Wagner himself:[3]

> Nevertheless, I decided on one drastic measure by adding a fourth major category to the three Schutz had set up: it was to contain writings dealing with the representative performing arts, that is, opera, chamber music, drama, literature in its several forms. Schutz had published two essays on music and on making music; he placed them into the "Applied Theory" section of *Collected Papers II*. By contrast, I found seven items falling under the topics of music and literature, three of them of considerable length, others quite short. Thus I had quantitatively ample materials for an additional dual section. Of course, even if one adds the two published items on music to the unpublished ones he would not have enough for a fourth volume of the Collected Papers in the original sense. For this reason alone I could not assume that Schutz would have subsumed them under the number IV. But maybe he would have brought them together in a third part of *Collected Papers II*.
>
> I am suggesting this possibility because Schutz was amazed to find that phenomenologists dealing with perception and apperception – from Husserl to Gurwitsch – worked exclusively with assumptions drawn from the areas of vision and non-musical acoustics and unjustifiably converted the results from observations in these partial areas into a universal theory of perception and apperception.
>
> In any case there can be no doubt that, for instance, operative performances, both in the part of the performers and their audiences, form their own quite specific provinces of meaning with their own unique, closed systems of relevances. The same goes for the writers of novels, short stories, and poems and the reception of their creations by listeners and/or readers. The separation of these – and other – areas of artistic experiences from the array of other provinces of meaning is not only justified but systematically necessary.

As George Psathas notes in a draft of his Preface to Volume IV, the one portion of Volume IV which unfortunately remained unfinished and unassembled by Wagner

[2]In this connection, see Helmut Wagner, *Alfred Schutz: An Intellectual Biography* (Chicago: University of Chicago Press, 1983), pp. 16ff.

[3]In his unfinished Introduction to Volume IV.

was just the section on music and literature; indeed, it is not at all clear exactly what materials Wagner intended to include, or how he would have set up the thematic subsections for them.[4] Thus the basic shape of Volume IV consists chiefly of writings that fit under the first three categories.

Those writings range from finished and published ones to almost finished and publishable drafts to unfinished and rough (often untitled) drafts to sets of notes and sequences of terms in catchword style, and finally in a few cases unpublished letters. In consultation with Ilse Schutz, Wagner selected those manuscripts he thought "publishable" (at times rejecting as "unpublishable" even more finished drafts such as those on Goethe's *Wilhelm Meister* or even the essay on Eliot's *Four Quartets* which Schutz himself deemed unpublishable). Of course, this does not mean that the manuscripts are at last "publishable" in any sense in which Schutz himself would have regarded them. But as a whole or in details, or in both, these manuscripts express ideas of value to Schutz as well as to students of his thought, especially to those who are familiar with his published work, his style of philosophizing and his unique approach to problems not just in philosophy but also in sociology, economics and legal theory.

Wagner had edited the manuscripts, at times reconstructing them. Wherever possible I have retained Wagner's editing which, however, was itself not finished at the time of his death. On occasion, therefore, I have had to edit his editing (just as, on occasion, I have found it necessary to revise his translations of Schutz's German writings into English). Still, I have always sought to retain both the spirit and substance of his editing and translating, referring the reader wherever possible to Wagner's discussion of the manuscripts in question to his intellectual biography of Schutz. Similarly, in the case of Schutz's manuscripts themselves I have made no further attempt to make them publishable in the way Schutz himself may have envisioned them. In most cases, what we have are *unpublished drafts* made readable by the least editing possible. Here I have taken my cue from Schutz himself in editing a manuscript of Edmund Husserl because what Schutz said about Husserl may be applied to Schutz himself in most of the writings in Volume IV.

In publishing an unfinished manuscript of Husserl, Schutz says, we believe that "a glimpse of Husserl at work will definitely be a source of emotion and interest to those students <of Husserl> in addition to the fundamental importance of the problem developed by the author in these notes. We are not presenting a finished work of Husserl but a fragment of work in progress – "quasi una fantasia" – to use the words of Beethoven. But where is the friend of music who would not be delighted to have a true record of an improvisation of Beethoven, played by him, offhand in the seclusion

[4]It is likely, although not at all certain, that Wagner would have followed the organization of the materials he published in the second part of *Life Forms and Meaning Structure* (London: Routledge & Kegan Paul, 1982); no doubt he would have added Schutz's "Fragments on the Phenomenology of Music" published in 1976 in *In Search of Musical Method*, edited by F.J. Smith (London: Gordon and Breach Science Publishers, pp. 5–72). In any case, in part because *Life Forms and Meaning Structure* is readily available, and because it is uncertain whether Wagner would have included the relevant sections in Volume IV, and because "Fragments on the Phenomenolgy of Music" is difficult to come by, only the latter has been included in the present volume, and as an appendix rather than as part of the main text of the volume.

of his workshop?"[5] And in most cases, precisely what we have are fragments of work in progress, glimpses of Schutz at work, perhaps more importantly a "true record" of improvisations of Schutz, played by him offhand in his own workshop.

Inevitably, however, some changes had to be made so as to shorten a volume already sizeable. The following manuscripts have been omitted from Wagner's original plan:

From Part II:

1. "From General Economic Theory to the Study of Meta-scientific Foundations"; aside from the incompleteness of the manuscript, it repeats the substance of "Political Economy: Conduct of Man in Social Life" (Chapter 10).
2. The various manuscripts making up "The Problem of Personality" and "Personality and the Social World" have been omitted; although Wagner had begun a very elaborate collation and reconstruction of both manuscripts, I found them to difficult to reconstruct in English without first reconstructing them in the original German – a task which I am not competent to do. (Should there ever be a Vth Volume of the *Collected Papers*, these substantial manuscripts should certainly be part of it.)
3. "Parsons' Theory of Social Action" and "Choice and the Social Sciences" have been omitted because the first was published by Richard Grathoff in *Alfred Schütz/Aron Gurwitsch: Briefwechsel 1939–1959* [6] while the second had already been published by Lester Embree.[7]

From Part III:

1. "Doubts and Derailments: Trouble with Noemata", which has been published in the Schutz/Gurwitsch Correspondence.
2. "Intentionality and Identity" and
3. "On the founding of Typifications" have been likewise omitted because of their prior publication in the Correspondence.
4. "Husserl and His Influence on Me" has been omitted because it too has been previously published.[8]

Together these omissions have made it possible to include, with some new editing, Schutz's "Fragments on the Phenomenology of Music" as an appendix.

All footnotes are either mine and/or adaptations of Wagner's and, in a few cases, those of Alfred Schutz. Those footnotes which Wagner would not have added are marked [FK]. The separate prefaces to each of the manuscripts are similarly adaptations of notes and comments of Helmut Wagner along with other material that I have been able to add. In order to indicate separately notes, additions and glosses in the texts, the following devices have been used: those of Helmut Wagner are in angle brackets (< >), those of Alfred Schutz are in parentheses (( )), and those by Fred

[5]Editor's Preface to Husserl, "Notizen zur Raumkonstitution", *Philosophy and Phenomenological Research* I (1940), p. 22. See below, Chapter Twenty One.

[6]Wilhelm Fink Verlag, 1985. English translation by J. Claude Evans, Forward by Maurice Natanson, *Philosophers in Exile. The Correspondence of Alfred Schutz and Aron Gurwitsch 1939–1959* (Bloomington and Indianapolis: University of Indiana Press, 1989).

[7]In *Life-World and Consciousness. Essays for Aron Gurwitsch*, edited by Lester E. Embree (Evanston: Northwestern University Press, 1972).

[8]In *Annals of Phenomenological Sociology* II (1977), edited by Lester E. Embree.

Kersten are in square brackets ([ ]). Throughout his many manuscripts Schutz refers to Weber's *verstehende Soziologie*. There would seem to be no fully adequate English translation of this term, and throughout I have followed Wagner's practice of translating it as "understanding sociology". Other German terms are placed in brackets after the translation. For the translation of Husserl's terms, I have followed, whenever possible, the suggestions of Dorion Cairns.

It remains to mention the following persons: George Psathas, Lester Embree and Claire Wagner-Kimball. Their help has been kind and generous, and is gratefully acknowledged here. I also wish to thank Helen Sebba for permission to use the translation of her late husband, Dr. Gregor Sebba, of Schutz's letter to Eric Voegelin.

The constant encouragement and support of Dr. Alexander Schimmelpenninck and Ms. Maja de Keijzer has been of great value to me. Without them the preparation and publication of this volume would not have been possible. I am especially grateful to Ingrid Lombaerts at the Husserl-Archives in Louvain for her careful proofreading of the manuscript.

Of Helmut Wagner George Psathas said that he "was a consummate scholar, a diligent and careful craftsman who had, in the last several years of his life, devoted himself to increasing our knowledge of Alfred Schutz's life and thought. . . . I think it is most appropriate to dedicate this volume, which represents Wagner's dedication to Alfred Schutz, to the memory also of Helmut Wagner." I wholeheartedly agree with George Psathas, and am honored to so dedicate this volume to Helmut Wagner: a friend and scholar to be sure, committed to advancing the thought of Alfred Schutz, but surely also a highly literate and original thinker in his own right.

Fred Kersten,
University of Wisconsin-Green Bay

PART ONE

The Problem of Social Reality

CHAPTER 1

Outline of a Theory of Relevance

Editor's Preface

Consisting of two pages of coherent outlines, one page of outline partly overlapping the others, and a fragment of an outline filling a fourth page, this manuscript was translated and assembled by Helmut Wagner so as to provide an orderly, readable text. With the title, "*Relevanz*", at the top of the first three pages, the manuscript contains sections written out alternating with telegraphic jottings. On occasion Wagner expanded upon the jottings and combined formulations found in different parts of the manuscript and added a few further simple editorial emendations to the text.

The manuscript pages are not dated. However, Walter Sprondel, who made the first complete inventory of Schutz's literary estate, surmised that it was written in 1929. Wagner suggested instead that it was written either at the end of 1927 or the beginning of 1928. The reason for the suggestion is that the content of the manuscript expresses the very beginning of Schutz's transition from a Bergsonian to a Husserlian phase in his thinking at the time when he started work on the book which would be published as *Der sinnhafte Aufbau der sozialen Welt*: *Eine Einleitung in die verstehende Soziologie* (1932). The manuscript, then, charts an important shift in thought from 1927/28.[1] For this reason Wagner selected this manuscript to head those comprising the first part of those included in this fourth volume of Schutz's *Collected Papers*.

The concept of relevance is the central concept of sociology and of the cultural sciences [*Geisteswissenschaften*]. However, the basic phenomenon of relevance reaches beyond them into every life; it permeates our existing, our living and cognizing experience.

[1]For this important shift in Schutz's thought, see Helmut Wagner, *Alfred Schutz: An Intellectual Biography*, pp. 21f., 35, 38ff.; Helmut Wagner, with Ilja Srubar, *A Bergsonian Bridge to Phenomenological Psychology* (Washington, D.C.: Center for Advanced Research in Phenomenology, 1984), especially Part II; and Alfred Schutz, *Life Forms and Meaning Structure*, Translated, Introduced and Annotated by Helmut Wagner (London: Routledge & Kegan Paul, 1982), especially Wagner's notes to Part I.

The Course of the Investigation

1. Demonstrating the setting of the problem of relevance in various spheres, notably in the social sciences;
2. discussing the typical formulations of the problem of relevance demonstrated in terms of objective possibility and of adequacy of meaning.

The basic *problem of relevance* concerns a selection from the totality of the world which is pregiven to life as well as to thinking. In itself the problem is a familiar one in the history of philosophy. There exists no area of philosophical speculation – ranging from the theory of sensations to metaphysics and from ontology to theodicy – which would not clearly point to the facts that such selections occur everywhere and there are no thinkers who would not practice such selections, be it in an idealistic or transcendental-critical way. This is shown as much in Hume's theory of perception as in pragmatism and in Bergson's theory of pure memory as it is in Husserl's intuition of essences [*Wesensschau*] or in Kant's separation of inner sense from apperception. It is in this connection that the opposition between thinking and living is to be considered.

Consider an example of relevance serving as a guide for selectivity in a relatively simple philosophical sphere. Philosophers frequently speak of *knowledge* as such <and treat it as self-sufficient if not explanatory>. A counter-example is found in the differentiation of three kinds of knowledge by Max Scheler: knowledge for the sake of domination, knowledge for the sake of knowing, and knowledge for the sake of salvation.

In the social sciences a rigid distinction is made between a) Science and b) Object. <This distinction is made manifest> in:

1. the selection of problems;
2. the ideal types and ideal-typical constructions (chance, interpretation of meaning, and so on). For example, consider Goethe's letter to Madame von Stein (chances of the Now);
3. the object of the social sciences itself: the sociological person. (This may be illustrated by examples from) the comedy of characters <which owes its success to> exaggeration <of features of persons encountered in daily life>;
4. the intended meaning: meaning meant (the pragmatic motive).

<The following examples may be drawn> from other sciences:

History: 1) the battle of Marathon; 2) Schiller and Christianity; 3) the nose of Cleopatra; 4) the apple of Newton; 5) Cesare Borgia.

Political Economy: economically relevant data *ceteris paribus*.

Jurisprudence: Establishment of the juridically relevant *Sachverhalt* and *Tatbestand* <factual circumstances and state of facts> as interpretations of reality.

Natural Sciences: the law of free-falling bodies <based on the conceptual and mathematical> idealization <of the space in which solid bodies can be observed under laboratory conditions which are, ideally, free of air but actually contain highly rarefied amounts of air which allow for some> air resistance <and thus make directly observable proof of the law impossible>. The law of free-fall is based on a reduction to categories.

Other concerns: 1) autobiography; 2) poetry and literature; 3) music; 4) Goethe's saying: "taking the first step we are free; taking the second step we are slaves."
Attempts at solution: 1) value consideration; 2) pragmatic criteria; 3) tangible interests; and 4) meaning in general: Meaning (or sense) and relevance are correlated. <The question of> what is meaning <must be divided into two groups of problems>: the temporality of meaning and the adequacy of meaning.
<Concerning temporality>: Only that which has passed is relevant. Examples can be taken from one's own life, from literature, from music.

<For proof of the directedness of relevance toward the past we will have to look at the temporal features of> the flow of duration – the spatio-temporality <of human experience> – the dual <past-future> constituting factors – and the constituted object – consult Husserl, Hofmann,[2] Heidegger.

Acting and Action

Modus perfecti of relevance and *modus futuri exacti*.[3] Relation between purpose [or end] and means. Intentions tending toward a value. In the Now everything is either relevant or trivial. Nevertheless the reference is directed upon the Now.

The illusionary circle of relevance <is connected with the assumption> that something has contributed to the constitution of the Now in such a manner that it could be eliminated in thought afterwards without changing the Now resulting from it into something "other."[4]

[2] Wagner found it difficult to identify the "Hofmann" referred to here. My guess is that it is Paul Hofmann, whose *Das Verstehen von Sinn und seine Allgemeingültigkeit* had appeared about the same time Schutz was writing this manuscript (c. 1928/29), and its mention would thus confirm Wagner's dating of the manuscript. Hofmann's work was also known to Aron Gurwitsch (see his *Human Encounters in the Social World* [Pittsburgh: Duquesne University Press, 1979], pp. 90ff. FK

[3] Wagner's gloss on this passage is: "the grammatical modes of the completed act and of the planned act imagined as having been accomplished at a time still belonging to the future."

[4] As recontructed and translated by Wagner, the manuscript breaks off here.

CHAPTER 2

The Problem of Rationality in the Social World. A Lecture Delivered at the Faculty Club of Harvard University on April 13th, 1940

Editors' Preface

The title is that of Alfred Schutz for a lecture he gave at the Harvard Faculty Club on the invitation of Joseph Schumpeter and Talcott Parsons. A shorter version of the lecture was published in 1943 by the British journal *Economica* (New Series, I, 1943, pp. 130–149), and reprinted in Alfred Schutz, *Collected Papers*, Vol. II, pp. 79–88 under the same title (although misdated as a lecture given in 1942).

Wagner notes that, historically, this was Schutz's first substantial manuscript written in English and therefore required more than the usual number of editorial changes. These changes are not identified except in a few unusual cases. The lecture itself, Wagner notes, marks the beginning of Schutz's enthusiastic but short-lived hopes for initiating an important dialogue with Talcott Parsons centered around Parsons' *The Structure of Social Action* (1937). Schutz had read the book before arriving in the United States and thought of it as a study by someone sympathetic to Max Weber and, as Wagner suggests, one who was well on his way to becoming Schutz's American counterpart: a sociologist of phenomenological persuasion. It is no longer a surprise that these expectations were unfounded. According to Wagner, Schutz had misinterpreted Parsons' intentions and thus conceived tendencies to correct Weber's subjective approach as signs of a struggle towards a social-psychological and phenomenological position akin to that of Schutz. In actuality, Parsons had rather acquired a kind of neo-Kantian position which served him in his attempt to establish a "structural-functional" sociological system.[1] In any case, the dialogue and exchange of ideas were unsuccessful. Yet, perhaps for this very reason the published correspondence of Schutz and Parsons remains of great importance for defining two very different views of "rationality in the social world".

[1]See *The Theory of Social Action. The Correspondence of Alfred Schutz and Talcott Parsons* (Bloomington: Indiana University Press, 1978), edited by Richard Grathoff, Foreword by Maurice Natanson, pp. xiif.; and Helmut Wagner, *Alfred Schutz: An Intellectual Biography*, pp. 75ff.

I

This paper deals with the problem of "Rationality in the Social World", or rather with the problem suggested by the term, "rationality". In fact, this term represents only inadequately a conceptual scheme which itself is central to the methodology and epistemology of the scientific observation of the social world. Therefore it is a rather difficult task to isolate the question of rationality from all surrounding problems. In addition, the term, "rational action", is used with many different meanings not only in the general literature but also frequently in the writings of the same author; so, for instance, by Max Weber. But ambiguous use is not the only thing that renders its interpretation uncertain. Taken alone this would be only a terminological discomfort which could be overcome by a conveniently broad definition.

You may remember the scheme of the many and heterogeneous concepts labelled "rationality" presented by Professor Schumpeter. In order to clarify these equivocations and varying connotations we have to penetrate deeper into the structure of the social world and to make extensive inquiries into the special attitudes social scientists have toward their subject matter.

I shall start by giving you the gist of my conclusions from my inquiries, and then will proceed to discuss the steps by which I reached those conclusions.

I want to defend the following thesis: In its *strict* meaning, rationality is a category of the scientific observation of the social world and not a category of the mind of the actor within the social world. Therefore, in its primary denotation, the conceptual scheme of rationality is valid only on the level of theoretical observation; its application to other levels of our experience of the social world is possible only in a modified and restricted sense. Its *restricted* meaning in general has been expressed best in the definition given by Professor Parsons in his most remarkable study, *The Structure of Social Action*: "Action is rational in so far as it pursues ends possible within the conditions of the situation, and by the means which, among those available to the actor, are intrinsically best adapted to the end for reasons understandable and verifiable by positive empirical science." In his careful manner, the author always indicates the methodological problem he is dealing with and comments on the definition as follows:

> Since science is the rational achievement par excellence, the mode of approach here outlined is in terms of the analogy between the scientific investigator and the actor in ordinary practical activities. The starting point is that of conceiving the actor as coming to know the facts of the situation in which he acts and thus the conditions necessary and means available for the realization of his ends. As applied to the means-end relationship this is essentially a matter of the accurate prediction of various possible ways of altering the situation (employment of alternative means) and the resultant choice among them. Apart from questions relating to the choice of ends and from those relating to 'effort', where the standard is applicable at all, there is little difficulty in conceiving the actor as thus analogous to the scientist whose knowledge is the principal determinant of his action in so far as his actual course conforms with the expectations of the observer who has, as Pareto says, 'a more extended knowledge of the circumstances'.

Based on these principles, Parsons developed his theory of "the rational unit act" which is described as "a concrete unit of concrete systems of action. It is a unit which is, within the framework of the general action scheme, arrived at by maximizing one important property of unit acts – rationality."

In my opinion, this abstract by Professor Parsons gives the best available resumé of the widely used concept of rational action. I have quoted Professor Parsons' statements verbatim in order to show that he clearly sees the great methodological difficulties he has indicated. My analysis is not aimed at criticizing Professor Parsons' statement of a broad theory but at examining this theory itself. To avoid any misunderstanding, I want to stress first of all that I fully agree with his chief thesis concerning the methodological significance of the conceptual scheme of the "rational unit act" in so far as what is in question is social theory. Once I have reached this theoretical level, I think that there is no important difference between Professor Parsons' interpretation of the conceptual scheme of the "rational unit act" and my own ideas.

Yet it seems important to me to accentuate and specify the particularity of this theoretical level in contrast to the other strata of our experience of the social world. Therefore I will start by examining what we really mean when we speak of different levels of scientific research. After this I shall try to give a short description of the social world as it appears in daily life to the man who lives in it naïvely among his fellow men. After having described the acting and thinking of this man, I shall answer the question as to whether this type of acting in daily life can be classified as rational or not. Furthermore, I shall analyze the conceptual scheme of deliberate and planned action of this man under the supposition that he has a choice among several alternatives.

With these preliminary considerations out of the way, I can now begin to consider how the social world appears to the scientific observer and ask the question of whether the world of scientific research, with all its categories of meaning interpretation and with all its conceptual schemes of action, is identical with the world in which the observed actor acts. Anticipating the result, I may state immediately that with the shift from one level to the other, all conceptual schemes and all the terms of interpretation must be modified.

II

Proceeding in this direction, I encounter several problems overlapping with the problem of rational action and the "rational act unit" in Professor Parsons' sense

First: The conceptual scheme of rational action presupposes a more or less definite knowledge of, or orientation within, the world in which this action is performed. In this sense the term, "rationality", is not specific to the conceptual scheme of action; it embraces the conceptual scheme of the world in general and is only one element in it. Therefore, we also must examine the problem of orientation in this world.

Second: We ought to keep in mind that all interpretation of the social world has to start from the actor's subjective point of view. Therefore, we cannot accept the term, "unit act", as such without trying to reduce it to its subjective meaning. Here I have to discuss in general why I insist on the subjective point of view. This is more than the whim of a few social scientists; social science cannot be built up except by taking cognizance of the subjective meaning the actor connects with his acting.

Third: Finally, I have to discuss the fact that there are social sciences operating on high theoretical levels which, like economics, apparently prefer to deal with statistical curves and mathematical formulae rather than with actions of human beings in the social world, yet they use the term, "rational action", as an indispensable element of their systems. I will have to show what modification this term undergoes in these types of social sciences.

III

The same object appears to different observers in different ways. Philosophers have illustrated this with the example of the same city that appears to different persons in different ways according to their individual vantage points. I don't wish to overuse this example, but it can be helpful in clarifying the difference between our view of the social world in which we naïvely live and the social world as an object of scientific observation. The man raised in a city will orient himself in its streets with the help of habits he has acquired in his daily life. He may not have a consistent concept of the geographical organization of the city. And if he uses the subway to go from his home to his office, a large part of the city may remain quite unknown to him. Nevertheless, he has a proper sense of the distances between different places and of the direction in which these places are situated in relation to the point he considers the center. Usually this center will be his home; it may suffice for him to know that he will find nearby a subway or a bus which will bring certain other points within his reach. Therefore he can say that he knows his city. And although his kind of knowledge is full of gaps it is practically sufficient for <his ordinary needs>.

When a foreigner comes to the city he has to acquire an orientation in and a knowledge of it. For him nothing is self-explanatory and he has to ask an expert – in this case, a native – to find out the direction in which he has to go from one point to another. Of course, he can refer to a map of the city. But to use this map correctly, he has to know first of all the meanings of the signs on the map. Furthermore, he has to know where he is in the city as well as the correlate of this point on the map and at least one more point in order to relate the signs on the map to the correct real objects in the city.

A cartographer must use entirely different means of orientation if he wants to draw a map of the city. There are several means open to him. He can start with an aerial photograph; he can place a theodolite at a known place in the city, measure a certain distance and calculate trigonometric functions, etc. The science of cartography has developed standard types of such researches which the cartographer must know before drawing his maps. Likewise he must observe the rules of his trade when drawing a map. By contrast we non-cartographers do not have to bother with the details of their technique. For our purposes it is sufficient that a science exists at all which prescribes methods and rules for the activities of cartographers.

The city is the same for all three types of persons we have mentioned: the native, the foreigner, and the cartographer. But for the native, it has a special meaning: "my home city". For the foreigner, it is a place in which he has to live and work for some time. For the cartographer, it is the object of his science; he is interested in it only for the purpose of drawing a map. We may say that the three consider the same object from different levels.

We would be astonished to learn of a cartographer who restricts himself to information collected from natives. However, social scientists frequently choose this strange method. No doubt they sense that their scientific work is done on another level of interpretation and understanding than that of the naive attitudes in orientation and interpretation characteristic of people in everyday life. When social scientists speak of different levels they think in general that the whole difference between the two levels consists in a different degree of concreteness or generality without considering that these two terms are only chapter headings for all complicated problems. The full depths of these problems cannot be fathomed in this survey, yet I have to try to render the question of different levels somewhat more intelligible.

As human beings we all have the tendency in our daily life as well as in our scientific work to presume naïvely that what we have verified once will continue to be valid for the future, and that what appeared to us beyond question yesterday will be beyond question tomorrow. We may make this presumption without danger if we deal with presuppositions of a purely logical character, or with empirical statements of very high generality, even though it can be shown that these kinds of propositions too have a limited realm of applicability. On the other hand, on what is called a concrete level, we are forced to admit many suppositions without questioning them. We may even consider the level of our actual research as being defined by the sum total of the unquestioned presuppositions which we make by taking the position from which we envisage the interrelation of the problems and aspects under scrutiny. Accordingly jumping from one level to another means that certain presuppositions of our research, formerly unquestioned, are being called into question now. What formerly was given datum for our problem now becomes problematic. With the shift in our point of view new problems and factual aspects emerge while others disappear even though before they had been in the center of our problematic. This fact alone suffices to initiate a thorough modification of the meaning of all the terms used on the former level. Therefore careful control of such modifications of meaning is indispensable in order to avoid the danger of naïvely transposing terms and propositions from one level to the other although their validity is essentially limited to one level and its implicated suppositions.

Phenomenological theory has made very particular and important contributions to a better understanding of the phenomena just characterized. But I do not intend to deal with this complicated problem from the phenomenological angle. I am able to refer to a great and well-established American tradition and to the powerful thought of one of the greatest philosophers of this century – to William James and his theory of conception. He taught us that each of our concepts has its fringes surrounding a nucleus of unmodified meaning. In all our voluntary thinking, he wrote, there is some topic or subject about which all the members of thought revolve. We constantly feel the relations of our concepts to our topics or interests in their fringes. Each word in a sentence is felt not only as a word but as having a meaning. Thus, taken dynamically in a sentence, the meaning of the word without context is quite different. (And, he adds, "The dynamic meaning is used usually reduced to the bare fringes we have described – of felt suitability for or unfitness within the context in question. The static meaning then is abstract, the meaning consists of other words surrounding the so-called definition.")

It is not our task to discuss James' theory of such fringes and their genesis in the stream of thought. It suffices for our purpose to state the context in which a concept or term is used and its relation to the topic of interest – in our case, the problem already creates specific modifications of the fringes surrounding the nucleus or even of the nucleus as such. Again, it was William James who explained that we do not apperceive isolated phenomena but rather a field of several interrelated and interwoven things as it emerges in the stream of our thought. For our purposes the theory satisfactorily explains the phenomenon of the modification of the meaning of a term by transposition to another level. It is hoped that these fugitive remarks will sufficiently characterize the problem with which we are dealing.

I want to state now that, in my opinion, the term, "rationality", or at least the concept at which it aims, occupies the specific place of a key concept within the framework of the social sciences. The particularity of key concepts is that, once introduced into an apparently uniform system, they constitute the differentiates between the points of view I call "levels". Therefore the meaning of key concepts does not depend on the level on which the actual research occurs. To the contrary, the level on which the research may be done depends on the meaning attributed to the key concepts. The construction of the latter, first of all, has been divided into several levels that formerly appeared as a homogeneous field of research. Anticipating what I will have to prove later, I shall characterize the level made accessible by the term, "rational action". It is a chief principle of the method of the social sciences and as such nothing else than the level of theoretical observation and interpretation of the social world.

IV

As scientifically trained observers of the social world, we are not practically but only cognitively interested in it. That means: we are not acting in it with full responsibility for the consequences. Rather we are contemplating the social world with the same detached equanimity with which physicists contemplate their experiments. But let us remember that in spite of our scientific activity we remain human beings in our daily life, men among fellow men with whom we are manifoldly interrelated. To be more precise: even our scientific activity itself is based on cooperation among us scientists, cooperation by mutual influence and mutual criticism.

Yet so far as our scientific activity is grounded in social relations it is one among other emanations of our human nature and certainly pertains to our daily life governed by the social relations and activities which we designate by the categories of vocation and avocation, of work and leisure, of planning and accomplishing. Scientific activity as a social phenomenon is one thing, the specific attitude toward his problems which the scientist has to adopt is another thing. Considered purely as human activity, scientific work is distinguished from other human activities by the mere fact that it constitutes the archetype of rational interpretation and rational action.

If we understand the term, "rationality", in the connotation given to it by Professor Parsons, as quoted, we must conclude that in daily life we seldom act rationally. Even more, we do not rationally interpret the social world surrounding us unless special circumstances compel us to abandon our basic attitude of just "living along". Let me examine this situation more closely, starting with a description of the structure of the social world as it seems to be given to each of us in his daily life.

It seems that, once upon a time, each of us naïvely organized his social world and his daily life in such a way that now he actually finds himself in the center of the social cosmos surrounding him. Or better: we are born into an organized social cosmos. It is organized for us in so far as it contains all the useful equipment to allow us and our fellow men to live routinely our daily lives. On the one hand, there are institutions of various kinds, tools, machines, etc., and, on the other hand, habits, traditions, rules and experiences both actual and vicarious. Furthermore, there is quite an agglomeration of systematized relations with members of our immediate families, with kin, personal friends, people we know personally, people we met once in our lives and relations with those anonymous men who work somewhere and in a way we cannot and need not imagine but who see to it that a letter we put in a mailbox reaches the addressee in time, or that the bulb in the lamp lights up with the turn of a switch.

The social world, with alter egos in their various degrees of intimacy, is arranged around the self as a center. Here am I and next to me are alter egos of whom, as Kipling says, I know "their naked souls". Then come those with whom I share time and space and who I know more or less intimately. Next in order are the manifold relations I have with people in whose personality I am interested, even if I should know them only indirectly through their writings or the reports of others: so my social relation to the author of the book I am reading now.

On the other hand, in the technical meaning of the term, I am in a social relation, albeit in a superficial and momentary way, with others who are of no interest to me as personalities but only because they happen to perform functions in which I am interested. So the sales girl in the department store where I buy my shaving cream or the man who shines my shoes. Perhaps they are much more interesting personalities than many of my friends. I don't ask. I am not interested in social contact with these people; I just want to get my shaving cream and have my shoes shined. In this sense it makes little difference to me when, in making a telephone call, an operator or a dial intervenes. Incidentally, to enter the remotest sphere of social relations, the dial too has its social function; it refers, as do all artifacts of human activities, to the man who invented, designed and promoted it. But it is not guided by a special motive; I do not ask for the history and genesis and technique of construction of the tools and institutions created by other people's activities. Likewise I do not ask about the personality and destiny of fellow men whose activities I consider as mere *typical* functions. In any case, it is important for our problem that I can use the telephone effectively without knowing how it functions; I am interested only in the fact that it functions. Only the accomplished function interests me whether it is due to the intervention of a human being whose motives remain undisclosed to me or to a mechanism whose operation I do not need to understand. What counts is the typicality of the occurrence in a typified situation.

In this organization of the social world by the human being living naïvely in it, we find the germ of the system of types and typical relations which we will recognize later in all its ramifications as the essential features of the scientific method. This typification progresses in the same proportion in which the personality of the fellowman disappears behind the undisclosed anonymity of his function. If one wishes to do so, he may interpret this process of progressive typifications also as one of rationalization. At least Max Weber had this in mind when he spoke about the "disenchantment of the world" as one variation of "rationalization". This term points to the transformation of an uncontrollable and unintelligible world into a seemingly depersonalized organization which we can understand and thereby master within a framework which makes forecasting possible.

Our fellowmen with their behavior and actions are given to us in different perspectives. In my opinion, this constitutes a fundamental problem which as yet has not received the attention of sociologists it merits. With few exceptions social scientists have failed to deal with this kind of rationalization within their conceptual framework. By contrast, each of us human beings who just lives along has mastered this task without planning to do so and without any effort in performing it. We did not need guidance through methodological considerations or conceptual schemes of means-end relations, nor were we guided by the notion that we had to live up to values. Our practical interests always arise in certain situations of our life and are modified by changes of these situations, the momentarily last of which occurs just now. This is the only relevant principle governing the building of the structure of perspectives in which the social world appears to us in daily life. All our visual apperceptions conform with the principles of this perspective and convey the impressions of depth and distance. In the same way, our apperceptions of the same social world necessarily occur in the basic mode of the perspectivist view.

Of course, the social world of a sixty-year old Chinese Buddhist during the time of the Ming dynasty is quite different from the social world of a twenty-year old American Christian in our day. But, and this is the point, both social worlds will be organized within the framework of the categories of familiarity and strangeness, personality and type, intimacy and anonymity. Furthermore, much of both worlds will be organized around the self who lives and acts in it.

V

Let me go further in the analysis of the knowledge that we have of the world in which we live naïvely – the social as well as the natural one. As healthy, grown-up and wide-awake human beings (we are not speaking of others) we have that knowledge, so to speak, automatically on hand. Our store of experience is built up from heritage and education, from the manifold sedimentations of traditions, habits of our own, and previous reflections. It embraces the most heterogeneous kinds of knowledge in a jumbled and confused state. Clear and distinct experiences are intermingled with vague conjectures; superstitions and prejudices cut across well-proven evidences; motives, means and ends as well as causes and effects are strung together without a clear understanding of their real connections. Everywhere there are gaps, intermissions, discontinuities. Apparently there is a kind of organization by habits, rules and principles which we use effectively. However, the origin of our habits for the most part is beyond our grasp; we therefore rely on rules of thumb whose validity has never been verified. In part, the principles with which we start have been taken over uncritically from parents or teachers. In part, we have distilled them from experiences in specific situations in our life or in the lives of others. We have accepted them without making any further inquiries into their consistency. Nowhere do we have a guarantee of the reliability of all the assumptions which govern our conduct.

Yet, on the other hand, these experiences and rules suffice for mastering our practical life. And normally we have to act and to reflect in order to comply with the demands of momentary situations that it is our task to master. We are not interested in a "quest for certainty". We are satisfied with having a fair chance to realize our purpose on hand; and we like to think that this chance is good when we set in motion the same mechanism of habits, rules and principles which formerly stood the test and assume that it will stand the test now. The store of our knowledge for daily life does not exclude hypotheses, inductions and predictions: but they all have the characteristics of the approximate and typical. The ideal of everyday knowledge is neither certainty nor probability in a mathematical sense but just likelihood.

Anticipations of future states of affairs are conjectures about what is to be hoped for or feared or at best about what reasonably can be expected. Later, when the anticipated state of affairs has taken form in actuality, we don't say that our prediction has come true or was proven false, or that our hypothesis has stood the test, but that our hopes were or were not well-founded. The consistency of this system of knowledge is not that of natural law but that of *typical* sequences and relations.

I would like to call this kind of knowledge "cookbook knowledge". The cookbook contains recipes, lists of ingredients, formulae for mixing them, and directions for compounding the ingredients and the procedures. This is all we need to bake an apple pie. In principle this is also all we need in order to deal with the routine matters in our daily lives. If we enjoy the apple pie as prepared, we do not ask whether the manner of preparing it as prescribed by the recipe is the most appropriate from the hygienic or alimentary point of view, or whether it is the shortest, the most economical, the most efficient one. We just eat and enjoy it.

Most of our daily activities, from rising in the morning to going to bed at night, are of this kind. They are performed by following recipes reduced to automatic habits or unquestioned platitudes. This kind of knowledge is concerned only with the regularity of events in the external world as such, regardless of their origin. If it is regular it can be reasonably expected: the sun will rise tomorrow. While not equally certain, I have good reasons for anticipating that the subway train will bring me to my office if I choose the right entrance and put the nickel in the slot.

VI

In a superficial manner, the foregoing remarks have characterized the conceptual scheme of our everyday behavior, if the term, "conceptual scheme", can be applied at all. Do we have to classify behavior of this type as rational or irrational? Answering this question involves an analysis of the various equivocal implications hidden in the term, "rationality", as applied to the levels of experiences in daily life.

1. "Rational" is frequently used as synonymous with "reasonable". Certainly we act in a reasonable way when we assume that the recipes in the store of our experiences have been tested in analogous situations. However, rationality often means avoiding mechanical application of precedents, dropping the use of analogies, and searching for new ways to master situations.

2. Sometimes rational action is put on a par with acting deliberately; but the term, "deliberate", itself implies equivocal elements.

a. Routine action in daily life is deliberate in so far as it refers back to the original act of deliberation which once preceded the construction of the formula now taken by the actor as standard for this concrete behavior.
b. Defined conveniently, the term, "deliberate", may block the insight into the applicability of a recipe to a concrete situation simply because it stood the test in the past.
c. "Deliberation" may mean merely the anticipation of the end. This anticipation is always the motive of the actor to get the action going.
d. On the other hand, "deliberation", as used by Dewey in *Human Nature and Conduct*, means "a dramatic rehearsal in imagination of various competing possible lines of action." This meaning is of greatest importance for the theory of rationality. Following it we cannot classify the types of actions in daily life, as examined up to now, as deliberate actions. Characteristically the problem of choice among different possibilities does not enter into the field of consciousness of the actor in routine situations. Presently we shall come back to the problem of choice.

3. Rational action is frequently defined as "planned" or "projected" action without an indication of the meaning ascribed to the term, "planned", or "projected". I cannot simply assert that the non-rational routine acts of daily life lack conscious planning. On the contrary, they are embedded into the framework of our plans and projects. And, in fact, they are instruments for realizing them. Planning presupposes an end to be realized in stages. From one or another point of view each of these stages may be called either means or intermediate ends. <The exception would be the first and last stages of a whole project>.

Now, the function all routine work is a standardization and mechanization of the means-ends relation by referring standardized means to standardized classes of ends. A consequence of this standardization is the ignoring of the intermediate ends when consciously envisaging the chain of means that have to be applied in order to reach the planned end. At this point we encounter the interference of the problem of subjective meaning that I have mentioned before. I cannot speak about the unit-act as if the unit were constituted or demarcated by the observer. If we earnestly ask: when does an act start and when is it accomplished, we see that only the actor is qualified to answer this question. Let us take the following example:

A businessman organizes and plans his vocational life with the intention of retiring after ten years. Continuing his business activities means that he regularly goes to his office. For this purpose he has to leave his home at a certain hour, buy a ticket and take the train. He did so yesterday and he will do so tomorrow if nothing out the ordinary intervenes. Let us assume one day that he is late and thinks, "I will miss my train, I will be late in my office. Mr. X will be there waiting for me. He will be in a bad humor and maybe he will not sign the contract on which so much of my future depends." Let us assume that an observer watches this man rushing to the train "as usual" (as he thinks). Only the actor can give the answer because he alone knows the span of his plans and projects. All routine work, we dare say, is an instrumental process moving toward ends which are beyond routine work and determine it.

4. Frequently "rational" is identified with "predictable". This has been discussed already on the occasion of the analysis of prediction as a form of likelihood.

5. According to some authors, rational refers to the logical. Professor Parsons' definition is one example and reference to Pareto's theory of non-logical action is another. As concerns the scientific concept of the rational act, the reference to the system of logic applies. On the level of everyday experience, however, traditional logic cannot render the needed and expected services. Traditional logic is a logic of concepts based on certain idealizations and generalizations. For instance, by enforcing the postulate of clearness and distinctness of the concepts, traditional logic disregards the fringes surrounding the nucleus within the stream of thought. In contrast, thinking in daily life gains its chief interest from the fringes which, attached to the nucleus, relate to the actual situation of the thinker.

This is a very important point. It explains why Husserl classified the greater part of propositions in the thought of everyday life as "occasional propositions", that is, as valid and understandable only relative to the speaker's situation and their place in his stream of thought. It explains too why we understand our everyday thoughts less in terms of the antithesis of "true-false" than in the sliding transition of "likely-unlikely". We do not use everyday propositions with the purpose of establishing their formal validity within a certain realm which would be accepted by others as true, as a logician does, but for gaining knowledge valid for ourselves and for furthering our practical aims. So far, but only so far, the principle of pragmatism is extremely well-founded. It fits the style of everyday thought, but is not a theory of cognition.

6. Following the interpretation by other authors, the concept of rational act presupposes a choice between two or more means for acting toward the same end or even between two different ends in an effort to determine the most appropriate one.

This is the case I want to analyze in the next section. Up to now I have considered the social world of daily life like a native considers his hometown. Now I have to adopt the attitude of the foreigner who seeks to orient himself in an unfamiliar environment.

VII

As John Dewey has pointed out, in daily life we are largely preoccupied with the next step. We stop and think only when the sequence of doing is interrupted; disjunction in the form of a problem forces us to stop and rehearse alternative ways over, around or through it as our past experiences in collision with this problem suggest. Dewey's image of a dramatic rehearsal of future action is very fortunate. Indeed, we cannot determine which alternative will lead to the best possible results without imagining the act as already accomplished. Thus we have to place ourselves mentally into a future state of affairs which we imagine as already realized even though its realization would come only at the end of the contemplated action. Whether the ways and means of bringing about the desired result are appropriate or not can only be judged by considering the act as accomplished. <This is also the only relatively sure way of checking> whether the end to be realized fits into the general plan for our life. I like to call this technique of self-deliberation thinking in the "future perfect tense".

But there is a great difference between an action once actually accomplished and an action only imagined as accomplished. The actually accomplished act is irrevocable and we must assume the responsibility of its consequences whether it was successful or not. Imagination is always revocable and can be revised time and again. Simply by rehearsing several projects I can ascribe to each a different probability of success but I can never be disappointed by its failure. Like all other anticipations, the rehearsed future action contains gaps which will be closed only accomplishing it. Therefore the actor will see only retrospectively whether his project has stood the test or turned out a failure.

The technique of choice is this: in his mind, the actor runs through one alternative and then through the other, repeating the process until, to use the words of Bergson, the decision falls from it like a ripe fruit from a tree. Prerequisite for this is that the actor knows clearly that alternatives of means or even of ends actually exist. It would be erroneous to assume that recognition of such alternatives and therefore of choice are necessarily given in any case of human action and that, in consequence, all acting involves deliberation and preference. This interpretation confuses selection without comparison and alternatives with choice in the sense described.

As James pointed out, selection is a cardinal function of human consciousness. Interest is nothing but selection, but it is not necessarily coupled with deliberate choice between alternatives. Deliberate choice presupposes reflection, volition and preferences. When I walk through the garden discussing a problem with a friend and turn left or right, I have not chosen to do so. It is a question of psychology to determine the motives for such behavior; I cannot say that I preferred one direction to the other.

But there are situations in which each of us sits down and reflects on his problems. Speaking generally, he will do so at critical points in his life in which his chief interest is not to analyze his situation but to master it. Trying to find the most suitable solution, he will consult his emotions and affects as well as conduct in rational, self-deliberations. He is correct in doing so because these emotions and affects also have their roots in his practical interests.

In addition he will appeal to his stock of recipes, to the rules and skills arising out of his vocational life or his practical experiences. Likely he will find many systematized solutions in his standardized knowledge. Perhaps he will consult an expert; but again he will get nothing but recipes and systematized solutions. His choice will be deliberate. Having rehearsed the possibilities of action open to him in the future he will put into action in the future perfect tense that solution which seems to having the greatest chance of success.

But what are the conditions under which we may classify a deliberate act of choice as a rational one? It seems that we have to distinguish between the rationality of knowledge which is a prerequisite of rational choice and the rationality of the choice itself. Rationality of knowledge is given only if all the elements from which the actor has to choose are clearly and distinctly conceived by him. The choice itself is rational then when the actor selects from all means within his reach the ones most appropriate for realizing the intended end.

As shown, clearness and distinctness in their strict formal-logical meaning are characteristics of the typical style of thinking in daily life. But it would be erroneous to conclude, therefore, that rational choice does not occur in daily life. It occurs provided we interpret the terms "clearness" and "distinctness" in a modified and restricted manner: clearness and distinctness adequate to the requirements of the actor's practical interests on hand. It is not my job to examine whether or not the mentioned characteristics appear frequently in daily life. There is no doubt that what Weber called "rational act" as well as what he defined as "traditional act" or "habitual act" represent rational types which are seldom found in pure form in actions occurring in daily life. I want to emphasize that the ideal of rationality is not a particular feature of everyday thinking. Therefore it cannot be the methodological principle of the interpretation of human acts in daily life. This will become clearer when I discuss the statement, or, better, the postulate, that rational choice occurs only if the actor has sufficient knowledge not only of the end to be realized but also of the different means needed to realize it. This postulate implies:

a. Knowledge of the place at which the end is to be realized within the framework of the plans of the actor (which also must be clearly known to him).
b. Knowledge of its interrelations with other ends and of its compatibility or incompatibility with them.
c. Knowledge of the desirable and undesirable consequences which may arise as by-products of the realization of the main end.
d. Knowledge of the different chains of means which are technically or even ontologically suitable for the accomplishment of this aim, regardless of whether the actor has control over all or only some of their elements.
e. Knowledge of the interference of such means with other ends or other chains of

means, including secondary effects and incidental consequences.

f. Knowledge of the actor's accessibility to those means: can he seize the means that are within his reach and use them actively?

These points do not exhaust the complicated analysis I should make in order to analyze the concept of rational choice in action. These complications increase enormously if the action is social, that means if it is oriented toward others. In this case, the following elements become additionally determinant in the considerations of the actor:

1. The interpretation or misinterpretation of his own act by his fellowman.
2. The other's reaction and his motivation for it.
3. All the outlined elements of knowledge (a to f) which, rightly or wrongly, the actor attributes to his partner.
4. All the categories of familiarity and strangeness, intimacy and anonymity, personality and type, which we have discovered on the occasion of our inventory of the organization of the social world.

This short analysis shows that we cannot speak of an *isolated* rational act, if we mean an act resulting from deliberate choice; we can only speak of a *system* of rational acts. I refer to the fine study Professor Parsons has devoted to this problem at the end of his book under the heading, "Systems of Action and Their Unity". I agree emphatically with his theory of the web and the knots of means-ends chains, and with his demonstration of the connection of this problem with those of relevance, personality and typology.

I disagree with him (1) in his conception of ultimate ends, values and norms as indispensable elements of the Act Unity Scheme and (2) in his manner of combining the conceptual scheme of the unit act with the subjective point of view. The second objection is fundamental but too general to be discussed here. The first one can be indicated only by the hint that in my opinion the whole problem group of ultimate ends, norms and values disappears when we introduce the conceptual scheme of subjective life plans, subsuming it under the principle of relevance.

Where do we find this *system* of the rational act? By way of anticipation I have pointed out that the concept of rationality has its native place not on the level of the social world of daily life, but on the theoretical level of its scientific observation. This is its realm of methodological application. Thus we have to move to the problem of the social world as object of the social sciences and to the scientific methods of its interpretation.

VIII

My analysis of the world in which we live has shown that each of us considers himself the center of this world; he groups it around himself following his own interests. The observer has quite another attitude towards this world. It is not the theatre of his activities but the object of contemplation at which he looks with detached equanimity. As scientist (not as human being dealing with science) the observer is essentially solitary. To become a social scientist, everyone must make up his mind and replace himself as the center of this world by another animate being: the observer.

With this shift in the central point the whole system has been transformed; if I may use this metaphor, all the equations proven valid in the former system have to be expressed in terms of the new one. If the social system in question were ideally perfect, it would be possible to establish a universal formula of transformation such as Einstein established for transposing propositions in terms of the Newtonian system of mechanics into those of the Theory of Relativity.

This shift in the point of view has a first, fundamental consequence: the scientist replaces the human actors he observes on the social stage by puppets he creates and manipulates himself. What I call "puppets" corresponds to the technical term, "ideal-types", which Weber introduced into the social sciences <provided these types are ideal types of actors>.

My analysis of the daily social world has shown the origin of typification. In daily life we typify human activities that interest us only as appropriate means for producing intended effects but not as expressions of the personality of our fellow man. The procedure of the scientific observer is the same. He observes certain events caused by human activities and begins to establish types of such proceedings. Later he co-ordinates typical actors with the typical acts they execute. In this way he constructs personal ideal types which he imaginatively endows with consciousness. He constructs this fictitious consciousness in such a way the fictitious actor, were he not a dummy but a human being, would swim in the same stream of thought as a living man acting in the same way. The important difference is that the artificial consciousness is not subject to the ontological conditions of human existence [such as birth, death, and growing older together].

The puppet is not born, will not grow up and will never die. It has no hopes, no fears; it does not know anxiety as a chief motive of its deeds. It is not free in the sense that its acting could transcend the limits established by its creator. Therefore it cannot have other conflicts of interest and of motives except those implanted into it by the social scientist. The personal ideal-type cannot err if erring is not its inbuilt feature. It cannot perform an act outside its typical motives, its typical means-ends relations and its typical situations as provided for by the scientist. In short, the ideal type is only a model of consciousness without the faculty of spontaneity and without a will of its own.

In typical situations of daily life we too assume certain typical roles. By isolating one of our activities from all other manifestations of our personality we disguise ourselves as consumers or taxpayers, citizens, members of churches and clubs, clients, smokers, bystanders, etc. As travelers, for instance, we have to conduct ourselves in ways we think the type, "railway agent", expects from typical passengers. In our daily lives these assumed attitudes are roles which we assume voluntarily as expedients and which we give up whenever we want to do so. Assuming roles does not change our general attitude toward the social world or toward our personal life. Our knowledge remains segmented, our propositions occasional, our future uncertain, our general situation unstable. The next moment may bring us the great cataclysm which will debunk our experiences, modify our plans, influence our choices. Yet even in a role we preserve the liberty of choice in so far as its exists at all within the scope of our human and social conditions. The liberty exists in the possibility of shedding our disguise, dropping a role, reordering our orientations in the social world. We continue to be subjects, centers of spontaneous activities, and actors.

In contrast the puppet called "personal ideal-type" is never a subject or a center of spontaneous activity. It does not have the task of mastering the world; strictly speaking, it has no world at all. Its fate is regulated and determined beforehand by its creator, the social scientist. He may manage this in that perfect pre-established harmony in which Leibniz imagined the world as created by God. By the grace of its constructor, the puppet actor is endowed with just that kind of knowledge it needs in order to perform the job for the sake of which it was brought into the scientific world.

The scientist distributes his own store of experience and that means [he distributes his own store] of scientific experience in its clear and distinct terms among the puppets with which he populates his constructions of the social world. And this social world is organized in a quite other way. It is not centered in personal ideal types; it lacks the categories of intimacy and anonymity, of familiarity and strangeness – in short, it lacks the basic character of perspective appearance. What counts in it is the point of view from which the *scientist* envisages the social world. This point of view defines the framework with its perspective in which the selected sector of the social world presents itself to him, the scientific observer, and through him to the type-puppet in its fictitious consciousness. The central point of view of the scientist is called his scientific problem under examination.

In a scientific system the problem has exactly the same function for the scientific activities in question that practical interests have for activities in everyday work. Once formulated, the scientific problem has a two-fold function:

a. It automatically limits the scope within which possible propositions become relevant for the inquiry. It creates the realm of the scientific subject matter within which all concepts must be compatible with one another.
b. The simple fact of raising a problem creates a scheme of reference for the construction of all ideal types which may be used as relevant for the problem.

In order to better understand the last remark we have to remember that the concept, "type", is not independent; it always needs a supplement. We cannot simply speak of an "ideal-type as such"; we must indicate the reference scheme within which this ideal-type may be used – that is, the problem for the sake of which it has been constructed. To borrow a mathematical term, I may say that the ideal-type always needs a subscript referring to the problem which determines the forming of all types to be used. In this sense the problem under scrutiny is the locus of all possible types which may pertain to the system under investigation.

Here I cannot deal further with the logical foundations of this thesis which I call the "principle of relevance". We can interpret it as an application of James' theory of the fringes of concepts. Like all other concepts, the ideal-type has fringes referring to the main topic about which revolve all members of the thought. It is easy to see that a shift in the main topic, that is, in the problem, automatically causes modifications in the fringes of each concept which is part of it. Since a shift in the problem means a modification in the scope of relevance we can explain that new facts emerge with any shift in the point of view, while facts disappear which before were in the center of our attention. This statement is nothing else than the explanation of the transition from one level to the other, which I offered earlier. To be sure, the term "level" is used only in reference to shifting whole systems of problems. Nevertheless, in principle the consequences are the same. It is important for the scientist to keep in mind that each shift in the problem involves a thorough modification of all concepts and all types he is dealing with. Many misunderstandings and controversies in the social sciences have their origin in the unmodified application of concepts and types on levels other than those for which they were created.

But why form ideal-types at all? Why not simply collect empirical facts? Or why not restrict ourselves to forming types of impersonal events or of impersonal collectivities and thus enhance the success of their application? Modern economics is the example of a social science which does not deal with personal ideal-types but with curves, with mathematical functions, with movements of prices, or with such institutions as bank systems or with currency fluctuations. Statisticians have done a great job by collecting information about the "behavior" of collectivities. Why go back to the scheme of social action and to the individual actor?

The answer is the following: It is correct to say that a good part of work in the social sciences can be done and has been performed on a level on which it is legitimate to abstract from everything that may happen within individual actors. But this operating with generalizations and idealizations on a high level of abstraction is nothing but a kind of intellectual shorthand. Whenever the problem on hand necessitates it, the social scientist must have the possibility of shifting his research to the level of individual human activities. Where real scientific work is done, this shift will always be possible.

The reason for this is that we cannot treat phenomena of the social world as if they were phenomena of the world of nature. In the latter we deal with facts and regularities which are not understandable in Weber's sense but to which we refer in terms of certain assumptions about this world. We never "understand" why the mercury rises when the sun shines on it. We can only interpret this phenomenon as compatible with the laws which have been deduced from some basic assumptions about the physical world. In contrast we want to understand social phenomena and we cannot understand them except through the scheme of human motives, human means and ends, human planning – in short, by means of the categories of human actions. Therefore the social scientist must ask, or at least have the possibility to ask, what happens in the mind of the individual actor whose action has brought about the phenomenon in question. We may formulate this "postulate of subjective interpretation" as follows: The social scientist has to ask what type of individual mind can be constructed and what typical thoughts must be attributed to it in order to explain the fact in question as a result of mental activities in an understandable context.

This postulate is complemented by another one which, borrowing a term from Max Weber, I call the "postulate of adequacy" [and define as follows]: "Each term in a scientific system referring to human action must be constructed in such a way that a human act performed in the life-world by an individual actor would be reasonable for and understandable by the actor himself but also for and by his fellow men." This postulate is of extreme importance for the methodology of the social sciences. What makes it at all possible for social scientists to refer to events in the life-world is the fact that their interpretation of any human act can be basically similar or analogous to its interpretation by the actor and his partner.

The principle of relevance, the postulate of the subjective interpretation, and the postulate of adequacy are applicable to all levels of the social sciences. Thus all historical sciences are governed by them. The next step would be to concentrate on the theoretical social sciences. Their outstanding feature is the interpretation of the social world in terms of a system of determinate logical structure (Parsons, p. 7). This system of means-ends relations is also ideal-typical; but as Professor Parsons has pointed out, it is analytical *and* deals with what he calls concrete actions. Once I formulated the same idea by stating that the personal ideal-types of action, constructed by the theoretical sciences, are of maximum anonymity. They typify the behavior of "people as such" or of "everybody". Whatever formulation may be used for characterizing the particularities of the theoretical realm, the following is clear: a logically interrelated system of means-ends relations together with the system of constant motives and the system of life plans must be constructed in such a way that

a. it remains fully compatible with the principles of formal logic;
b. all its elements can be perceived in full clearness and distinctness;
c. it contains only scientifically verifiable assumptions which have to be fully compatible with the whole body of our scientific knowledge.

These three postulates may be condensed into another postulate for constructing ideal-types, that of rationality. It may be formulated as follows: "The ideal-types of social action must be constructed in such a way that the actor in the life-world would perform the typified act (in the ideal-typical form) if he had a clear and distinct knowledge of all the elements relevant for his choice and persistently tended to choose the most appropriate means for the realization of the most appropriate ends."

As I anticipated at the beginning, only by introducing the key concept of rationality may we provide all the elements needed for the constitution of the level called "pure theory". Furthermore, the postulate of rationality implies that all other behavior has to be considered a derivative of the basic scheme of rational acting. The reason for this is that action can be scientifically discussed only within the framework of rational categories. Scientists have at their disposal no other methods than rational ones; therefore they cannot verify or falsify purely occasional propositions.

As stated before, each type formed by the scientist has a subscript referring to the main problem. Thus only pure rational types are admitted into a theoretical system. But where may a scientist find the guarantee for establishing a truly unified system? And where the scientific tools for performing this difficult task? The answer is: Each branch of the social sciences which has reached the theoretical stage contains a fundamental hypothesis both defining its field of research and offering the regulative principles for constructing a system of ideal-types. Such a fundamental hypothesis, for instance, is the utilitarian principle in classical economics and the principle of marginality in modern economics. The meaning of this postulate is the following: "Construct your ideal-type as if all actors had oriented their life plans and therefore all their activities on the chief end of achieving the greatest utility with a minimum of costs. Human activity oriented in such a way (and only this kind of human activity) is the subject-matter of your science."

Behind all of these statements arises a disturbing question: If the social world, as our object of scientific research, is but a typical construction of the scientist, why bother with this intellectual game? Our scientific activity, too, in particular if it deals with the social world, is performed within a certain means-end relation: that of acquiring knowledge for mastering the real world, not the world created by the scientists. We want to find out what happens in this real world but not what goes on in the fantasies of a few sophisticated and strange fellows.

There are a few arguments for quieting such an interlocutor. First of all: The construction of the scientific world is not an arbitrary act which a scientist can perform at this discretion.

1. Each scientist has inherited from his predecessors a stock of approved propositions which present the historical boundaries of his science.
2. The postulate of adequacy requires that constructed types are compatible with the totality of both our daily life and our scientific experiences.

Should a person not be satisfied with these guarantees and ask for more "reality", I have to answer, "Sorry, I don't know exactly what reality is." My only comfort in this calamitous situation is that I share this ignorance with the greatest philosophers of all times. Again I will refer to William James and his profound theory of the different realities in which we live simultaneously. One misunderstands the essence of science if he thinks that it deals with Reality, understood as the reality of the world of daily life. The worlds both of the natural and the social scientists are neither more nor less real than the world of thought can be in general. The latter is not the world within which we act and in which we are born and die. But it is the home of those important events and achievements which we call culture.

Social scientists may continue to work in full confidence. Governed by the aforementioned postulates their clarified methods offer them the assurance that they will never lose contact with the world of daily life. As long as they successfully use methods which have stood the test and still do so, they are justified in continuing their work without bothering with methodological problems. I have no intention to share the presumptiousness of certain methodologists who criticize what is performed in the social sciences with genuine workmanship. Max Weber, one of the greatest methodologists, coined the adage: "I hate the constant sharpening of methodological knives if there is nothing on the table to be carved." Methodology plays a humbler part. It is not the preceptor or tutor of scientists; the methodologists are always their pupils.

There is no great master in any scientific field who could not teach the methodologists how they should proceed. Yet the truly great teacher has always to learn from his pupils. Arnold Schoenberg, the famous composer, started the preface to his masterly book on the theory of harmony with the sentence: "I have learned this book from my pupils." The methodologist in his role has to ask the intelligent questions about the techniques of his teachers. He has performed his task if his questions help others to reflect on what they actually do and perhaps induce them to eliminate certain intrinsic difficulties hidden in the foundations of the scientific edifice which the scientists themselves have never inspected.

CHAPTER 3

Realities from Daily Life to Theoretical Contemplation

Editors' Preface

The title is Helmut Wagner's for an early draft of Schutz's "On Multiple Realities", published in 1945.[1] Adapted by Wagner for inclusion in this volume, the text, dating from 1943, was transcribed by Lester Embree. According to Wagner, Schutz worked on this particular draft until August, 1943, when he put it aside to prepare his first academic course. It was at least a year later before he returned to the draft, writing a new version which was eventually published. Unlike Schutz's usual practice of multiple revisions of a given draft, he apparently revised the present draft but once. It therefore required more editing than usual as well as more footnotes. In Embree's transcription there were gaps left for unreadable words, and these have been filled in by Wagner, if not always with Schutz's words, at least with words that can be reasonably assumed to convey Schutz's intended meanings.

In a famous chapter of his *Psychology*, William James analyzes the notion of Reality.[2] He comes to the conclusion that there is not one single Reality but an indefinite number of different Realities, some of which he enumerates. Among them are: the reality of daily life, the reality of dreams, the reality of science, and the reality of personal opinion.

As usual, William James' view of the problem touches on one of the most important philosophical problems. However, intentionally restricting himself to the psychological aspects of the question he did not embark upon a radical inquiry into the implications of the problem. Fragmentary as they are, the following pages attempt to outline a first approach towards the analysis of these implications with the specific aim of clarifying the relationship between the reality of the world of daily life with that of science. Although phenomenological methods will be used for this purpose, we do not claim to outline a "phenomenology of reality" or to make any contributions to "phenomenological philosophy" in the restricted meaning of the

[1]First published in *Philosophy and Phenomenological Research*, Vol. V, 1945, "On Multiple Realities" was reprinted in Alfred Schutz, *Collected Papers*, Vol. I, pp. 207–259. See also Helmut Wagner, *Alfred Schutz. An Intellectual Biography* pp. 90f., 225f.

[2]William James, *Principles of Psychology*, Vol. II, chapter XXI, "The Perception of Reality".

term. To the contrary, our problem will be exclusively posed within the mundane sphere of the natural attitude. Therefore it will belong to the field of phenomenological psychology; that is, it will be restricted to the constitutional analysis of the natural attitude.

I. The Reality of the World of Daily Life

We start with the analysis of the world of daily life as reality given in the natural attitude of the wide-awake, grown-up man who lives and acts in it and works upon it amid his fellow men. Several of these terms require further comments.

1. *The world of daily life* shall mean the intersubjective world into which we were born and within which we grew up. This world existed before we were born; it is given to our experiences and interpretations. At any age we have at our disposal a certain stock of knowledge of this world; it has been constituted by our own actions of interpretation, by learning from others, by habits formed and traditions handed down from parents and teachers and from teachers of our teachers. This stock of acquired experiences functions as our scheme of reference. Philosophical or psychological analyses of the constitution of our knowledge may show how elements of this world effect our senses, how we perceive them passively in indistinct and confused ways, how our minds single out certain features from the perceptual field by active apperceptions and how thus the notions of real objects stand out over against more or less inarticulated backgrounds or horizons. But this constitutive process is a mere product of analysis in hindsight and does not account for the ways in which we experience our world in daily life. To us this world is not a sum (total) of colored spots, incoherent noises, separate centers of warm and cold, of hard and soft places; it is a world of well-circumscribed objects with definite qualities, or objects among which we may move around, which resist us, and upon which we may act.

2. *The Natural Attitude and Its Epoché*. We experience this world in the *natural attitude* just characterized. That means that we have not a theoretical but an eminently practical interest in it. In the first place, "world" is to us not an object of thought but a field of dominations, of action: we may pursue our goals within it; and we have to change it in order to realize our purposes. Therefore we may trust our experiences as long as they may remain consistent in themselves but also consistent with the warranted experiences of others – for the world of daily life is essentially intersubjective, common to all of us, and not the private world of any individual. Characteristically, persons in the natural attitude take the world and its objects for granted until counterproof. As long as the once established schemes of reference work as systems of our warranted experiences, and as long as the actions and operations performed under its guidance yield the desired results, in the natural attitude we are not interested whether this world does "really" exist or whether it is only a coherent system of consistent appearances.

We have no reason to cast doubt either upon our past experiences or upon our senses which, or so we believe, represent things to us as they "really" are. If a new experience pops up and proves to be "strange" and is not subsumable under the existing stock of my previous experiences, or if the inconsistency of such new experiences compels us to revise our former beliefs – these facts do not change anything in the basic fact: while maintaining our natural attitude we take our beliefs for granted unless a specific motivation forces us to "stop and think". Phenomenology has taught us the concept of the phenomenological *epoché*, the suspension of our belief in the reality of the world by "placing the world within brackets". This *epoché* is necessary in order to overcome the natural attitude and in order to radicalize the Cartesian method of philosophical doubt. We venture to state that in our natural attitude we also use a specific *epoché*, although one quite different from the transcendental *epoché* of phenomenology. We do not suspend belief in the outer world and its objects; to the contrary, we suspend doubt in its existence. What we put between brackets is the doubt that the world and its objects might be otherwise than they appear to us. We suggest calling this *epoché* the *epoché* of the natural attitude.

3. *The Performance of Spontaneity*. It might be said that in a certain sense the natural attitude and its *epoché* are based on pragmatic motives. The world of our everyday life is not only the scene of our actions but also their object. We work and operate not only within but also upon the world. Our bodily movements – kinaesthetic, locomotive, operative – so to speak gear into the world and its objects. They modify them, change them and, on the other hand, are regulated by their resistance which they have to master or to which they have to yield. In this pragmatic world, objects of the world therefore are things that we have to modify by our actions or which modify our actions.

However, some terminological caution is indicated here. For the most part, the term, "action", is used for purposive conduct in respect to purposively overt, covert and sub-overt behavior. Certainly the customary distinction among these three kinds of behavior is very inadequate for a non-behaviorist interpretation. This terminology has been formed from the point of view of the observing behaviorist and not from the point of view of the actor. However, our study has to deal with the latter. We are not interested in considering the activities of man according to a relational scheme accessible only to the observer, as organism, environment, or stimulus-response, but we are asking what meaning man bestows upon his activities. Therefore we prefer the term "conduct" to that of "behavior". The former refers to the so-called subjective meaning that an act has for the actor; the latter points to the objective meaning of the act according to the observer's interpretation. Furthermore, the term, "conduct", is applicable only to manifestations of intended spontaneity whereas "behavior" includes mere physiological reflexes. Those reflexes, like certain passive reactions provoked by what Leibniz called the surf of confused small perceptions, lack the character of intention which is essential for conscious conduct. The latter occurs as a psycho-physiological unity or response to it. But my adopted attitude toward these occurrences and the steering of my so-called responses by intended spontaneous acts constitutes meaningful conduct. If conduct is correlated with some project it shall be called action regardless of whether this conduct is overt or covert, whether or not it leads to bodily movements and changes in the outer world.

In terms of the suggested terminology, a process of projected thinking, say the attempt at solving a scientific problem, is certainly action. It is not essential for the notion of action whether or not the intention to realize the project is added. If it supervenes we may speak of purposive action. However, if conduct shows the character of what behaviorists call overt behavior, if conduct entails bodily movements gearing into the outer world, for our purposes it shall be called "working".

Let us mention once more the different stages of spontaneity since they point beyond terminological subtleties to serious philosophical problems:

a. Performances of spontaneity without meaning for the performer, without project and without the intention to realize anything.[3] In so far as these performances are connected with bodily movements we may call them *mere doing*. To this class belong mere physiological reactions provoked by physiological stimuli, so for instance blinking <of the eyelids> or reflexes of the <*patella*>, etc.[4] Moreover facial expressions and other expressive gestures occur during movements accompanying working acts without being noticed separately; thus they remain unperceived. Furthermore there are the indiscernible small perceptions which remain unstable and elusive. Being what they are, they can neither be apperceived nor recollected by the performing individual.

   Meaning always refers to a past which can be recollected in isolation. This also holds for the doings with which it is connected. <However>, small perceptions are subjectively meaningless. Such "essentially actual experiences" exist only in the actuality of experiencing and therefore are ineffable in the true sense of the term. That is what separates them from conduct which is always meaningful because it can be recollected beyond its actuality. Thus it can be questioned about its implications.

b. The term, "conduct", <refers to> performances of spontaneity which have meaning <and are executed> with the intention to realize the latter. Two subclasses have to be distinguished: i) unperceived conduct (conduct without a project): all kinds of habitual, traditional, affective behavior fall into this class, so walking, eating, greeting, caressing, moving the fingers while playing the piano. Leibniz called this the "class of empirical behavior". ii) Conduct according to a preconceived project: *action* in the full meaning of the term. Acting may be covert: acting that is not performed by bodily movements (mere thinking) or overt physical acting, gearing into the outer world. In the latter case it shall be called *working*.[5]

c. Meaningful performances of spontaneity, projected and preconceived without the intention to realize them: mere imaginaries (fantasms), daydreams. In addition,

[3]The typescript has "intention to realize them"; Wagner replaced "them" with "anything", which would seem to make more sense.

[4]The typescript has "pretella", apparently a typing error for "patella".

[5]Next to the bottom line of this typescript page are found the words: "Imagining!" and "Imaginary!" Wagner suggested that they are reminders of the planned content of the next sub-section.

[6]At this point in the typescript the following note appears in parentheses: "(diagram to be inserted)". No such diagram has been found among Schutz's papers, and the published version of this essay does not contain a diagram.

any intention to realize the project remains imaginary.[6]

Among all these forms of spontaneity that of working is the most important for the constitution of the reality of the everyday life-world. According to the above scheme, working is characterized by an underlying project and the intention to realize it. There it is a subcategory of action, namely, action performed by physical movements of my body. The importance of our bodily movements for the constitution of the outer world has been emphasized in Bergson's investigations. We experience our bodily movements simultaneously on two different planes: in so far as they are movements in the outer world we look at them as events happening in space and spatial time, measurable in terms of distances covered <during the time elapsed>. In so far as they are events in inner time (*durée*) we experience them as happening changes, as manifestations of our spontaneity.

Thereby we find the transition from our *durée* to the spatial time that governs our everyday life-world. On the other hand, Husserl has shown that we group our world around our body together with its perspectives and horizons; it constitutes the "hic" ("here") that is the center of the system of co-ordinates that we apply to the <surrounding> world. By our locomotion we shift this center and therewith our entire system of co-ordinates. What previously was an "over there", an "illic", now becomes a "hic". Distances, perspectives and horizons of all the surrounding objects have changed accordingly. Furthermore, only by bodily movements may we bring distance objects into contact, experience their resistance and, hence, their reality. We may manipulate or evade them.

The characteristics given so far refer to all bodily movements whether or not they are performed according to an underlying project. However, as bodily action, working opens an additional dimension for the constitution of the life-world. As unrolling action it belongs to the specious present of the actor, as projected it refers to its future, as motivated to its past. Thus the working self is constituted as the center of the world of action; it determines its habitualities and automatisms; it delineates the segment of the world which is relevant for the actual situation in hand and for the scope of contemplated projects; it constitutes, by its working and in its working, the unity of the self; and it creates the state of mind which we call "wide-awakeness" and which now we have to characterize.

4. *The Tensions of Consciousness and the Attention to Life*. As Bergson has pointed out, our stream of thought shows in its different phases manifold degrees of strain and relaxation. He calls these different stages of mental energy, ranging from concentration to inattention, the *tensions* of our consciousness. According to him they are the equivalent of our varying attitude towards life and its requirements. *Attention à la vie*, attention to life, is therefore the basic regulative principle for our approach to our world, the outer as well as the inner stream of thought. It determines the realm of our different interests and therewith the selection of those elements of the world which are relevant for us. It articulates our continuously flowing stream of thought, constituting within its permanent transitions what James calls "resting places". It directs us either to live within the unrolling passages from one state of mind to another, hence to life within the ongoing transitions themselves, or to turn back to our past by acts of reflection. In other words, it makes us live within our present

experiences directed toward their objects or else to turn back to our past experiences and ask about their meanings.[7]

As we used it before, with the term, "wide-awakeness", we want to characterize states of mind of highest tension originating in an attitude of full attention to life and its tasks. In this attitude, the self lives within its acts as directed toward their objects. The latter can only be mastered and dealt with if the self "pulls itself together" and concentrates all its energy in the "fiat" that gets its working acts going.

Thus working is the highest performance of spontaneity. Only the working self is fully interested in life. Its attentions are exclusively directed upon bringing about the effects of this working: the realization of its projects. This is not a passive but an active attention. Passive attention is the opposite of full-awakeness. For instance, in passive attention I experience the surf of indiscernible small perceptions. As stated before, they are essentially actual experiences in their instability; they do not lead to meaningful spontaneous performances.

Meaningful spontaneity may be defined, as did Leibniz, as the effort to arrive at other and ever other perceptions. This means in its lower form to extol distinct perceptions and to transform them into apperceptions by an act of active attention. <This transformation is> performable only by a change in the tension of consciousness. In its highest form this means modifying the world by working acts that can be performed only in the tension of creative volition. – These brief remarks by no means aim at circumscribing the role of spontaneity in constituting consciousness. But they show clearly the possible starting point for the pragmatic interpretation of our cognitive life.[8]

5. *The Time Perspectives of the Ego Agens and Their Unification*. We stated before that the working self lives within its acts directed toward the preconceived objects of its working and that therefore it lives only within its specious present. This statement calls for some additional comments.

Let us start with an analysis of the time perspectives of action in general, whether this acting occurs in what is commonly called overt or covert behavior. Our statements hold for both cases. However, we have to distinguish between acting in progress (*actio*) and action performed (*actum*). Acting in progress is necessarily *present* action. If, having performed an action, I turn back to my acting, I perceive it always as performed act, as what it was while I performed it. This is part of my vivid present. Now this present has turned into a past; the vivid experience of my acting had yielded to recollections of having acted. Seen from my actual present, my past acting is conceivable by me only in terms of <finished> acts <once> performed by me

[7]The sentence in the typescript which follows forms a separate paragraph in Schutz's text, and which Wagner places as a footnote: "It seems that the true importance of this Bergsonian concept thus far has not been recognized. This is probably due to the aphoristic character of Bergson's presentation; it is quite possible that even the brief indications given by me transcend Bergson's original concept."

[8]Footnote of Alfred Schutz: "What is commonly called Pragmatism or pragmatic philosophy, save for a few exceptions, does not go back to the constitutional problems of constitutional life, or action and of work. It starts with an analysis of *ego agens* (the acting I) or the *homo faber* (tool-making and tool-using man) as givens. My remarks in the text <merely serve the purpose of> indicating to what degree the pragmatic motive is justified <at its point of> origin."

<but now belonging to the past>. This even holds for past initial phases of an acting that still continues.

This distinction is rooted in the time perspective involved. During the performance of the act I anticipate its outcome. These anticipations are empty and may not be fulfilled. A past act shows no such empty anticipations. My anticipations were or have not been fulfilled. Nothing remains unsettled, nothing undecided. Certainly I may remember the open anticipations which I had when I acted. But I am doing this in terms of past anticipations that have come true or else not. Therefore only the performed action can turn out as success or as failure. The action in progress <cannot be subject to such judgments>.

However, here our distinctions between acting in general and working become important. In the case of mere overt acting – for instance, when attempting the solution of a mathematical problem by mental mathematics – I may cancel the whole process of operations and start over from the beginning whenever I am dissatisfied with the results. Nothing will have changed in the outer world: mere mental acts are revocable. Working, however, is irrevocable. By my working I have changed the world. Sometimes I may restore the initial situation by countermoves but I cannot make undone what I have done. From the moral and legal point of view I am responsible for my deeds but not for my thoughts. Only in present working do I have the freedom of choice among several possibilities. In terms of the past tense there is no choice. I have chosen once and for all and now have to bear the consequences. I cannot choose what I wish I had done <after I had done otherwise>.

This difference in the time perspective is of greatest importance for the manner in which the self regards itself. The working self is an undivided unity only in the performance of its working activities.[9] This is merely another formulation of the thesis that the working self lives within its acts *modo presente* (the grammatical form of the present). It not only experiences its bodily movements from within but it is also directed by its essentially-actual experiences which it cannot recollect. Its world is an open world of choices and of open anticipations. In and through its working the working self realizes not only its work but also and entirely itself.

However, if, in an act of reflection, the self turns toward the past, it does not experience itself as acting. It steps out of the stream of its thinking, so to speak, and regards its performed acts: it is no longer directed toward the object of its acting. With this reflective turn the unity of the self goes to pieces. The self which had performed past acts is no longer the undivided self but a partial self, the performer of a role. Or, to use a rather equivocal term of the necessary precaution: a Me. Here we cannot enter into a thorough discussion of this difficult implication. But the mere consideration that the essentially-actual experiences are bound to the present makes it sufficiently clear for our purposes that the self in the past is not the total one. Although starting from quite another point of departure, we can therefore agree with G. H. Mead that only the present is real and the self experiences itself in vivid experiences only as acting self.

[9]Schutz wrote, "work experiences", for which Wagner substituted "working activities".

6. *The Social Structure of the World of the Working Self.* The world of everyday life into which we are born is, from the outself, an intersubjective world common to all of us. I not only work[10] upon inanimate things but also upon my fellow men, inducing them to re-act and being induced by them to act. Thus an interrelationship between us subsists. Here it is not possible to detail the mechanism of this interrelationship. It must suffice to point out that my performed actions motivate the Other to re-act and vice versa. I question him with the intention to provoke his answer and he answers, motivated by my question. Speaking roughly, the "in order to" motives of my actions become the "because" motives of his reactions. If this is actually the case, we speak of social action.

Social actions presuppose communication and communication necessarily is grounded in working acts. I have to perform overt acts in the outer world that are supposed to be interpreted by others as signs of what I mean. Gestures, speech, writing are based on bodily movements gearing into the outer world. To this degree the behaviorist interpretation is justified. [It errs] by identifying the prerequisite of communication, namely the *founding* working act, with the communicated meaning itself.

Here again the time perspective in which the communicative work unrolls is of great importance. I talk to my partner and he listens to me. My talk, the meaning of the words uttered by me, are open to my partner's interpretation. So are also my facial expressions, the inflections of my voice, the involuntary gestures I make. As talker I am living in my present directed toward my goal – which is to communicate to my partner what I mean. Thus I am working and living in my present. However, my working activity is limited to the delivery of my speech. The accompanying gestures, facial expressions, etc., are what we have called mere doing, reflexes by my state of mind that do not originate in intended spontaneous acts which are meaningful to me, the speaker. (We disregard special cases like the play-actor or the public speaker.) <Mere doing is> only meaningful to the interpreting listener. He will get quite another impression if he shares with me the vivid present and can follow my acting in simultaneity than he would have had he just the outcome of my act for this interpretation: the signs established by me, the letter written by me, the implement produced by me.

If he shares my vivid present in simultaneity it makes a difference whether he does so face-to-face with me, whether he shares the same surroundings and is subject to many of the same impressions from the outer world to which I am subjected,[11]

[10]In his transcription of the typescript, Wagner appended the following footnote: "At this point it is necessary to remark that the phrase, 'I work', and its variations, appear here only because there is no English equivalent for the word Schutz would have used had he written this essay in German. 'To work' is the adequate equivalent for the German verb, *arbeiten*. But in the present context the German equivalent would have been '*wirken*', standing for 'exercising an *effect* upon a thing or a person'. The term aims not at the activity but at the *results* of an activity – a difference as striking as that between the verb 'to cause' and the noun 'result' as the lasting tangible consequence of a finished causative action. Schutz elevated the difference to the intersubjective level when he wrote, ' I work . . . upon . . . things' and 'I work . . . upon . . . my fellow men'."

[11]A marginal note by Schutz in the margin opposite these lines reads: "Any theory of the environment must start here."

or whether he listens to my talk at another place, such as over the telephone or the radio. Only the face-to-face relationship permits us to participate in the same stream of present time. Only <under this condition> does the other follow step-by-step the building-up of my working performance. And, finally, only in the face-to-face situation does the self of my fellow man appear to me in its unbroken totality. Any other social situation is derived from the experiencing of the *alter ego* in the vivid present of a face-to-face situation; it does not reveal the total self of the partner but breaks it down into partial selves, performers of roles, or of Me's.

7. *The Strata of Reality in the Everyday World of Working.* The wide-awake man in the natural attitude is, first of all, interested in that segment of the world of his in everyday life which is within his scope and which is centered in himself both in space and time. The place which my body occupies within the actual world, my actual Here, is the starting point from which I take my bearings in space. It is, so to speak, the center 0 of my system of co-ordinates. I group the elements of my surroundings relative to my body under the categories of right and left, before and behind, above and below, near and far, and so on. And in a similar way my actual Now is the starting point of all the time perspectives under which I group the events within the world as before and after, past and future, simultaneity and succession, etc.

However, within the basic categories of orientation the real world of working is organized in manifold ways. It is the great merit of G. H. Mead to have analyzed what he calls the "manipulatory area".[12] This area includes the objects both seen and handled in distinction from distant objects which are out of reach but still remain in the visual perspective. Mead stressed the overwhelming importance of the experiences of the manipulatory area for the constitution of reality. Only such experiences are subject to the test of contacts, only they permit the basic experience of the reality of physical things, namely by resistance, only they define what he calls the "standard sizes" of things appearing outside the manipulatory area in the distortions of optical perspectives.

Whether or not we accept all the conclusions drawn by Mead from this basic fact, his theory of the predominance of the manipulatory area converges certainly with the suggested thesis that the world of our working, of bodily movements, of gearing into the outer world, of manipulating objects, and of handling things and men constitutes the kernel of our experiences of reality. However we deviate for our purposes from Mead's pragmatic point of view in so far as we favor the analysis of the natural attitude and refrain from over-emphasizing the otherwise most important distinction between objects experienced by <manual> contacts and distant objects experienced only by vision and hearing.

Because we do not share Mead's basic proposition that any experience is based on the interrelationship between stimuli and responses, we are justified in linking our analysis of the natural attitude to a trust in the stock of our experiences of which man always disposes, and teaching that in principle he may always bring distant visual objects of the world of working into a contact situation by his own locomotive acts. It is true that the manipulatory area does not coincide with, say, the area of

[12]In the margin opposite this sentence Schutz wrote: "Present 125." The reference is to George Herbert Mead, *The Philosophy of the Present* (1932), p. 125.

things in view. However, any visual experience of a distant object refers to a set of former experiences that constituted our notion of distance as such. This notion includes [the idea] that distance can be overcome by acts of working, namely locomotions. <If we manage to move close enough>, the distorted perspectives will disappear and the "standard sizes" of the objects will be re-established. Therefore the visual apperception of distant objects in the natural attitude implies the anticipation that they can be brought into contact. Like any anticipation it may be verified or falsified by supervening experiences. Its falsification would mean that the object under consideration does not pertain to the world of working. A child may want to touch the moon or the stars. To the naïve grown-up the stars are points of light outside the sphere of his working. That holds true even if he uses their positions as means for finding his bearings in the universe. Therefore, for our purposes, we suggest calling the stratum of the world of working that of the individual experiences as kernels of reality, "the world within reach". As center, this world includes Mead's manipulatory area but also the things within the scope of a person's view and within the range of this hearing – briefly not only the segment of the world open to this actual working but also the adjacent spheres of his *potential* working. Of course, these spheres have no rigid borders, they have their halos and open horizons and these are subject to time perspectives, modifications of interest and attentional attitudes, and so on. It is clear that this whole system of the world within my reach shifts with any locomotions by which I, displacing my body, transfer the center 0 of the system of my coordinates.

However, so far we have only considered the spatial perspective of the reality of my world of working. Turning to the time perspectives we may say that the world within my actual reach has essentially the character of the present. It is connected with the world within my possible reach in a two-fold way. At first it is potentiality; to it belong what for me was in the past the world within my actual reach. All working, as any conduct in the natural sphere, is guided by the idealization that I may continue to act as I did so far and that I may again and again recommence to act in the same way under the same conditions. Husserl calls these assumptions the idealizations of the "and so on" and of the "I can do it again".

What formerly was to me the world within my actual reach is now beyond my reach due to locomotion and shifting of the center of my co-ordinate system. It turned from a world in the "*hic*" into a world in the *"illic"*. But under the idealization of the "I can do it again", I may assume that I can re-transform the actual *"illic"* into a new *"hic"*. The idealization of the "I can do it again" bestows upon the past world within my reach the character of a world that again can be brought within my reach. For instance, the past actual manipulatory area continues to function in the present as a potential manipulatory area or better a manipulatory area in the mode of the *"illic"*. It now has the specific character of a chance.

Over against this first potentiality, which originates in the past, there is the sphere of a second potentiality derived from anticipation. It is not the world within my actual or former reach but the world within attainability.[13] This is a world which

[13]In the margin opposite this sentence, Schutz wrote: "the realm of the attainable."

neither is nor ever has been within my reach but which I may bring within my reach according to the idealization of the "and so on". The most important instance of this sphere of the second potentiality is the world within the actual reach of my fellow man. For instance, the manipulatory area <appears to him> in the mode of the "*hic*" but to me in the mode of the "*illic*". Nevertheless, it is my potential manipulatory area; and it could be and may become my actual manipulatory area if I were in his place.[14]

And what has been stated about the manipulatory area of the fellow man holds good for the world in your, in their, in someone's actual reach. This includes the reference to the worlds in the other's past reach. The whole system is subject to all the shades originating in the various perspectives of the social world with regard to intimacy and anonymity, social proximity and social distance as prevailing in my relations with others. All this cannot be treated here. May it suffice for the purpose on hand that the second zone of potentiality just described is for me also a possible world within my reach with the specific character of a chance of attainability.

However, the chances of attaining the first and second zones of potentiality are by no means equal. As to the first zone we have to keep in mind that what is now a mere chance for me was formerly experienced reality. Working acts performed and even mere projected actions are recollections and belong to my present state of mind which is what it is because the former reality was once a present reality. Therefore the anticipated re-actualizations of the once actual world within my reach are founded upon reproductions and retentions of my own past experiences. This gives the zone of the first potentiality the character of a maximal chance.

Quite otherwise is the structure of the world in attainability, which constitutes the second zone of potentiality. This zone refers anticipatorily to future states of mind. It is not connected with my past except by the fact that its anticipations (like all anticipations) are founded within, and have to be compatible with past, stocks of experiences actually at hand. To the experiences belong, for instance, those which enable me to weigh the likelihood of effectuating my plans or to estimate my own powers. However, the chances of transforming the world in attainability into a world within my reach will diminish in proportion with its increasing spatial, temporal and social distance from the actual center of my world of working. The greater the distance the more uncertain are my anticipations of it until they become entirely empty and unrealizable.

8. *The World of Working as Paramount Reality*. The world of everyday work, so to speak, constitutes one of the many finite provinces of meaning upon which we bestow the accent of reality. However, this reality is marked out for several reasons. It is that world within reach in which there are physical things and <other> tangible <objects>; that means the world in which I can effectuate my plans and attain my purposes; the world that places tasks before me. I share this world and its objects with others; I have with them in common the whole undivided world of co-working, of social acts, and of social interrelationships, of means and ends, of space and time.

[14]An "X" appears in the typescript here, presumably indicating an absent footnote. In the corresponding published text, there is a footnote to Mead, *The Philosophy of the Present*, p. 225, note 15.

The time element in the social world would deserve a special study. Here we want only to state that the time which is constituted in the everyday world is an intersection of individual inner *durée* and cosmic time, which is the synthesis of all imaginable time perspectives. I shall call the time of the everyday life world the standard time. It is common to all of us. That is, all our systems of plans under which we subsume our actions, social or not, are elements of it: plans for life, for work and leisure, for the week or the next hour. Thus standard time is a real element of the everyday world, measurable in space but nevertheless coincident with our inner sense of time. This coincidence is particular to the state of mind which we have called wide-awakeness. Standard time is as much an intersubjective structure of the everyday world as the spatial structure of the earth that embraces the private environments of all of us.

Another reason for the pre-eminence of the reality of everyday working is the following fact: communications and interpretations, which can be tested as to their motives, projects and purposes, become possible only within <this reality of everyday working>. Such rational reconstructions are based on the assumption that acts or communications to be interpreted were performed by actors in wide-awakeness and with the intention to [set in motion] the interplay of mutual motivations lying at the bottom of all social interrelationships. The world of working, furthermore, is explicable by schemes of reference based on both the causality of motives and the teleology of purposes.

This world is the sphere within which reality is taken for granted and not questioned as to existence or mere appearance. Working involves changes in the outer world and these changes remain and can be tested even if their meanings and relevances have shifted in the subjective meaning of the actor. Within the unified field of this reality the *ego agens* appears as unified self. An act of interpretation is necessary in order to break this self down into roles. – All this will become very important for our later investigations of the world of science and especially of the social sciences.

II. The Many Realities and Their Constitution

We have found in the analysis of the world of working that there are certain basic assumptions which induce us to consider this world as a real one. These basic assumptions are: 1) a state of mind of wide-awakeness, originating in a certain *attention to life* ; 2) a specific *epoché*, namely the suspension of doubt; 3) *a prevalent form of spontaneity*, namely working: meaningful spontaneity based upon a preconceived project and the intention to realize it by bodily movements gearing into the outer world; 4) a specific *time perspective* (the standard time as intersection between the inner *durée* and the universal cosmic time); 5) a specific *form of sociality* (the common intersubjective world of social actions); 6) a specific concept of the experiencing *self* (*ego agens* as the total personality).

But otherwise we may say that, by making these assumptions, we bestow upon the world of working the accent of reality. We can do that because all our experiences of this world are not only consistent in themselves but also compatible with one another and because they all show a specific cognitive style. We are entitled to do so because our practical experiences have proven the unity and uniqueness of the world of working: the hypothesis of its reality is irrefutable. Even more, this reality seems to us to be the natural one and we are not ready to abandon our attitudes toward it without having experienced a specific shock which induces us to break through the limits of this "finite province of meaning" and to put its reality in question.

To be sure, experiences of shock befall me frequently amidst my daily life; they themselves pertain to the reality of daily life. They show me that the world of work in standard time is not the only finite province of meaning of my intentional life but only one among other provinces with which I am familiar too, although they are not of the same practical importance for me.

There are as many kinds of different experiences of shocks as there are different finite provinces of meaning upon which I may bestow the accent of reality. Some instances are: the shock of falling asleep as a leap into the world of dreams; the inner transformation we incur when the curtain in the theater raises as transition to the world of fiction; the radical change of our attitudes when we view a painting. <In the last case, we permit> the limitation of our visual field <by what we see> within the picture frame <which offers us a> passage into the world of art. <Or consider> our laughing after hearing the punchline of a comic story <to which we were> listening (attentively). For a short while we are ready to accept the fictitious world of the joke as reality in which the world of our daily life takes on the character of tomfoolery. <Or we may watch a> child turning toward his or her toys as transition to the play-world; and so on. <There are also> religious experiences in all their varieties – for instance, Kierkegaard's experiences of the "instant" leap into the religious sphere in such a shock. Or there is the decision of the scientist to replace all passionate participation in the affairs of "this world" by a disinterested contemplative attitude.

Our thesis is:

1. All of these worlds – the worlds of dreams, of imageries, of fantasms, especially the worlds of the arts, the worlds of religious experiences, of scientific contemplation, the play world of the child, and the worlds of the insane – are finite provinces of meaning. That means that all experiences within each world a) are consistent in themselves and compatible with one another (although not compatible with the meaning of everyday life); b) have their particular style of experiencing (although not that of the civic world of working); and c) may receive a specific accent of reality (although not the reality accent of the world of working).
2. All the aforementioned characteristics – consistency and compatibility, style of experiencing, accent of reality – are valid only *within* the boundaries of the particular province of meaning <in which they occur>. For instance, what is compatible for the province of meaning A will be by no means compatible with the province of meaning B. On the contrary, if a <person> supposes A to be real, B would appear to him as fictitious and inconsistent, and *vice versa*.
3. This very reason entitles us to call these <provinces of meaning> "finite": none of them is reducible to any other. Consequently, there is no possibility of a transition from one to the other by the introduction of a formula of transformation. <Each of

them> is only accessible by a "leap" – as Kierkegaard called it – or by an experience of shock, which is its subjective counterpart.

4. What was called a "leap" or a "shock" is nothing else than a radical modification of the tension of our consciousness; it is founded in a different "*attention à la vie*".
5. A specific *epoché*, a specific form of spontaneity, a specific time perspective, a specific form of sociality, and a specific concept of the experiencing self are particular to each of these provinces of different realities.
6. In daily life the world of working is the archetype of our experiences of reality; all the other provinces of meaning may be considered its modifications.

It would be an interesting task to try a systematic grouping of these finite provinces of meaning according to their constitutive principles [and] the diminishing tensions of our consciousness founded in a turning-away of our attention from life. Such an analysis would prove that the more mind turns away from life the more of the everyday world of working is put in brackets and included in the *epoché* of the <non-skeptic> attitude.[15] In other words, a typology of the different provinces would start from an analysis of that moment of the world within the center of our attentional interest in life. What remains outside the brackets could be defined as the constituents of the style of experience particular to the province of meaning thus delineated. In its turn it may obtain another accent of reality – or in the language of the archetype of all reality, namely that of our daily life, or quasi-reality.

The last remark reveals a specific difficulty inherent in all attempts at describing these quasi-realities. It consists in the fact that language – any language – pertains to communication *kat exochen* (held separate from) the intersubjective world of working and therefore resists [becoming] a vehicle for meanings that transcend the presuppositions upon which its system subsists. Therefore everything which can be communicated about the derivative provinces of meaning has an incidental and metaphorical character and is rather a hint than a statement.[16]

First of all we are interested in the difference between the world of working in daily life and the world of science, especially of social sciences. However, we cannot work out this problem in all its implications in a single step.[17] [Therefore] we shall proceed in stages and start [by] confronting the world of working with two typical examples of other finite provinces of meaning, namely the world of imageries and the world of dreams. Afterwards and based on the results of our investigations concerning the modifications of the meanings of experiences in passing from one province to the other we shall embark upon a description of the world of scientific contemplation.

[15]In the margin of the typescript, opposite the preceding nine words, there is a question mark.

[16]Footnote of Alfred Schutz: "This certainly holds true also for the philosophical attitude. Scientific terminology is a special device for overcoming the outlined difficulty within <its own sphere>."

[17]About seven lines of repetition of the previous paragraph have been omitted here [FK].

III. The Worlds of Imageries[18]

Under this heading we shall try to describe the general characteristics of a whole group of finite provinces of meaning; all of them originate in modifications which the world-conceived-in-full-awakeness undergoes when our minds turn away from full attention towards life and its tasks – in other words, when the tensions of our consciousness gradually diminish. We have no longer to master the outer world and to overcome the resistance of its objects; we have no longer to choose between issues derived from occurrences within it and we are free from the bondage of inter-objective space and inter-subjective standard time. However, the indicated modifications show the most manifold shadings. The latter depend on the degrees of attention toward life between full awakeness and mere dreaming – <attentions> which function as constitutive regulators for the limitation of the particular province of meaning under consideration, for instance, for the worlds of daydreams, of play, of the arts, of jest, and so on. They differ from one another by their different ways in which the accent of reality is withdrawn from that of the world of daily life in order to be replaced by a context of supposedly quasi-real fantasms.

They all have in common that the imagining self does not work. It does not even act in accordance with the earlier definition. Although imagining may be projected, it always lacks the intention to realize the project; that is, it lacks the purposive "fiat". However, we have to sharply distinguish between imagining as a performance of spontaneity and the imagined imageries. Although I am not acting when imagining a performance of spontaneity I may imagine myself as acting and even working. Thus the imagined acting may refer to a project, it may have its in-order-to and because motives, it may originate in choice and decision. Even more, it may show intentions to be realized and it may be fancied to be gearing into the outer world. However, all this belongs to the imageries produced by the imagining, etc. Imagining itself is necessarily inefficient and remains outside the hierarchies of plans and purposes that are valid in the world of working. The imagining self does not transform the outer world.

But how? Does not Don Quixote act and even work when he attacks the windmills, imagining that they were giants? Is not his in-order-to motive that of killing giants and his because-motive that of complying with his knightly code which obliges him to fight bad giants wherever he meets them? Is what he does not included in the hierarchy of his life-plan and does it not gear into the outer world? The answer is that Don Quixote, when acting as described, does not transgress the boundaries of the world of working. He is a fantasm confronted with realities (as Eulenspiegel is a realist confronted with fantasms). For him there are no imagined giants in the reality of his world of working but real giants. Afterward he will recognize that his interpretation of the objects of his chivalrous deeds is falsified by the events. But for him this is <not> the same experience all we others make when it turns out that something in the distance that we believed to be a tree is in reality a man. Don Quixote

[18]In the printed version of this text, Schutz replaced the word, "Imageries", with the word, "Phantasms".

reacts otherwise than we would in similar situations: he does not admit that "his experience exploded" and he does not acknowledge his delusion by concluding that the attacked object was always a windmill and not a giant. He comes to the result that his archenemy, the Magician, in the last moment transformed the giant into a windmill. Merely by drawing this conclusion, Don Quixote performed the leap into the world of imageries. He is compelled to accept the reality of the windmill but he interprets this fact as not belonging to the world of everyday life. What within this world is incompatible, namely the existence of magicians and giants and the transformation of the latter into windmills, is very well compatible within the finite province of imageries. *Mutatis mutandis* similar analyses could be made concerning the magic world of primitive man and the make-believe worlds of children at play.

By analyzing Don Quixote's conduct we have obtained another important result. The compatibilities of experience that belong to the world of working in everyday life do not subsist within the finite province of imagery; however, the logical consistency of experiences in themselves remains valid. I can imagine giants, magicians, centaurs, even a *perpetuum mobile* (a self-propelling machine never running down), but not a regular decahedron – unless I am satisfied with the blind juxtaposition of empty words, as I may do in full awakeness. Put otherwise: within the realm of imagery the logical incompatibilities hold good but not the factual ones.

The corollary of this statement is that "chances" in the proper meaning of the term do not exist within the province of imageries in the same manner in which they exist in the world of working. What in the latter is a chance is in the former what jurists call a *conditio potestativa* (wilful condition); that is, it depends on the imagining individual whether or not he wants to fill the empty anticipations of the future with any content. Thus the scope of the "freedom of discretion" is larger by far in the world of fantasms than in the world of daily life.

The time perspective within the world of imageries is of great importance. The imagining self can eliminate all the features of standard time except its irreversibility. It may imagine all occurrences as if viewed, so to speak, through a time retarder or through a time accelerator. However, irreversibility eludes any variation by imagery because it originates within the *durée* which also subsists in the world of imageries. Imagining and even dreaming I continue to grow older. The fact that I can remodel my past by a present imagining is no counter argument against this statement. In my imageries I may fancy myself in any role I wish to assume. But doing so I have no doubt that the imagined self is only a part of my personality: a Me existing only by my grace. In my fantasms I may even vary my bodily appearance but this freedom of discretion has its barrier at the primordial experience of the boundaries of my body. They exist whether I imagine myself a dwarf or a giant.

Imagining may occur lonely or social. An instance of the first kind is day-dreaming; one of the second kind is the mutually oriented intersubjective make-believe of the playing of children, or some of the phenomena uncovered by the study of the psychology of donning masks. On the other hand, other persons and all kinds of social relationships of social actions and reactions, may become objects of imagining. The freedom of discretion of the imagining self is a very large one. It is even possible that the imagined fantasms include imagined cooperations of imagined fellow men to such a degree that the latter's imagined reactions may corroborate or annihilate one's own fantasms.

IV. The World of Dreams

Deep sleep is the opposite of full-awakeness. If the latter is considered the highest degree of the tension of consciousness that corresponds to a maximum *"attention à la vie"*, the former is the outcome of complete relaxation. Sleep is that state of consciousness which is free from all apperceptions although not from perception of all kinds. In contradistinction to any form of awakeness the sleeping self has no pragmatic interest whatever to transform its principally confused conceptions into some state of clarity and distinctness – in other words, to transform them into apperceptions. However, the sleeping self continues to perceive. There are the somatic perceptions of the self's own body, its position, its weight, its boundaries; perceptions of light, of sound, of warmth occur without any activities of regarding, listening, attending to them which alone would transform them into apperceptions. Furthermore they continue in small perceptions that in the state of wide-awakeness remain indiscernible and ineffable within the pragmatic orientations towards the tasks of life – or as we like to call this in modern usage: the unconscious. But exactly these small perceptions, escaping the censorship of the attention to life, gain high importance in the world of dreams. To be sure, they do not become clear and distinct; they remain in a state of confusion. Yet the passive attentions, which are nothing else than the totality of the effects exercised by the small perceptions upon the intimate order of the personality, are no longer concealed and disturbed by the active attentional acts that are conscious and pragmatically conditioned. Therefore passive attention alone determines the interest of the dreamer and the topics that become themes of his dreams. It is the incomparable performance of Freud and his school to have clarified the reference of dream life to the unconscious – although his concept of the unconscious itself, and also his theory of the three selves (Id, Ego, Superego), misunderstands the basic character of the intentionality of the stream of thought.

The dreaming self neither works nor acts. This statement would be a mere truism had we not applied it also to the world of imageries. Therefore we have the task to show the principal modifications which the "bracketing of the world of working" undergoes both within the province of imageries and that of dreams. I submit that the world of imageries is characterized by what we called a high degree of freedom of discretion whereas the world of dreams lacks such a freedom. The imagining self bestows the accent of reality – and may integrate "chances" lying within its mastery. None of these features of *potestativity* (power or ability)[19] prevail for the dreamer. There exists no freedom of discretion, no arbitrariness in the evaluation of changes, no possibility of filling in empty anticipations. For instance, the nightmare shows clearly that the happenings in the world of dreams are inescapable and the dreamer is powerless to influence them. However, all this does not mean that the experiences

[19]In the typescript, the word "discretion" was written above the word, *"potestativity"*.

of the dreamer do not have the character of intentionality. To the contrary, active intentionalities subsist although they are not directed toward the outer world of working and not steered by active attention. But among these experiences are none[20] of apperceiving or of volition. The life of dreams is without purpose and project.

In general, the world of working is safeguarded as object of the world of dreams in the form of recollections and retentions, or at least fragments of it are. We may say in this sense that the *attention à la vie* is directed toward the self in the past tense. The happenings in dream life are the re-interpretation of past experiences by transforming previously confused experiences into distinctness by explicating their implied horizons, by shifting their anticipations into the past and their reproductions into the future. The sedimented experiences of the world of awakeness are thus, so to speak, broken down and reconstructed otherwise. In dream life the self has no longer any pragmatic interest to keep together its stock of knowledge as a consistent unity. For the same reason, the postulates of the consistency of experience and of what is commonly called *adequatio rei ac intellectus* (adequacy controls the intellect) are not valid within the realm of dreams since these postulates <do not appear> in the tense of the future past.[21] Consequently the rules of compatibility are eliminated and even logical axioms (for instance, the axiom of identity) do not hold good in the sphere of the dream. Frequently the dreamer is astonished to see now as compatible what he remembers to have been incompatible in the world of wide-awake life. Freud and other psychoanalysts have worked this out thoroughly. It was merely our intention to translate some of their results – those which are important for the topic at hand – into our language and to give them their place within our system.

I may dream of myself as working or acting, frequently accompanied by the knowledge in reality that I am not working or acting. My dream-working has its quasi-projets, its quasi-plans and their hierarchies, all originating in pre-experienced sedimentations in the world of daily life. When a dreamer dreams himself working it happens frequently that he dreams he can perform his work without any intention to realize it, without any volitive fiat. He may effectuate results with improportionally either great or small efforts.

The analysis of the time perspective particular to the realm of dreams is very difficult. Seemingly, but not only seemingly, the happenings during the dream are no longer embedded in the stream of the inner *durée*. However they are merely detached from the arrangements of standard time. They unroll in the subjectivity of inner *durée* although parts of the standard time are snatched into the world of dreams: they were <originally> experienced by the past self <as coherent time units> but that have now fallen to pieces. However, even within the happenings of dreams the irreversibility of *durée* persists. Only: sometimes the awakened person has the illusion of possible reversibility when remembering his dreams.

The last remark reveals a serious difficulty for all dealings with the phenomena of dream but also of imagery. As soon as I think about them I no longer dream or

[20]Wagner substituted the word, "none", for the word, "more", found in the typescript. The latter runs counter to Schutz's argument, the former being consistent with the argument and the published version of the text. [FK]

[21]About eleven lines of repetition of the foregoing paragraphs have been omitted here. [FK]

imagine. Speaking and thinking, I am wide-awake and use the implements of the world of working, and they are subject to the principles of consistency and compatibility. Are we sure that the awakened person, he who no longer dreams, really tells of his dreams? Probably it will be of a certain importance whether he recollects his dream in vivid retention or whether he has to reproduce it. Whatever the case may be, we encounter here the eminent dialectic difficulty that no possibility of direct communication exists which would not transcend the sphere to which it refers. We can approach the provinces of dreams and of imageries only by way of "indirect communication", to borrow this term from Kierkegaard who, in an unsurpassable way, has analyzed the phenomenon it suggests. Poets and artists are by far closer to an interpretation of the worlds of dreams and fantasms than scientists and philosophers. The categories of the former refer themselves to the realm of imagery. They can, if not overcome it, so at least show forth the underlying dialectical conflict.

Within the modest limits of our purpose we have no reason to shrink away from the outlined difficulties. Our topic is the style of experiences particular to the provinces of imageries and dreams as modifications of the style of experiencing the world of everyday life. Therefore we feel entitled to apply categories derived from this world to the phenomena of imagery and dream. However, as outlined, the dialectic difficulty has to be understood by us in its full importance. We shall meet the same problems again in our analysis of the world of scientific contemplation and we shall have to study the specific device that science has developed for overcoming it, namely the scientific method.

Concluding our fugitive remarks about the realm of dreams we want to state that dreaming, in contradistinction to imagining, is essentially lonely. We cannot dream together and the *alter ego* remains always an object of my dreams, incapable of <sharing> them. The *alter ego* of whom I dream does not appear in its vivid presence but in an empty fictitious quasi-we-relation. The other of whom I dream is always typified – and that even when I dream him to be in a very close relationship to my intimate self. He is an *alter ego* only by my grace. Thus the monad with all its mirroring of the universe is indeed without windows when it dreams.

V. The World of Theoretical Contemplation

We have studied the general style of experiencing in the provinces of imageries and dreams and <contrasted it to> the world of working. This was a preliminary step toward an analysis of the realm of the experiences of the practical actor. However, we encounter considerable difficulties when <circumscribing> the province of meaning to be investigated. Our daily life within what we called the world of working does not exclusively consist in working and acting, in kinaesthetic, locomotive and other bodily movements. It is a permanent oscillating between contemplative and practical attitudes, between interpreting the surrounding world and practical reaction to it, between deliberating and planning and the execution of these plans. And in great crises of our lives we sit down and analyze our problems as objectively and theoretically as possible. "We stop and think", as Dewey put it. How, then, is it possible to separate the level of contemplation from the level of our working activities since both belong equally to our existence as human beings within this world? For what reason should we consider the realm of theoretical contemplation as a finite province of meaning, separated from the everyday life-world by a shifting of the accent of reality? Obviously, in daily life we continually cross the borderline of this province, if any, without hesitation and without experiencing a shock.

The answer to this question is: of course, our daily life in the world is not <occurring> on one single level of reality. During a single day or even <a few hours> we run through several levels. Performing our daily duties we do not live exclusively in that tension of consciousness that we called "full-awakeness". To the contrary, our consciousness shows a permanent oscillation among all possible degrees of tensions; it runs through the whole gamut of *attention à la vie*. As long as we live naïvely along in the vivid presence of our stream of thought our life is a totality of possible performances of spontaneity. However, when we turn to an attitude of reflection towards our life, when we abandon the tendency to float with the stream of our experiences and step out of it, the seeming unity of our experiences goes to pieces. We have to reconstruct it by artificial devices: by abstractions, formalizations, idealizations, by isolating what seems to be typical for a cross-section of our existence.

We break down the unity of our life and single out certain finite provinces of meanings on which we place the accent of reality. This attempt shows all the shortcomings of typification. However, in this special case we feel entitled to pay attention to what we called the world of theoretical contemplation since it is the home of scientific activity in so far as it is systematical-theoretical. We take as model of our analysis this theoretic-scientific thinking and its special attitude toward its objects. <Yet> we remain well aware of the fact that daily life also shows enclaves of purely theoretical contemplation.

All theoretical cogitations are actions within the meaning of our definition. Thinking as scientific contemplation is a performance of spontaneity according to a project. It has its in-order-to and because motives and its hierarchies of plans that are established with the decision to pursue and carry out scientific activities. Furthermore, theoretical thinking has its special form of volition: It is purposive thinking, the purpose being the intention to reach the solution of the problem on hand. However, theoretical thinking does not gear into the outer world. Therefore it is not "working" as defined above. Scientific thinking can only be communicated by acts of working (writing a paper, delivering a lecture); it is based upon or checked by working activities. These facts do not contradict our statement. All these activities are performed in the world of working; they are conditions or consequences of the purely theoretic activity of contemplative thinking but can easily be separated from it.

In the same manner we have to distinguish between the scientist as human being who acts and lives his daily life among his fellowmen, and the scientist as theoretical thinker whose aim is not to master the pregiven world but to observe and possibly to understand it.

Here I wish to anticipate another possible objection. Is it not the ultimate aim of science to master the world? Are not the sciences of nature designed to dominate the forces of the universe, and the social sciences to exercise control, the medical sciences to fight disease? And is not the only reason why man bothers with science his desire to develop the necessary tools in order to improve everyday life and to help humanity in its pursuit of happiness? Certainly all this is as true as it is banal and has nothing to do with our problem. The desire to improve the world is one of the strongest motives for men to occupy themselves with science. All applied sciences have the goal to invent <workable> devices for the mastery of the world. But it neither injures the dignity of science nor impairs the merits of applied sciences if we separate the mere theoretical attitude of contemplation – which is an integral element of the scientific process – from their practical application. <In other words, we> abstract from the fact that <scientific-contemplative> results may be used for "worldly" purposes. Scientific theorizing is one thing, dealing with <aspects of scientific knowledge that are applicable> within the world is another. Our topic is "theorizing" and our problem is a most serious one: How can the life-world of all of us be made an object of theoretical contemplation and how can the outcome of this contemplation be used within the world of working?

We repeat: the pure, theoretical sphere of science is marked by the fact that the thinker is not interested in the mastery of the world but in its observation and the knowledge <gained thereby>. This attitude of the "disinterested observer" is based on a particular *attention à la vie* as a prerequisite of all theorizing. It consists in the abandoning of the system of relevances which prevails in the practical sphere. The whole universe of life – what Husserl calls the *"Lebenswelt"* – is pregiven to both man in the world of working and the theorizing thinker. But for the former other sections and other elements of this world are relevant than for the latter.

The necessities of physical life require the handling of physical things and the overcoming of obstacles in order to comply with the basic requirements of life. The interest in life as task to be performed builds up the system of relevances that selects the objects of the world in the world within my reach. As we have seen, it is *the* center of reality of the world of working; it corresponds to the full-awakeness of the practical attitude. In the world within my reach those objects become important that are useful or dangerous or otherwise relevant to my basic experiences. I know that I have to die and I fear death: This experience lies at the basis of my system of relevances. I wish to call it the fundamental anxiety. It is the origin of my many interrelated hopes and fears, my wants and <illusions> of my system of chances and dangers, of my ideals of success and <my fears of failure>, all of which guide me in any of my attempts at mastering the world, at overcoming obstacles, at drafting my projects, and at realizing them. I am always anticipating the future with opposite expectations <concerning the outcome> of my intended work either according to plan or else in consequence of <the failure of my expectations and [resulting]> in repercussions for the objects.

I am persistently interested in the results of my actions and in the question of whether my anticipations will stand the practical test. Of course, these anticipations and plans refer to previous experiences that have taught me to evaluate the changes of occurrences <that I wish to bring about by my actions>. But that is only half the story. *What* I am anticipating is one thing; the other thing is *why* I anticipate certain occurrences at all. The question, what may happen under certain conditions and circumstances is one thing; the other is why I am interested in these happenings and why I should passionately expect the outcome of my <expectations>.[22]

Only the first part of these dichotomies is answered by a reference to the stock of experiences at hand <which, in turn, is to be seen> as sediment of previous experiences. The second part of the dichotomies refers to the system of relevances by which the working man is guided by his daily life. This system originates in the fundamental anxiety; it is the regulator for the selective activity of our consciousness. To describe its constitution requires toilsome analyses. To carry them out is not the purpose of the present paper. But we had to indicate the problem involved in order to delineate the specific attitude toward life that is particular to the theoretical thinker. As I have already said, this thinker does not use the system of relevance of man within the world of working. He is free from the fundamental anxiety[23] and free from all the hopes and fears arising from it.

He also makes his anticipations, on the one hand, by referring back to the stock of experiences and, on the other hand, <by using> a special system of relevances which shall be discussed later. But he is not passionately interested in the practical question whether the anticipation is fulfilled: If the anticipation is fulfilled, will it prove to be practically useful? He is solely interested in whether or not it will stand the test, whether or not it will be verified or falsified by supervening experiences. His passionate interest is the truth, regardless of whether it is pleasant or unpleasant, helpful or dangerous for the process of life. In the well-understood meaning of the definition given above, this involves a certain detachment of interest in life and a turning-away from what we called the state of full-awakeness.[24]

Another characteristic of the world pregiven to the theoretical thinker is the fact that it is independent of the scope of his reach. As we have seen, the concept, "world within reach", depends on our body as the center O of the system of coordinates through which we group this world. In turning to the sphere of theoretical thinking, however, the human being puts his physical existence and therewith also his body between brackets. Unlike the man in daily life he is not interested in finding a solu-

[22]For Schutz's word, "prophesies", Wagner substituted the more appropriate word, "expectations".

[23]Footnote of Alfred Schutz: "This does not mean that the fundamental anxiety is not the chief motive inducing human beings to philosophize. To the contrary, philosophy is one of the attempts – perhaps the principal one – to escape the fundamental anxiety. An immortal being, say an angel in the system of Thomas Aquinas, need not turn philosopher. But the human being, having performed the 'leap' into the realm of theoretical contemplation, exercises a particular *epoché* of the fundamental anxiety by putting it and its implications between brackets."

[24]Footnote of Alfred Schutz: "I hope that this proposition will not be misunderstood. It contains no pejorative connotation. The term, 'full-awakeness' – as used in this paper – does not involve any valuations. Nothing could be more wrong than to conclude that the writer intended to declare that mere life has a higher dignity than philosophical thinking as is the point of view of certain faddish 'Philosophies of Life' especially modish in Germany. If there is any reason at all to prefer the system of relevances of the living world over other attitudes, it is a methodological one: it is easier to communicate (in everyday language). We have to keep in mind that communication originates within the world of working." Helmut Wagner added a further note to remind the reader to bear in mind that the "present essay was written in 1943, that is, at the height of World War II. Obviously Schutz felt it necessary to distance himself from slogans such as 'Germany Awake!' and from the 'Blood and Soil' mystique of the National-Socialist Party whose leaders had set the Western World on fire."

tion fit for his personal and private problems depending on the particular circumstances of his situation. The theoretical thinker is interested in the truth, in problems and solutions valid in their own right and for everyone. Therefore he has made up his mind to abstract from the subjective point of view.

Summing up: The *epoché* particular to the theoretical attitude refers 1) to the subjectivity of the thinker as man among fellowmen in the world of working; 2) to the pragmatic system of relevances valid within this world; and 3) to our fundamental anxiety and its implications. They all are put between brackets. But in this modified sphere the life-world of us all subsists as the object of theoretical contemplation but, as pointed out, not as object of practical interests. However, with this shift in the system of relevances all terms change their meanings <in so far as they> refer to manifestations in the world of working, such as "plan", "motive", "project".

Now we have to describe the system of relevances that prevails in the field of theoretical contemplation. It is created in a voluntary act of the scientist in which he selects his objects for further inquiry. In other words: it is created by *stating the problem*. As soon as the problem has been stated its solution becomes the supreme goal of theorizing activities. However, by stating the problem at hand the sections or elements of the life-world that are of theoretical interest in respect to it are likewise defined. Henceforth this delimitation will serve as guidelines for the progress of the inquiry. Most of all it determines the level of research. Secondly, it demarcates the parts of the life-world that can be considered mere data to be accepted without question and what other parts have to be made into subject-matters of further investigations. In the third place, the <delimitation> reveals the open horizon – the influence of connected problems which will have to be stated <later>. On the other hand, <we find the cluster> of all the implications within the problem itself; they have to be explicated in order to solve <the problem>. By stating the problem the elements of the pregiven life-world have been divided into groups. One group is constituted by those that belong to the problem stated. <They comprise> its <characteristics> and <effects> which are supposed to be investigated, explicated, clarified. The other <group contains items that> are irrelevant with respect to the problems at hand. They have to be accepted in their mere givenness and they are mere data.

The <preceding> presentation shows a two-fold shortcoming. First it seems that the scientist has the same full "freedom in discretion" in choosing his problems that the imagining self has in filling out its anticipations. This is not true at all. Of course, the theoretical thinker may choose at his discretion – a choosing solely determined by inclinations rooted in his intimate personality – the science in which he wants to carry out his investigations. But as soon as he has made up his mind in this respect, the scientist enters a pre-constituted world of scientific contemplation handed down to him by the historical tradition of this science.

Henceforth he will participate in a universe of discourse determined by the results obtained by others, problems stated by others, solutions suggested by others, methods worked out by others. This theoretical universe itself is a finite province of meaning, having its particular style of experience with particular implications of problems and horizons to be explicated. The regulative principle of the constitution of this province is <the following>: any emergent problem has to participate in this universal style of experiences by either accepting or rejecting the subsisting problems and their solutions or demonstrating them to be merely apparent problems. Therefore each stating of a problem is connected with the whole universe of scientific experiences. As a matter of fact a scientist's latitude of discretion in stating his problem is very small.

However, as soon as the problem has been stated and the inquiry started there is no latitude left at all. The [second] of the aforementioned shortcomings of our presentation is that it represents the process of scientific thinking too statically. This process is going on according to strict rules of scientific procedure. It is not without our present purpose to describe the epistemology and methodology <of this procedure>. The postulate of consistency and compatibility of all propositions prevails not only within the field of the particular science. It also [prevails in] all the other scientific experiences and even with [respect to] experiences of the life-world: the postulate that all scientific acts must be traced back to or tested by genuine experiences; the postulate of a maximum of clarity and distinctness of all terms and notions; and, as a corollary of it, the postulate of explicating the hidden implications of pre-scientific thought, and so on. Science and the methodologies of the single sciences have established the necessary rules and devices in order to guarantee the operational procedures of scientific work and of the testing of its results. The totality of these rules sets forth the conditions under which scientific propositions and the totality of scientific [thought] can be considered as guaranteed and tested.

The perspective of time particular to the activities of contemplative theorizing is a very complicated structure. The theoretical thinker lives also within his inner *durée*; he also grows older since his stock of experiences changes <continuously> with the emergence and sedimentation of new experiences. Therefore the theorizing self has its particular history which refers to its past. It also has its own perspective of the future since it projects future tasks arising from the open horizon of other problems and methods to which its present problems refer. The theorizing self lacks the time perspective of the specious present, the time-form particular to the working self. The specious present is inseparably connected with, and the project of, standard time, which may become the object of thinking but is not its medium. In so far as scientific activities take place in the standard time of working hours, time tables, and so on, they consist of working in the outer world and of dealing with science but in the acts of pure theorizing. If, on the other hand, we define the present by the spread of the projects conceived at a certain moment by the acting self we may say that the theorizing self has its particular present, constituted with the stating of the problem; <it defines> the spread of the projects that <are the subject-matter> to be <dealt with> by the theorizing activities planned for their solution.

Everything (?)[25] described so far refers to the world of the theorizing itself and not to the world of the objects of such theorizing. We had to distinguish between the world of imagining and the world of imageries; now we have to distinguish between theorizing cogitations and the theoretical *cogitata* (the content of the theoretical thoughts) of such theorizing. By their intentionality the latter refer to the one life-

[25]The question mark is in square brackets in the typescript.

world within which we all work and think – to the intersubjective life-world that is pregiven to all our forms of conscious living and therefore also to our thinking.

Here now arises a dialectical problem similar to that which we encountered in our analysis of the world of dreams. But in the sphere of theoretical contemplation this dialectical problem has a twofold aspect.

In the world of working, including the working self, both the thinker as human being and his working fellow man belong to the objects of potential theoretical cogitations. The existence of fellow men, the question as to how I may get knowledge of them in the natural attitude, and the question of what the object of this knowledge can be – <all of these questions> may become theoretical problems. Great difficulties arise when the world of working in its intersubjectivity and its particular form of existence within standard time become the topic of theoretical thoughts. <And that occurs> in those sciences that are commonly called the social sciences. As long as thinking deals with objects in universal time which do not recur in the theorizing activities of the consciousness of the thinker[26] himself – and this is the case in the sciences of nature and especially in those that are suitable for mathematical treatment – the dialectical problem outlined does not appear in its full <seriousness>. But how should it be possible that the thinker who remains in theoretical disinterestedness and refrains from all working activities should find the approach to the world of working accessible only in the very natural attitude he has abandoned? How could this be possible since all working happens within the specious present of standard time?

As we have seen, [the specious present] is the dimension which does not enter into the system of the time perspectives of theoretical contemplation. Furthermore, only by working and in working does the unity and <complexity> of the self in its totality become established when all the other approaches break this unity down into the roles of different "Me's". How, then, can the acting self in its totality become an object of theoretical contemplation? Yet this is the very presupposition of all theoretical social sciences. Moreover, the theoretical social scientist can only refer to his own subjectivity as source of all experiences of the existence of others, of their acting and working, and of the meaning they bestow upon their acts and their works. His subjectivity can only become a source of knowledge because he is a human being living with other humans in the same world of the natural attitude. But this is the same "innerworldly" subjectivity that he had to put between brackets which <we encountered> in our analysis of dream life: the problem of the person who awakened and attempts to communicate his experiences as a dreamer. However, here we have to face this dialectical difficulty in its full <seriousness> in order to understand that the theoretical thinker in his necessary aloofness cannot find access to the naïve life-world within which I, you, Peter and Paul, anyone and everyone acts, plans, worries, hopes – and in which <nearly everyone> is interested and pays attention or

[26]Footnote of Alfred Schutz: "However, the problem does appear as soon as the scientific observer includes himself in the observational field. For instance, <this was done by> Heisenberg, the world-famous physicist who postulated the famous 'relation of uncertainty'. If <events of this kind occur in the natural sciences> so-called crises in the fundamental problems of these sciences emerge. They are just one form of the dialectical situation outlined in the text."

else has at least confused and ineffable perceptions. In one word: <it is the world in which they all live> their lives as unbroken selves in their full humanity.

In order to understand the artificiality of indirect communication we have to face the fact that this life-world is inaccessible to the theoretical social scientist. It is only by means of <communication in terms of the artificial languages of their sciences that> the theoretical social scientists manage to bring the intersubjective life-world into view – or better (a quite simplified) <and rigidly mechanized> likeness of it.

<In this likeness> the human world is deprived of its liveliness, and the men living in it are deprived of their humanity. This artificial device is called "the Method of the Social Sciences". <With its help social scientists> overcome the outlined dialectical difficulty by substituting a model of the life-world for the life-world itself. <They [populate]> this model not with human beings in their full humanity but with puppets, with *types* that are constructed in such a way that their supposed actions and re-actions are not performed in spontaneity. <Rather> they are bestowed upon them by the grace of the social scientist. <By design> they are supposed to become consistent in themselves as well as compatible with our experiences that originated in the world of daily life. We do not have to develop here the outlines of this typifying method; we only have to show the dialectical difficulties <that beset> any theoretical social science.

Theorizing itself, however, reveals another aspect of the dialectical difficulties involved. It consists in the fact that theorizing itself is an activity performable only by human beings in intersubjectivity. To be sure, theorizing is lonely as long as we consider only the ongoing stream of cogitations. But, as mentioned before, for the theorizing self the theoretical universe of discourse is pregiven as the outcome of other persons' theorizing acts. Moreover, it is founded on the assumption that other persons too theorize, have experiences, have the possibility to verify or falsify my own results.

However, such mutual corroborating and refuting presupposes communication and is only possible outside of the purely theoretical sphere, namely the world of working and by acts of man in his unbroken living humanity. A scientist turns back from his theoretical attitude to the natural one in order to communicate as a human being with his fellow men. This is a highly paradoxical situation: the full display of theorizing activities becomes possible only after dropping the pure, theoretical attitude in the world of everyday life that, on its part, remains inaccessible to the direct approach of theorizing. Yet it is exactly this paradoxical situation which prevents theorizing from <freezing into> a strange solipsism by which any thinking self would remain secluded in its own private and fictitious world. Only [by virtue of] this paradox, originating in the dialectical situation of theorizing itself, does science become again included in the life-world. And, conversely, the miracle of *symphilosophein* brings the full humanity of the thinker into the theoretical field.

CHAPTER 4

Teiresias or Our Knowledge of Future Events

Editors' Preface

In his "Editor's Note" to the second volume of Schutz's *Collected Papers*, which contains the published version of this essay (1959), Arvin Brodersen refers to two earlier drafts which Schutz had written in 1942 and 1943.[1] There was yet a third draft of 1944/45 which superseded them. Because it yields the most extensive text of the whole, Wagner selected it for inclusion in this volume.[2]

II

In the following an attempt is made to analyze some of the forms in which the man who lives among his fellow men in the natural attitude of everyday life anticipates things to come. Thus problems of scientific prediction and of calculable probability are excluded from the present investigation. The preceding inquiry[3] – how the consciousness of a fictitious seer might be conceived to work – serves the mere purpose to pinpoint certain aspects of the problem which are incompatible with the natural attitude.

To start with: Teiresias' knowledge of future events is not related to his present or past experiences or to his considerably elaborated vision of things to come; at no

[1]Alfred Schutz, *Collected Papers*, Volume II, pp. xivf.

[2]Because the first four and a half pages of the printed text of 1959 (designated Section I) are essentially identical with the first pages of the first part of the 1944/45 text, those pages have been omitted here. The text printed in *Collected Papers*, Volume II, was first published in *Social Research*, 26 (1), 1959, where the spelling of "Teiresias" is "Tiresias". The text published here is dated by Schutz, "Delaware Watergap, July 31–August 6, 1944", and "New York, July 12 –August 5, 1945". In his notes to the editing of this text Wagner observes that the "or" of the title does not indicate that "our knowledge of future events" is the same sort as that of Teiresias; "our knowledge of future events" is public foresight, he says, that may be expressed by one person but the formation of which can be shared by many persons. In contrast, Teiresias' gift is utterly private. The "or", then, "separates ordinary foresight of predictable events . . . from the terrifying flash of the seer's seizure of the unpredictable event beyond any human horizon."

[3]The first section of this essay, published in *Collected Papers*, Volume II, pp. 277–281.

given moment did it originate in the stock of his knowledge at hand. Teiresias, taken as a seer but not as a man in everyday life, does not have a present in which to live, not even a specious one. Even his past is irrelevant for his prophecies because it is unrelated to them. By contrast, man in his everyday life lives in the actuality of Now which is the terminus of his past and the starting point of his future. The organized stock of his knowledge on hand in any such Now – though changing in content and structure from any Now to any other Now – serves him as a scheme of reference for interpreting his past, present and future experiences.

Second: Teiresias is not an interested party to the events which he forecasts. In daily life, man is eminently interested in what he anticipates. His prognoses refer to the very world which will become his and his children's actual life-world. He has to be prepared for it, ready to dominate or endure it. What will come interests him now; everything he predicts is related to and relevant for the actual state of affairs he lives in. This relevance expresses itself in his fears and hopes. Motivated by them, he selects from all imaginable future occurrences some which he brings anticipatorily before his mind. But he does not only think about such future events; within the limits of his powers he tries to bring them forth or at least to modify them through his actions. Thus, what he anticipates becomes determinative for the motives, projects and plans which govern such actions.

Third: What will happen Teiresias sees as certainty. His knowledge of future events is no less originary and self-giving than our perceptions. However, none of our perceptions has this character <of Teiresian expectations>. We think of things to come in terms of chances and probabilities of various degrees. Ours is not a knowledge of certitude but merely a belief in likelihood; <this belief> can either transform itself into certainty or is annulled before the anticipated event occurs, whether or not it occurs as expected. All this has been analyzed by Hume with unsurpassable clarity.

Fourth: Like all our knowledge, our knowledge [of future events] is from the outset intersubjective. My present and past experiences upon which I base my expectations are not isolated and inaccessible to others as are those of Teiresias. To the contrary, at the least they refer to the possibility of being checked against and tested or refuted by present or past experiences of others.

Let us examine more closely these arguments in their interconnections.

III

Man in daily life, I have said, finds at any given moment a certain stock of knowledge on hand, ready to be used as scheme of interpretation of what he is doing and what is occurring to him. This stock of knowledge has its history and its particular form of organization. It is historical because any of its elements and bits of knowledge refer back to previous acts of experiencing in which and by which they have been formed. In describing the constitutional processes involved, Husserl speaks of the "sedimentations" of meanings. Any reference to past experiencing acts presupposes memory and all its functions, such as retentions, recollections, recognitions, etc. This does not mean that we have to reactivate our past acts of experiencing step by step in order to catch their outcomes. What has been constituted in previous activities of experiencing is the result of these past processes and can now be grasped in one single glance as this and that particular <piece of> knowledge.

This knowledge will be of various degrees of completeness, and it may or may not be compatible with all other particular experiences at hand in the same Now. Although organized in a specific way, this stock of knowledge on hand is by no means homogeneous. There is a relatively small kernel of knowledge which is distinct, clear and consistent in itself. Such particular knowledge is distinct if we can refer it back at any time to the past experiencing acts in which it has been constituted and of which it is a sediment. It is clear if we have full insight into the operational functions of these constitutive acts and their implications. It is consistent in itself if it is compatible not only with all of our own experiences but also with those of others – our contemporaries and predecessors.

However, this kernel is surrounded by layers of knowledge characterized by a decreasing degree of distinctive clarity and consistency. To use William James' terminology, such knowledge is merely "knowledge of acquaintance" without "knowledge about". For instance, we are familiar with certain facts, we have experienced them frequently but we are unable to break down this knowledge into the single phases in which it has been constituted or to explicate its hidden implications. Or we take a particular <piece of> knowledge for granted because others, whom we believe to be better informed, tell us that they have a distinct and clear insight in its object and we trust them. Other elements of our knowledge consists of vague notions not of particular facts but of the general type to which facts are allocated. A zone of blind belief follows, of mere impressions, assumptions, guesswork, hearsay. We have no interest whatever to transform them into clearness and distinctness. Our knowledge of this zone in its inherent vagueness suffices because this zone is irrelevant for the central problems with which we are dealing in this specific Now. We need not know more only about *this* subject. It is our changing interest and, as I will show presently, first of all our changing practical interest which determines the structurization of the stock of our knowledge at hand into layers of different relevance. Thus it delimits the borderlines between the various types of knowledge just characterized.

Any actually emerging experience is referred back to the stock of knowledge at hand by calling it a "familiar" or a "strange" experience. Familiar experiences are related to sameness, likeness, similarity, analogy to or with experiences already known to us. An emerging experience may be conceived as a pre-experienced "same which recurs" or as the "same but modified", as similar in type as pre-experienced; and so on. A "strange" experience cannot be referred back to a type or particularity of previous experiences. In order to understand it either we have to try analyzing it so as to find some elements or implications which refer to something pre-known to us or we have to re-group and re-interpret our stock of knowledge at hand in such a way that it becomes a scheme of interpretation applicable also to the new. If we do not succeed either way, we will carry this new experience in our memory as a strange one which we are incapable of understanding or explaining.

"Familiarity" and "strangeness", the terms used, merely point to the two opposite poles I have selected for the sake of a clearer presentation of the problem. They themselves are "types". As a matter of fact, there is no such thing as *pure* familiarity or *pure* strangeness. Even if the "same" experience recurs it is a novel experience by virtue of the mere fact that the sameness is *recurring*. Even if a strange experience is seen as unrelated to the pre-known it is by this very fact referred back to the stock of knowledge at hand. And solely by this reference does it become problematic.

Our previous statement about the cognition of the same calls for further qualification. As Husserl has shown, all forms of recognition and identification of objects, even of objects of the outer world, are based on a generalized knowledge of the type of these objects or of the typical way in which they manifest themselves. I recognize this particular cherry tree in my garden as being the same tree I saw yesterday, although in another light and shade of color. This is only possible because I know the typical way in which this object, "this particular cherry tree", refers to the pre-experienced types of "cherry-trees in general", "trees", "plants", "extended objects", and so on. Each of these types has its typical style of being experienced; the knowledge of this typical style itself is an element of our stock of knowledge at hand.

This account is still incomplete. No type or style is restricted to a single individual object. But more, there is no such thing as an isolated type or style pertaining to one class of generalized objects within the stock of our knowledge. All the types or styles of our experiencing form systems in which each type or style is interrelated with others in manifold ways; so, for instance, types of sequences of experiences of the forms "if-then", "either-or", and so on. The organization of our stock of knowledge at hand into systems of types is of highest importance for our anticipating the future.[4]

So far I have related the emergent experience to the stock of knowledge presently at hand, and thereby also to the past, namely the previous experiences which are sedimented in the present. The very fact that in any Now the stock of knowledge at hand is preconstituted shows that the present, in which the emergent experience is interpreted as being strange or familiar, is by no means a mere instant, a demarcation point between the past and the future. It is what James called a specious present which includes actual remembrances of things past in the form of the organized stock of knowledge at hand. But likewise any actual experience refers to the future: protentions of occurrences are expected to follow immediately as are anticipations of more distant events. These future events also belong to our specious present whose structure I will have to describe later. At this point, it is pertinent to deal with the underlying idealizations that make anticipations in daily life possible.

Husserl proved convincingly that idealizations and formalizations are not restricted to the realm of scientific thinking but also pervade our consciousness in the natural attitude of daily life. He called them idealizations of "and so on" and, in a subjective correlate, of "I can do it again". The former implies that I can continue to assume that what has been proven itself to be adequate knowledge so far will also be adequate in the future until an instance to the contrary comes up – a "strange experience" in

[4]There follow 19 lines of text in the manuscript crossed out by two diagonal lines; because their content is repeated a little later on with only slight variations and revisions, these lines are omitted here.

my terminology. To repeat, the latter refers to my ability until counterproof to repeat the experiencing steps which are sedimented in the particular knowledge in question.

Together the two idealizations entail the basic assumption of all our thinking in daily life: until invalidated by a novel experience, my stock of knowledge at hand will be applicable to events and experiences occurring in the future. In other words, common to both is the assumption that the basic structure of the world as I know it will not change. Therefore the types and the style of experiencing this world will not change either. They will remain available as a scheme of interpretation of future experiences. In still other words, all our anticipations of future events are subject to the *"clausula rebus sic stantibus"*(" other things remaining the same").

Strictly speaking, with respect to anticipations in everyday life, this assumption is inconsistent in itself. First, it is obvious that the stock of knowledge continuously changes not only its extent but also its structure from one Now to another Now. Any supervening experiencing enlarges it even if this experience is strange and remains unrelated to the body of pre-known things. In addition, the emergence of a supervening experience as such by necessity causes a change – be it ever so small – in our prevailing interest and therefore of our system of relevances. Now, as we have seen, it is this system of relevances which, on the one hand, determines the zones of various degrees of distinctiveness, clarity and consistency of our knowledge. Any intervening shift in the system of relevance dislocates[5] these layers and redistributes our knowledge. Some elements which previously belonged to the borderzones enter the central domain of optimal clarity and distinctness, some are removed from it to the layers of increasing vagueness, still others are entirely "forgotten" and no longer at hand. Still others are transformed from knowledge *at* hand into knowledge *in* hand by newly formed habits, by learning and routine.

On the other hand, it is the very system of relevances which determines the system of types under which our stock of knowledge on hand is organized. The types in this system have been selected according to my present knowledge of what so far has been typically relevant. This is the same system of types and of the same types which are valid at the moment of anticipating and are available for the interpretation of future events under the idealizations of "and so on" and "I can do it again". However, when the anticipated event occurs, when it becomes an actual element of my vivid present, the system of relevance and with it the types valid at the moment of anticipating <the planned future action as having been done> will necessarily have changed.

Second, what is anticipated is not the particular occurrence in its uniqueness and its unique setting within a unique constellation but an occurrence of such and such a type, placed typically in a typical constellation. On account of their typicality, all anticipations are more or less empty, and the empty places will be filled by exactly those features of the actual event which will render it a unique individual occurrence that cannot repeat itself.

[5]In a note Wagner suggested that the term, "dislocates", may be too strong and at best appropriate only to the extreme case but not to other variations in the degree of the intervention of the factors governing relevance.

Using the terms in their strict meaning we therefore may say paradoxically: Whatever occurs in the thinking of everyday life could not have been expected; and whatever has been expected will never occur. Thus prediction would turn out to be a category restricted to scientific thinking. In a set of procedural rules are fixed, once and for all, the system of relevances, the types to be used, the required degree of clarity, distinctness and consistency, the formulation of the problem at hand and the type of solution <acceptable by the community of scientists in the particular field>. Also fixed in advance is the prevailing interest governing scientific thought. Certainty, probability, impossibility are modes of scientific prediction. By contrast, all anticipations of daily life are made *modo potentiali* in terms of chance: it is likely, presumable, conceivable, imaginable that what we expect will occur.

But even this way of putting it is merely an abbreviation. For instance, we may anticipate with a relatively high chance of likelihood that something of this or that typical kind will occur. But such an anticipation refers merely to the "That" but not to the "What" and "How" and "When" of this occurrence. In daily life, the degree of the likelihood of our forecasts depends on the degree of precision pertaining to the particular layer of our knowledge to which the pre-constituted typicalities belong and upon which we base our anticipations. The more distinct, clear and consistent these pre-constituted types are, the greater the "weight" they have in defining the likelihood of anticipated chances. Ascertaining this "weight" itself belongs to the stock of our knowledge at hand. In this sense it may be said that an occurrent event was expected if what actually happens corresponds with typicalities which were or could have been pre-constituted at the time of the anticipation. An unexpected event may turn out to be either atypical or, in the extreme case, "strange". It is important to understand that judging an occurrence as expected or unexpected is possible only in hindsight – *ex eventu.*

In the present tense, the verb, "I expect", has an entirely different meaning. It always refers to typicalities in the potential mode of chance which carries along with it its open horizons and unclarified implications. Again, this discrepancy between our expectations and their fulfilment or non-fulfilment by later facts becomes itself an element of our stock of knowledge at hand. And, in its turn, it displays a typical cognitive style.

Anticipations in daily life are not mere fancies, such as daydreams. They still refer us to events possible in the paramount reality of the world of our daily life and are continuously corroborated or refuted by occurrences in this life. In a daydream I may anticipate future events at my fancy: I no longer accept the structure of the world in which I live and act and ignore my pre-constituted knowledge of it as scheme of reference which usually governs all my experiences of this world – actual, past, and future ones. Now, I do not consider myself bound by the framework of goals that are attainable by means which are practically at my disposal. I disregard the obstacles to overcome and the efforts required; I am free in my decisions but also from responsibility. Thus I withdraw the accent of reality from my world of practical experiences and bestow it upon the quasi-reality of the realm of my daydreams. To be sure, phantasying I may even "predict" future occurrences in this quasi-real world. But these "predictions" are not based on pre-constituted knowledge of their typicality or on chance of actualization; they did not result from consistent experiences – my own or those of others!

After having shifted the accent of reality from the world of daily life to that of daydreams, all anticipations are made in the optative mode, so to speak, in oblique language governed by "I wish" or "I fear". While daydreaming, I believe in my predictions – but merely within the limits of the optative form. This is quasi-belief, capable of being tested not by real occurrences but by other quasi-beliefs. If we inspect more closely these dimensions of daydreaming (and, of course, also of all other kinds of fantasms) we will discover the possibility of fancying future and past events, but also that this quasi-future and quasi-past are not connected with one another in a unified and deliberate specious present as would be the case in the world of practical experience, the world of our real and possible action.

Before I turn to a closer examination of the latter, one remark seems indicated in respect to the predominant anticipation that governs human thought and is the reason for the very existence of systems of relevances: Every man's anticipation of his own death. The "That" of this occurrence is anticipated with certainty – it is the only anticipation in the mode of certainty. The "How" and "When" of this occurrence remains open. It escapes any anticipation and during our lifetime it is essentially unfulfilled and unrealized.

IV

So far I have not distinguished between expectations and events which will occur without our interference and those that will be brought about by our actions. We adopt a merely interpretative attitude toward the first category; we are unable or unwilling to steer <events falling under it>, we just accept them. Events falling under the second category originate in or are influenced by our decisions and our purposive behavior. At least in part it is within our power to produce or to prevent them; and we have to bear the responsibility for our commissions and omissions.

Without entering into a discussion of the different forms in which our spontaneous life manifests itself, I define "action" for the present purpose as behavior governed by a project which presupposes a volitive decision. All forms of so-called overt, covert and sub-overt purposive behavior fall within this definition – which also includes purposive non-acting that is purposively refraining from doing what could or should be done. Furthermore, I disregard here the distinction made by some sociologists, that between rational acts, on the one hand, and traditional or habitual ones on the other hand. It can always be shown that routine work also originates in projected actions whose projects are no longer in view but have been replaced by habitual or traditional standards of conduct.

However, what is the project of an action? Before tackling this question, I have to carefully distinguish among our acting, the ongoing process in time in which our spontaneous behavior manifests itself, and the action once performed, the work done, the state of affairs resulting from our acting. For the sake of convenience, I shall call the former "action" (*actio*) and the latter "act" (*actum*). While acting we are living in the unfolding experiences of our ongoing action, directed upon its objective, the goal to be obtained, the task to be performed, etc. However, we may stop at will the flux of acting and turn back to our action itself. Yet doing so we are no longer directed toward our initial goal. The object of our reflective attitude is not the task to be performed by our acting but this acting itself, or more precisely an acting which had been present just now as an ongoing flux but has become a "Now" past, namely in the Now of the reflective attitude. Therefore what we actually grasp in the reflective attitude is not the ongoing flux of action but merely the outcome of our former acting, the performed act or at least the initial phases of the still incomplete act. In other words, we look at our action always in hindsight, in the Past or Past-Perfect tense.

Before our action started we had projected it: that is, we anticipated the goal to be obtained, the means to be applied, the specific manner in which to get the process going. To cite Dewey again: We perform (in imagination) a dramatic rehearsal of our action. But, as used here, the term, "action", does not seem to conform with the terminology just suggested. What I anticipate in projecting any action is not the ongoing flux of the acting to be embarked upon, but its terminus, its outcome, the state of affairs to be brought about: the future act imagined as what it will be after having been performed. In my fantasy, I place myself in a future Now in which the projected act will have been performed and can be viewed in hindsight. Doing so, I construct in retrogression the steps of acting that will have brought about this imagined act. Thus I go through the same procedure as if I had to analyze in hindsight a concrete act I did actually perform in the past. The questions: *quid faciem* or *quid fecisserim [futurus]*[6] *sum* should correctly read: *quid fecisserim.*[7] In other words, all projecting of action consists of the anticipation of the act to be performed through this action in the future [perfect][8] tense. It is an anticipation *modo futuri exacti.*

It can easily be shown that the opposite assumption does not obtain. In projecting a future action we do not look at it as an ongoing flux without having preconceived its outcome. To assume this would be absurd. I can neither live in my actions nor imagine myself living in them without being directed toward and having in view the state of affairs to be brought about by this action. The anticipation of having performed the act to be performed constitutes and determines the meaning of all purposive behavior.

Like any other anticipation, the anticipation of future acts *modo futuri exacti* refers to the stock of knowledge at hand at the time of projecting the act. All the analyses offered in the preceding section, which pertain to the structure of this stock of knowledge but also those pertaining to the discrepancy between expectation and fulfilment hold additionally for the relationship between projected and performed

[6]The text reads *furus*", which is not a word in Latin, although it has the correct ending of the future active participle. It is, I believe, a typographical error for *"futurus"*, and I have so corrected the text. [FK]

[7]Wagner rendered the meaning of the Latin expressions as follows: What external form; What will it be when completed at a time in the future; and What will be. He adds that in all three cases "what" does not denote a question but instead "that which will have resulted", that is, the future state imagined as accomplished.

[8]The text has "future-past tense". [FK]

act. The latter will necessarily differ from the former: If nothing else, experiencing the ongoing action has modified content and structure of the knowledge at hand while planning the action used for interpreting the accomplished act. Yet, if this were true without qualifications, it would lead to a paradox: we would be unable to explain how we succeed frequently in carrying out an intended project.

In order to overcome this difficulty we have to investigate the time dimension to which projecting belongs. Earlier, I mentioned the specious present as the time dimension of our interpreting emergent experiences. By occurring in the specious present, such an experience is related to both the past and the future: to the past by referring to our stock of knowledge at hand and thereby to the preceding experiences in which this stock of knowledge has been constituted; to the future by its inherent protentions and anticipations.

Of course, to this specious present belongs our projecting but also the projected action in its particular form of "what-I-shall-have-performed-in-the-future" (and by implication the single phases of this, my future, which can be retrogressively disclosed from my thus projected act). They have specious existence. In projecting, so to speak, we pull that which is not, but will be, into quasi-existence in the specious present. As we have seen, in general it is the universal function of the specious present to connect expectations with past experiences in as much as the latter have been sedimented in the same stock of knowledge at hand in which the former originated. But, except in the case of projected action, both expectations and experiences belong to different dimensions of the specious present – one to its fore, the other to its aft. Each of them is <governed>[9] by hierarchies of interest and relevances: their zones of clarity and distinctness, their different forms of potentiality, and their various degrees of idealizations of "and so on".

Except in the case of projected action, the specious present is neither unified nor delimited. If it is not unified it displays juxtapositions of specious and actual experiences that appear in zones of varying degrees of vagueness; it shows a juxtaposition of specious and actual experiences in different modal forms such as "it is possible", "there is a chance", and so on. It is not delimited because its "fringes" reach into the past in irregular configurations: here by retention into the immediate past, there by secondary recollections – recollections of recollections – into the past perfect. <In the opposite direction of time it may> touch here protentions of the imminent future which is just about to become present; there, it may reach into a remote time to come by way of anticipations of indefinite range. The unifications and delimitations of this specious present is the unique contribution of acting and projecting.

This unification is brought about first by the fact that acting and projecting introduce a paramount denominator to which the system of interest and relevances can be reduced. The goal to be attained, the act to be accomplished, the problem to be solved – they all become of dominant interest and thereby decide what is and what is not relevant in the stock of knowledge then at hand. To be sure, neither this predominating interest nor the projecting in which it originates are isolated. Both are elements

[9]At this point the text is garbled, and the word, "governed", was inserted by Wagner to make sense out of the rest of the sentence; it makes the content roughly equivalent to the text published in *Collected Papers*, Volume II, p. 291, lines 2–7.

of *systems* of projects, interests, goals to be attained, problems to be solved; these are based one upon the other and are interdependent in manifold ways. Using ordinary language, I call these systems my plans, plans for the hour, plans for the day, for work and leisure, for life. These plans themselves are flexible and determine my interests presently at hand. The latter in turn delimit the relevant section of the stock of knowledge which concerns me in this particular specious present.

Second: all acting and projecting has a particular modal character in the form of "I can" and "it is within my power". (In its essentially optative form, the daydream lacks any specious present; in this sense, it is the opposite of the project.) In this specious present, I bestow this modal form upon the past, present, and future experiences which are relevant to the project in hand. Thereby the present section of my stock of knowledge in this particular specious present becomes one single unified realm of knowledge; in it, specious and actual experiences – past, present, and future – become commensurate with one another regardless to what zone of precision[10] they belong and regardless of the temporal dimension within which they have originated. Moreover, by and in our acting and projecting we establish borderlines of the specious present with respect to past and future.

Its past dimensions are limited by the remotest past experiences – now sedimented and preserved – in that section of our stock of knowledge at hand that is still relevant for the present projecting. Its limits toward the future are defined by the span of the projects presently conceived; that is, by the remotest acts still anticipated *modo futuri exacti*. There exists a certain chance that our future actions will fulfil the anticipations of our projecting – provided we succeed in keeping our projects consistent within this unified and delimited realm of the specious present; and provided we keep our projects compatible both with one another and with the stock of knowledge pertinent within this specious present.

However, such a chance is subjective; that is, it will exist merely for me, the actor, in the forms of reasonable likelihood, calculable risk, reasonable assumption, and so on. This concept of subjective chance does not connote that the chance is warranted, that the underlying assumptions are correct, that this subjective chance – chance for me – will coincide with objective probability. The importance of this distinction will emerge when we turn to an analysis of the intersubjective specious present.

Before doing so, let me consider an additional point: The unification and delimitation of the specious present and the stock of knowledge pertaining to it in the type of constellation under discussion originates in the particular modal form of "I can" and "it is within my power". This modal form belongs exclusively to projecting and acting in progress; it makes our knowledge of future events-to-brought-about by our own activities entirely different from our knowledge of other future events which may or may not occur without our interference.

It is not possible to enter here into the ethical problems involved. But it seems

[10]Wagner notes that with the expression, "zone of precision", Schutz sought to express the ideal-typically constructed degree of clarity or vagueness that a sociologist may ascribe to a type of clarity or vagueness in a descriptive or explanatory scheme set up for a theoretical purpose.

that the analysis of responsibility, repentance, joy, fear, anxiousness, despair, <hope> has its starting point here. On the other hand, the unified and delimited specious present is merely created by our projected acts and by the ongoing actions to which it leads. Anticipated acts and actions in progress alone carry the open expectations of the modal form of "I can" and "it is within my power". Once the flux of action stops, be it by the completion of the action or by its interruption, the unified knowledge pertaining to this specious present breaks asunder. (Of course, other projects, other actions may then supervene and bring about other unifications and delimitations of the stock of knowledge pertaining to the then given specious present.)

What once has been performed in my actions remains in its sedimented results: in the case of outer action, a change occurs in the outer world which from now on will belong to the dimension of physical or mundane time; in the case of "covert" action, a supervening experience will be integrated into my stock of knowledge at hand. In other words, I experience the outcome of my actions in the same way as I experience any other event: Simply, I am the interpreting observer of my own deeds. The difference is that I also know the anticipations I formed when projecting my acts and thus I know whether the outcome of the materialized acts brought their fulfilment or nonfulfilment. These insights have now become elements of my potential scheme of interpretation in future cases.

V

From the outset, the world of daily life is not my private but an intersubjective world. Not only are fellowmen objects of my knowledge, of my social actions, of my expectations – I am also theirs. My experiences of the world show that they are shared or may be shared by others and are open to verification or refutation by others. The world to which these experiences refer is not my private world, it is common to us all. And so, to a certain extent, are the forms of structurization of my stock of knowledge at hand: its distribution in layers of varying precision, its idealizations, its typifications, its modal forms, and even its belonging to a specific specious present.

This is not the place to embark upon a thorough study of these highly complicated problems. I will restrict the discussion to a few remarks which are important for the topic in hand: our knowledge of future events.

First: We have to investigate how far other people's experiences can become possible elements of our stock of knowledge at hand. It is correct to state that my past immediate and originary experiences have been sedimented into my stock of knowledge at hand. But these experiences represent only the core of the actualities of my knowledge. Other people – my contemporaries or predecessors – have actually and originarily experienced what others are experiencing now; this also becomes part of my stock of knowledge at hand if I hear about and pay attention to it even though not in immediate actuality but merely in derived potentiality.

To start with, the other's actual experiences are my potential experiences and take the form: If I were in his place I would have the same experience he has. Would I have the same chance, I could do the same. Thus, what to him is or was an actually existing object of his actual experience is to me a specious object of a possible experience. Even more: the other's potential experiences and his anticipations are to me potential experiences of a second degree and have the form: If I were in his place, I would have this and that possible experience; I would anticipate this or that.

I call this kind of knowledge socially derived knowledge. The idealization underlying it is but a special case of the general idealization of "and so on". It has its particular typical style because it is experienced by me. For instance, I do not accept the other's subjective chances as my own chances without modifications. I may say, "If I were in the place of X and had his special opportunities I would do the same or even better – but I do not have his opportunities".

Furthermore, socially derived knowledge has its typical ways of verification, namely my trusting the other, my belief in his veracity, authority, prestige. Taking for granted what others assert to be true <provided I am convinced that they know things better> is an essential feature of my own stock of socially derived knowledge at hand. A few examples are: our beliefs in eyewitnesses and experts but also in history, in doctrines, folkways, mores, and finally in hearsay.

Second, let us consider the following: Some parts of my own stock of knowledge at hand that are shared by others – tested or verified or merely believed by them – acquire additional "weight" by this very fact <of being shared knowledge>. They gain higher credibility. Private knowledge is surpassed by "socially approved knowledge". Such knowledge is neither less vague nor more relevant on account of being approved by others. In fact, such approval does not improve the subjective chance that expectations based on it will be justified by the events. But the consensus of others bestows upon socially approved knowledge a great objective likelihood if the proposition is sufficiently clear, distinct and consistent with regard to the given anticipation.

Again, the authority of the approving Other enters the picture and contributes to a kind of looking-glass effect to my own prestige: "If a man like X confirms my experience it must be well-founded". This is the origin of the importance of socially tested recipes for my stock of knowledge at hand. It creates a particular style of anticipations based on it in the form of different types of habitual or traditional acts, etc.

Third: I have to point out the importance of so-called social actions for the constitution of the stock of knowledge at hand and the anticipations of things to come. Roughly, I may define an action as "social" if it is either motivated by the behavior of a fellowman or directed toward him in order to motivate him to react. The latter case deserves our special attention. Instead of discussing the casuistics of sociology as relating to the classification of social actions, let us analyze the example of the anticipations involved in my intention to ask someone a question. Among many others things, I expect 1) that I shall succeed in formulating my question clearly enough to make myself understandable to the other; provided 2) that he understands the language used by me; 3) that the other will interpret my utterance as a question, namely as the expression of my wish to receive an answer; 4) that this understanding will induce him to answer; 5) that his answer will be understandable by me; and so on.

All this future behavior of the other is anticipated *modo futuri exacti* in my project to ask him a question in order to get an answer. Each of these anticipations is empty and leaves it open whether or how it will be fulfilled. Nevertheless, I take for granted that the typical question-answer scheme will be workable in this case. I know from past experience that this scheme works and that likely it will be followed by the other as I am following it. This itself is an ingredient of my stock of knowledge at hand. What remains open in my expectation is merely what the other's answer will be. But even with regard to this "What" I have expectations which afterwards enable me to say that my interlocutor answered what I expected, or gave me a strange and unexpected answer, or that what he said was no answer at all to my question.

This is one example of what sociologists call a social relationship. It is a problem of theoretical sociology to investigate the different forms of social relationships from the most intimate to the most anonymous ones. All of them can be derived from the archetype of all social relationships, the pure We-relation. Something should be said about the latter because it is of special importance for the problem of the specious present.

Roughly, I shall define a pure We-relation as a social relationship in which the consociates share a community of space and time and are mutually "tuned into" each other. The community of space – the so-called face-to-face relationship – is important because each consociate has maximum access to the other's body as an expressional field and because a sector of the outer world serves as the common environment of the consociates. This common environment serves as a shared frame of reference for a mutual scheme of expression, interpretation, verification, etc.

But what does community of time mean? Since social intercourse is based upon actions within the meaning of our definition, I may say that there is a common specious present which the consociates share. Each of them can follow the other's action in its ongoing flux as it unrolls phase by phase. In the rigorous sense, what is given to me for interpretation (*modo presenti*) is not the other's act but his action. By contrast, I can turn back to my own actions only by way of reflection. Thus I bring into view not my ongoing action but my performed act or at best the past initial phases of a still ongoing and incomplete action.

When I look at my consociate's ongoing action, by protentions and anticipations I may expect its outcome even if I do not know his underlying project. Of course, this expectation is also based on our stock of knowledge on hand and will still be empty; it may or may not be fulfilled. But while the other's action goes on, it is an element of his as well as of my specious present: I participate in the ongoing flux of his action as directed toward its terminus, the goal to be attained, the act to be accomplished, the problem to be solved, the state of affairs to be brought about. In short, with the other I anticipate the projected end as a speciously existent ingredient of my stock of knowledge at hand in a shared specious present. To a certain extent, this common specious present is unified, although not in the same way in which my own specious present is unified through my projecting and acting. The fact that we are mutually "tuned in" to one another constitutes a common interest, a common environment, a common relevance bestowed upon the ongoing action and, by implication, even a common stock of knowledge at hand.

VI

Before concluding these considerations, I wish to remind my readers that I have intentionally restricted my topic to our knowledge of future events in daily life. I have not dealt with scientific-theoretical knowledge and scientific forecasting. Theoretical-scientific knowledge may be as an analogon[11] to the stock of knowledge at hand as a body of interrelated, verified and tested propositions showing an optimum of clarity, distinctness and consistency. In it, the predominant interest is the problem to be solved. Accordingly, the relevant types are defined by a set of procedural rules which compose the scientific method.

Scientific knowledge is anonymous, independent of the hopes and fears to which the individual is subjected, and therefore independent of his system of relevances. As theorist, not as a human being dealing with science, he does not have any pragmatic interest in which he observes. Scientific knowledge lacks any pragmatic interest – period. It is detached from any individual's specious present; it does not partake of inner time. Strictly speaking, it also lacks a social dimension. To be sure, scientific knowledge is necessarily socially approved knowledge within the meaning of my definition. That is, it refers to cooperation with others and is subject to their inspection and criticism. But these activities of checking and criticizing do not belong to the realm of theoretical-scientific knowledge; only the outcome of these actions, the actions performed, do. The individual, the man among men, entirely disappears behind the anonymous result.

After these much too fugitive remarks we may say that scientific forecasts are always based on the tested and verified body of scientific knowledge at hand. If an event is observed that does not correspond to scientific expectations because it is inconsistent with the body of propositions and the procedural rules accepted as scientific knowledge at hand, this body is to be modified and adapted until the strange fact becomes explicable. The chance of a scientific prediction being correct depends on whether it is based on an empirical law (a synthetic universal proposition – [Felix] Kaufmann, [*The Methodology of the Social Sciences*, New York, 1947,] Chapter IV and p. 233), or a theoretical [law] (procedural rule in terms of which "warranted prediction" is defined), or whether it is restricted to a prognosis of typical occurrences of typical events, such as frequently [employed] in meteorology or medicine. The character of prediction in those sciences which deal with human action comes close to the category of expectations in daily life – unless, as in economics, they succeed in exclusively ascribing relevance to well-defined types of human acts or behavior <that is, to solely concentrate either on statistical averages or on typifications of economic actions constructed according to theoretical principles>.

However, our knowledge of future events in daily life does not have the form of objective predictions but that of subjective expectations. With regard to the structure

[11]Wagner suggested substituting "may be compared" for Schutz's "as an analogon", a formulation Wagner found misleading because it may not be a matter of analogy at all but instead a matter of consistency and precision which distinguishes Schutz's category of scientific from everyday knowledge. Here the reader will have to decide what is appropriate.

of these expectations, as pointed out, we have to distinguish between events that will occur without our interference and such that will be brought about by our actions. The former refer to the pre-constituted typicalities and their systems as we find them ready-made in the stock of our knowledge at hand. According to the idealization of "and so on" we take for granted that the anticipated event will be of the same typicality. The latter are anticipated as if they had already materialized. Our project refers *modo futuri exacti* not to our future actions but to the acts.[12]

Thus we are brought back to the problem of Teiresias. Is it possible in daily life to have knowledge of future events other than in the form of anticipated hindsight? Are we in the role of mere spectators? Are we the makers of future events or are we retroverted historians?[13]

As to future events that we are unable to control or to influence, we are mere observers of what goes on and what will happen. We may anticipate the future merely by assuming that what as a rule turned out to be correct in the past will also be correct in the future. We do not and we cannot expect anything to be typically recurring if we did not learn to do so from past events. Like the spectator in the theatre we do our best to make sense of what we have lived through thus far, and we remain confident that the author of the play will reveal its sense at the end. The end itself is not yet disclosed to us. It gives free rein to our hopes and fears; we may approach it in terms of our religious beliefs or our metaphysical convictions – but it is not known to us.

However, within our vision of the future open to our domination there are possible events which could be influenced by our actions. Thus we assume that we are truly the makers of these events. But what we preconceive in the project of our actions is their terminus – nothing else than an anticipated state of affairs which we imagine as having been materialized. Nevertheless, when projecting future actions we are not merely retroverted historians. We are historians when we look back from any Now to our past experiences and interpret them according to our stock of knowledge now at hand. But in this case there is nothing open and emptily anticipated. What in it was formerly anticipated has or has not been fulfilled.

[Even so,] when we project we know that what we anticipate carries along its open horizons. The materialized state of affairs brought about by our actions will have quite other aspects than the projected ones. Foresight is distinguished from hindsight not by the dimensions of time in which we place the event: In both cases, we look at it as having occurred; in hindsight as having occurred in the past, in foresight as having become quasi-existent in an anticipated past. What constitutes the decisive difference is the mere fact that genuine hindsight does not leave anything open and undefined but refers to something irrevocable that can be *undone* by counteroperations, yet cannot be cancelled. Foresight is anticipated hindsight depending on the stock of our knowledge presently at hand. Therefore, it leaves open

[12]Wagner rightly calls attention to the fact that Schutz uses the term, "act", here in the technical and very narrow sense defined above, pp. 57f.

[13]For a discussion of this and related issues, especially as it pertains to Teiresias, see Fred Kersten, "Phenomenology, History, Myth", in *Phenomenology and Social Reality. Essays in Memory of Alfred Schutz*, edited by Maurice Natanson (The Hague: Martinus Nijhoff, 1970, pp. 234–269).

what can be irrevocably fulfilled only by the occurrence of the anticipated event itself.

We who have not received the gift of seerdom by the deity cannot obtain immediate and originary knowledge of future events. “For now we see through a glass, darkly; now we know in part, and we prophesy in part.”

CHAPTER 5

Relevance: Knowledge on Hand and in Hand

EDITORS' PREFACE

The title is by Helmut Wagner for a collection of pages from the end of the manuscript used by Richard Zaner when he prepared for publication most of the first (and only) part of a book manuscript originally intended to comprise five parts.[1] The manuscript was written during the summers of 1947 to 1951, chiefly during vacations Schutz spent at Lake Placid in New York and at Estes Park in Colorado.[2]

When Schutz approached the conclusion to the first part of the project, he wrote to Aron Gurwitsch (4 October, 1950) that "one more thing happened to me, something which shouldn't happen at my age and which one can only blushingly whisper to a good friend as a sweet secret: 'I am with book.' I have two chapters finished, roughly 27,000 words, perhaps a fifth of the whole, which given my way of life will need six or seven years for completion."[3]

The text printed from the manuscript came to 182 printed pages. The remaining pages assembled by Wagner for inclusion in this volume are either single pages or a sequence of pages, which, if not unnumbered, bear numbers above 160 and go beyond 180 of the original manuscript. Wagner assumed that these pages were written at the end of the summer of 1951 and would seem to form a textually coherent unity even though they do not belong to the main text stylistically or textually.

Why Alfred Schutz did not complete the book on relevance is not clear. In part it may have been his realization that, with his "way of life", he would need six or more years to complete it. In his letter to Gurwitsch, Schutz also seems somewhat unsure of his work, a "first draft" of which, he says, he will send to Gurwitsch "with the request that you tell me whether I should continue with my efforts."[4] For whatever reason, Schutz did not continue the manuscript and may have even abandoned all together the idea of the book. Of course, the problem of relevance continued to

[1]Alfred Schutz, *Reflections on the Problem of Relevance*, edited, annotated, and with an Introduction by Richard M. Zaner (New Haven: Yale University Press, 1970).

[2]See Zaner's Introduction, p. viii.

[3]See *Philosophers in Exile. The Correspondence of Alfred Schutz and Aron Gurwitsch. 1939–1959*, p. 118. (German edition, p. 194.)

[4] *Ibid.*, p. 119 (German edition, p. 194).

occupy his thought, surfacing again, for instance, in his comments on the last part of Gurwitsch's *The Field of Consciousness*.[5]

In general terms: both the sufficiency of our knowledge and the required degree of familiarity with things and events depend on the adequacy of this knowledge to further our purposes on hand. In turn, this is determined by the system of motivational relevances originating in the autobiographical definition of circumstances at a particular moment. So far, Scheler and some other philosophers are correct in emphasizing the pragmatical motive in our knowledge. But the radical pragmatist is wrong because he considers the system of motivational relevances the only one that governs our knowledge, and because he interprets action in too narrow a sense – most frequently in terms of biological needs and their satisfaction.

Thus familiarity has its degrees and – as stated on an earlier page – the term should always be conceived in its full sense, namely "familiarity sufficient for the purpose at hand". This justifies our previous remark that familiarity defines the demarcation line not only between things which have to be known and those "not worthwhile" to be known, but also between those aspects of things which are and those which are not topically or interpretatively of interest. Sufficient familiarity designates that point up to which inquiry and research are necessary and desirable.[6] I have to "familiarize" myself with the topic or problem at hand merely to an extent <required by the purpose at hand>.

These considerations enable us to gain a clearer insight into the organization of the stock of knowledge at hand at any given moment of our conscious life. This stock of knowledge consists of stored-away pre-experiences of a sufficient degree of familiarity. <It is complemented by a> sufficiently well-circumscribed typicality (and sufficiently determined expectations).[7] The latter term refers also to a set of more or less empty expectations that this neutralized habitual possession will be reactivated if typically the same or like experiences turn up in the future. What has been stored away in this manner is no longer problematic and for the time being does not need further inquiry. The known life-world – known in all these various degrees of sufficient familiarity – is just taken for granted until further notice. Unquestioned as it is, it is the general frame of open possibilities of further questioning. Being the locus of all things with which we are sufficiently familiar, the world taken-for-granted forms the horizon of a principally determinable indeterminacy; against it the topics with which I am concerned at this particular moment stand out as thematically relevant.

Thus at any given moment the stock of knowledge at hand is not a closed realm but it is open in various dimensions – as described in the preceding paragraph. The knowledge actually at hand refers to potential knowledge of things, once known but meanwhile dropped and therefore forgotten (restorable knowledge) and to things never known but knowable under certain conditions of inquiry (attainable knowledge).

[5]See for example the comments published as addendum to Schutz's letter to Gurwitsch of 25 January, 1952, pp. 154ff. (German edition, pp. 247ff.).

[6]This sentence was crossed out in the manuscript.

[7]The passage in parentheses was crossed out by Schutz in the manuscript.

Also it is always possible that the relevances determining the sufficiency of our knowledge are shifted and that new topical problems occur.

A metaphor might be helpful to make more graphic the structurization of our stock of knowledge at hand at any given moment. Cartographers represent on their maps mountain ranges by drawing lines connecting points of equal altitude. They call these lines contour lines or isohypses. Let us imagine, if this were possible at all, that we could make a similar graph of our stock of knowledge of equal degrees of familiarity or of what, according to what has been stated before, is equivalent or of equal relevance. We would then obtain a map showing the contour lines of our life-world as taken for granted beyond question <and we may speak> of relevance-isohypses. However, the mountains representing the profiles of our world taken for granted would not be arranged in the form of a more or less continuous range. They would be spread all over the map, here a few peaks emerging immediately out of the plains, there a range of hills with interspersed valleys, there again highlands emerging from rising grounds. At any given moment such a map of our relevance-isohypses would show a particular configuration. Of course, <any such map> would be just a snapshot, catching an instant of a continuously ongoing process; but it is the purpose of our present investigation to describe the structure of the stock of knowledge at hand in static terms.

We do not want to overload this metaphor but from time to time we will use the term, "relevance-isohypses", as an innocent and convenient expression for the description of the structurization of our stock of knowledge at hand. Yet in the light of our metaphor we do not feel entitled to speak of the stock of knowledge at hand without making some distinctions. Among the habitual knowledge stored away some elements are merely at hand – that is, <they are> readily available for being transformed from neutrality into actuality as soon as required by recurrent typical experiences. Others, however, are more permanently present, are more frequently used: the business of living does not permit us to let them entirely out of grip, and to keep them neutralized and dormant.

We may say that these elements of our knowledge are not only *at* hand but *in* hand. They are of outstanding relevance and of permanent relevance even though by having been transformed into routine knowledge these topics *in* hand are no longer consciously <registered and noted> as being in the thematic field. As said before, apparently they lost their outer and inner horizons. They are of highest familiarity, they have their fixed place in the habitually possessed chain of means for well-circumscribed specific ends. <They remain> unquestioned as long as they fulfil their specific functions; they do not need interpretations or definitions of their functional character. Being vitally relevant for the fulfilment of other activities of the mind, they seem to have lost their own particular relevance. They are no longer experienced as topics in themselves but it seems that they are objects pertaining to the life-world itself, having their well-defined place and function in it. By continued usage, the elements of our knowledge *in* hand have acquired the character of tools or utensils. We will refer to them by these terms from now on.

Sometimes the transformation of elements of knowledge *at* hand into such *in* hand is clearly discernible. Every student of a foreign language, if he continues long enough to work at it, can determine the moment at which the vernacular ceases to be habitual expression at hand and can be freely mastered as a tool for conveying thoughts. This is precisely the moment when the passive so-called reading knowledge of a language turns into its active use: The foreign terms are no longer recognized by me; they are no longer at hand. As it were, they offer their services when needed. They are present for active use; <they became> utensils *in* hand.[8]

[8]The manuscript breaks off here. I find it difficult to decide whether Schutz intended these pages as a continuation of the larger manuscript, or whether they were intended as additions and clarifications of what he had already written. They seem to presuppose and expand his discussions in *Reflections on the Problem of Relevance*, Chapter 3, section E, p. 66, and F, p. 70. [FK]

CHAPTER 6

The Problem of Social Reality

Editors' Preface

The text is a prospectus that Alfred Schutz wrote to support his application for a sabbatical leave from the Graduate Faculty of the New School for Social Research for the Fall of 1958 and the Spring of 1959. There exist two other shorter versions of the prospectus, the contents of which dovetailed into the longer version presented here. Schutz's leave was granted, but he was unable to carry out the task proposed in the prospectus because of his final illness and death in May of 1959.[1]

During the forthcoming eight-months leave of absence the writer plans to finish at least the first draft of his projected work (tentative title: *The Problem of Social Reality*). He has accumulated over the years about 600 pages of notes which have to be condensed and organized.[2] He intends to spend a part of his leave of absence in Louvain in order to study the unpublished manuscripts of Husserl dealing with the problems of the *Lebenswelt* and of intersubjectivity.

The main topic to be elaborated can be stated in rather simple terms: Philosophers as different as William James, Bergson, Dewey, Husserl and Whitehead agree that the common-sense knowledge of everyday life is the unquestioned but always questionable background within which inquiry starts and within which alone it can be carried out. It is this *Lebenswelt*, as Husserl calls it, within which according to them all scientific and even logical concepts originate; it is the social matrix within which, according Dewey, unclarified situations emerge which have to be transformed

[1]For details of Schutz's various writing projects during his last years, see Helmut Wagner, *Alfred Schutz. An Intellectual Biography*, pp. 106ff.

[2]For the nature and status of these notes, see Wagner, pp. 110f. Much of the 600 pages, in five notebooks, was assembled, reconstructed and edited by Thomas Luckmann in Alfred Schutz/Thomas Luckmann, *Strukturen der Lebenswelt* (Frankfurt am Main: Suhrkamp), Volume 1 (1979) and Volume 2 (1984). A detailed outline of the notebooks is given in Volume 2, pp. 241ff. The first volume has been translated into English by Richard M. Zaner and H. Tristram Engelhardt, Jr., Alfred Schutz and Thomas Luckmann, *The Structures of the Life-World* (Evanston: Northwestern University Press, 1973); the second volume has been translated into English by Richard M. Zaner and David J. Parent, *The Structures of the Life-World II* (Evanston: Northwestern University Press, 1985); this second volume contains, as an appendix, all the material of the five notebooks.

by the process of inquiry into warranted assertibility. And Whitehead has pointed out that it is the aim of science to produce a theory which agrees with experience by explaining the thought-objects constructed by common-sense through the mental constructs or thought-objects of Science.

If, according to this view, all scientific constructs are designed to supercede the constructs of common-sense thought, a principal difference between the natural and social sciences becomes apparent. It is up to the natural scientists to determine which sector of the universe of nature, which facts and events therein, and which aspects of such facts and events are typically and interpretationally relevant to their specific purpose. These facts and events are neither pre-selected nor pre-interpreted. They are just facts and events within his observational field – but this field does not "mean" anything to the molecules, atoms and electrons therein.

Yet the facts, events and data before the social scientist are of an entirely different structure. The primary goal of the social sciences is to obtain organized knowledge of social reality, that is, of the sum total of objects and occurrences within the social-cultural world as experienced in the common-sense thinking of men living their daily lives among their fellowmen, connected with them in manifold relations of interaction. The observational field of the social scientist thus is the world of cultural objects and social institutions into which we all are born, within which we have to find our bearings, and with which we have to come to terms. This world – our *Lebenswelt* – has particular meaning and relevance structure to us human beings, living, thinking and acting therein. We have pre-selected and pre-interpreted this world by a series of common-sense constructs of the reality of daily life and it is these thought-objects which determine our behavior, define the goal of our actions, the means available for attaining them and so forth. The thought-objects constructed by the social sciences in order to grasp this social reality have to be founded upon the thought-objects constructed by the common-sense thinking of men, living their daily life within the social world. The social sciences – as all empirical sciences – have to develop systems of explanatory theory through processes of controlled inferences, statable in propositional form and capable of being verified by observation. Yet in contradistinction to the natural sciences, the constructs of the social sciences are, so to speak, constructs of the second degree – namely constructs of the constructs made by the actors on the social scene, whose behavior the social scientist has to observe and to explain in accordance with the procedural rules of his science.

It is the writer's conviction – supported by the results of his studies during the last twenty years – that any science dealing with human affairs and eager to grasp human reality has to be founded on the interpretation of the *Lebenswelt* by human beings living within it. The description and elucidation of the *Lebenswelt* by phenomenological techniques is the main theme of Husserl's later philosophy. Mainly, it is dealt with in still unpublished manuscripts preserved in the Husserl-Archive in Louvain (Belgium).

PART TWO

A

Studies in Social Theory

CHAPTER 7

Toward a Viable Sociology

EDITORS' PREFACE

The title is by Helmut Wagner for a series of four lectures that Alfred Schutz gave to the members of a private seminar of the economist, Ludwig von Mises; three of the lectures were given in December of 1928, and the fourth in March of 1929. Schutz provided no general title, and only the first lecture carries a title note: *Pragmatismus und Soziologie, besser Sozialwissenschaften: Zu Scheler, Erkenntnis und Arbeit* ("Pragmatism and Sociology, better, the Social Sciences: On Scheler's *Cognition and Work*).[1]

The original German text consists of eight densely written pages of exposition interspersed with outline headings and telegraphic formulations. Truncated passages have been completed by Wagner and then translated into English. Wagner's translation has been revised for readability, and following Schutz's own arrangement, the lectures are marked with the corresponding Roman numeral.

Von Mises' private seminar was a weekly, occasionally bi-weekly, gathering of a select group of his former students, all of whom had obtained their doctoral degrees under him and were pursuing their professional careers in the commercial world. All members of the seminar offered lectures on many different topics but very few, it would seem, dealing with economics.[2]

I

However sociology may be defined, it is certain that its subject-matter is the knowledge of human actions and specifically of socially oriented actions. In Understanding Sociology the problem of the relationship between knowledge and action is intertwined in two ways:

[1]The reference is to Scheler's essay, *Erkenntnis und Arbeit. Eine Studie über Wert und Grenzen des pragmatischen Motivs in der Erkenntnis der Welt* ["Cognition and Work. A Study of Value and Limits of the Pragmatic Motive in Cognition of the World"], first published in Max Scheler, *Die Wissensformen und die Gesellschaft* (Munich, 1926 [2nd ed., 1960]).

[2]See Helmut Wagner, *Alfred Schutz. An Intellectual Biography*, pp. 11ff. for further discussion of von Mises' seminar and Schutz's participation in it.

1. The term, "knowledge", contains and presupposes conduct *oriented* toward others. (Knowledge here is not that of the sociologist but instead of the person who is located in the social world.)
2. According to the postulate of the investigation of the meaning *intended*, the knowledge of the sociologist is based on the knowledge that the actor has of the "subject of orientation".

Max Scheler posed the pragmatic problem. (He differentiated between knowledge and action as well as between natural science and the machine; that is, between theoretical knowledge and pragmatic procedures or instrumentalities. Accordingly, he spoke of two kinds of knowledge: knowledge for the sake of knowing and knowledge for the sake of domination. In applying this distinction to sociology we have to say that sociology aims at theoretical and "value-neutral" knowledge.) In contrast, the knowledge of the social actor is knowledge for the sake of domination.

<Themes for continuation of these considerations are>: Main tenets of pragmatism; development of these notions; positive and negative critique; methodical pragmatism; theory of foundation. (It would be desirable to continue these considerations into the theory of perception and its modification by Bergson. But this will not be carried out here.)

What is the relationship between social conduct (acting in the larger sense) to the knowledge of the actor?

Understanding sociologists define social conduct as conduct oriented toward another person. The expression, "oriented toward", implicitly already contains "knowledge" of the other. It would seem that the pragmatic thesis would be fully effective here. Attempts <at interpretations in this direction have been made by> Gumplowicz, Jerusalem,[3] and also Marx. They imply that we only have "knowledge" about the other that is *relevant* for our own conduct. This problem of *relevance* is the fundamental problem of sociology.

Here, too, acting <is measured according to> success and failure; here, too, the validity of the interpretative scheme of the type of reality is tested by its purposiveness.

The correlation between relevance and type <leads to consideration of three major problems>:

A) <Knowledge for the sake of domination> is relevant for the orientation of the social actor for the following reasons:
   1. The "person" of the other <as sociological person appears> to the actor as an "ideal type" of other <in contrast to> the actor's "ideal type" of the I, of his self, which in turn has to be examined in its relationship to the intimate person.
   2. The type of reality of the conduct of the other <is subject to the pragmatic test>. Types of deviation <may have to be formed and the possibility of> misunderstanding <will have to be considered>.
   3. Rational action presupposes as known the typical conduct of the other. <This becomes complicated if one faces planned> actions with imagined intermediate goals.

[3]Ludwig Gumplowicz (1838–1909) was a Polish-born Austrian lawyer who later taught Administrative Theory at the University of Graz. Wilhelm Jerusalem (1854–1923) taught philosophy and pedagogy at the University of Vienna.

4. <Instead of certainty we deal with> chance: the objective chance that the reaction of the other <occurs as imagined>.

Thus we also see that social conduct in daily life obviously is based on a knowledge that – without introducing a different foundation – seems to be controlled only by practical orientations and their relevance for the interpretation of the conduct of the other.

However, all occurring social conduct is explained relative to the existence of the Thou, and therefore it is also explainable only as being existentially relative to the existence of the Thou. And that means it is never explainable by those ontological and existential insights guiding social action. Already the "stratification" <of the individual in typifiable actor and> intimate person demonstrates the inadequacy of the pragmatic view.

B) What is relevant to a group (for its members and for outsiders)? We should deal here with types of conduct and the positing of goals. What else do we know about groups?

C) The social sciences have to be considered in their choices of objects, their choices of methods, and by the <principle of> value neutrality. Examples <could be shown demonstrating the selection, use, and treatment of> *data*. <We have to deal further with Scheler's conception of> ideal-factors which become "effective" only thanks to real-factors <which favor and allow the conversion of ideals into effective social action with lasting effects.> Further, we should pose the question: What is the "meaning" of a development <with lasting social consequences>?

II

Leopold von Wiese[4] <developed a> sociology of relationships. Relationships among whom? <The main topics are>: Action – process; catalogue of *motives*. Special distance (Sander).[5]

I. Concerning Reality. Problem of resistance. *Hypostatization as would-be Reality*. Chance <as treated in> Scheler's theory of ideal and real factors: Burckhardt's "Potentialities".

Intended meaning? Chance? Who knows anything about the I? What enters into it?[6] Concerning wishes: What are the values? Why these four?[7] Implicitly, they all contain parts of the formula.

[4] Leopold von Wiese und Kaiserswaldau (1876–1969) was co-founder with Max Weber of the German Society for Sociology.

[5] Wagner found Sander a somewhat elusive figure to identify; apparently he was a student of Max Weber, and Schutz may have had in mind Fritz Sander, "Der Gegenstand der reinen Gesellschaftslehre", published in 1925, also discussed in *Der sinnhafte Aufbau der sozialen Welt*, pp. 163ff. (English translation, pp. 145ff.)

[6] The manuscript copy is badly blurred at this place, and "What enters into it?" is a guess on Wagner's part as to what Schutz was saying.

[7] The reference is to the theory of the "four wishes" of William I. Thomas and Florian Znaniecki, *The Polish Peasant in Europe and America* (Chicago, 1918), Vol. I, p. 73.

II. Principle: Explaining as understanding, as describing or even theorizing. *Definition of Formations*.[8] Why <does von Wiese speak of> running idle [*Leerlauf*]? Who grasps <such a period> as unity and as what kind of unity?

Classification:	<What is its> justification?
Mass:	Social relations of individuals?
Directedness <of a formation:>	open, closed.
Group:	Social relations with one another.

Chance <of the acting of their staff members according to formally> pre-established rules. There is a real staff of administrators <authorized> to enforce actions. – Later we will have to consider overlaps: class – mass – proletariat.

Type <construction> of specifically abstract collectives <reveals that> they cannot be grasped otherwise.[9]

The practical-actual experience <stands in contrast to its memory. There are> limits of remembering. <They are set by the possibilities of> positing its own I <as an I which has had experiences in the past>. Beneath this <lies nothing but> an inarticulate sphere.

Spheres of orders: Art, Eros, etc. The sphere of values.

<What we are able> to remember is that which had been, and also the attitude of the I to what had been – but not how-it-had-been. Nevertheless, essentially-actual experiences are accompanied by a consciousness of being-other. Actual experiences continue to be effective even though we cannot remember them.

The symbolic sphere reaches memories in transformation <of past experiences but it> cannot reach below. <The question is whether> the sphere of the unarticulated how-[it-had-been] is *sui generis*. Is everything else only a special case? (For example: mechanisms of atoms.)

<There is an inverse relationship between a> tool and the depth of strata <that can be reached by it>. The idea of heuristic purposiveness contradicts this insight. – (Nouns with time indices.)

III

Spheres of the I are: the Thou-relationship with the I; the stratification of the life-forms (within the individual, reaching from the biological life-functions in systematic progression up to the most rational operations:
What are the limits of the social I?
<What are the> relations between bundles of relations?
How is the Thou possible?[10]

[8]"Formation" translates von Wiese's term, *"Gebilde"*, which has a very broad meaning comprising all sorts of social associations, consociations and even the many forms of social contracts of whatever kind and description.

[9]There follows a note in the manuscript covering about half a page; it is not clear whether Schutz used it as the end of the second lecture or whether he reserved it for a different use. The note, in translation, is included here as the end of the second lecture.

[10]Wagner notes that from here on Schutz's system of subdividing the manuscript by way of Roman numerals is in disarray. Moreover, the manuscript pages themselves are unnumbered and it would

(iv) “Abstract mass” <to be seen in the light of> inner experience; objective chances; experience of meaning, of linguistic community – <but also holders of weekly or monthly> travel cards, <or of the distinction between> the public and the members of special-interest groups; <or the references to members of> high society. <A consideration of> the chances <of encountering typically expected conduct in meetings of “members” of such abstract collectives>.

<Mass-behavior by Max> Weber: <it begins to> drizzle. <One person opens his or her> umbrella. <As on signal, all the others follow his or her example.>

Mostly the behavior of the mass is not related to meaning. But <in contrast to that the behavior of a> demagogue is; <he deliberately incites a mass of emotionally aroused people to unthinking aggressive and destructive behavior.> Kraus[11] affronts everyone.

(v) Pair: Thou

B. Quantum-quale (quantity and quality): Simmel <wrote about> marginal members <of groups and> levels <of group participation by> various kinds of members. <What is> the standard of <membership>? How does it originate? Ideal type.

(vi) Burckhardt: What does one want? Description or interpretation of meaning – or <dealing with> external developments or with intellectual-spiritual history?

(vii) The Prussian State and the Protestant Church.

(viii) What do relations between formations signify? – What are these formations? Do they “live” at all? Reality dissolves itself in individual positing of meanings. One has to give up <the notion of the> interpretation of meanings by society. Collective happenings and connections between the specific actions of individual human beings who <interact as different from another as constructs from concrete events>.

Collectives are important a) terminologically and b) as ideology: Notions of particularly valid rules <existing> in the heads of the actors.

(ix)[12] <Laws in the natural and the social sciences>.

In contrast to the natural sciences, laws in the social and humanistic sciences are laws of meaning. This is so because they occur in consciousness but not in <objective> time.

For this reason they are necessarily “subject-founded” (while physics, according to Einstein, manages to exclude the observer in a far-reaching way. Compare also to Planck’s attempts to construct laws of objective reality – analysis of worlds).

Specifically, only action that has occurred is meaningful. In its essence, the category of meaning monopolizes the index, *“modo perfecti”*.

---

seem that their exact sequence has been disturbed in such a way that it may not be possible to restore it. Schutz also began to use the Roman numerals from IV to VIII to mark sections despite the fact that the first of the manuscript pages belonging to the fourth lecture carries as well the designation “IV”. To retain the numerical value of IV to VIII they have been placed in parentheses: (iv) to (viii).

[11]Schutz probably refers to Karl Kraus, the acerbic publisher of *Die Fackel*, of which Schutz owned an almost complete set.

[12]The placement of (ix) is not entirely clear; it is marked “III”, but does not belong to the section bearing that number. Wagner therefore placed it at the end, chiefly because of its methodological content.

It follows that both the attempt to construct or to postulate laws of meaning for the future are necessarily paradoxical. That I, <as an astronomer>, can predict astronomical constellations is rooted in the fact that physical occurrences take their course in a time without consciousness. However, if consciousness is added as the center of the index of inquiry, it becomes impossible to meaningfully construct the *modo futuri*.

I simply "understand" only that which has passed. This is possibly so because of the "fulfilled protentions and the retentional intentions" which constitute the problem of meaning (Husserl, 457[13]).

What, for example, concerns laws in political economy? 1) For the most part, they offer only a scaffolding for <establishing> causal adequacy; or 2) they are heuristic instructions <functioning> as a collection of economically relevant facts *certeris paribus* : Both 1) and 2) are possible because political economy no longer deals with pure courses of happenings in consciousness but with spatial-temporal social processes. <In other words>, the general validity of laws in this social science is rooted in its selection of problems.

Concerning Understanding – Wesenschau [seeing of essences]: Perhaps all phenomena of understanding are of a pre-phenomenological nature because they belong to the pre-phenomenological consciousness of inner time (which alone conditions all seeing of essences).

Perhaps understanding is exclusively directed to that which exists but not to the how of its existence, which is exemplified by that which exists.

IV[14]

A. *Group Soul and Group Spirit [Gruppenseele, Gruppengeist]*

Leopold von Wiese distinguished between a) the feelings and ideas which group members have, and b) those which members *should* have. Therefore <he dealt with> 1) different existing ideas, 2) common ideas <of the majority of members>, and 3) the idea of the group. Indeed, conceptually we can differentiate this content of ideas <about the group> from conceptions as notions of events[; we] direct ourselves toward them as something independent, namely as group spirit.

The latter is not a mystical essence detached from human beings and [which] hovers over them. Rather it is an idea that can be formed in lesser or greater clarity; group members think it with different intensity and in <varying degrees of> clarity. In this manner <the notion of> an abstract collective prepares itself within the group. Yet it is questionable whether this tendency inheres in every group of card-players. In any case, the tendency toward the formation <of the idea of an abstract collective> is the criterion of the group.

[13]The reference is to Edmund Husserl, "Vorlesungen zur Phänomenologie des inneren Zeitbewusstseins", *Jahrbuch für Philosophie und phänomenologische Forschung*, IX (1928), p. 457. (*Husserliana*, X, pp. 105f.; English translation by John Barnett Brough, Edmund Husserl, *Collected Works*, Vol. IV, pp. 111f.)

[14]The manuscript copies of the fourth lecture consist of two dated (March 27, 1929) but unnumbered pages; the order of the pages here is Wagner's.

Max Scheler <speaks of> Group Soul and Group Spirit. <He aims> not at metaphysical entities which substantially precede the life-with-one-another <nor does he focus on how Group Soul and Group Spirit> are experienced. Instead <he thinks> about subjects of the spiritual – respectively, the *ideal* [*geistigen*] content that reproduces itself ever anew in <the members'> being-together. Group Soul is merely the collective subject of those spiritual activities which are not spontaneously performed but take place "by themselves". Group Spirit is the subject which constitutes itself in performing together fully conscious, spontaneous acts (that are substantially-intentionally referring to one another).

Group Soul is impersonal and anonymous. Group Spirit <is related to a> small number of idealized examples = <the group's> elite (Pareto, Wieser). (Means of the analyses of group structures.) Max Adler[15] <declared that> in human experience the relationship among spirits belongs to the transcendental potentialities of theoretical consciousness. From the outset all thinking and experience is directed upon general validity. Thus it belongs to the species. The similarity of the spiritual life of all humans is not an empirical mass-phenomenon: to the contrary, it is given *a priori*. Certainly the individual is not a fiction; but from the outset it exists not so much as individual consciousness but as consciousness of the species. <It exists> not so much as I but as consciousness as such. This <species->relatedness of consciousness determines a specific being on the same basis of being as <that of> natural experiences for the social being.

Vossler[16] <argues that required are> two roles or persons and three moments (speaking, comprehending and answering are necessary for the vernacular; but only one individual is required). The notion that a dialogue between individuals takes place in the soul of the people <to which they belong> issues from the erroneous opinion that the psychic happenings in speaking a vernacular transcends the point of view of individual psychology. Speaking itself passes through the (space of the) environment <but is> not the environment. <The latter> speaks no more than do telephone wires. <What takes place is> a slowly getting-accustomed by the I", etc. The Crowd Soul is not the soul of the crowd but a crowd-like propensity of individual persons.

Bergson <assumes that> the whole universe participates in our *durée*. Thus was born the idea of a *durée* of the universe – that is to say, of an impersonal consciousness which is the uniting thread among all individual consciousnesses and the rest of the universe.[17]

[15]The reference is to Friedrich Freiherr von Wieser (1851–1926), an Austrian economist; and Max Adler (1873–1937), an Austrian social philosopher at the University of Vienna.

[16]The reference is to Karl Vossler (1872–1949) whose work on language and linguistics had considerable influence on Schutz.

[17]Schutz wrote the second sentence of this short paragraph in French. It is difficult to tell whether it is a direct quotation from Bergson or a paraphrase.

<b. Second Part of Lecture>[18]

<Left Column>
1. Totem Taboo
2. Chosen People
3. Antiquity, Kelsen
4. <left open>
5. Herder, Lessing
6. Goethe citat

<Right Column>
1. Organic Sociology and evolutionary position
2. Concept of Society, for instance by Spann
3. History. Humanity, Conception of predecessors and successors. German Idealism, Herder, etc. "Movements", "Tendencies", etc. Theological-Cosmological Moment.
4. Objectivations: Art, Language, Culture. <Arrow pointing to an additional but not numbered line:> Presuppositions of all Sociology.

<Simmel's Five Reasons for Social Psychology>
1. The developments of Language, State, Law, Religion – all point beyond the individual soul. The participation of the individual <does not seem to have been postulated by Simmel> as the meaning of, or the necessity for, the formations. However, as a whole <social formations of any kind> must have their creators and bearers. <Tribal or national legends or other forms of hallowed traditions have it that the latter> arrived from Heaven, or else <there is the idea that> society is an animate object which is its own bearer.

   Conversely, happenings or origins are <thought of as being> "separate from [their] contents". <The latter> are psychologically assumed to be existent by themselves. Both lexicon and language <must be treated as the means of> individual processes of realization. Separate from these processes they cannot be validated as creations of society. This conclusion is false. But <they display> a third <kind of> objective mental content. <The latter is> no more a psychological plus than the Pythagorean tenet <in geometry>. Both are capable of gaining reality only within the consciousness of the individual. The origin <of both> is an individual-psychological manifold; considered as unities, they have no *origins* but are ideal contents.
2. Action is manifold, but the result of action assumes unity. The uniformity of the resulting phenomenon reflects itself in the presupposed unity of its psychological cause.
3. <There is a> qualitative difference between the actor who finds himself in a mass of people and the isolated individual: mass stupidity. <But this is still> acting of individuals who are influenced by the fact of being surrounded by others.

[18]Because the catch-words and catch-word-like formulations of the two columns on these pages do not parallel each other, and because their content seems independent of one another, the columns are perhaps best presented here consecutively rather than side-by-side.

4. The problem of suicide: Sometimes <there is talk about> an epidemic of suicide. By consensus of "on-lookers," a seemingly social connection is established <between occurring cases which form merely a> statistical unity.
5. Ethnological unity: Average, synopsis. "The Greeks at Marathon".

<c. Third Part of Lecture>

a) Necessity of the interpretation of meaning in contrast to abstract collectives presupposes a correct positing of meaning. <This is so> on account of the aprioristic Thou-conditioning of human cognition.
b) To be born later: the problem of the world of predecessors.
c) Ideology of the "exponents of meaning" as means of ruling the masses on the basis of "charisma".
d) The experience of resistance as motivation for action oriented by meaning (chances . . .)

Toward a Viable Sociology[19]

<d. Fourth Part of Lecture>

It would be <desirable> to investigate:
a) the relationship of the vital sphere (the bodily I) to actual experiences (pain, sex).
b) The relationship of the intimate person, notably to the absolutely intimate person – <and in connection with it> the understandability of the intimate person.
c) Formation of <these> strata presupposed, does logical priority belong to the intimate person of the Thou?
d) With Dilthey, silent thinking
e) Death by aging is seen as a fundamental existential fact by Heidegger.
f) The Teiresias Motif.

[19]The title is that of Schutz. Wagner notes that he placed this section at the end although it does not seem to resemble a summary of the lectures nor a conclusion in the ordinary sense. It would rather seem to be a list of problems which represent basic concerns of Schutz.

CHAPTER 8

Understanding and Acting in Political Economy and Other Social Sciences

Editors' Preface

Schutz's own title was *"Leitsätze zur Diskussion über meinen Vortrag vom 22. Mai vorbereitet für den Seminarabend am 27. Juni 1930"* ("Guidelines for the discussion of my lecture of 22 May, prepared for the seminar-evening of 27 June, 1930"). This is another lecture given in the private seminar of Ludwig von Mises and announced with the heading of *Verstehen und Handeln* (*Understanding and Acting*). If Schutz had made further notes for the lectures they have not been preserved. Nevertheless, the guidelines provide a condensed picture of the major themes he treated. To the title Wagner added, "in Political Economy and Other Social Sciences", in order to indicate the broad focus of the guidelines. In the copy of the typescript used for the translation by Wagner, the last sentence has been lined out with pencil by Schutz.

1. Like understanding sociology, history, and other social sciences, political economy claims that its subject-matter is meaningful human action in the social world. Among these sciences, only political economy postulates "universally valid propositions". It is necessary that we inquire into the circumstances under which this is possible. Most importantly we must try to discover whether the meaningful action which is the subject-matter of political economy is identical with that upon which understanding sociology focuses. For this purpose, it is necessary to undertake

2. An analysis of Weber's conception of the "understanding of the subjectively intended meaning that the actor connects with his action". According to Weber, the inner nature of understanding sociology consists in the thematic focus upon the intended meaning. My analysis shows that the Weberian conceptual pairs

a) actual and motivational understanding, and
b) subjective and objective meaning

can be transposed into each other. A sufficiently precise investigation will <demonstrate that these pairs> under no circumstances yield sufficiently sharp and useful distinctions. The reason for this confusion of concepts chiefly is a disregard for the set of problems pertaining to intersubjectivity and time. In principle, however,

3. The expression, "the actor connects meaning with an action", is merely a

linguistic metaphor. The meaning of one's own conduct or acting is under no circumstances an "experience" which is independent of the acting and, so to speak, merely accompanies it. <The assumed experience> is connected with the conduct <under consideration> in a fashion which is not further explained. Neither is it a predicate of a specific conduct – that which is immediately one's own. Obviously this seems to be expressed in metaphorical phrases saying that a specific conduct "has" meaning, "is meaningful" or "makes sense". Actually, such "acting" and "carrying out action" is merely a linguistic hypostatization of one's own experience. This is brought into focus in a certain way: the "meaning" that (likewise, metaphorically) is predicated of such action is nothing but the "how" of this turning-toward-one's-own-experience. That is, it is that which constitutes acting in the first place.

4. Every action is experienced as a process of acts being built up phase-by-phase. Husserl designated such acts "polythetically articulated syntheses of a higher order". Essential for them is that, after having taken place, retrospectively they can be viewed "monothetically" as something unitary in one ray of regard. We must therefore distinguish between *acting* (*actio*) in its course and the finished *action* (*actum*) after it has run its course. Thus the question to be posed is: To which of the two "accrues meaning"?

5. Weber's conception of action is marred by a further unclarity. Even though the question is directed upon the "subjective meaning" of action, the delimitation of the acting that is to be interpreted is left to the interpreter – just as if it were completely obvious that the momentarily selected segment of the external course of an action forms a "unity" whose meaning now can be explored. However, the considerations offered under (3) and (4) show that this is not at all the case. Only the actor (speaking popularly) can establish when his concrete action starts and when it is finished, provided that he turns his attention toward the course of his own experiencing. This is so because he alone has "designed" this action and he alone can, in monothetical retrospection, look upon the polythetical acts of his acting (of the *actio*) and constitute the unity of the action (of the *actum*) and therewith its meaning.

6. About our meaningful experiences E_1, E_2, . . . E_n we say that they are found within one context of meaning provided these experiences constitute themselves in polythetically articulated acts phase-by-phase building up to a synthesis of a higher order and we are able to regard them monothetically as a constituted unity. In this fashion, the individual phases of our *acting* enter into a context of meaning: we are able to regard them as a unitary *action* as it flows along.

7. What has been said thus far ((3) to (6)) is valid above all for one's own action. However, in the social sphere we deal with the "meaning" of the acting of someone else. Now, the observation of the acting of someone else can be carried out in two ways.

a) *Subjective Meaning*: We grasp the context of meaning in the regard in which the actor places the course of experience which is called acting. We thereby apprehend the experiences of someone else in their course within someone else's duration as they are built up in polythetical acts in the consciousness of Thou, enabling this Thou to look upon them monothetically after they have run their course. Under this condition, the courses of experience called "acting" occur in a context of meaning for the experiencing Thou, and this Thou is a special Thou in its Being-thus at every Now-point of its duration: It is not "interchangeable"; it cannot be replaced by any other Thou, nor even by the same Thou at a different point of duration. However, we can also consider

b) *Objective Meaning*: just in its "finished" *actions* without regarding the polythetical acts in which they are constituted in the course of experiencings of the Thou. More particularly we also place this action into the context of meaning, although not into that context in which the actor places them. We place it instead in the context of meaning just of our own experiences (that is, into the context of experiences in daily life if we are partners in the social relationship, or else into the context of experiences in our science if we pursue social-scientific objectives). Thus we place the action of someone else into a context of meaning which (in contrast to (a)) is *only* pregiven *to us*. Nothing is changed by the concept of *"action of someone else"* pointing back to the existence of an other Thou who has posited precisely that action.

If we ask about the objective meaning we do not at all come to regard this Thou and its experiences: in principle, in its being-thus the Thou remains anonymous in its individual peculiarities. The Thou becomes an impersonal "someone" [*"Man"*]. I or anyone else can replace this Thou by any real *alter ego* or an "ideal type" or "everyone" without thereby being able to change anything in the context of meaning in which we fit the action. But it is just for this reason that the "objective meaning" of the action, its place in the context of meaning of *our* experience, remains invariable in the fact of any context of meaning whatever in which the action happened to be built up polythetically: who executed the action under regard and when it was done is in principle irrelevant for this mode of observation; it is sufficient that such an action does not contradict our experiences.

In recapitulation we may say that the objective meaning (of an action or of a sign) is exclusively integrated into a context of meaning in the consciousness of the "observer" (or, more generally, the interpreter). Beyond this, subjective meaning also stands in a context of meaning in the consciousness of the actor (more generally, the one who posits meaning). The observer concentrates on this subjective meaning with the help of a technique (not further discussed in this lecture).

8. Only a science of objective meaning is capable of forming "laws of universal validity". Political economy is a science of objective meaning. It does not deal with action which is built up phase-by-phase in the course of consciousness pertaining to the Thou; it deals instead with the anonymous processes of actions by an impersonal "someone". Just this sets off the subject-matter of political economy from that of understanding sociology (and also that of history).[1]

[1]The last sentence has been lined out with a pencil. Because it expresses a main point of Schutz it has been retained.

Perhaps a brief comment may be permitted about this remarkable text of Alfred Schutz, especially because of a very special problem of translation. So far as I can make out, this is the earliest example of Schutz's attempt to systematically express his own special Weberian concept of social action in terms of the concepts of Husserl's phenomenology (stemming, no doubt, from *Ideas*, First Book, but also from the then recently published *Formal and Transcendental Logic*).

The gist of Schutz's view would seem to be that social action turns out to be a special case of what Husserl calls "polythetical" and "monothetical" *acts of consciousness*. Social *acting* is constituted and articulated polythetically, and objectivated and apprehended monothetically as social *action* in just the same way, e.g., a collection is constituted and articulated polythetically, step-by-step, and objectivated as a collectivum (see F. Kersten, *Phenomenological Method: Theory and Practice* [Kluwer, 1989], pp. 54f., 338f.). The consequence is that *Handeln* and *Handlung*, acting (*actio*) and action (*actum*), would seem to be special cases of acts of consciousness in Husserl's pregnant meaning of "act".

Now, "act" in the pregnant meaning is a special case of an *Erlebnis*, a mental process which has the "quality" of being lived in by the ego. Similarly, social acting is an acting I initiate, plan, the consequences of which I foresee, which I manage and carry out to its conclusion – in just the same way I collect things, or carry out a judgment, or count things. Thus while *Erlebnis* can be translated as "mental process" for Husserl, it cannot be so for Schutz; a term must be found in English which also covers *Handlung* as well; with Wagner I have opted for "experience", although this would not work for Husserl (see in this connection, F. Kersten, "Discussion. *Ideas II*", *JBSP*, 22 (No. 2), May, 1991, p. 90).

Schutz eventually came to criticize Husserl's concept of polythetic and monothetic acts as inadequate to understand special cases of social acting, such as "making music together" (see F. Kersten, Preface to "Fragments on the Phenomenology of Music", *In Search of Musical Method*, edited by F.J. Smith [Gordon and Breach, 1976], pp. 9ff.). Although Schutz's criticism is clear, I have often puzzled over it:

For Schutz, the monothetic apprehension is always introspective and retrospective, whereas for Husserl it is not – objectivating, even thematizing and reflection, are of necessity neither introspective nor retrospective. However, in Schutz's "Guidelines" it is clear that not only is social acting a special case of the polythetic act and a synthesis of a higher order, but for Schutz, action (*actum*) is always only apprehended retrospectively: I only know what I am doing when I am done, the acting is "known" by the deed, hence is always retrospective. If we take acting, *Handeln*, as a paradigm of a polythetic synthesis of a higher order, then indeed it would seem to follow that all polythetic acts, of which social acting is a special case, are apprehended monothetically only in retrospect. It seems to me that this is just what Schutz does here. Expressed most broadly, the paradigm of every mental act is its special case, social acting. Although this would seem false, at least logically and phenomenologically, I think that it is a view, an "operative concept" perhaps, that pervades the rest of Schutz's thinking. [FK]

CHAPTER 9

Basic Problems of Political Economy

Editors' Preface

This is an English translation by Helmut Wagner of a review article by Schutz of Ludwig von Mises' *Grundprobleme der Nationalökonomie. Untersuchungen über Verfahren, Aufgaben und Inhalt der Wirtschafts- und Gesellschaftslehre [Basic Problems of Political Economy. Investigations of Procedures, Tasks, and Content of the Theory of Economy and Society]*(Jena, 1933). The review was published in *Deutsche Literaturzeitung*, Third Series, V, 1934, pp. 36–42.

Ludwig von Mises was Schutz's principal teacher of economics at the University of Vienna and represented the third generation of the Viennese School of the theory of marginal utility (a theory noted for its adherence to an utterly unrestrained principle of free competition, yet emphasizing the demand side of market operations). Schutz himself would not seem to have been enthusiastic about the theory of unrestrained (better, cut-throat) competition. In his book von Mises develops not so much an economic theory in the narrow sense of "economics" as he does his broad social theories in the hope of providing them with a philosophical foundation. For Schutz, reviewing the book provided the occasion for laying out his own position with respect to economics as the foundation of all the social sciences.

Representing the Austrian School of Political Economy, Ludwig von Mises is known far beyond the boundaries of the German language. Sociology too owes him many basic contributions, not the least of which is the most significant and radical critique of recent Marxist theory of society. In this volume von Mises offers a collection of his articles with a critical-methodological content that have appeared in various German journals and which are complemented by several more recent writings.

At first sight the title of the book does not seem to do justice to the broad framework of its content. The author's investigation pursues no less a task than "to present the logical justification of that science which aims at universally valid laws of human action". It is the author's opinion that such a science does not have to be developed because it already exists: theoretical political economy and sociology, developed in several generations of research, has no other goal than to be an aprioristic science of human action. In this connection, von Mises encounters such different writers as

John Stuart Mill, John Elliott Cairnes, Walter Bagehot, Karl Menger, Friedrich von Wieser and Max Weber.

The author emphasizes that with his approach he shares the position that German historians and the philosophical school founded by Windelband have taken in their opposition to the attempt to constitute the science of history as a natural science. Thus the author faces two tasks: first, to clarify the subject matter and method of a theoretical science of human action and, second, to set his concept of a theoretical social science apart from the approach of the historical school <which had made historical interpretations of economic affairs and of social relations into the guiding principles of their undertaking>. Accordingly, he is compelled to discuss in detail the difficult question of the relationship between sociology and history and further to lay bare the specific logical structure of social sciences in contrast to the so-called "cultural sciences" *[Geisteswissenschaften]*.

The theme of the first article is the task and range of the general science of human action (pp. 1–63). Initially it shows how the social sciences developed during the eighteenth century from historical and normative beginnings into a theory of human action, and that notably by means of the maturing of political economy. As theory, and that means as *a priori* cognition prior to all experience, it is to be sharply contrasted with all historism[1] and most of all with that "understanding" characteristic of all historical reflection: "What we know about the basic categories of action, about acting, managing economic affairs, preferences *[Vorziehen]*, about the relationships between means and ends, and everything else which all together constitutes the 'system of human action' – all this does not issue from experience. We recognize all this by ourselves like we do logical and mathematical truths: *a priori* and without relationship to any experience" (p. 13). In the unfolding of this system the role of experience is restricted to informing us of whether the concepts, as they are developed in the aprioristic analysis of the basic category of action, find their correlate in given conditions under which we work and act. We recognize in aprioristic analysis what are free goods and what are economic goods. However, only experience teaches us that not all things of the outer world are free goods. This circumstance informs us about the importance that theoretical insight has for the practice of life. "Experience can achieve no more than the separation of these problems which we eye with interest from problems which we wish to leave aside because they are of no interest to our urge to know" (p. 14).

Consequently it is not the economy but economic conduct which becomes the starting point of analysis – or, more generally, the concept of (rational) action with which are co-posited the pairs of concepts of path and goal, means and end, cause and effect, and with them the concepts of values, goods, exchange, price, costs but also order of rank and importance, scarcity and abundance, advantage and disadvantage, success, gain and loss (pp. 22f.). The logical development of these concepts

[1]Wagner notes that "historism" has no counterpart in English, and that it signifies one kind of explanation of social institutions which considers an account of their history a sufficient interpretation of their characteristics without claiming that the historical factors in question are rigidly causal factors. Thus historism has to be contrasted with "historicism", a generic label for the Hegelian concept of history as an unfolding dialectical process of historical necessity in the guise of the "world spirit".

from the basic category of "action" yields the elementary theory of values and prices in purely aprioristic deduction. Without exception all of these elementary laws of value are valid for all human action (p. 25). The propositions about *"Katallaktik,"*[2] about the theory of money and circulation, about the theory of cartel and monopoly prices, etc., are valid "in so far as the conditions are given that are presupposed and exactly prescribed by them" (p. 24).

Thus characterized, the task of economic theory is subsequently defended against a number of objections. First it is shown that the opinion of historists that one could grasp facts without theory is false because the empiricists, who pretend to work without theory, necessarily use a theory themselves.

Theoretical knowledge has to be verifiable by empirical facts. Nevertheless, a correct theoretical realization, if correctly deduced from aprioristic insights, can never be refuted by experience. Von Mises also discusses the objection that next to so-called rational action driven by purpose there occurs irrational action as well. He tries to show that the idea of irrational action is based on an erroneous idea of the separation of means from ends. Finally, he lays out the scientific character of the aprioristic theory of action and thereby emphasizes its value-neutrality in contrast to politics and world-view philosophies. Von Mises refutes the universalist critique of Othmar Spann and his criticism of fostering individualism; he argues that science, whether it proceeds aprioristically or empirically, can only proceed causally and rationally. In violation of this principle, any universalistic concept <of economic matters> is based on a "vision" of the whole which is discursively visible. In a polemic against Vierkandt, Myrdal and Eduart Hahn, von Mises rejects the objections against pure theory which it is now fashionable to make and which originates in an erroneous notion, namely a materialist utilitarianism which is falsely connected with this theory.

The second article in the volume is called "Sociology and History" (pp. 64–121). After a short exposition of the logical and methodological problems behind the so-called "conflict about methods" *["Methodenstreit"]*,[3] the article concentrates on a critical discussion of Max Weber's theory of the ideal type. Essentially, von Mises refers to that theory of ideal types which Weber developed in his famous essay of 1904 about the objectivity of social-scientific knowledge. Von Mises acknowledges Weber's efforts to clarify the logical-conceptual form of scientific-historical research. He fully agrees with the rejection of all tendencies to establish historical laws or to apply natural-scientific concept-formations to the realm of history. However, von Mises criticizes Weber for an alleged misinterpretation of the character of sociological research: he understood by sociology something else than the normative science

[2]This would seem to be a key term in von Mises' economic theory. Wagner's surmise is that the term is derived from the Greek *"katallage"*, which means "exchange" in its various connotations, among them "profit made on exchange". Thus von Mises' *Katallaktik* as a theory of economic gain made in the exchange and use of goods and services obtained on the free market.

[3]Wagner identifies this long-standing conflict among economists with that version of it which surfaced in the controversy between Max Weber and Gustav Schmoller; the latter insisted that moral and other value judgments enter into all social-scientific knowledge, the former insisted on the value-neutrality of political economy and sociology.

of human action (p. 74). For von Mises every kind of acting falls exclusively under the principle of economy *[Wirtschaftlichkeit]* and thus is necessarily purposive and rational. "All action is economic managing with the means available for achievable ends" (p. 77). Consequently he has to reject all other categories of action introduced by Weber (value-rational, affectional, traditional). Following this point of view, von Mises also opposes the notion that the "laws" of sociology are ideal types or that the concepts of sociology are ideal-typical constructions. <The sociological concepts> "are rather the sum of the characteristics which are found in the same manner in every single object to which they refer". Causal sociological propositions do not express what will occur as a rule; they "are expressions of what necessarily has to occur in so far as the presupposed conditions obtain"(pp. 87f.).

It is my opinion that von Mises does not do justice to Weber in this polemic. This is not the place to present this in detail. What sociology is for Weber is something else again for von Mises; it may adequately be called "general theories of history or general history". All historism is based on the heresy of believing that "science" could do without theoretical propositions. History without sociology, in the sense of the author, is unthinkable. The historian always lets himself be guided by theories when selecting and analyzing his materials. These theories have been created by thinking – although mostly extra-scientific thinking – <and are presented> with a claim to general validity. Historical "laws" have been attempted for instance in theories of economic stages (Bücher) or laws of progress (Breysig). They lack that universal validity which inheres in – genuine – sociological laws by virtue of their aprioricity (for instance, the proposition of the higher productivity of work achieved through division of labor). History "either has to develop theory itself or else it has to take its position wherever theory is developed already with all the means at the disposal of the human spirit". It is clear that so far all theorizing has achieved nothing for history. However, history itself can begin its own tasks only after the means of theory have been completely exhausted. Its realm starts only "with the realm of the individual, of the temporary, of the historically whole. History can cross the threshold of this reality only after it has been brought to this threshold by the force of rational thinking" (p. 120).

The third article bears the title, "Comprehending and Understanding" (pp. 120–136). It develops the method that rational thinking has to use. Here von Mises concisely lays out the basic features of his scientific-theoretical approach. First he juxtaposes the science of human conduct to the science of nature. The former aims at grasping the meaning which the actor linked to his acting. This task is not recognized by behaviorism; it considers the behavior of humans from the outside, that is, as a reaction to specific situations. Behaviorism fails completely in its critique of idealist psychology. However, the procedure of grasping meaning should not simply be identified with "understanding" [*Verstehen*]. In contemporary German sciences, the latter expression does not at all connote every sort of procedures directed upon the grasping of meaning. Rather it refers to that specific procedure that tries to grasp meanings in empathic participation in life in a whole [*in einfühlendem Sicheinleben*]. The opposite of this is "comprehending"; it tries to seize upon meaning by way of discursive thinking (p. 125).

Understanding is always subjectively conditioned. Its logical realm exists exclusively in a region which comprehending cannot penetrate, that is, in the seizing upon the quality of values: "For the science of human action, human evolution and the establishment of goals of ultimate order are givens which it is unable to explain further" (p. 127). But the grasping of these values by understanding still is not an "explanation". Values are the irrational as such; the latter never can be an object of science. From this position, von Mises quite properly criticizes [Werner] Sombart who, as is well known, propagates a political economy of "understanding". Von Mises instead demands that the social sciences adhere to that conceptual rigor which alone allows the <adequate> theoretical treatment of any object.

These considerations give rise to the following comments. The polemic is pertinent in so far as it directs itself against that hermeneutics which tries to avoid theoretical rigor by appealing to some sort of mystical vision [*Schau*]. Their "understanding" of cultural science rests almost completely on an erroneous interpretation of the writings of Dilthey. However, one must warn against the misunderstanding that the sociology of understanding, as established by Max Weber, renounces genuine sociological comprehension and therefore is not a theoretical science.

The preceding considerations report on the methodologically most important part of the book. The remaining articles concern themselves chiefly with the subjectivist theory of values and with the concept of fixed capital. Written in an unusually attractive manner, they apply to specific problems of theoretical political economy the methodological principles that were established in the first three writings. They offer a mass of suggestions and much edification not only for experts in this area but to everyone interested in the method of the cultural sciences. I may mention specifically the article which treats the "psychological roots of the resistence against economic theory" (pp. 170–189). In it the author attends to the critique of Marx which he had offered originally in his book, *Die Gemeinwirtschaft* [*Communal Economy*]. Here von Mises directs strong arguments against Marx and the interpretations of cultural phenomena in the Marxist sociology of knowledge. In a sound analysis he also deals with the conflict between belief and science as it is revealed in positions taken toward theoretical cognition; he reduces the conflict to the basic problem of freedom and necessity.

Like all of the author's writings, the present book is distinguished by a clear and concise language. Most happily it emphasizes the special gift of the author to present difficult ideas in easily understood, yet strictly scientific form. In his expositions he analyzes the character and methods of the social sciences in a fine manner even though he deliberately abstains from a discussion of the question of a general epistemology basic to the problems of the social sciences. His book merits attention and discussion all the more because <most specialists in economic and social-scientific areas of> our times know all too little about the goal and path of social-scientific research. Whatever one's position may be toward details of the concepts offered by von Mises, every unprejudiced reader will have to agree that sociology and political economy either will have to be pursued as theoretical sciences or they will not be sciences.

CHAPTER 10

Political Economy: Human Conduct in Social Life

EDITORS' PREFACE

The original title of this unpublished essay was *Nationalökonomie: Verhalten des Menschen im sozialen Leben*. The English translation is by Helmut Wagner. The essay was occasioned by Friedrich von Hayek's visit to Vienna in 1936, where he gave a lecture to the Viennese *Gesellschaft für Wirtswissenschaft*. The topic was *"Wissen und Wirtschaft"* ["Knowledge and Economics"]. In his discussion, Schutz addressed not so much the points von Hayek made, but instead developed ideas occasioned by some of von Hayek's remarks, sending typed copies of them to Ludwig von Mises, Felix Kaufmann and Fritz Machlup. Von Hayek requested a copy which he intended to have translated and published in the journal *Economica*. Agreeing to write an appropriate essay for the journal, Schutz wrote a hand-written introduction of seven pages and a longer draft of his discussion which his wife typed in several copies, each of which came to about twenty-five pages. Schutz made corrections by hand to bring the manuscript into final form. There are also changes made by Machlup, some of which Wagner has incorporated into his translation.[1]

For reasons not known, Schutz never sent the finished manuscript to *Economica*. It was Wagner's surmise that Schutz withheld it from publication because he feared that an exposition of his views on economic theory would be misleading without first establishing the foundations of his own work in phenomenology and sociology.

(1) Von Mises and Hayek rightly agree that it is false to speak of a static or stationary economy or even of a state of equilibrium. To be correct one would have to speak of a static method. In the present context it can be left open whether the conceptual model of a state of equilibrium is pedagogically or heuristically purposeful. The history of theory seems to answer in the affirmative. However, the important question is whether the conceptual model of a state of equilibrium can be constructed without contradictions and, should this be the case, what explicit and implicit

[1]Machlup's copy had originally been in the possession of Aron Gurwitsch who probably received it from Schutz sometime after they met in Paris in 1935. Machlup made the copy of the manuscript available to Wagner around 1980. For Schutz's relationship with von Hayek and Machlup, see Wagner, *Alfred Schutz. An Intellectual Biography*, pp. 158f., and 166ff.

preconditions are then presupposed. Such questions belong to the realm of the logic of pure economics.

If this sphere is abandoned and if the attempt is made to search within the social economy of exchange for a possible state of equilibrium, then the same investigations have to be carried out anew. This must be done, however, on the level now reached – a completely different thematic level (here the political economists speak of a higher "level of abstraction"). Again, the question has to be raised whether now the model of a state of equilibrium holds without inner contradictions with the social economy of exchange. Should this question be answered in the affirmative, it must be asked whether the preconditions then postulated are the same as the ones assumed by the logic of pure economics.

(2a) Like other social-scientific problems, in principle phenomena of the economy can be viewed in two ways: first, one confines oneself to the description of the external course of the phenomena which become visible and yet are of a highly complex structure. For instance, we design curves of supply and demand; we occupy ourselves with the observations of price fluctuations and establish the relation between the prices of the final products and their costs. According to experience, this observational method suffices for the observation of many problems, provided we waive the attempt to make thematic additional and deeper strata.

<The question of> which strata become thematic is decided once and for all by the selection of the problem when it is made with deliberation and clearly executed. (Of course the serious researcher cannot choose his problems at will: the formulations of the questions that are of interest are also predesigned in his factual materials. This is a difficult set of problems which I shall ignore here.) Such a manner of observation works with types of economic processes. Concerning some observations we can call this the question about the objective sense of the phenomena that offer themselves to the observer. However, this term has still other connotations.

But even when the investigation aims at penetrating deeper layers of problems, it is often useful to speak about curves of supply and demand, and the like, but only in the sense of an abbreviation: It is to be supposed that we have recognized in full distinctness and clarity the content of these terms which present the results of long chains of thinking <and that we make sure> that we always mean the same things when using the same expressions. Should a mathematician, for reasons of the technical simplification of his calculations, represent a complicated equation by a single symbol, he must use this symbol exclusively in its originally established meaning. He may not forget what the original sense of this symbol had been.

(2b) All social phenomena can be traced back to actions of actors in the social world who, in turn, may be observed by social scientists. Therefore it is possible at any time to pose the further question: What possible meanings did the actors connect with these actions which present themselves to us, the observers, as courses of social phenomena? Posing this question we will no longer be satisfied with establishing a certain form of curves of supply and demand. Beyond this we ask, What considerations must have caused sellers and buyers to behave in the market place so that the resulting curves of supply and demand acquired this or that shape? We will no longer be satisfied with the prices of end-products and the statistical establishment of the producers when setting up the plans of production. Of course, one ingredient of the producers' plans will be their expectations of the considerations of the consumers.

This perspective of research may appropriately be called the subjective direction, or better the question about the subjective meaning of social phenomena. This is not a matter of forming types of courses of action but of personalities whose motives are described or postulated as constant.

At no stage of our social-scientific investigations can we be prohibited from referring back to the subjects of the social world. We can object to this information only if, for reason of one or another problem, this turn of attention will yield little information of interest, perhaps none at all. Conversely it can be said that the same turn of attention is unavoidable when we aim at the exact recognition of phenomena which are not even viable on the level of objective meaning and become thematic only at a deeper level of inquiry. To these phenomena, in my opinion, belong not only the problems of equilibrium respectively of the static method, but also the problems of data, of prediction, of risk, of misinvestments *[Fehlinvestitationen]*.

(3) When reaching back to the subject matter of social life, specifically with respect to economic life, do we not have to fear becoming entrapped in that psychologism which our "rational age" is proud to have overcome? I think that social scientists should not be worried by this question. They may leave that to the philosophers whose best contemporary representatives have convinced themselves that a good amount of psychologism is also contained in so-called pure logic.

(4) If we open at random any selected treatise on political economy whose author claims to have exhausted its topic, or even if we read only one monograph <making the same claim>, we will find long stretches in which the author concentrates on that research method we characterized as "objective". But then subsequently the author gets occupied with subjective aspects of the problems. Is this not an impermissible syncretism of methods? There was a time during which it was fashionable, under the influence of neo-Kantians, to cut up into small pieces any comprehensive area of knowledge. It was alleged that each of these pieces required its own method. What could not be pressed into these beds of Procrustes by being labelled something like "meta-economic" or "meta-juristic" was pushed into the realm of other sciences (mostly into sociology or history). Exponents of these disciplines, <should they take these neo-Kantian, self-appointed advisers seriously>, would be cautioned to find out for themselves how they may deal with such assignments by relying on their own specific methods. The exponents of this trend never went far enough to even hint at a method with the help of which they might treat those sets of problems transcending the special sciences.

Fortunately political economy has always rejected attempts of this sort and did not allow itself to be confused by the postulate of the purity of methods. The latter has a very limited validity outside the mathematical natural sciences. More particularly, the originators of the school of marginal utility had no inclination to create a mere brainchild, a non-Euclidean political economy, so to speak; they wanted to provide a useable machinery for the description of the concrete economic life. Anyone familiar with the problems of political economy has realized that work had to be carried out at "different levels of abstraction", as it was called. According to our research situation, new "data" could be inserted into our scheme of thought or else we would be subjected to the principle of *"ceteris paribus"*.

Political economists should not be blamed for this attitude. On the contrary, it must be said that this often naïvely executed procedure protected their science from the sad fate which, for instance, befell the theory of pure law. Nevertheless, the vacillation between various thematic positions is accompanied by a series of dangers. It becomes disastrous in the case of the transition from a "level of higher abstraction" to one of "decreasing abstraction" when the researcher does not realize which modifications his original points of departure have to undergo because "other things" become thematic or are implicitly intended on the newly gained level. Finally, if it happens that outstanding researchers disagree on matters of basic principles – a stage through which any science has to pass at a specific stage of its development – there is no other way out than by methodologically recalling how we must actually proceed in our own scientific work.

(5) An especially good example of the importance of such reflection is the problem of "data" in political economy. It is certainly time to stop using the concept of "data", or even of the "given datum", as a refuge for ignorance. The definitely legitimate question is: To whom are such data given? To me, living my everyday life, the whole environment is, as it were, given as an environment of data. It is a datum for me that the sun will rise tomorrow, but also that the streetcar will work, and that I can buy merchandise in a store for my money. It is a datum for me, further, that the stockmarket in Paris is in disorder and that the price of tea will rise because of the poor harvest in India. In this sense, all my experiences of the external situation on which I have no influence are data.

According to my given situation of interest, I will pay attention to one or another factor; I will even analyze sufficiently the phenomena of importance for me to the extent called for by the situation and allowed by my experience. For instance, it will suffice for me as passenger to be informed about travel-times and frequencies of the streetcar lines. However, if I am not a technician and if it is not relevant for me for other reasons, I am not concerned with the construction and technical layout of the electric streetcar – even though these too are data or me. Thus, what is a datum for us in daily life and what we keep in view in our considerations is what is relevant for us in the given case. We are ready to analyze it and do this either on the basis of a review of the actual stock of our experiences in the matter or on hand by way of potential information. (This occurs when he informs himself about this matter by asking others or by consulting a handbook.)

However, all of the data of daily life and my knowledge about them are given to me beforehand in the mode of chance. This point will gain significance for a problem I shall treat later. Whether these data are actually given to me or whether my earlier experiences with them are still useful or will apply in the future is not certain and most of all not necessarily certain. Merely this is more or less possible. Any reference to experiences occurs under the silent assumption that nothing has changed since last I took notice of the matter. Phenomenologists call this thinking in the form of the idealities of the "and so on" and the "I can always again".

By comparison, what does "datum" mean when not given to a person in daily life but instead to the social scientist, e.g., the economist? In my opinion, there is only one answer possible, and it is one which simultaneously offers a precise definition of the term, "datum": social scientists designate as data those phenomena which remain unproblematic for a specifically posited problem-position. However, we must be aware that, just because it remains unproblematic, from now on the so-called datum presents an unexplored manifold. In no way can it be seen within clear limitations. To use a phenomenological expression, it always carries with it an "open horizon".

Calling something unproblematic from the perspective of a specific formulation of a problem is not saying that we know nothing about it or that at present we cannot say anything about it. As persons in daily life – which we also are – we know a lot about it. Aside from this, as economists we too could make a series of <more or less> precise statements, let us say, about population shifts. When we call certain phenomena "data", we indicate that, in the present state of our investigation, we do not wish to make a statement and we want to leave some data as they are, and that they are irrelevant for the present problem at hand. In short, we consider them extra-thematic.

As anywhere else, the situation complicates itself in the social sciences by the fact that social scientists, when turning back to the subjective sphere, must also deal with those phenomena that are given as "data" to actors whom they observe in the social world. It may happen that what is given to the actor is also a datum given for the observer; thus it remains extra-thematic for the observer's investigation. But in no way does this have to be the case. It may well be that in sociological investigation of economic convictions a sociologist treats as theme what appears as mere datum to actors in the social world.

(6) Important consequences follow from the notions discussed about the nature of data. Most important of all, as long as we remain within the realm in which we started we will never encounter the question whether or which data are given to a social scientist. There are no data within the given sphere. Nothing is "given", everything must be determined by definitions, axioms, so-called tautologies, or else it must be derived from them. The question of data emerges first when the original problem-formation is abandoned (expanded) and when the set of insights gained so far is now to be applied to other strata of problems. What formerly was non-problematic now becomes the datum if the formerly acquired set of insights becomes the object of a new theme. Political scientists regularly encounter the question of data; so, for instance, when they apply insights found in the logic of pure economy to the concrete economy of exchange, or when they apply propositions of the social economy of exchange to the economy of money; or when they are to apply a general proposition belonging to the economy of money to the concrete exchange rate of the pound sterling in 1936. (Here we talk about "reductive layers of abstraction" through which given concrete "data" can be integrated into tautologically gained superordinated propositions. This is misleading because it clarifies only a part of the problem, and does so inadequately. I shall discuss this in a special section.)

In addition, the problem of the datum also occurs when we cling to the same layer of problems but change the basic methodological position. This may be owing to deviation from the objective method of the forming of personality types or its converse. Or it may be that the point in time is not unequivocally fixed and exact in the application of the subjective method. The latter is frequently the case. An excellent example of the errors thereby committed is offered by the theory of misinvestments. On the one hand, misinvestments are viewed as investments which the economic subject in question was rationally justified in making according to the situation at the time of planning (more exactly, according to the information at his disposal at that time) but which *afterwards* turned out to be misdirected – the course of events did not justify the expectations. On the other hand, we speak of misinvestments when the investment program was unjustifiable from the start, perhaps because the calculations of the entrepreneur in question were contradictory in themselves. Both misinterpretations <in spite of their difference> share the same mistake: one did not distinguish between the project and the executed action with all its consequences.

In the one case, <the investor> places himself in the time span of the project but <in anticipation> introduces into it all the experiences which can be acquired only when the project has grown into its execution. At this time, the consequences of this act are known together with everything that happened in the meantime in the relevant "environment"; it has become known and can be appraised. In the other case, <in anticipation the investor> is placed into a point of time in which it already has been revealed that a misinvestment took place. <The unlucky investor> now assumes that there still exist expectations, plans, calculations of risk and that which long since has been established as unequivocal and unalterable is still uncertain and in question.

This is only one, although typical, example of the trick of *hysteron proteron*, a trick often performed in economic discussions. That which might turn out later to have been a misinvestment should not be confused with what was already before an obvious mistake. One cannot prophesy the past, and one cannot describe the future in historical retrospection. What has occurred is not only unequivocally determined, it is also unchangeable. What is situated in the future is in principle uncertain. Even the imaginary dictator of global economy (who conspicuously resembles the *demiurge* of the Scholastics) is not omniscient with the exception of the given moment. In spite of his omniscience, with regard to the future, he thinks only in terms of the idealities of "and so forth" and "always again", as phenomenologists say, or else with the reservation of the *clausula rebus sic stantibus* <(under the condition that other things remain the same)> as the jurists postulate.

(7) The preceding remarks brought to light the particular importance of the problem of knowledge and prediction in economics. Hayek's investigations were first of all intended to serve this purpose. At the outset I posed the question: whose knowledge is of such relevance for the science of economy? Whoever views the objective method as characteristic of the economic sciences will be able to answer this question unequivocally. Most of all he will trust statistics, the phenomena of price fluctuations, the formula of market equilibrium, etc. He will be of the opinion that the knowledge of economists about these interrelations is the only relevant knowledge for their science.

The school of marginal utility has especially emphasized that such a conception is insufficient for the deeper explanation of the phenomena of economics. <The suggestion of> applying the conception of the subjective method <to economic matters> as developed above does not amount to a coarse equivocation. Already the founders of the school of marginal utility designated it as a subjective problematic even though with very different intentions. It can be demonstrated that the "Copernican turn" of the theory of marginal utility resulted in a more radical comprehension of economic life. Once this turn is carried out, the question of the problem of knowledge in economics expands itself to that of grasping the knowledge characteristic of one economic subject or else some or all of them at a specific time.

(8) In political economy, models are customarily constructed in order to illuminate this problem; as a rule, they suffice only for one specific layer of depth, whether we are concerned with Robinson Crusoe or with the omniscient economic dictator, or with that *"solus ipse economicus"* (the "solipcistic economic self") of which exponents of general praxeology[2] or of pure economics like to speak. The reason for this complexity is that economists treat these conceptual models, on the one hand, as though they were humans of flesh and blood like you and I and Peter and Paul and everyone who encounters them in daily life; on the other hand, they endow them with that preknowledge, with those experiences, and even with that specific orientation of interest which are characteristic only for a few, namely the theorizing economic scientists themselves.

This peculiar constellation leads to many beautiful controversies: whether non-rational acting is thinkable at all, whether the economy would take a different course if the economic subjects would not commit errors, whether the expectations of the economic subjects would be satisfied or disappointed, and even whether free will can be ascribed to them. All of these problems can be posed legitimately when we deal with you and me, with Peter and Paul, or finally with everyone who is a human being in daily life and as such is also producer or consumer, householder or economic leader or employee. Anyone classified here plans, acts, expects, is disappointed in all his rational and non-rational thinking; he can err and, as an actor and thinker, he may feel himself free in one respect and bound in another.

But neither I nor you nor anyone in the fullness of his existence is identical with those subjects of economic life of which economists speak. We are related to this construction as to merely *one* side of our being human, <the side> that responds to those schemes which economists posit as economic subjects. What economists consider subjects of economic life are not humans in the fullness of their existence, but are rather ideal types. That is, they are fictive beings imagined to be equipped with conscious experiences (goals of action, motives, actions, etc.) and they are considered sufficient for acting out those economic events which the economist considers sufficiently relevant for his problem.

Here a fictive world comes into existence alongside the actual world. No danger will arise from this fact as long as the economists keep the rules of typification

[2]According to Wagner, this term would seem to be von Mises' general term for the principle governing his economic theory as a whole.

constant and their types correspond sufficiently to empirical realities. We pursue political economy merely in order to recognize and control this economic reality. Yet economists should avoid the fate of Pygmalion whose sculpture gained a weird life of its own. Economists should not transpose their models into the mundane world and treat them like humans with knowledge, experience, error, and freedom. This basic remark will have to be inspected more closely.

(9) As social science, political economy is a science of human action. Therefore economists view courses of action as standardized forms and use them as conceptual models in the manner discussed. As said before (section 2) we can be satisfied with treating the objective course of action in the external world and make nothing else thematic. Who posits the action is an extra-thematic question and therefore considered irrelevant; thus it will not be asked. Strictly speaking, in this attitude we do not even ask whether the external course of events does actually qualify as human action, even though this is mostly presupposed. By asking explicitly whether an observed event was in actuality human conduct, we execute the turn to the subjective mode of consideration.

With this turn a decisive, methodological step is taken. Now we no longer speak of a simple process in the external world but are concerned with the conscious experiences of the individual who has acted in the external world. We no longer speak of causes and effects as we would if our task were the description of a purely physical phenomenon. We inquire into the motive that urged an actor to operate in the external world and into his intention and purpose as well as into the meaning which the actor may have linked to his acting. With this decisive turn we reduce an event of the external world to conscious inner experiences of that person who produced it or at least would have produced it. Now the correct methodological question is: what kind of conscious experiences of an actor do we have to presuppose in order to plausibly explain his actions?

Previously I had posited as typical the external course of action and therefore a type of occurrence (so the typical course of the economic cycle as it results from the Harvard schemes[3]). With this subjective turn I am now turning back to the question of the personal type whose acting allows the interpretations of the presupposed typical courses of action. In addition, I am asking about the experiences of a consciousness that must be typical for such a manner of acting.

(This methodological turn may be carried out anywhere. Currently natural scientists limit themselves to view the natural world in terms of external happenings. Yet even in the seventeenth century it was still considered legitimate to pursue <the objectives of the> natural sciences by inquiring into the intentions of the Creator. Even the adherents of Newton interpreted space as the *sensorium* of God.)

(10) To construct a personal type means to postulate as invariant certain goals of and motives for action. All construction of these types is subject to the laws of possibility and compossibility. Possibility posits that the type in question does not display inner contradictions. This would be the case if motives and goals were considered

[3]Wagner, like others consulted, admits that he was at a loss to establish what, in 1936, Viennese economists called the "Harvard schemes".

constant but contradict one another. The law of compossibility dictates first that the types formed for dealing with one problem are compatible with one another. These laws hold not only for the forming of types but for any kind of formation of concepts. However, when the task is to grasp empirically actual happenings, it is also necessary that the applied types are compossible with the totality of our experiences of the world as such. In the sociology of understanding the terms possibility and compossibility correspond to the terms "meaning adequacy" and "causal adequacy". However, in the present context it is better not to use these terms because they include the notion of causality in an unclarified manner.

In the social sciences the forming of types is especially complicated because the principle of compossibility demands that the types of actors who stand in social relations to one another have to be synchronized in so far as the action of A is supposed to evoke a reaction of B which, however, already is part of A's expectations. This holds not just for the scientific formation of types but as well for the forming of types in everyday life as we continuously carry it out.

If someone wants to take a railroad trip he has to conduct himself in the way that he imagines the type, "railroad conductor", expects from him. Conversely, to the type, "railroad conductor", there also belongs the expectation that there is orientation to the type called "passenger". In order to inform myself I may ask a railroad conductor among my acquaintance or an acquaintance who has made railroad trips before, or else I ask for information in a travel bureau. Finally, I may study the principles that are suitable for the construction of types, may they be normative like the rules of transportation or consist of a time table. (An aside: This example shows that all norms for the consideration of the formation of types are merely a variation of standardization and that there is no logical difference between goal-adequate selection of a means and abiding by a norm. Felix Kaufmann has worked this out very clearly.)

Neither in daily life nor in science is there "type formation as such" or "type as such". Every type, so to speak, carries an index; it points to the purpose for which it was formed. This functional aspect of the formation of types is frequently overlooked. In daily life I form the types, "railroad conductor" and "passenger", as a potentially interested traveller. The same goes for the types formed by social scientists. Their situations of interest are determined by the problems they had posed themselves and by the layers of depth on which they wished to deal with these problems. This is no empty phrase. As I have shown, with the selection of a problem and the determination of the layer on which to treat it, what is thematically relevant is already established as well as what can be treated as a datum – and, accordingly, what is considered extra-thematic and thus invariant. This is what economists mean by the expression, *"ceteris paribus"*.

One basic attitude will be determinant for the social scientist under all circumstances: the social scientist is and remains *observer* of the social world. As social scientist he does not at all interfere in it. He also does not deal with living individual human beings but always with types of various grades of anonymity. In daily life inadequately formed types correct themselves immediately whenever the actor enters into a direct relation with an *alter ego* <representing for him a certain type>. This method of substantiation and correction is not available to the social scientist. Therefore he must pay particular attention to establishing a regulative principle that will teach how to carry out correctly the formation of types according to the laws of possibility and compossibility in the sense discussed. The economist has such a principle at his disposal: the Law of Marginal Utility.

(11) Unfortunately, we have an overabundant choice of variations of the principle of marginal utility. But whichever variation we consider, it remains easy to comprehend that we deal with a specific section out of the fullness of human conduct. For instance, if one wants to see the marginal principle at work in selective or preferential acting one has to consider thematic only a specific realm of social existence while other areas remain unproblematic for one's theme.[4] In this sense Felix Kaufmann has said that the principle of marginal utility delimits the realm of definition. This statement is correct, although it is in need of additional explanation. In any case, it establishes the thematic realm of political economy and with it the posing of problems in terms of which all types receive their indices.

By setting typical courses for establishing goals, for determining the corresponding motives, but also by circumscribing the typical relations between goal systems and intermediate systems among and between themselves, the theory of marginal utility offers regulative principles for the forming of all types which are supposed to delimit the realm of descriptions thereby created. Consequently, the principle of marginal utility attains a universal character by way of marking out theoretical realms of social life.

An economist who subscribes to the principle of marginal utility must make sure not to introduce directly or implicitly premises that are incompatible with that layer of abstraction he has chosen. <Only then> can he be sure not to have stepped outside the marked circle of problems and not to have abandoned its unitary character through which everything is connected with everything. The principle of marginal utility does not contain inner contradictions and agrees with the postulate of possibility. And more: a good chance exists that you and I and everyone orients his conduct to it.

Applied to the present theory of the forming of personality types, it follows that the principle of marginal utility is a postulate directed at economists that can be circumscribed as follows: 1) Supply the conceptual models of actors in the social world as such, which you are to form, with experiences of consciousness (goals of action and motives) so that the resulting actions appear oriented to the principle of marginal utility; 2) construct only ideal types which conform to this postulate.

The fundamental role of the principle of marginal utility is to serve as regulator of the forming of all its concepts and as definitional principle for the delimitation of its thematic realm. This explains why the propositions of this political economy

[4]Footnote of Alfred Schutz: Authors who consider all acting "preferential acting" do not realize that with this thesis they provide a definition of acting as such and that thereby <unwittingly> have set themselves the task of separating this acting from other manners of human existence. Should one – as many philosophers do for pertinent reasons – consider *cogitare* (thinking) a form of acting, then one would arrive at completely absurd results if the intention is to interpret thinking as preferential or selective action. And what kind of acting shall this preferring and selecting be if it is considered acting on its part?

appear with the claim of "always and everywhere being valid [propositions] if and only if the conditions exist which they presuppose" (von Mises).

Furthermore it becomes clear that universal validity is ascribed to these propositions in the sense "that they are not an expression of what may occur as a rule but of what will occur always and necessarily". And that means that such is the case provided the theoretical realm, as delimited by the principle of marginal utility, will not be abandoned. This is nothing but a consequence of the universality of the principle of marginal utility for the realm of invariance defined by it. To the laws of political economy accrue universality and objectivity in the same sense in which the laws of physics are "universally valid" – but also only within their established realms of invariance. Both types are hypothetical in character.

(12) Various authors, notably von Mises, are not satisfied with this assertion. They insist that laws of political economy, or more exactly of general social science, of which political economy is a special case, are of aprioristic character. In the light of the works of von Mises published so far it cannot be seen whether his conception of the *apriori* is designed to go beyond the general validity and universality which I discussed before. Should that not be the case, it would be better to avoid the term, "aprioristic". Propositions that are within certain realms fixed by the definition of invariance are in no way aprioristic propositions. Should von Mises use the concept of the *apriori* in the sense of one of the great systems of philosophy, he will certainly explain that himself.

The concept of the *apriori* not only has undergone dogmatic and historically radical changes, but it is also used today by philosophers in completely different ways. The neo-positivists are inclined to view any *apriori* as a founded convention (see the discussion in Kaufmann's last book). Recently Husserl has spoken of the relativity of the *apriori* as a thematic task of phenomenology. For Bergson and his circle there is only one genuine *apriori*: inner duration.

There is no reason why the question of the current philosophical meaning of the *apriori* should intensely occupy methodologists of the social sciences. He who knows the current problematics of the *apriori* will have to admit that this form of cognition warrants no more dignity than the properly understood empirical position. Both enter into "primal instituting experience" [*urstiftende Erfahrung*] and the "having of something as it itself" [*Selbsthabe der Sachen*] only afterwards. Aside from this, the phenomenon of the genuine *apriori* is revealed only in the so-called transcendental sphere. We social scientists deal with mundane phenomena and their realities within the world. We do not ask about the being of the world as such but are satisfied that our propositions are of general and universal validity within the pregiven world of mundane phenomena – no matter whether this world hangs together without contradiction as a world of appearance or as one of genuine being.

(13) The talk about the *apriori* in political economy has a still different meaning. With it the idea shall be expressed that no action is conceivable that does not occur following the principles of marginal utility: all acting is economic acting because it implicates preference and planning. In response to this assertion I say: this seems to be a terminological question. If one wants to qualify all acting as economic, one must state in what way this action differs from other manifest cases of human conduct

which are called actions or activities in psychology and philosophy. However, if one does not deprive the term "action" of its general connotation, one faces in turn the task of deciding what *differentia specificae* are characteristic of economic actions. Whichever alternative I may choose, it seems purposeful to separate acting turned toward so-called economic goods from other acting. Of course I am aware of the multiple meanings attached to the term itself, "economic goods"; they can be comprehended only after far-reaching preparation. One cannot be satisfied with the concepts of choosing and preferring without careful analyses. As mentioned before, choosing and preferring themselves are actions.

When I walk with a friend in a park and turn into the left instead of the right path, can I meaningfully say that I preferred the left path? And are not what we call choosing and preferring complex processes occurring in elapsing time? Undergoing them the one who chooses reciprocally imagines alternative projected actions as having occurred already. We continue the imaginary comparison until, as Bergson said, the decision falls from our consciousness like a ripe fruit. If one inspects this highly complex structure of preferential action he will doubt that any argument about the preferentiality <or non-preferentiality> of a <concretely occurring> acting will contribute to the clarification of the burning social-scientific question: on whose account did the controversy begin?

(14) After the digressions of points (12) and (13) let us return to those of the significance of the principle of marginal utility as regulator of the formation of economic types. It would not do to declare that the principle of marginal utility is a tautology. On p. 273 of his *Methodenlehre [der Sozialwissenschaften]* (Vienna, 1936) Felix Kaufmann dwelled on the effacement of the difference between a hypothetically deductive system which is crowned by certain assumptions about the world and a calculation of proofs beginning with definitions (tautologies).

Now, the principle of marginal utility is a statement about the world. As such it fixes the definition of the realm of invariance included in its sphere. Yet this is not a definition in the sense of an analytical judgment. I completely agree with Felix Kaufmann on this point.

However, it is wrong to consider the propositions of marginal utility major terms under which are subsumed the different statements about data as minor propositions. The talk about diminishing abstractions, as it occurs in current economic discussions, is naïve. What modifications occur in the ideal-typical schemata through the shift of thematic realm must be retested time and again; any unnoticed shift in the previously established state of affairs must be prevented.

(15) The economic subject with which economists deal are not humans of flesh and blood like you and me, Peter and Paul and everyone. They exist only by the grace of economists. The latter created these *homunculi* (artificially animated man-like machines) in order to experiment with them. Such ideal types set into the world in this way cannot know, intend and expect anything else but what has been predestined for them by those economists <who designed them>. It is impossible for them to display any other action or conduct than that for which they were designed. In short, like any other ideal type, the ideal type of economic subject cannot transcend the realm assigned to it; it cannot act atypically. <In the light of

all of this> the problem of "knowledge" in political economy acquires an entirely new character.

We should not be surprised when this ideal type, imagined as being involved in social relations, should now, in marvellous harmony, be in command of knowledge of such a kind and have at its disposal such corresponding experiences and such change and risk calculations which belong to the whole situation. Out of these factors an acting has to arise the final result of which would be an economic equilibrium. Indeed, this wonderful harmony is pre-established – and that by the sage economist who designed the whole machinery and its parts in the manner in which Leibniz imagined that God the Creator established the world.

The economist is not only the puppeteer who assigns the roles to all his marionettes but who also made the puppets himself as needed for presenting his play. He alone knows the whole play. When the performance begins and unfolds, the marionette knows nothing; and in most cases the child in front of the show booth does not know the end of the play before its end has been acted out.

In daily economic life, in which I meet Peter and Paul in the market place, I have to rely on my spontaneous project which I design with the help of my own insight and calculation. Even if I choose means adequate for reaching my goal, I know and everyone else knows that we may hope and err, that we may be lucky or unlucky. In this world of everyday life such knowledge is not distributed according to the principles of pre-established harmony. There is no state of equilibrium in the economic world of everyday life.

Does that mean that what economists do is nothing but a figment of their imagination and that it is thus without any connection with the realities of daily life? Certainly not. Adequately modified, the propositions of political economy are valid in economic reality. This is guaranteed not only by the circumstance that the chief regulator of economic conceptual formations – the principle of marginal utility – is free from inner contradictions and concurs with our everyday experiences of the economic world. It also follows from the fact that the harmony based on this basic assumption has an extraordinarily high chance for <securing> the comprehension and control of economic life.

CHAPTER 11

Phenomenology and Cultural Science

Editors' Preface

The title is a translation of Schutz's title in German, *"Phänomenologie und Kulturwissenschaft"*. In 1938 Schutz was invited by Marvin Farber to contribute an essay to *Philosophical Essays in Memory of Edmund Husserl.*[1] Schutz prepared an essay in German for this purpose and sent it to Farber in August of 1939. It was translated into English by Richard H. Williams under the title, "Phenomenology and the Social Sciences".[2] While still in Paris, Schutz also mailed to Farber a five-page outline of the essay with the title, *"Phänomenologie und Kulturwissenschaft"*. Because the outline is quite different from the structure of the published essay, it was decided to include it in this volume of the *Collected Papers*. According to Wagner, it is a "document manifesting Schutz's confidence that this potential audience in the United States would be able to comprehend his basic ideas as much as his virtual audience in Central Europe". The outline is dated "Paris, 15th January, 1939". The translation is a slightly edited version of that by Helmut Wagner; the section divisions are those of Schutz.

I

Phenomenological philosophy is most of all a Philosophy of Man. It is a "rigorous science", and like all science refers to the world of human existence it has to make comprehensible. The mathematical natural sciences in their orientation to rational objectivism have forgotten that this life-world is the meaning-foundation of all science. The life-world is constituted solely by phenomena of productive subjectivity which, for reasons of existence, remain inaccessible to the mathematical natural-scientific approach. The natural scientist forgets that he cannot find in any objective science an appreciation of himself, of his activities and of his subjectivity which produces [*leistet*] science. Both the liberation of the mathematical natural sciences

[1]*Philosophical Essays in Memory of Edmund Husserl*, edited by Marvin Farber (Cambridge: Harvard University Press, 1940), pp. 164–186.

[2]Schutz's essay was reprinted in his *Collected Papers*, Volume I, edited by Maurice Natanson, pp. 118–139.

from the crisis in their foundations and the founding of a true cultural science can be attained only by referring back to the sphere of subjectivity taken for granted by a psychology oriented to the natural sciences and which it has never brought to self-understanding.

The path to the understanding of the meaning of the life-world is that of transcendental phenomenology. For this reason the latter alone can create the foundations for all cultural and social sciences. All phenomena with which these sciences deal are phenomena of this, our life-world. And the transcendental subjectivity in whose productions the world is constituted is from the beginning related to other subjectivities with respect to whose productions and achievements it "confirms and corrects" itself. From the outset, the life-world and its meaning are related to others: it is our common life-world the meaning of which is founded by our common productions and achievements; it is collectively assigned to us for interpretation.

The preceding theses restate in a very condensed way the themes that form the thought of Edmund Husserl. Starting points for them already occur in the sixth Logical Investigation and in the <First Book> of *Ideas*. But they are only fully developed in later writings (*Formal and Transcendental Logic*; far more strongly in the Afterword to the *Ideas,* in the *Cartesian Meditations*, and most of all in the highly important essay on "The Crisis of the European Sciences and Transcendental Phenomenology"). The *first* part of this article will be devoted to exhibiting these motives.

II

On the one hand, transcendental phenomenology limits the constitution of the life-world to the productions of transcendental subjectivity. On the other hand, it co-posits from the beginning the *alter ego* as co-constituent of this life-world, and thereby of the basic phenomena of all cultural and social sciences. Thus the latter have the task of demonstrating how the solipsism of the first thesis can be overcome. Among Husserl's writings this attempt is chiefly assigned to the sixth Cartesian Meditation.[3] Its basic argument will be clarified as well as criticized. The result will be that Husserl's attempt at a solution is not satisfactory, at least not in the expositions found in his writings which have been published up to now. But this problem of formulation remains outside the realm of the cultural and social sciences. Therefore the significance of [transcendental] phenomenology for the clarification of the meaning of these sciences cannot be influenced by the failure of Husserl's attempts at a solution.[4]

[3]It is of interest to note Schutz's reference to Husserl's (then) unpublished sixth Cartesian Meditation. For the "underground" history of the circulation of the sixth Cartesian Meditation, see Fred Kersten, "Notes from the Underground", in *The Prism of the Self: Philosophical Essays in Honor of Maurice Natanson*, edited by Steven Crowell (Dordrecht: Kluwer Academic Publishers, 1995).[FK]

[4]It is interesting that Aron Gurwitsch in *Die mitmenschlichen Begegnungen in der Milieuwelt* (herausgegeben und eingeleitet von A. Métraux, Berlin: Walter de Gruyter, 1977) of 1931 already made the same point in almost the same context, pp. 46f. (English translation by Fred Kersten, *Human Encounters in the Social World*, Pittsburgh: Duquesne University Press, 1979, pp. 32f.). See also Alfred Schutz, "The Problem of Transcendental Intersubjectivity in Husserl", of 1957 (reprinted in *Collected Papers*, Volume III, pp. 51–84. [FK]

III

In principle all cultural and social science is mundane and therefore not related to the transcendental ego or the transcendental *alter ego* except as they concern mundane intersubjectivity. These sciences have nothing to do directly with the phenomena of constitution in the phenomenologically reduced sphere but only with the corresponding correlates in the natural attitude. Here we pursue that *genuine psychology of intentionality* which, according to Husserl, is nothing else than the constitutive phenomenology of the natural attitude. Yet psychology understood in this sense is not a science of actualities but a science of essences. For instance, it asks about the invariant characteristic peculiar to the structure of the soul with respect to the communality of psychical (spiritual) life: that is, about its *apriori* ("Afterword" to *Ideas*, especially, p. 555[5]). Such an eidetic-mundane science of the phenomena of the cultural and social worlds stands at the beginning of all methodological and scientific-theoretical problems of the corresponding special sciences. In this science (thus in the psychological apperception of the natural attitude) all analyses that have been executed in the phenomenological reduction essentially maintain their validity. In this factor is rooted the immense significance of the results worked out by Husserl for the foundation of the theory of the social and cultural sciences.

IV

What are these results? The limited space allotted to the present essay only allows for a few hints:

a) Application of Husserl's analysis of time to the problem of the "structure of social action" in the sense of Weber and Parsons.
b) Husserl's theory of signs and symbols and their relation to positing and interpreting of meanings.
c) Husserl's theory of sedimented experiences and its significance for the problem of the social world.
d) Formal logic and the theory of the ideal-type.
e) Theory of ideal objects and the objective meaning-contents (objective spirit).
f) Husserl's teleological interpretation of history.

V

Indication of future analyses of constitution in the natural attitude which concern foundational problems of all cultural (social) sciences:

[5]Schutz refers specifically to Husserl's *Nachwort zu meinen "Ideen zu einer reinen Phänomenologie und phänomenologische Philosophie"*, first published in *Jahrbuch für Philosophie und phänomenologische Forschung*, Vol. XI, p. 555. (Reprinted in *Husserliana*, Vol. V, Den Haag: Martinus Nijhoff, 1952, pp. 145f.; English translation by Richard Rojcewicz and André Schuwer, Husserl, *Collected Works*, Vol. III, Dordrecht: Kluwer Academic Publishers, 1989, pp. 412f.)

a) The theory of the social person.
b) The problem of interest and relevance.
c) The world of social environment, the world of contemporaries, the world of predecessors, the world of successors.[6]

[6]It is of interest to compare Schutz's list of results and prospects of Husserl's phenomenology with that offered by Dorion Cairns at about the same time, published in *The Journal of Philosophy*, 36 (27 April, 1939), pp. 236–238. Cairns' list is longer chiefly because it includes topics other than those pertaining to the social and cultural sciences. Among those results on Cairns' list that overlap Schutz's are the "differentiation between individual objects and essences", "analysis of the constitution of other minds and the world as intersubjective", "rudimentary analyses of the social and cultural worlds", and the "clarification of the nature of phenomenology and its relation to other sciences". [FK]

CHAPTER 12

The Life-World and Scientific Experience

Editors' Preface

This text consists of an unpublished letter to Felix Kaufmann of 17 September, 1945.[1] The translation and the title are by Helmut Wagner who surmised that Schutz responds in the letter to Kaufmann's criticism of a paper written by Schutz and sent to Kaufmann. The paper is not named, nor does the letter provide certain identification of the paper in question. It was Wagner's surmise that the paper is "On Multiple Realities" which was published in 1945 and certainly deals with the themes of experience in the life-world and scientific interpretation (among others). The letter has been edited to isolate its specifically scientific content and make even more explicit some of the ideas Schutz had been concerned with up to this time.

. . . I had not hoped that you would agree with certain of my results. Still it was my hope to be understood, if not praised, by a reader such as you. You have kindly conveyed to me your comments on two essential points and given me the opportunity to clarify my position.

What you say about the relation between the *epoché* and scepticism, about the different levels of the meaning of existence and the supposed doubt about existential positings [*Existenzsetzungen*] I fully accept. However, this is a problem of the theoretical sphere, of science, of logic, of phenomenology. As the context unequivocally shows, the section cited from <Husserl's> *Formal and Transcendental Logic* aims at the scientist's concepts of truth and reality, at the scientific-apophantic (presentational?) judgment which, under constant criticism, deliberately become themselves evidentially and adequately given. Reality, then, is that which truly is; and the real is a specific case of this "broadest" analytical-formal conception of reality. Everything you say is valid within this problem-stratum. But I cannot comprehend why this admission would be incompatible with my interpretation of the natural attitude.

The natural attitude relates to the life-world which, being one and unitary, is also

[1]For a discussion of this and other letters of Kaufmann and Schutz, see Wagner, *Alfred Schutz. An Intellectual Biography*, pp. 169ff.

the substratum of apophantic and eventually of critical-scientific judging. However, it is not by judging that the conception of the reality of the natural attitude is acquired. From the outset the life-world is accepted without question and just as what it appears to be. <It is presupposed> as long as there do not appear motives which run counter to this general supposition [*Generalansetzung*]. I have called this general supposition the "epoché of the natural attitude". This epoché is not a suspension of belief but one of doubt. It is a matter of our naïve attitude *in* the world simply presupposing its reality as a province of meaning which would still have to be contrasted with the theoretical realm of meaning because both issue from basically different "attitudes" (tensions of consciousness) and [because] both are incommensurable in their styles as well as in their productions. This is not contradicted <by the fact> that both spheres are founded in the life-world as one and unitary; <nor by the fact> that their coherence systems display similar structures or at least can do so. The last-named factor is the less astonishing as theoretical thinking and working are both "performances" and thus point back to a coherent pre-experience and so follow the same principles entailed (by this fact).

CHAPTER 13

The Scope and Function of the Department of Philosophy within the Graduate Faculty

Editors' Preface

The title is that given by Alfred Schutz to a memorandum he wrote at the request of the administration of the Graduate Faculty of Social and Political Science of the New School for Social Research after its Department of Philosophy had lost its strength through the departure, retirement or death of its original faculty. In the memorandum Schutz offers his ideas about the general principles of the New School's graduate school and reformulates their consequences along with the obligations of the faculty for the implementation of its curriculum given budgetary and personnel conditions then existing at the Graduate Faculty. The memorandum provides an especially clear picture of how Schutz thought of the new academic setting in which he found himself and how he proposed to realize his ideas in that new setting tailored to the unusual student body of the time (and of which he gives a very accurate picture).

As presented here, about seven pages of the memorandum are omitted because they contained matters specific to the situation of the Graduate Faculty at that time. The memorandum is dated 22 May, 1953. The section headings are those of Alfred Schutz.

A. The Particular Contribution of the Graduate Faculty to the Teaching of the Social Sciences

We have to start with an analysis of this preliminary question because it will prove of particular significance for our main problem. It seems that three factors determine the special approach of the Graduate Faculty to the teaching of the social sciences, and enable it to fulfil its unique function: first, its unique position among other academic institutions of equal rank; second, the composition of its teaching staff; and third, the composition of its student body.

1. *The Faculty's Position among Other Institutions*

Our faculty cannot offer our students certain advantages that they might find at other institutions:

a) Our teaching staff is small, and many standard courses in the curriculum of other universities – especially those dealing with the applied social sciences and their methods – are not given by our faculty.
b) In certain departments the opportunities for laboratory work are limited.
c) Opportunities for training student groups in carrying out research projects are limited.
d) Library facilities are limited.

In these respects and many others our Faculty cannot and should not try to compete with Columbia, New York University, Fordham, and similar institutions.

But, on the other hand, we offer our students an approach to the social sciences which they will hardly find elsewhere:

a) We do not impose a rigid study program on them, but try to shape the curriculum for each graduate student in accordance with his individual interests and needs.
b) Each member of the teaching staff is available for the student's advice and guidance to a much greater extent than in other institutions; the customary textbook system is thus replaced by a kind of personal tutorship.
c) The unique educational advantage we have to offer is that we are teaching the social sciences as a *faculty*, that is, on an interdepartmental basis. Our "departments" are merely administrative units. We are convinced that the study of human affairs is only possible within the unified field of the social sciences in their totality, not within a particular discipline alone; and that this principle applies even to scientific inquiry into very concrete problems. Elsewhere it is possible to study social psychology without sociology, sociology without the history of ideas, government without political philosophy, economics without reference to the other disciplines; but Graduate Faculty students become aware of the social sciences as an integrated whole.
d) In nearly all of our courses special emphasis is placed on problems of theory and the theoretical approach. It seems to the present writer that the teaching of theoretical thinking in the social sciences is the foremost educational contribution of the Graduate Faculty to the study of human affairs on the graduate level. Twenty years ago this was a unique contribution, and it remains a speciality of our teaching that is highly appreciated by our students even today, when the need for "basic research" in the social sciences as well as in the physical sciences is slowly winning recognition at other institutions. A gratifying proof of the truth of this statement is the fact that many students from other universities enroll in our Graduate Faculty for the specific purpose of attending one or two of our purely theoretical courses, which they cannot find at their own institutions.

2. *Composition of the Staff of the Graduate Faculty*

Our teaching of the social sciences as an integrated whole, and our emphasis on theory, have been made possible by the fact that nearly every member of our teaching staff is not only competent in his "departmental" field proper, but also conversant by training, inclination, and scientific conviction with the study of human affairs from a universal vantage point – the vantage point of theoretical perspectives of the anticipation of later conclusions, of the philosophical approach.

3. *Composition of the Student Body*

This particular approach became successful because of the special structure of our student body. Most of [our students] are mature men and women, from many walks of life, who know from experience how limited all insights into human affairs are when restricted to the mere practical level. Most of them take up their graduate studies at considerable personal sacrifice, often in addition to a full-time job. Their main motive is their desire to learn from what deeper reasons the social world is what it is. They are mature enough to acquire *information* on data and facts by reading a text; however, they want something more than information, namely *knowledge* – that is, the disclosure of the central points from which the particular facts with which they are concerned become transparent and understandable. Their intellectual curiosity incites them to look for the place their particular problem has in the total situation of our society, and to find out how the particular features of our society are interrelated with the destiny of "man, mutable and immutable".[1] Any help offered in this respect, any tool proposed for the solution of questions of this kind, is accepted by our students with enthusiasm.

In other words, what our students want is the philosophical enlightenment of human affairs; philosophical, that is, in terms of a method and a way of life – the "theoretical life". This is precisely what has been understood under the name of *"theoria"* since the beginning of philosophy in the Ancient World. And in this respect our students' needs and the particular aims of our teaching staff meet in the happiest way.

On the other hand, the very fact that our students are of quite another type and background than young college students who just want to continue their studies by postgraduate work involves a considerable setback. As far as scholarly background is concerned, our student body is by no means homogeneous. Their knowledge is frequently not integrated. Some of them left college years ago and have forgotten what little insight was then offered to them into human affairs – even that little often

[1]The phrase, twice referred to by Schutz, is the title of Kurt Riezler's last book, *Man, Mutable and Immutable* (Chicago: Henry Regnery Company, 1950; reprint by Greenwood Press, 1975). This no doubt also explains Schutz' emphasis on "philosophical anthropology" later on as the core of the discipline of philosophy relative to the integration of the social sciences. Kurt Riezler (1882–1955) had been Dean and Professor of Philosophy at the Graduate Faculty. For more on Riezler, see the Introduction by Richard Grathoff to *Philosophers in Exile. The Correspondence of Alfred Schutz and Aron Gurwitsch 1939–1959*, translated by J. Claude Evans, Foreword by Maurice Natanson (Indiana University Press, 1989), p. xxiv, note 24. (FK)

having consisted merely of imposed reading of an undergraduate textbook. For a teaching system that emphasizes the theoretical and philosophical approach, this unevenness in the preparation of the students is a particular handicap, and special teaching methods must be provided in order to overcome this obstacle.

B. The Role of the Department of Philosophy within the Educational Scope of the Graduate Faculty

If the preceding analysis is correct, it leads to the conclusion that the teaching of the theoretical approach to the social sciences as an integrated field is not only the unique contribution which the Graduate Faculty can and does make to the system of higher education, but also the Faculty's very *raison d'être*. It follows, furthermore, that both these special goals of the educational program of the Graduate Faculty – the insight into the integration of the social sciences and their theoretical treatment – can be achieved only by basing them on an underlying philosophy. This does not mean in any way that some particular school of thought in philosophy must be selected and taught as the center and starting point. *Which* particular philosophy should be chosen is a question for the responsible student's personal decision, and no teacher of philosophy can do more than show his students what the choices are and what implications each choice has.

The student does have to learn, however, that the social sciences did not start with *his* thinking on human affairs, or with that of this teachers. He must learn that the whole process of inquiry occurs within a great tradition, that our actual problems are new only as to their shape, and as old as mankind in their substance. He has also to learn that, in Dewey's words, all inquiry occurs within a given social matrix, and that for this very reason philosophy itself is a social science – perhaps *the* social science from which all the other disciplines originated. He has also to understand that philosophy is involved, explicitly or implicitly, in all human affairs he may study; and that the social scientist depends upon philosophy in his endeavors to a far greater extent than does the physicist, who studies the nuclear structure of matter regardless of whether this leads to the atomic bomb or to cancer research, or the chemist, whose compounds are medicine in the hands of the healer and poison in those of the murderer.

The founders of the Graduate Faculty saw this situation clearly. As Alvin Johnson says in *Pioneer's Progress*:[2]

> In setting up the University in Exile I conceived that while the faculty as a unit would become assimilated to American conditions, the group organization would protect the individual member against the conventional mutilating process of individual assimilation. I hoped that these European scholars would retain the values of the European university discipline.

[2] Alvin Johnson, *Pioneer's Progress* (New York, 1952), p. 347. For Alvin Johnson and the context of the passage cited, see Anthony Heilbut, *Exiled in Paradise. German Refugee Artists and Intellectuals in America from the 1930's to the Present* (New York: Viking Press, 1983), Chapter 4, especially pp. 80ff. (FK)

> Philosophy lay at the center of that discipline, philosophy extending to the state and society. There was indeed intense specialization in the German university, but the speciality was conceived of as a branch of the philosophical tree, not as an autonomous growth. The scholar, whatever his branch of the social sciences, felt himself responsible for the whole cultural system. And this gave the scholar a mission . . . the scholar felt the obligation to help the student to think his way through to an inner order of mind.

The role of philosophy in the educational program of the Graduate Faculty could hardly be stated in a more succinct way. To be sure, the teaching of philosophy, in the sense outlined by Dr. Johnson, need not be restricted to a *department* of philosophy. Indeed, it can safely be stated that all the instructors of the Graduate Faculty, teaching any of the various disciplines, are aware of the fact that their specialities are merely branches of the philosophical tree. This explains the considerable number of courses given in the departments of sociology, political science, psychology and even economics which are actually, as to their nature and content, courses in philosophy, and which at other learned institutions would be taught in the department of philosophy. But the founders of our Graduate Faculty were not concerned merely with the branches but also with the tree itself. They felt that the essential goal of our Faculty could be reached only by creating a full-fledged department of philosophy in which the ideal integration of the theoretical approach could be taught systematically. The success of the department of philosophy justified this basic idea. At the time when Dr. Horace Kallen, Dr. Kurt Riezler, Dr. Felix Kaufmann, and Dr. Leo Strauss were members of our Faculty, we doubtless had one of the best departments of philosophy in the country.

C. The Minimum Program for a Department of Philosophy at the Graduate Faculty

The program of the teaching of philosophy at the Graduate Faculty should be centered around the discipline that nowadays is called "Philosophical Anthropology". This is just a "new name for some old ways of thinking". It is the philosophical science of "man, mutable and immutable": of his station in the universe, the conditions of his existence, his interrelationship with nature, culture, and society in its various organizational forms, his historical existence and his freedom and bondage. Characterized in this way, philosophical anthropology has always been the main topic of all philosophical inquiry and has indeed been developed in various forms. It crosses the customary boundaries of school-philosophy, partaking of epistemology and metaphysics as well as of ethics and political philosophy. In this sense, philosophical anthropology was at the center of the thought of Plato and Aristotle, St. Augustine and Aquinas, Spinoza and Leibniz, Kant and Hegel, and it has been revived by many outstanding modern thinkers in the most varied forms. Thus this central problem can be treated from various approaches, starting from quite different philosophical positions, but all leading to insight into the importance of the topic and its manifold ramifications. A contemporary author in this field has rightly maintained that the various forms of the concept of man's position in the universe, as developed in the course of history by various religions, philosophies and sciences, became in each form decisive in shaping the particular culture within which it originated.

The suggestion that philosophical anthropology be given the central place in the teaching of philosophy in our Department is by no means an innovation. It can safely be maintained that most of the courses taught by the eminent men who have been members of our Department – Dr. Kallen, Dr. Riezler, Dr. Löwith, and Dr. Strauss – dealt in essence with this central group of problems, although under various headings and starting from different basic positions. Philosophical anthropology in the sense outlined (which is of course far broader than what is meant by certain fashionable slogans) should be treated both systematically and historically. Further, the teaching of this history of philosophy should be planned around the historical development of the concept of man, a concept which is indispensable to the integration of the social sciences and to understanding our present spiritual situation. And even the study of a particular philosopher or philosophical school, of whatever century or cultural background, should be organized with these fundamental problems in view.

PART TWO

B

Studies in the Methodology of Social Theory

CHAPTER 14

Basic Concepts and Methods of the Social Sciences

Editors' Preface

The original manuscript, probably written in or about 1936, is untitled and undated. The title is Helmut Wagner's, taken from the first sentence, and the translation is also his with some minor revisions. The manuscript may be considered a sequel or even as an alternative to Chapter Ten, "Political Economy: Human Conduct in Social Life", which Schutz had prepared for the journal *Economica*. As we mentioned in our note to Chapter Ten, it is not clear why Schutz's article remained unsubmitted. Whether the present manuscript represents yet another attempt to write it, or develop its ideas further and perhaps in terms more congenial to Schutz at the time, it nevertheless provides important insights into Schutz's attempt to overcome the idea that the social sciences can be reduced to the basics of economic theory as developed by the "Vienna School" with its theory of marginal utility.

Many intellectual circles are adverse to investigations concerning basic concepts and methods of the social sciences. One frequently hears the opinion that such considerations hamper rather than advance the sciences of matters of fact and that it is intolerable to conduct fruitless discussions about the goal and nature of method instead of working on actual tasks. To become entangled with ancillary preparations prevents the <execution of> the work itself. These and other unfriendly arguments <are frequently advanced>.

Such criticisms may not be completely misplaced with regard to a certain kind of theoretical-scientific approach. However, he who believes that such arguments dispose of the social-scientific theory of method itself overlooks a crucial factor: it is a basic characteristic of the social sciences to ever and ever again pose the question of the meaning of their basic concepts and procedures. All attempts to solve this problem are not merely preparations for social-scientific thinking; they are an everlasting theme of this thinking itself. The researcher who occupies himself scientifically with the objects of the world of nature is in no way in the same relationship to the objects of his interest as the sociologist, the economist, the theorist of law or the historian. Any well-founded consideration of the methodological problems of the social sciences needs to begin with the clarification of this difference. Simultaneously such a clarification leads immediately to the center of the whole complex of problems belonging to the social sciences.

This clarification may be attempted in various ways. The most reliable but also most difficult way would be that of philosophical investigations into the nature of sociality, of the relation between I and thou, of human actions, and of the concepts of the motivation of action, of objective and subjective meaning. Yet this may prove itself an insecure point of departure, thus necessitating further investigations concerning the temporality of human action and the steps of the constitution of consciousness in which the processes of the positing and interpreting of meanings occur.

To reassure the reader, we hasten to add that we do *not* intend to pursue this path in the following investigations. Yet, this decision was not made on the assumption that the problems in question are neither accessible to, nor in need of, rigorous philosophical inspection. Elsewhere I myself have tried to subject this problem to systematic treatment in the sense of that phenomenology which was introduced by Edmund Husserl. However, an undertaking like this demands such an elaborate philosophical equipment that <its treatment> would provide more trouble than benefit for any reader who is not prepared for such considerations. I shall forego many a clarification even though they are almost indispensable. Instead I will chose a path which – as far as possible – will circumvent deeper philosophical strata, strata feared by all exponents of the sciences of matters of fact. Instead of departing from philosophically fundamental considerations, I will begin with a few general facts which are familiar to anyone who is at all involved with the thematics of any social science, for instance, political economy.

I

What distinguishes scientific thinking from thinking in daily life? Without risking contradiction we may assert that scientific thinking is necessarily *clear and distinct thinking*. But what do clarity and distinctness mean here? It would be extremely difficult to describe this exactly; <the attempt> would lead us into that basic philosophical set of problems which we decided to avoid. Nevertheless we hope to gain general consent when we characterize clear and distinct thinking in the following manner.

It must seize upon its objects in clear separation from all other objects. Yet, simultaneously, it must be aware of all relevant relations of this object to other objects. Further, clear and distinct thinking about an object presupposes that it be "explicit", that is, that it can be comprehended in its own characteristic structure. According to the formulation of the problem and the factual situation this may be a matter of the recognition of its parts or characteristics, or of its genesis, or of the chain of causes or motivations related to it.

But do we not think clearly and distinctly in daily life? (Doubtlessly this is not always the case. In everyday life, most of all, we try to clarify the concrete situation in so far as, for whatever reason, they provoke our attention. If this is the case we find ourselves face to face with <the necessity of> having to make a decision of importance to us, or else we have to design a plan for decisive action in all the details necessary for us. But even then we only think clearly and distinctly to the degree necessary for any given situation. We may say that we are concerned with parts and contexts of the object of our thinking only to the degree to which that is interesting or relevant for us under the given circumstances.)

Aside from this, there exist large areas of our everyday life which are matters only of unclear and vague thinking on our part: there are the habits of conduct but also of our thinking which are simply pregiven in daily life and which we take for granted. Further there is the large realm of our impulses and emotions which govern our acting. There are our needs and drives which – if at all – become objects of thinking only in the modes of unclarity and confusion. But there are also our experiences of the external world, of animate and inanimate nature, and most of all of our consociates. In daily life these experiences are taken for granted to a high degree. If not, they become objects of distinct and clear thinking only to the degree to which this is warranted by the given state of our interests.

These examples may suffice for the justification of our assumption of the existence of areas of unclear and vague thinking in everyday life. Yet next to them exist wide areas that are made objects of *relatively* clear and *relatively* distinct thinking. So it is for most of our own modes of conduct, or those of others, which are oriented on a predesigned plan. For this reason these are <usually> called "rational", to use a term which itself is in greatest need of clarification.

We will be in a position to establish the precise meaning of the term, "rational", only in a later part of this investigation. Certainly the businessman who acts according to a certain plan makes an effort to comprehend with "sufficient" clarity and distinctness the objectives of his actions as well as the means required <for their execution>. Likewise he tries to anticipate the effects as well as the side-effects of the conduct he has planned. However, in daily life this clarity and distinctness remains relative: relative not only to the thinking subject but also to the subject's state of interest at the moment.

Most misunderstandings between the theorists of political economy and business practitioners arise because both ignore this simple state of affairs. As a consequence, the theorists accuse the practitioners of lack of insight into the basic facts of economic life and thus of ignoring the postulate of distinct and clear thinking. The practitioners <on their part> accuse the theorists of "ignorance of the facts of <economic> life" – that is, of rejecting the perspective issuing from the interest obtaining in the situation of the businessman.

However, it would be an error to believe that everything which is thought of only in the mode of (relative) unclarity and vagueness is devoid of sense or is even meaningless. What is simply experienced and only vaguely conceived too is meaningful. And [this is true] both for the experiencing and thinking subject and his consociate who deals with him, be it as observer or as partner. But this meaning itself occurs in the modes of vagueness or unclarity. In order to gain meaning in full clarity and distinctness we need clarification by way of interpretative explanation.

With these considerations we have now clarified one essential characteristic of the particular relation between the social sciences and their subject matter. In the natural sciences thinking means to convert experiences of inanimate nature into objects of the clearest and most distinct thinking possible. The experiences of these natural objects are gained through the objects themselves by way of observation, measurement and experiment. The natural scientist operates within the framework of the total approach and the state of knowledge of his science. He follows his particular scientific interests within these limits. He may view the object which he selects to study, either in isolation or in combination with other natural objects. Between the natural scientist and the objects themselves stand no pregiven results of pre-scientific thinking, no meanings formed in earlier vague and unclear thinking.

As science, the social sciences too must satisfy the postulate of the greatest clarity and distinctness possible. What, however, is the object of the social sciences? (Not the objects of inanimate nature but instead human conduct, modes of conduct in daily life [make up the subject matter of the social sciences]. With this deliberately vague circumscription we try to characterize the theme of social-scientific thinking in its greatest generality.) Specifically, one may be inclined to designate human actions or facts of human consciousness as objects of the social sciences; acts of positing meanings or interpreting meanings; human operations or products of human efforts. In any case, one thing is certain: everything that can be the object of social-scientific thinking which aims at optimal clarity and distinctness must already have been an act or content of thinking in daily life within the social world and thus an act or content of relatively vague or unclear thinking. In other words, the raw material of social-scientific thinking is necessarily preformed in its meaning, and this by way of acts of forming meanings in the daily life of the social world. And that is in the mode of vagueness. In contrast, in scientific thinking no precondition or pregivenness can be accepted as simply given, as not in need of further clarification. Therefore, the first objective of the social sciences has to be the maximal clarification and explanation of what, in general, persons living in the social world think about this world.

In no way is this thesis a postulate imposed upon social scientists by epistemologists. They would not be sufficiently justified in doing so. The thesis is merely an exact description of what all social scientists and most theoretical economists have in fact done and do. Moreover, it can be asserted that the methodological problems characteristic of the social sciences merely serve one task: to demonstrate the specific techniques these sciences have to use in order to transpose their materials, which are necessarily pregiven to them in the mode of vagueness, into the mode of explicit clarity. In this form the problem is foreign to the natural sciences. Their materials do not consist of preformed meanings; the questions posed speak to a thematic of clarification concerned very specifically with problems of a general logical and epistemological nature common to all science.

Our intention is to demonstrate the specific methodological problems belonging to the social sciences using the example of theoretical economics. However, before doing so, we will try to deepen our insight into the structure of the social sciences which deviates radically from that of the natural sciences. We will approach this problem from a different angle.

II

A natural event is explained by its unambiguous integration into the total context of experience. Here "experience" means not just my personal experience but also yours and that of all of us. Finally, it also means experience of that clear and distinct thinking which has been subsumed under "laws" and which is commonly called "natural science". Experience is intersubjective experience from the outset. Accordingly, the natural event to be explained does not occur in my private world but in the intersubjective world accessible to all of us. In principle this world can be checked by everyone.

Instead of reserving the term, "meaning", for those phenomena which refer back to human beings and to human society, one may be inclined to apply it also to the realm of nature. It may then be said that Nature is a total context which is equally in need of explanation for everyone and which is amenable to explanation. In other words, the meaning-context that is established with the explanation of a natural phenomenon is *objective*. The meaning-interpretation of a natural phenomenon creates meaning for everyone; in principle it is accessible to everyone. It affirms itself only when – properly understood – it agrees uncontroversially with everyone's experience.

Now let us look at the world of social phenomena: not that aspect of this world which social scientists have selected for the purposes of processing <their observations and conclusions> scientifically, but instead at that totality and fullness of social phenomena as we humans experience them in the experience of everyday life simply by living with others.

Simply living in the social world I notice a series of phenomena upon which I bestow meaning by integrating them into the total context of my experience. I become aware of human bodies and bestow upon them the meaning, "these are consociates with a structure of consciousness similar to my own". I interpret their bodily movements as courses of action of consociates. I interpret certain objects as artifacts made by human hands for certain purposes (tools, machines, objects of art, etc.). All of this, so to speak, is assigned to me as a task of interpretation. I have to integrate all of it into the total context of my experiences; I can ask about the meaning <of each sign or thing thus encountered>. This meaning will be objective; it is not only accessible to me but to all those of my consociates who approach these data in terms of the same scheme of interpretation that has been acquired in prior experiences. Everybody who has learned English will be able to read the meaning of a sentence formed according to the rules of the English language composed, for instance, by letters found in the columns of the New York Times. The same is true, although with highly complex modifications which we refrain from discussing here, for the comprehension of the objective meaning of a machine as an apparatus for the production of specific effects. And it is true for grasping the meanings of innumerable performances and courses of actions of our consociates in everyday life. We (you and I and everyone) can observe and interpret all these meaning contexts. And more: as soon as we have absorbed them we tend to include them, as self-understood data of our existence, into the calculus of our own actions.

We who live straightforwardly in our everyday lives expect as a matter of course that the subway starts operating at a fixed hour as much as we expect that the sun rises. Likewise, we have not the slightest doubt that the owner of a store will hand over to us a piece of merchandise when we have given him a number of small metal discs called "coins". No less do we doubt that an object which we hold in our hand will fall to the ground as soon as we open our fingers. All of this is self-understood only as a result of a long series of meaning-interpretations.

At this moment we leave open the question of whether we deal with the interpretation of signs, of artifacts, of motions of an individual human being, or of social institutions. <At present> only one thing is important for our considerations: namely, that the meanings of all of these data are objective. They are accessible not only to me as an individual observer or partner but in principle to all of us who live in the same community tied together by a common culture. It follows that the social phenomena, of which we have spoken up to now, are not different from the phenomena of the natural world in so far as the objective character of their meaning structure is concerned.

But this objective meaning is neither the only nor the most important phenomenon which the social world offers us. In order to instruct ourselves about this we have to devote some closer considerations to the "meaning of human action". For reasons mentioned previously, we single out human action not only because it presents a fundamental concept of theoretical economics in the form of economic action,[1] but also because it can be easily demonstrated that all the previously mentioned phenomena of the social world can be either reduced to the concept of social action or else they can be derived from it.[2]

Initially I notice actions of my consociates as events in the outer world. I can appraise the individual phases of such actions as well as their effects in the outer world in terms of their objective meanings. When a traffic officer makes a certain gesture, I can establish that all cars stop when coming from a certain direction. Frequently in my simple straightforward living in daily life I will be satisfied with interpretations of this kind. <In such cases> my practical interest does not urge me to reflect back beyond taking notice of the external process. Actually, a great part of the actions of others in everyday life have themselves become "standarized" and "normed" by law and usage. This occurs to such a degree that in a simple grasp I can read the objective meaning of actions of others which I apperceive in the same manner in which I read terms indicated by printed letters. In other also less frequent cases, however, my state of interest will force me not to be satisfied with the objective meanings which offer themselves in this manner. For example, my attempts to interpret the actions of others may fail because they run courses different from the assumed and standard course. If this is the case, I do not merely inquire into the outer courses and effects of the actions of others. Going beyond this <merely external interest> I pose the question: What does the actor mean with his acting? While I naïvely live straightforwardly in the social world I pose this question only on special

[1]Footnote of Alfred Schutz: Whether all action is necessarily economic action is a question which can be decided only at a later stage of this investigation.

[2]Footnote of Alfred Schutz: However, this shall not be done within the framework of this essay.

occasions. Yet in principle I can pose it anytime with respect to any actions of others whom I observe. <If I do so> the question reveals to me a completely new stratum of specific problems characteristic only of the social world and totally overlooked by naïve behaviorism: the problem-stratum of subjective meaning.[3]

This turn is so significant that it forces us to remain with it a while longer. As observer of the acting of another person, I ask: What is the meaning of his action for *him*, the actor, not for me the observer. Doing so, I reason from the premise that the actor as *alter ego* experiences his acting in the same fashion in which I would experience the same acting, should it have been my own. Thus every interpretation of the subjective meaning of the acting of another person refers to the meaning which acting in a similar fashion has *for me* or possibly *could* have for me.

Now, closer consideration shows that I experience my own actions first of all in a dimension which is completely different from the scheme of interpretation of the actions of others, as previously described. What will present itself after the fact to an observer and also to myself as an external course of action and as effect of this action, I experience <during the actual course of its execution> as design of a goal of action. To bring this goal about is the motive of my acting <by way of planning the execution of> the project in a series of actions as posited by me just in order to realize that goal of action. I project the effects which my acting is to produce prior to the positing of <individual steps of> acting themselves. The projected effects lead me to realize them through my acting – or, what amounts to the same, the projected aim of the action becomes my motive for mobilizing the required means for my acting. The subjective and therefore actual meaning of human action reveals itself only in such "motivational understanding".

But is not the objective meaning of the action of others, deduced from its external course and effects identical with the subjective meaning as revealed in motivational understanding? In all cases, this question must be categorically denied.

We will now have to prove this thesis.

In some frequent cases the discrepancies between objective and subjective meaning of action are so obvious that their enumeration will sound trite. Anyone can point to a number of examples taken from his own life which showed him how little the projected effects of his actions agreed with the actually occurring effects. He will have to report disappointments, misunderstandings, errors in the choice of means, unforeseen external difficulties and obstacles in the execution of the action, erroneous calculations, etc.[4] In some cases he even will be unable to name the motives of his own actions because the original goals were supplanted by other goals in the course of the execution of his actions. Further we refer to the folk saying, "when two do the same it is not the same". This <proverb> indicates that basically different subjective motives can be ascribed to the same objective courses of actions. Nevertheless, these examples alone do not entitle us to deny on principle the possible

[3]Footnote of Alfred Schutz: The great achievement of Max Weber is to have decisively clarified the combining of the dual problem of subjective and objective meaning. Anyone acquainted with Weber's writings will recognize the great degree to which the present expositions depend on his theory.

[4]Footnote of Alfred Schutz: We may refer here to the economic concept of "miscalculated investments" as a typical example of such discrepancies.

agreement between the subjective and the objective meaning of actions. If we <wish to> deny this we have to muster other arguments which contain the given examples but are rooted in deeper strata.

Above all here we have to point to the fact that in principle the motivational context of one's own acting is never closed. What is seen from a particular point in time and out of a goal of our acting in a situation of specific interest, presents itself from the perspective of another point in time as a means or intermediate goal within a larger context. In different words we may say that our motivational contexts carry with themselves open horizons which in turn point to infinite further motivational contexts. For example, every single action I carry out in my professional activities may display a closed motivational context if viewed in and by itself. The businessman writes a letter in order to conclude a certain business transaction; yet the conclusion of this specific transaction itself falls within the motivational context of the general business plan of this businessman.

This business plan itself is subordinated to the total context which is given to the businessman with the choice of his profession. His professional life itself is articulated into the rhythms of working day and leisure time, of professional and private interests; <it is woven into> the life plan of this man. But related considerations have to be made which point in a different direction. The composition of this letter itself is a goal for a number of actions: the content must be planned, its train of thought specified, the linguistic expression of it formulated, the act of writing executed, etc. These are simple considerations. Yet their systematic justification provides unsuspected difficulties. Consequently it is unexpectedly problematic to speak simply of human action as if it were self-evident that this action reveals itself <to an observer> as an obvious unit.

In actuality no observer can ever decide what makes an action into a unity. He has before him merely a segment of a motivational context that is open in both directions[5] yet is in its nature closed for all investigations of objective meaning. <This is said apart from the fact that the observer often may be> satisfied with mediating the objective meaning <of that acting of others which he does observe>. That which makes an acting into a unit can be understood solely and exclusively in terms of subjective meaning and that is in terms of the scope of the project which for the actor is the motive of his acting. Of course, the scope of the project is a function of the total situation of interest to the actor. So, our businessman may think, "I will now dictate this unimportant letter". But he may also say, "if this letter evokes the reaction hoped for in the addressee a large business deal will be realized and I will be able to retire". By contrast, for the secretary to whom the letter was dictated, the objective course of the act of dictation will be the same in either case.[6]

As presented, the necessity of reducing the unity of action exclusively to the scope of the subjective project would be by itself a weighty argument for our thesis

[5]Footnote of Helmut Wagner: I take it that Schutz meant not merely temporal directions, open with respect to its past and future, but also with respect to its because and in-order-to motivations.

[6]Footnote of Alfred Schutz: In the continuation of our investigation we will show which lanes of access to the subjective meaning of action are open to the observer.

of the incommensurability of subjective and objective meaning. But this argument is not the only one to be developed. Further consideration shows that the subjective motivational context of the actor points back to the total stock of experience that at this moment is at this disposal.

The positing of the goal itself, the selection of means, the establishing of access to the means – all of this has occurred as much on the basis of the given total experiences of the person in question as through his interpretation of the open horizons of his motivational contexts and accordingly <circumscribes> the reach of his project.

However, this treasure of experience is not only described as the sum of all that which I have experienced, learned, practised, and suffered; it also will depend essentially on when, how, in what sequence and intensity the individual elements of experiences have been received by this person. Just this constitutes the individuality of each person. Accordingly and strictly speaking, one can assert that no two persons have the same stock of experience at their disposal. (If this were not the case, there would not be two persons but only one.)[7] The motivational context and thus the subjective meaning context of an action is anchored in the total stock of experience of the actor. It follows with necessity that the objective meaning, which the observer imputed interpretatively to the action of an other is necessarily incommensurable with the subjective meaning that is meant by the actor with his acting.

We may also express this factual constellation in this manner: The phenomena of subjective meaning and of motivational context do not unfold in the intersubjective world but in the private world of the acting person. (To be sure, a private world is nothing else than a private perspective opening up upon the intersubjective world common to us all. It remains one and the same in its being-for-us and its being-in-itself.)

Now, the social sciences have to face the following dilemma: if the intention is to understand human acting clearly and distinctly, then it is necessary to reach back to the subjective meaning of the acting. Already the understanding of acting as a unity presupposes the explication of the subjective context of motivation. However, as *science* the social sciences naturally belong to the intersubjective world and are themselves an objective constellation of meaning. Therefore the basic question of any specifically social-scientific methodology has to be, How is it possible to establish objective contexts of meaning about subjective contexts of meaning? It does not take a lengthy discussion in order to demonstrate that this question is merely a specific case of the basic problem of social-scientific methodology, namely how to transpose pregiven materials, offered necessarily in the mode of confusion, into explicit clarity. In anticipation I will now show that the method of the ideal-typical formation of concepts is available to <exponents of> the social sciences as the specific instrument for the performance of this task.

Our next objective is to derive the characteristics of this method from that particular attitude which social scientists are compelled to adopt in the face of everyday life.

[7]This sentence is bracketed and marked for deletion in the manuscript.

Doubtlessly in daily life we try constantly to practice motivational understanding and do so always when our interest in comprehending actions of others is not satisfied by the mere interpretation of its objective meaning. Similarly it goes without saying that we can be sufficiently successful, and as a rule are successful, in satisfying our practical interest in the subjective interpretation of meanings <of the conduct of others which have become part of our situational concerns>.[8]

[8]The manuscript breaks off at this point.

CHAPTER 15

A Note on Behaviorism

Editors' Preface

The title is by Helmut Wagner replacing Schutz's title, "Behaviorism". Schutz had divided his manuscript into four sections, giving a title only to the third; Wagner provided the other subtitles. The manuscript itself is drawn from the extensive notes Schutz wrote in preparation for his first course, "The Theory of Social Action", at the Graduate Faculty of the New School in 1943. Schutz's notes are very condensed and cover about three pages, with short addenda scattered on other pages. The first page is divided into two columns, identified as "pro" and "con" arguments about behaviorism. On the other pages the arguments are dovetailed into each other. The reconstruction of Schutz's abbreviated notes into a coherent whole for presentation here is by Wagner, his textual additions indicated in the usual way (< >).

Behavioristic Arguments

Behaviorism deals with a) overt, b) covert, and c) subovert behavior.[1] <The basic behaviorist assumption is that the> organism reacts or responds toward its environment. It is responding to <external> stimuli. All three terms, <organism, stimulus and response, environment>, are headlines for chapters full of enigmas.

The basic view of behaviorists is not that "ideas" do not exist but that reality is only defined by human behavior towards the objects: both reality and existence are relative to some responding organism. If "wall" is defined as that which obstructs the movement of a person towards a given place, the existence of the wall is predicated upon that behavior of a person. The same holds true for the magic force of a

[1] Wagner notes that the first term refers to conditioned or unconditioned reflexes, the second, on early behaviorist theory, e.g., to thinking caused by the movement of the "speech muscle". For the third term, Wagner refers to Watson's essay on "behaviorism" in the 1946 edition of the *Encyclopedia Britannica*, Vol. 3, pp. 327–329, where "subovert behavior" is a case of "unconditioning" which Watson describes in the light of a "recent experiment". Wagner summarizes the "experiment" as follows: A child who is continuously talking to himself is subjected to consistent parental threats which first reduce speaking to mumbling and, after bodily punishment, to merely talking silently to himself. Here the observable reflex action is repressed but the reflex itself is not extinct (and, we may add, subovert).

stone venerated by a primitive tribe as an idol. But <behaviorists emphasize that> imaginations, thoughts, and feelings manifest themselves, if at all, through <symbolizing[2]> or other neuro-muscular behavior.

The only metaphysical position necessary and compatible with <behavioral> science is a postulate conceding the existence of *whatever* precipitates our responses but making no further statements about the absolute nature, the characteristics of temporal-spatial qualities of the postulated entities. Objective science has to stick to behavior, has to measure it, has to make experiments, and has to predict <the future behavior of organisms>.

Four General and Methodological Assumptions about Behaviorism

1. Introspection is a mysterious faculty of understanding. As a source of knowledge it is *not accessible to objective control* by science <and thus must be ignored by it>.
2. Only experimentation (as inductive inference) and mathematics (as deductive reasoning) are scientific methods.
3. The unity of the sciences <must be established> under the hegemony of physics.
4. Symbols, signs, language conventions <are to be treated as resulting from or caused by environmental stimuli which evoke them as responses>.[3]

Individual Responding to the Environment

1. Who is this individual?
2. Environment – for whom?
3. Response. And scientific activity itself?

To 1: Biological unity as sensory-motoric circuit. Our interest in this biological question: In so far as biology is concerned, we are not interested.

To call a bottle of fine Bordeaux "alcohol" is as preposterous as calling one's sweetheart a "mammal".

The Rommel Plan in Africa.[4]

How do I know of my brain and of neuro-muscular movements? Why should the sensory-motor circuit of the conditioned reflex be better understood than human motives, wishes, desires?

"Thou knowest not what is the way of the spirit nor how the bones grow in the womb of her who is with child".

[2]Schutz had written "symbolic", which Wagner changed to "symbolizing" because "symbolic" suggests that ordinary behavior stands for symbolic meanings, while the behaviorist theory Schutz considered here stands for just the opposite view: physiological behavior as observed is misinterpreted as having symbolic meanings.

[3]Schutz's main exposition of behaviorism ends with the fourth point. The section which follows is constructed from outlines and phrases on a subsequent page of the manuscript and points to the themes which Schutz developed during his lectures. Of his construction Wagner says that the sentences "are then not literal renderings of Schutz's thinking but should be taken as possible 'free variations' of Schutz's themes as developed from his clues."

[4]Schutz, of course, was writing in 1943 when Rommel sought to capture North Africa.

Not behaving may be planned and even rational action.

Metaphysical problem: birth – growing older – death.

To 2: Organism, stimulus and response, the terms of environment and situation have to be defined.

Example: Prejudice reads: "A conditioned response which predisposes an individual to make his observations fit the previously established system of evaluations and habituations". In contrast, see Merton: How the Negro thinks.[5]

To 3: The behaviorist's behavior: how can he build up his theory? An automaton cannot theorize. Signs and symbols <in communication are interpreted as mere indicators of> neuro-muscular reactions. <Yet the principle obtains:> *nihil est in sensibus*.[6]

Intelligence of fellowmen.

Solipsism.

[5]The reference to Robert K. Merton is difficult to identify; Schutz may have been referring to Merton's "Fact and Factitiousness in Ethnic Opinionnaires", *American Sociological Review*, Vol. 5, pp. 13–28. Schutz was acquainted with Merton during the early years of his life in New York City.

[6]Schutz refers to Leibniz's response to Locke's view that there is nothing in the mind which was not first in the senses – nothing, that is, except the mind itself.

CHAPTER 16

A Scholar of Multiple Involvements: Felix Kaufmann

EDITORS' PREFACE

The title is by Helmut Wagner for a memorial address given by Schutz to the Graduate Faculty of the New School for Social Research on 4 January, 1950. Schutz's title was "In Memory of Felix Kaufmann", and the manuscript is dated at the bottom of the title page, December 31, 1949. A shorter version of Schutz's address was published in *Social Research*, Vol. 17, 1950, pp. 1–7 with the title, "Felix Kaufmann: 1895–1949". Another editing of the longer version is to be found in Harry P. Reeder, *The Work of Felix Kaufmann* (Washington, D.C.: Center for Advanced Research in Phenomenology and University Press of America, 1991), pp. vii–xiv.[1] In the main, Wagner's editing has been followed here for the sake of consistency with the rest of his editing of Schutz's manuscripts.

Schutz did not list either this manuscript or the published version to be included in his *Collected Papers*, and at this late date it does not seem possible to determine whether this was due to an oversight or some other reason. In any case, the longer version certainly qualifies for inclusion here and contains much more in the way of theoretical substance than the shorter, published version. To Wagner's knowledge, this manuscript is the most comprehensive appraisal of Kaufmann's remarkable multidisciplinary knowledge that Schutz committed to paper. Felix Kaufmann had been Schutz's mentor during his university years and thereafter his friend. Kaufmann's unexpected death at the end of 1949 prematurely cut short a brilliant career that still demands attention.[2]

Only a few weeks ago Felix Kaufmann addressed this General Seminar on the occasion of John Dewey's ninetieth birthday. Many of you will remember his masterful representation of Dewey's logical achievements. They will remember the extraordinary precision and the remarkable skill he showed in condensing and illuminating

[1]Reeder's version first appeared in the *Proceedings* of the 8th annual meeting of the Husserl Circle, at Ohio University, Athens, Ohio, April 9–11th, 1976.

[2]For details of the relationship between Alfred Schutz and Felix Kaufmann, see Helmut Wagner, *Alfred Schutz. An Intellectual Biography*, pp. 169–172. See also Part I of Harry F. Reeder, *The Work of Felix Kaufmann* for a survey of Kaufmann's many contributions to philosophy and the social sciences.

an intricate set of problems which had become dearer and dearer to his heart. I wish that in this hour the same power of the word were at my disposal. Only then could I hope to succeed in giving you within the short time of this evening an impression of the thought and character of Felix Kaufmann. He had to leave his work at an age at which a philosopher reaches the point of drawing the sum-total of his various attempts; the book which our friend had outlined and partially draft when death came was planned by him to be such a summary. We can only hope that the fragments of this manuscript will permit a reconstruction of his thought.

The German philosopher Georg Simmel once formulated a profound insight when he said that every man is not only just a fragment of humanity but also a fragment of himself, since he materializes only a part of his possibilities.

Yet, fragmentary as the life work of our friend must be in this sense, in another sense it is a consistent whole and this in spite of its astonishing diversity. Only seemingly does it deal with the most heterogeneous matters which range from problems of responsibility in criminal law to those of the concept of the infinite in mathematics, from the postulates of economic theory to the phenomenological analysis of formal and transcendental logic, from the methodology of the social sciences to the problem of probability. In truth, all these manifold topics were handled from a single point of view and therefore show a rare unity. Kaufmann believed in deductive logic as a fundamental science from which the methodology of both the so-called natural sciences and the social sciences can be derived as a logic of scientific procedure. He was convinced that many, nay, even most of the controversies arising within the domain of the particular disciplines can be overcome if their logical structure is understood and if the pertinent rules for taking correct scientific decisions are properly determined.

This was one basic trait of his thinking. The other was the strong interest in, and a rare gift for, pedagogical issues which led him to the Socratic belief that anyone can be brought to the full understanding even of the most complicated problems and that agreement can be achieved only if the underlying basic positions are clearly enough analyzed and clearly enough formulated. Clarity of thought, precision of formulation, radical analysis of equivocal terms and concepts – briefly, the highest discipline of thinking – these were Kaufmann's postulates for everyone who aimed at the honor of being considered a scientist. In this respect, he was as rigorous with others as he was with himself. As a human being he was the kindest man, ready to help anyone, full of understanding of human weakness, intolerant only of intolerance itself. As a thinker, however, he did not tolerate any fallacy, any subterfuge, any dodging of the issues. He was entitled to do so. His rare intellectual integrity was matched only by the integrity of his character.

Of course, I cannot claim to be competent in all of the fields handled so competently by our friend; I even doubt strongly that there are living scholars who, by training and inclinations, are able to follow him in all of his endeavors. Yet, I am perhaps for *one* reason qualified to give you something like an outline of his spiritual biography. From our student-days in Vienna and for nearly twenty years I had the privilege of following closely the development of this extraordinary mind – mostly with admiration, ever with the greatest respect. These were also the years in which a deep personal friendship bound us together – a friendship nourished by the many intellectual adventures we had in common. I might be forgiven if at this moment I feel deeply the need to acknowledge my gratitude to Felix for having led me to the decisive experience in my intellectual development: it was he who called my attention to phenomenology. I shall always remember the evenings and nights during which we read and discussed section by section Edmund Husserl's just published books: the lectures on *Consciousness of Inner Time*, the *Formal and Transcendental Logic*, and the *Cartesian Meditations*.

To be sure, his attitude toward Edmund Husserl's work was in many respects different from mine; there are many dwellings in the mansion of phenomenology.

Felix was first of all attracted by the logical achievements of Husserl's early writings and by his rigorous method of philosophizing. Husserl's interpretation of formal logic as an analytical *apriori*, his revival of Leibniz's idea of a *"mathesis universalis"*, his theory of signification and meaning was closer to him than the theory of noema and noesis or the concept of a transcendental ego. This is certainly not the place to enter into the difficult and fundamental questions involved here. Yet, this I would have to do in order to characterize Kaufmann's outstanding place in the development of the phenomenological movement. It might be sufficient to say that not only Husserl, the philosopher, but also Husserl, the man, was one of the dominant factors in the life of our friend. Rightly, Husserl considered Kaufmann one of the most competent logicians among his followers as well as one of his most loyal friends. This loyality, so characteristic of Felix, found its expression not only in his devotion to the philosopher's person but also in his indefatigable life-long endeavors in the interest of his work.

Felix was one of the first to actively join Professor Marvin Farber in founding and organizing, under the auspices of the University of Buffalo, the *International Phenomenological Society* and in editing the journal, *Philosophy and Phenomenological Research*. The papers which he contributed to this journal, and especially the two symposia on Meaning and Truth and on Probability, which he organized <for the journal>, were certainly remarkable events in the philosophical life of this country.

Kaufmann was an eminent phenomenologist and never ceased to consider himself a phenomenologist. But because of his deep understanding of the true intentions of Husserl he never viewed phenomenology as a kind of sectarian creed, incompatible with and aloof from all the other great philosophical movements of our time. On the contrary, he believed that a broad common ground could be found on which empiricists, operationalists, neo-positivists, neo-Kantians might meet with phenomenologists: In spite of all striking differences of these various schools of thought, each of them has made its valuable contributions to the *"philosophia perennis"*. Felix considered it his most important task, not to reconcile in a superficial eclectic way what cannot be reconciled, but to lay bare, by critical analysis, the fundamental issues common to all of them. This explains from the personal angle why he could be an understanding although sometimes critical friend of such different thinkers as Moritz Schlick, Rudolf Carnap, Ernst Cassirer, Edmund Husserl and, in the later years of his life, John Dewey. He saw Dewey's eminent role in the philosophy of our time more clearly than most scholars with a European background.

In 1919 I met Felix for the first time in an economics seminar at the University of Vienna. We both had just been released from the defeated Austrian Army and we both studied law. Nearly four years older than I, he prepared for his doctoral examinations. Being rather a freshman, I accepted his competent knowledge of philosophy, especially of Locke, Leibniz, Hume, Kant, the neo-Kantian School of Rickert, and further Simmel, Husserl and Scheler.

Yet I also became aware that Felix considered himself a mathematician by avocation and had chosen the study of law, as so many of us did in that desperate period, in order to earn his living as soon as possible. His knowledge of the philosophies of mathematics and physics was stupendous. He lived in the world of Russell-Whitehead's *Principia Mathematica*, of Wittgenstein's *Tractatus*, of Hilbert's *Axiomatics of Geometry*. The works of the great mathematicians – of Cantor, Felix Klein, Dedekind, Weierstrass, Borel, Brouwer – were at his fingertips. What knowledge, however poor, I might have of Einstein's general theory of relativity and of Planck's and Schroedinger's, of Heisenberg's and de Broglie's contributions to the science of physics, is due to Felix Kaufmann's tutorship.

Next to phenomenology, Kaufmann's training in mathematics and physics and in the methodological problems of these sciences was a second basic factor in Kaufmann's development. His interest in these problems brought him in contact with the group around Schlick which is known under the name of the "Vienna Circle". But Kaufmann was never a member of this circle and refused to be considered as such. However, he attended more or less regularly their meetings, although he was always in strong opposition to certain basic tenets of Neo-positivism. Felix Kaufmann made his own contribution to the logical problems of mathematics in his book, *Das Unendliche in der Mathematik und seine Ausschaltung* (1929).[3] I hope that Professor Nagel will give us his competent view on the merits of Kaufmann's theory. Not being a mathematician, I know only that the book met with the greatest interest and that Felix received many gratifying letters from outstanding scholars in this field.

This was the fourth book he published. Before I can speak about the three preceding ones, I have to say a few words about the third determining factor in the intellectual biography of our friend: his acquaintance with Hans Kelsen and his "Pure Theory of Law" (*Reine Rechtslehre*). It was this experience which made Felix a social scientist. Kelsen was not only a fascinating personality and teacher, he offered his students a unique approach to the social sciences. The pure theory of law was in the true sense a theoretical system designed to explain concrete human behavior, in so far as it is relevant for the jurist. Based upon the epistemological teachings of the neo-Kantian school, according to which it is the method that constitutes the object of inquiry, Kelsen's theory distinguishes between the sociological and the juridical aspect of law. The latter consists in a body of propositions of specific character, called norms, the normative validity of which cannot be derived from facts. The "is" and the "ought", Kelsen says, lie in different planes.

[3]Translated into English by Paul Foulkes, *The Infinite in Mathematics: Logico-Mathematical Writings*, edited by B. MacGuinness, along with a translation of "Logischen Prinzipienfragen in der mathematischen Grundlagenforschung", with an Introduction by E. Nagel (Reidel: Dordrecht and Boston, 1978).

Kaufmann recognized immediately the merits and shortcomings of this theory. He familiarized himself in the shortest time with the literature and became one of the prominent members of the circle around Kelsen. His main contributions to the development of Kelsen's theory consist in the replacing of the neo-kantian epistemology by the phenomenological one, in a clear analysis of the double character of the norm which is both, substantive norm and sanction, in the reduction of the realm of the "ought", (the norm) to the realm of the "is" (the underlying human behavior), and in a careful elaboration of the criteria of the legal norm, based upon human conduct. The outcome of this work are three books: *Logic and the Science of Law*, 1922, *The Criteria of the Law*, 1924, and the *Types of Intent in Criminal Law*, 1929.

The second of these books was at the same time his thesis for obtaining his degree as a doctor of philosophy – his law degree he had obtained already in 1920.

Already the brilliant first book gave Kelsen the opportunity to obtain for his favorite student an appointment as *Privatdozent* of Philosophy of Law at the juridical faculty of the University of Vienna. At that time Kaufmann was 27 years old. This position was unsalaried and Kaufmann had to enter a business career in order to make his living. Also in this field his extraordinary gifts brought him full success. Within a few years he became the responsible manager of the Austrian representation of the Anglo-Iranian Oil Company. This did not hinder him from delivering his lectures at the university and from participating eagerly in the discussion of various groups of economists, sociologists, jurists, mathematicians. It was his endeavor to test his basic concepts on the concrete work of these scientists and to find the way from them to a general methodology of the social sciences. The German book, carrying this title,[4] is the same which was recently translated into Spanish.[5] But it should not be confused with the entirely rewritten book published in English eight years later by Oxford University Press [1944]. A comparison of these two books reveals the great progress in the development of Kaufmann's basic concept of knowledge and of scientific procedure, mainly due to his study of John Dewey's *Logic: The Theory of Inquiry*. He was deeply impressed by Dewey's analysis of scientific procedure, though he could not accept his theory of meaning.[6]

It is characteristic of the manner in which Kaufmann's mind worked that all of his books and many of his articles are divided into a general and a special section. In the former he dealt with fundamental problems of deductive logic and methodology, in the latter he applies the insights secured by such analysis to the particular concrete problems of the individual science under consideration.

The German *Methodologie* [*sic*] was published in 1936. Two years later Hitler invaded Austria and our world broke asunder. Felix received the call from Dr. [Alvin] Johnson. What he achieved here you have heard from Dr. [Horace] Kallen and you will hear more I am sure from the following speakers.

[4]*Methodenlehre der Sozialwissenschaften* (Vienna, 1936).

[5]*Methodologia de las ciencias sociales*, translated by E. Imoz (Mexico City: Fondo de Cultura Economica, 1946).

[6]The last sentence, and the last half of the previous one, were interpolated by Wagner from Schutz's published version in *Social Research* in view of the importance, Wagner says, of Schutz's references to Dewey's works.

I may be permitted to close with two personal recollections.

When Hitler invaded Austria I happened to be in Paris. There I received Felix and his family when, only two months later, they came through this city on their way from Vienna to London, from where they embarked for the United States. It was a meeting between two trains, lasting two hours. I could not persuade him to take a few days of rest, so eager was he to go to New York and to start a new life. I shall not forget the hurried dinner we had together. With deep emotion he showed me Dr. Johnson's telegram and told me what it meant for him. It was not only the possibility to escape hell and to reach heaven in a free country. He was enthusiastic because Dr. Johnson's invitation gave him the possibility of pursuing his scientific mission with all his energy liberated from the yoke of a disliked business activity which had absorbed a great deal of his energy. "If the great catastrophe were not so terrible", he said, "and if the misery of all my friends permitted me to rejoice, I would consider this turn in my life a blessing in disguise". He never forgot what Dr. Johnson did for him in this most critical moment in his life. The words with which he dedicated the book he wrote <in the United States> came, I am sure, from the bottom of his heart.

When Kaufmann sent me a copy of this book I wrote him a lengthy letter. After due appreciation of its outstanding merits I pointed out that I consider it as basically unfair to reproach an author for writing the book that he, the author, wanted to write instead of the book the reader would have liked to receive from him. Nevertheless, I uttered my regret that he had not dealt with certain problems, which I enumerated and which I considered vital for the social sciences. He answered with a charming letter which I may be permitted to quote in part since it shows his character as a man and a scientist. "You will understand", he wrote, "that it was one of my most difficult problems to determine the depth of the level I should select for the foundation of my theory and the width I should give its superstructure. The only possible solution was a compromise. My job as I see it was to define the distinction between deductive logic and methodology to such an extent that my results could serve as a starting point for future investigations. Please do not forget that I limited my task intentionally to the investigation of the logical structure of scientific inquiry and that within the frame of this program the underlying level which you had in mind cannot become thematic. The methodologist, too, has his 'brackets' and has to accept limitations. *But to limit oneself intentionally to a problem does not mean to be limited.* Especially during the last months I have worked hard on the problem of the constitution of ideal objects and my thoughts centered around the criticism of Plato in Aristotle's Metaphysics. I hope to be able in a not too distant future to present my pertinent ideas in an acceptable form."

"To limit oneself intentionally to a problem": If this is limitation at all, it is of that kind in which, according to Goethe, the master shows himself most of all. And if, as Husserl believed, it is the criterion of any true philosopher to approach his problem in full awareness of his tremendous responsibility and with fearless intellectual integrity, then Felix Kaufmann deserves indeed to be called a true philosopher.

CHAPTER 17

Social Science and the Social World

EDITORS' PREFACE

This chapter consists of an untitled letter in English to Adolph Lowe, and is dated 17 October, 1955. The letter owes its existence to an exchange of ideas carried out by telephone and letters between Schutz and Lowe. Adolph Lowe had studied economics in Germany before coming to the Graduate Faculty, and was influenced by Franz Oppenheimer. Oppenheimer, whose interests were quite broad and included the social sciences in general, had opposed the theory of marginal utility, a mild form of which was endorsed by Schutz. According to Wagner,[1] until 1955 Schutz's discussions with economists had been confined to the theory of marginal utility. But this letter largely ignores differences in economic theory and concentrates instead on Lowe's efforts to understand the principles which underlie Schutz's general approach to the social sciences. The title of the chapter was supplied by Helmut Wagner.

I just received your letter of October 10th and I am really very happy that the ideas developed in my paper, "Choosing Among Projects of Action", found your warm interest. As I told you, it was originally my intention to add a second part of this article which should deal exclusively with problems of economic theory and then apply some of the findings of the general part to the domain of economics.[2] The whole paper turned out to be a mongrel – the philosophical part of no interest for economists and the economic part of no interest for philosophers. With the exception of my friend Fritz Machlup, you are the only one whom I found to be interested in both levels of the pertinent question. I decided therefore to rewrite the first part and to publish it in a philosophical journal and just to refer at the end of this paper to the

[1]For details of the relationship between Alfred Schutz and Adolph Lowe, as well as a discussion of this letter, see Helmut Wagner, *Alfred Schutz. An Intellectual Biography*, pp. 164–166.

[2]The second part of "Choosing Among Projects of Action" was published by Lester Embree as "Choice and the Social Sciences", in *Life-World and Consciousness. Essays for Aron Gurwitsch*, edited by Lester Embree (Evanston: Northwestern University Press, 1972), pp. 565–590; see Embree's "Editor's Note", p. 565. "Choosing Among Projects of Action" was first published in *Philosophy and Phenomenological Research*, XII, No. 2 (December, 1951), and reprinted in Alfred Schutz, *Collected Papers*, Vol. I.

open problem in the methodology of the social sciences and especially of economics to which the findings of the philosophical part could probably make some contribution. The economic part of my paper, which was written in 1945, constitutes just a first draft that was never brought into shape. Since you are kind enough to be interested in it I dictated it in my tape recorder and I will ask Ilse to type it as soon as she'll find the time and to let you have a copy.

As usual, the questions you raise are truly fundamental questions and I regret that the circumstances of my life didn't permit me so far to present my ideas in a consistent context in the framework of a book. What I have to say to this topic is dispersed in various articles and it is only too understandable that even a reader of your competence and carefulness finds himself confronted with serious difficulties. In the following I shall try to answer your questions as well as I can.

Your first question is whether the social scientist can and does refer to the same reality of the social world that appears to the actor. Obviously you expect an answer of yes or no. But neither you nor I are americanized enough to believe that all scientific questions can be answered in such a way. I would be happy if I could answer your question by a simple yes and then go on to explain that my second level is just an aspect of the same full-blooded all-embracing reality of the social world as it appears to the actor. But precisely here is the root of the great difficulty: I would deny that to the actor within the social world this social world appears as a full-blooded all-embracing reality. He too has to deal merely with selected aspects of this all-embracing "reality" which are the result of his interpretation of his own situation within the social world. It seems to me that this is precisely what W. I. Thomas understood by his term, "to define the situation". Any definition of the situation involves a selection of a particular sector of the social world which is of interest to the actor. This selection depends on the system of interests and relevances originating in the biographical situation of the actor within his actual environment or, as I sometimes preferred to say, in his life plan. The interpretation of this selected sector occurs in the form of typifications which frequently and to the greater part are elements of the world taken for granted and socially derived as well as socially approved. Thus the social world as a whole is experienced by the actor within it in form of preconstituted types and preconstituted interpretations. Within this social world the actor has to find his bearings and he has to come to terms with it. He has an eminent interest in the outcome of his practical or theoretical actions. And let us not forget that these typifications and relevances depend on the practical or theoretical problems to be solved by the actor. Perhaps this is the teleological element by which the actor is guided.

The interpretation of this selected sector occurs in the form of typifications which frequently and to the greater part are elements of the world taken for granted and socially derived as well as socially approved. Thus the social world as a whole is experienced by the actor within it in the form of preconstituted types and preconstituted interpretations. Within this social world the actor has to find his bearings and he has to come to terms with it. He has an eminent interest in the outcome of his practical or theoretical actions. And let us not forget that these typifications and relevances depend on the practical or theoretical problems to be solved by the actor. Perhaps this is the teleological element by which the actor is guided.

I have to insert here some statements concerning another fundamental question with which I hope you will be in agreement. It has to be pointed out that to the actor on the social scene the social-cultural world is a meaningful world from the outset. The meaning of this world and its elements can be understood.

Now it is one of my leading ideas that understanding involves the referring of all social-cultural objects and events to human actions and, in particular, to the in-order-to and because-motives of those actions. That is what we are indeed doing in our intercourse with social-cultural objects and events and with our fellow men. If we want to understand what the other fellow means with his actions we ask about their why and wherefore. But this type of inquiry is only very rarely based on the laws of formal logic and does not have to have the ideal of clear, distinct, and consistent thinking. In common-sense thinking we break off the definition of the situation and the understanding of the meaning as soon as we have reached the understanding sufficient for our purposes. Common-sense thinking is not governed by the ideal of finding the truth. We are satisfied if we come to a plausible explanation and understanding. We do not want to make predictions but to take our chances and our risks in terms of reasonable likelihood. Moreover, in one single day we are running through a set of social roles, that is, a set of typifications, which are not only not fully integrated but frequently contradict each other. And if amidst of our passions and of our hopes and fears and of contradicting attitudes we achieve a certain degree of reasonableness of our actions and our interpretations sufficient for several useful purposes we have reason to believe that we are prudent men. Perfect rationality in our actions cannot be achieved on a common-sense level as I have tried to prove in several of my papers.

But I am not alone in the social-cultural world and my interpretation of it is not my private affair. It is from the outset intersubjective and shared with my fellow men who also use socially derived and socially approved schemes of typifications and relevances taken by them for granted, as I take them for granted. The more standardized and the more anonymous these typifications and structures of relevances are, the greater is the likelihod that my and their systems of relevances and typifications will coincide.

All this is more or less the mechanism of experiencing the social world on the first level, that is from the point of view of the actor living within it. Now, what is the attitude of the social scientist to this social world? When speaking of the social scientist I mean the theoretical scientist in his selective attitude. For the time being let us forget that he, the scientist, too is man among fellow men and let us keep in mind that one thing is the theoretical activity of the scientist and another thing is dealing with science within the social world; for instance, in the form of the correspondence or of the discussions in which we are both engaged.

You will certainly agree with me that the purpose of the social sciences is to describe, analyze and if possible explain what really happens in the socio-cultural world. These again are human motives, human actions originating therein, and the results of these actions – be they cultural objects, social institutions, etc. In this sense, but only in this sense, the social reality is the same to the scientist as to the actor living on the social scene. But between us no further explanation is necessary to the effect that to the social reality which the scientist has to examine belong also all the interpretations of the social world which those acting within it have bestowed upon it, that is, of the typifications, systems of relevances, etc., constructed by the actors in the social world in order to find their bearing in it and come to terms with it. These constructs formed by the actors within the social world are themselves elements of the social reality given to the social scientist for examination and explanation. In order to do so the social scientist has to form constructs in accordance with what <Felix> Kaufmann calls the rules of procedure common to all empirical sciences. I meant this when stating that the constructs of the social scientists are constructs of the second level, that is, constructs of constructs by which the actor on the social scene interprets the social world. More or less, this statement conforms with the statement by Whitehead that it is the purpose of scientific activity to replace the thought-object of common-sense by the thought-object of scientific thinking. I believe that his statement is especially important for the methodology of the social sciences because the social scientist – in contradistinction to the natural scientist – has to deal with the pre-structures, pre-constructs, pre-interpreted world; that the natural scientist does not have to do.

What is the decisive difference between the constructs on the second (the scientific) level and those formed on the first level by the actors on the social scene? As far as I can see, there are two decisive points. The first is that the social scientist takes the attitude of a disinterested observer. To him – always as theoretical scientist – the world is no longer a field of action but a field of observation. The scientist's interests do not depend on his wish to come to terms with the social world and to find his bearing in it. Strictly speaking, they do not depend on this integrated system of relevances which constitute his life plan in so far as he is not a scientist but a human being living in the social world among his fellow men. He has replaced his system of interests by the system of scientific interests. He has replaced his personal situation in the world by his scientific situation, that is, by defining the locus of his particular problem and his particular methods to solve this <problem> within the sum total of his particular science as he finds it in order to carry out its <unending task>. Consequently, all constructs and all typifications which the social scientist will use have to depend on the scientific problem and its level with which he is concerned. Therefore his first job will be to formulate his problem as clearly as possible; and as soon as he had done so successfully he has found the locus for all problem typifications and constructions which might be helpful for its solution.

The second feature distinguishing scientific constructs from constructs of common-sense thinking is the fact that scientific constructs have to live up to the ideals of clarity, distinctness, consistency. Of course, the scientist is governed by the idealized rule of not being satisfied with simple plausibility and likelihood but with searching for the truth. This would correspond to the "quest for certainty" of which Dewey speaks, although it is not my belief that it is the business of science to arrive at laws in the sense of natural laws as the basis for the prediction of singular events.

Of course, this does not mean that scientific constructs are nothing but consistent propositions in a vacuum. Like all empirical sciences the social sciences formulate hypotheses and theories which are subject to validation by empirical verification.

The object is and must always be that social reality which social scientists want to describe, analyze, explain and possibly understand. Yet, a considerable dilemma arises here: On the one hand, I state that understanding of the social reality always involves reference to human actions and human motives. On the other hand, I state that the social scientist as theoretician has withdrawn himself from participating in the social world and has assumed the attitude of a disinterested observer. In this attitude, he is no longer man among fellow men; he is no longer permitted to take things for granted as actors do within the social world. To the contrary, it is his job to put in question what seems to be unquestionable to the actor on the social scene. Incidentally, this explains why the findings of the social scientist can never coincide with the interpretations of social reality by common-sense thinking. Of course, this does not exclude the broad realm of applicability of theoretical findings to the social world as interpreted in terms of common-sense thinking. If the social scientist has to understand to explain the events in the social world, and if such explanation and understanding are only possible by referring the events in the social world to human actions and their motives, how does the social scientist proceed?

He begins by observing certain events within the social world. He interprets these events as the outcome of human actions. He constructs a model of action which might bring about this state of affairs. He adds to this model of action the model of the consciousness of an actor which contains all the motives leading to such action – but only these. All these constructs are typifying constructs; which features have to be typified and which remain untypified depends on the particular problem for the sake of which the types have to be constructed. It has to be kept in mind that these typifications have to follow the rules of procedure of all the empirical sciences. They are subject to the laws of formal logic; they have to be consistent with one another; they have to be as clear and distinct as possible; they have to be relevant to the problem involved. In addition, they have to be compatible with the common-sense interpretation which real actors on the social scene bestow upon the social world and their own actions in it. This last postulate is particularly important because it guarantees the applicability of these typifications to events within the social sciences which Max Weber called an interpretative understanding of meaning.

What I have said so far refers to all social sciences. Particular social sciences – at least some of them – have to form their typifications or constructs in accordance with additional conditions. For instance, the constructs of economics have to assume that the fictitious consciousness of the model of the economic actor has to choose any moment between pre-given problematic possibilities and more over <must postulate> that choosing among these possibilities occurs in perfect rationality. This is so because the very definition of the field of economics – I believe that is what you call the economic system – involves the axiom that such a system can only survive if this principle is adhered to within the range of tolerance. Of course, in order to ascertain this range of tolerance, the economist has to build deviation-types of actors who do not act purely rationally. This procedure will help him to find out what "requirements" have to be fulfilled so that the economic system may survive in case of the occurrence of less than rational actions.

Let me sum up. I stated here <conceptions> in my own language but translated them into your terms as I understand them. You formulate a certain problem, for example: how may the observed ratio between consumer goods output and capital goods output of ten to one be maintained. This involves certain requirements. You distinguish here between "required conditions" relating to a particular order and factors which are compatible with it. This is a *"trouvaille"* (discovery). You find, for instance, that this ratio can only be maintained if certain sellers raise their supply whenever the price exceeds a certain level. Now, by stating that sellers will raise their supply when the price exceeds a certain level you have referred to typical motives of typical sellers who act in such a way that the supply will be increased. Strictly speaking, the statement that there is a certain ratio between consumer goods output and capital output is nothing else but a statement about typical actions of typical producers which lead to the statement of affairs ascertained by the economist in his statistically established prevailing ratio.

Of course, it is well understood between us that there is no necessity for using this language instead of studying appropriate curves of supply, demand, and indifference. But you may always recur to the behavior patterns and motivations of economic actors and for certain particular purposes you must do so. If my theory is sound, the marginal principle involves the assumption that all participants in the economic process at any moment find themselves in the face of problematic possibilities among which they have to choose rationally. Thus they determine their course of action. But I may safely continue to operate with the principle of marginality at any level without referring to the underlying actions and motives.

This procedure can be repeated on any level of concreteness or abstraction. Your former idea of a postulational economic theory or, in the present version, of a theory of environments, coincides with and originates in the scientific problem as formulated by you. Of course, you do not formulate problems and theories as a kind of abstract chess problem or, as Mr Hicks[3] naïvely assumed, as a good assumption to start with. Of course as a theoretical economist you remain subject to the rules of procedure of all the empirical sciences. Therefore, you will live up to the postulate of adequacy, which means that all your assumptions and all your constructs have to be not only consistent and compatible with one another but also compatible with the empirically observed social reality to which they refer. It might be possible to construct a theoretical economic system on purely counterfactual assumptions, for instance, <the assumption> that everybody buys at the highest prices and sells at the lowest. Although the layman has the impression that certain international trade agreements aim precisely at such a situation, no economist would ever try to develop the requirements to which such a system has to live up in order to survive.

I assume that by the correct formulation of the problem in economic theory the relationship to the social reality is already established – if that were not the case, the problem would not have been formulated correctly according to the rules of procedure of economic science. Further, I assume that the formulation of the problem itself already contains the requirements which have to be fulfilled by the system under scrutiny with its particular conditions. Should you agree with me, I cannot see

[3]Schutz probably refers to the British economist, John Richard Hicks (co-recipient of the Nobel Prize in Economics in 1972).

the necessity for introducing functional-structural conceptualizations, and I do not see why you have to worry about the nature of the wholes or entities or subsystems with which you have to deal. If I deposit 10 dollars in my savings account I have in my common-sense thinking no idea that I made a small contribution to the change in the relationship between savings and capital production within the economy of the United States. Nevertheless, I have lived up to the requirements for the maintenance or change of the ratio between saving and capital formation in general as well as with respect to the United States as of October, 1955. And if this ratio is found unsatisfactory, let us say by government agencies, appropriate measures should be taken in order to induce people like me to increase their savings. The trained economist will make such suggestions easily without recurring to my particular situation and without asking Mr. Gallup to take a poll among people in order to find out what kind of circumstances might induce them to deposit $20 instead of $10 in their savings accounts.

Let me repeat what I told you during our conversation last Sunday: It is my conviction that methodologists have neither the job nor the authority to prescribe to social scientists what they have to do. Humbly he has to learn from social scientists and to interpret for them what they are doing. It seems to me that all the great masters of our social sciences proceeded as I have outlined in my general scheme. And it is also my belief that the serious questions raised by you in the manuscript you kindly gave to me aim also in the same direction.

CHAPTER 18

In Search of the Middle Ground

EDITORS' PREFACE

In December of 1954 Alfred Schutz attended the fourteenth meeting of the Conference on Science, Philosophy, and Religion held at Harvard University. One of the objectives of this conference, largely a civic organization composed of prominent scholars, was the fostering of tolerance and cooperation among Christians and Jews. To this end Robert MacIver of Columbia University and Rabbi Louis Finkelstein of the Jewish Theological Seminary of America were co-leaders of the permanent conference committee. The Fourteenth Meeting convened at the very end of 1954, at which time Schutz delivered his paper, "Symbol, Reality and Society".[1] And in the next year, 1955, Schutz also contributed a paper, "Equality and the Meaning Structure of the Social World"[2] to the fifteenth meeting of the Conference, which met at Columbia University.

It is not widely known that, on the request mailed to speakers at the latter conference, Schutz summed up his impressions of the deliberations, setting them down in a seven-page response. The response is published here with the omission of a short introductory remark of no scholarly interest. Wagner found this document unique among Schutz's papers because it shows Schutz "in a state in which he abandoned his stance of aloofness from partisanship in practical social issues. . . . No longer the impartial, and that is uninvolved, 'scientific observer', he assumed the role of sympathetic observer lending advice to those for whom active involvement is a personal and moral obligation." The title is that of Alfred Schutz.

A reading of the report of our meeting reveals that there was rather unanimous agreement that a "middle ground" has to be found which should be explored in the future

[1]The paper was included in the volume of the proceedings of the Conference, published under the editorship of Lyman Bryson in the volume, *Symbols and Society: Fourteenth Symposium of the Conference of Science, Philosophy and Religion* (New York: Harper & Row, 1955). Schutz's paper was republished in *Collected Papers*, Vol. I, pp. 287–356.

[2]The paper was presented at the Fifteenth Symposium of the Conference on Science, Philosophy and Religion, at Columbia University, and published as Chapter III of the proceedings, *Aspects of Human Equality*, edited by Lyman Bryson, Clarence H. Faust, Louis Finkelstein and R. M. MacIver (New York: Harper & Row, 1957); the paper was subsequently published in *Collected Papers*, Vol. II, pp. 226–273. Schutz's comments are printed on pp. 392–397.

work of the Conference. However, it seems that the term, "middle ground", was used in a rather equivocal way by the various speakers, and frequently by the same speaker in various contexts. There are at least three different meanings which were attributed to this term and their analysis might be found to be of some help.

1. Middle Ground in the Sense of Common Language

<Such a middle ground was thought of as> enabling the participants in the conference to achieve a meeting of minds within a well-established universe of discourse with a view of mutual clarifications of the thoughts of the discussants. The hope was expressed: In terms of such a common language a conceptualization and delimitation of the topic could be <reached> with which we all are concerned in our ways <according to our> diversified backgrounds and varying interests.

However, it was never determined in what capacities – technically speaking, in what social roles – the participants in these discussions wanted to approach the common enterprise and to look for the middle ground of a common language. In the first place: we all are human beings, men of good will, who have a rather keen sense of ethical responsibility and who try to establish the principles of an "ethics for our time". For this purpose <we use> all the intelligence and discipline of thinking within our power.

In the second place we are worried citizens of the United States of 1955, deeply troubled by the many manifestations of discrimination, prejudices, and other social evils prevailing in our particular social environments and we are looking for appropriate remedies. Last but not least we are scholars – philosophers, theologians, educators, social and natural scientists – who are eager to investigate *theoretically* the problem of equality and its place within our *theoretical* interests and to use for this purpose the methods of our particular disciplines. Is it then our intention to investigate equality (or equality of opportunity) as one of the "ethical principles for our time" which ought to guide *all* mankind and which ought to encompass the globe or at least the community constituted by the United Nations? Or is it our strategic political goal to transform the United States into a "more perfect Union" in the sense of Professor MacIver's book? Or is it our goal to find theoretical access to a central problem common to all of our various fields of study in the hope that if our individual approaches are sound they will fit into one another and form a unified picture like parts of a jigsaw puzzle? It seems that our discussion oscillated among these three groups of problems. Thus a determination and clarification of both the topics to be investigated and the social role to be assumed by the participants might facilitate the determination of further procedures.

In order to avoid misunderstandings I want to state my conviction that these three groups of problems are by no means mutually exclusive; on the contrary, they are interrelated in many ways. Moreover, I believe that each of them is of highest importance and deserves our best efforts. <I believe> also that for each of them a universe of discourse can be found. However, I submit that his universe of discourse, this common ground, will be different for each group of problems to be approached. It will also vary with the social role into which we place ourselves. This is necessarily so because any topic <dealing with> equality will present different relevance structures for the theorist using the methods of his field, for the common-sense approach of the citizen, and for a man who has committed himself to a set of ethical principles, axioms, or postulates. All typifications and constructs used by common-sense or by scientific thinkers depend on the problem for the solution of which they were formulated; and all relevance structures depend on the system of our theoretical and practical interests. To prove these statements was one of the principal aims of my paper.

2. Middle Ground in the Epistemological Sense

The papers submitted deal with philosophical topics of a high level of abstraction on the one hand, and with concrete questions such as equality of education on the other hand. The term, "middle ground", was frequently used in order to denote the level of investigation at which the ideas or ideals of the philosopher and the religionist come in close contact with concrete situations within the social reality as studied in several monographs. In the course of the discussion it has been rightly stated that all these levels should not be considered sets of sharply divided groups but rather elements of an interconnected continuum and that it would be wise to look for the middle realm.

Doubtlessly this is a promising approach. However, it is advisable to suggest that a series of rather difficult problems enters the picture if the "same" phenomena are studied on various levels of abstraction. To give an example: The ideas and ideals of the philosopher have their history and tradition, and so has any religious attitude. However, the concrete life of the concrete social group – the social reality as I suggest calling it – is of a rather different historical structure. As pointed out in my paper, it is determined by factors which Max Scheler called the *"Realfaktoren"*, that is, the world of everyday life taken for granted in the common-sense thinking of the actors on the social scene with which they have to come to terms. Surely, under certain conditions the ideas and ideals of the philosophical or religious thinkers influence common-sense thinking. But if and in so far as they do so, they have undergone transformations. As I said in my paper,[3] they become secularized, or as Professor [Richard] Mckeon called it, they have to pass into the dimensions of institutionalization. As demonstrated convincingly in several excellent papers, the idea of equality shows a continuous development in its own right from the beginning of occidental philosophical thought up to the present day. It is an element of *philosophia perennis*.

The concepts of Hobbes, Locke, Rousseau and other thinkers that influenced the framing of the American and the French Constitutions were secularized in different ways in either case. To the philosophical insight in the dignity of man corresponds the notion of "fair play" in American common-sense thinking – a term that certainly is [more] closely related to sportsmanship than to philosophy in the mind of the man in the street: "Let's give the other fellow a break". And the Calvinist churchgoer

[3]Perhaps a reference to the fourth part of Schutz's paper (*Collected Papers*, Vol. II, 243ff.). The reference is probably to MacIver's *The Web of Government* (1947).

does not have to grapple with the subtle and exceedingly difficult <social> problems connected with the doctrine of original sin and predestination as developed in Calvin's writings – he just has to listen to the teachings of the minister who translates them into common-sense terms.

It seems to me that this region of secularized common-sense thinking is indeed the "epistemological middle ground" where ideas and ideals – transformed into taken-for-granted notions of social reality – become springs of social interaction. It is the task of the theoretical social sciences to study the rather complicated structure of this social reality and the forms of these transformations. It is the task of empirical research to apply such theoretical findings <in the study of> concrete social groups and social relations in a given setting at a given historical moment. It is understood that theory and empirical research are corroborating and correcting one another. To be sure, the theoretical social sciences are as deeply rooted in philosophical presuppositions as any other theoretical endeavor. However, at least to a certain extent, they can perform their task without immediate recourse to philosophical problems.

To do this precisely was the aim of my paper that – so I hope – contributes to the analysis of the epistemological middle ground by showing some of the features of the structure of social reality. Again several levels have to be distinguished, dependent on the various forms of typification of structures of relevance, of subjective and objective interpretations of the situation both from the points of view of in-groups and out-groups and from the points of view of individuals. The past part of my paper makes certain applications of this conceptual framework to concrete problems, such as discrimination and equality of opportunity.

<I submit> that philosophical analysis of the underlying principles requires supplementation by findings of the theoretical and empirical social sciences in order to find the epistemological middle ground for further research. Applied to the problems of our conference this means that we have to substitute the question, "What do we, the members of the conference, understand by equality?" by the questions, "What do the actors on the social scene – either in general or in particular settings – say, in present-day American society – understand by equality? What is, in this respect, the self-interpretation by the in-group and the interpretation by the out-group? What is the relationship between group and individual member seen from the point of view of either one? How are the underlying typifications institutionalized (for instance, by law, mores, rituals, etc.)?"

If this approach is considered sound, a concrete problem – say, that of educational opportunities in present-day America – should be investigated in terms of the philosophical principles as well as in terms of the theoretical social sciences. If attacked correctly from both ends, the tunnel must meet.

3. Middle Ground in the Pragmatic Sense

The term, "middle ground", was also used in order to determine the region where the theoretical attitude of the thinker can be translated into the practical attitude of the man of action, or, as it has been said, of the decision-maker. It is obvious that the solution of this problem is intimately connected with those solutions dealt with under 1) and 2). On the one hand, the question was raised how we, members of the Conference, can communicate our findings to the man in the street who neither uses nor understands our language. On the other hand, several members emphasized the necessity for giving a series of practical answers applying to education, equality of opportunity in choosing work, international relations, etc. All this is <solely> possible if we have some knowledge of the particular structure of the common-sense thinking within the social group addressed by us, that is, the systems of typifications, the relevance structures, the schemes of interpretation, etc., that prevail in it. To convey our message to the common man and be understood by him we have to use his language and to translate our thoughts into the conceptual framework accepted by him. In order to change social attitudes and to promote, say, racial equality or equal opportunity of education, we have to know more about the mechanism of discrimination of all kinds.

My paper brought some illustrative materials, showing for example that it would be in vain to reduce all kinds of discrimination to so-called prejudices. We have to attack the prevailing central myth, as Professor MacIver calls it, and its various particularizations. How this can be done has been shown again in a masterly way by MacIver in the book, *The More Perfect Union* (1948).

PART THREE

Studies in Phenomenological Philosophy

CHAPTER 19

Husserl's *Cartesian Meditations*

Editor's Preface

Schutz's book, *Der sinnhafte Aufbau der sozialen Welt*, was published and reached the market in the Spring of 1932. Next to Max Weber, the main inspiration for the study was Edmund Husserl. Because he was not certain whether his book was important enough, Schutz had not planned to send a copy to Husserl. However, Schutz's friend, Felix Kaufmann, who corresponded with Husserl, insisted that Schutz send a copy of the book to Husserl. Upon receiving the book, Husserl wrote Schutz the following letter, dated 3 May, 1932:[1]

> Dear Dr. Schutz,
>
> I was just on the verge of writing to you that I was very delighted by your book, *Der sinnhafte Aufbau der sozialen Welt*, as well as by your friendly accompanying letter, when I learned from Professor Otaka, who visited me to say goodbye, that you will soon come to Basle and that you plan to make a detour to Freiburg. I am eager to make the acquaintance of such a serious and thorough phenomenologist, one of the very few who have penetrated to the deepest and unfortunately so difficult to penetrate sense of my life work and whom I view hopefully as its continuers and as representatives of the genuine *philosophia perennis*. Please come, I will find time for you. It shall turn into a beautiful *symphilosophein*.
>
> Yours, E. Husserl.[2]

While reading and correcting the proofs for *Der sinnhafte Aufbau* Schutz read the just published French translation of Husserl's *Méditations Cartésiennes. Introduction à la Phénoménologie*.[3] He cited the French text and provided comments on it in

[1]The translation is by Helmut Wagner.

[2]For information about Schutz's meetings with Husserl, see Helmut Wagner, *Alfred Schutz. An Intellectual Biography*, pp. 45ff.

[3]The text was translated by Mlle Gabrielle Peiffer and M. Emmanuel Levinas, Paris: Vrin, 1931. The German text was first published in 1950: Edmund Husserl, *Cartesianische Meditationen und Pariser Vorträge*, herausgegeben und eingeleitet von Prof. Dr. S. Strasser (Den Haag: Martinus Nijhoff, 1950).

German in footnotes added to the galley proofs.[4] Presumably some time after his visit to Husserl, Schutz wrote a review of the *Méditations Cartésiennes* for the *Deutsche Literaturzeitung* and which was published 18 December, 1932 (Heft 51). The review was republished in an appendix to the German edition of the third volume of the *Collected Papers*, introduced and edited by Alexander von Baeyer.[5] Because the English-language edition of the third volume of the *Collected Papers* appeared without a translation of the text, it appears here for the first time. The translation is a revised version of one by Helmut Wagner.

I will try to retrace the course of the investigations contained in this book even though they can hardly be exhausted in a short exposition and even though <I have to confine myself to> broad outlines while omitting whole groups of problems. Nevertheless, <I shall proceed> as far as possible with formulations which have come from Husserl himself.

So far not published in German, this is the French translation of an extended transcript of two lectures presented by Husserl at the Sorbonne in 1929. In it's subtitle the book is modestly called *An Introduction to Phenomenology*. It is nothing less than the basic foundation of Philosophy from the perspective of transcendental subjectivity in its absolute cognition, and it is a systematic interpretation of this subjectivity in its full range. Husserl had already developed his method of "phenomenological reduction" in his *Ideas Pertaining to a Pure Phenomenology and to a Phenomenological Philosophy*. With its help Husserl now systematically explores – in the first four meditations – the fields of transcendental egological experience in its dual structure as field of flowing experiences of the world and as field of habitualities. However, in the last meditation he treats transcendental intersubjectivity and the problem of "empathy".

Because these problems serve solely as means for disclosing transcendental intersubjectivity as a thematic field of philosophy, all the investigations are of a merely preparatory character; they contain no final concretely-constitutive analyses. Nevertheless, in particular the last two meditations lead to completely new ideas which are extraordinarily daring and difficult. They prepare an expansion of our philosophical knowledge that, in its radicality, cannot as yet be fathomed. Here indeed scientifically virgin land is penetrated and the path toward a significant new world is cleared.

Husserl took his point of departure from the meditations of Descartes. This was not just a polite gesture in front of a French audience. It was the aim of Descartes to radically reform philosophy and to make it a science of absolute foundations by way of "ascertaining a first beginning": Any person seriously philosophizing must "at least once in his life" retreat into himself and attempt the revolution of all sciences which so far were valid for him and seek their refoundation. Thereby he has to follow the well-known method of doubt which recognizes as indubitable precisely the ego and its cogitationes.

[4]The relevant notes added in the galley proofs are p. 31, fn. 1; p. 41, fn. 1; p. 53, fn. 1; p. 106, fn. 2; p. 111, fn. 2; p. 113, fn 3; p. 114, fn 1; p. 184, fn. 2; p. 190, fn. 1.

[5]Den Haag: Martinus Nijhoff, 1971.

By posing the question of the ultimate existence of apodictic evidence, which can be found in the life of consciousness of the meditating person, the *Cartesian Meditations* becomes the prototype of every radical-philosophical self-examination; it lends it "eternal value". As a truly new "beginning" of philosophy, phenomenology will retrace the path of Descartes without, however, falling into Cartesian errors. Prominently featured among the errors is the retention of the deductive system of science and the idea of the goal of science *more geometrico* by the application of the method of doubt. If one wants to carry out the Cartesian revolution in a radical way, then not only must the *de facto* validity of all sciences be included but also the idea of their purpose. The latter reveals itself as an ordering of its earlier cognitions into its later ones, that is, as a construction of steps or a sequence of ranks of evidences the constitution of which can be systematically disclosed. To see the truly first beginning, thus, means to ask for the first complete and in truth apodictic evidence.

Now, such an evidence obtains neither for the belief in the existence of the "world", which is the basis of all naïve world-experience, nor for the belief in the existence of other egos which belong to this world. Therefore, not just corporeal nature but the whole concrete surrounding life-world must be subjected to the Cartesian revolution. It is not that it is the intention of phenomenology to deny the existence of the world as such or that of "others". But a truly beginning philosophy must "refrain" from every judging about their existence and from every experiential believing in them. It has to "put out of action" all position-taking toward the pregiven objective world; it has to exercise a *"phenomenological epoché"* – to use a term which Husserl first introduced in his *Ideas*.

The objective world is "bracketed" in the epoché. To it belong not only transcendent objects [*Objekte*] but also the mundane human ego of the meditating person as something existing in the world and, therefore, as a *"psychological subject"* of inner experience. Yet, while achieved in the epoché, this *phenomenological reduction* in no way places the meditating person opposite a void. It merely refers him to the pure life of consciousness of the *transcendental ego cogitans* which exists for itself "prior" to all mundane existence as well as to the latter's real mental processes [*reale Erlebnisse*] in and through which mundane existence alone achieves the validity of being. As a result, the questionable assumptions of the existence of the objective world are reduced to the indubitable experiences [*Erlebnisse*] (to the cogitationes in the Cartesian sense) of the world by the meditating person. At the same time, the transcendental subjectivity of the cognizing ego is revealed as the originary ground of cognition: in apodictic evidence, but only in the universality of an "open horizon" of the past, of transcendental capacities and habitualities which belong to it.

In a certain way Descartes had also realized this. But he missed the meaning of his great discovery when he identified the cognizing ego, by which he assumed he had grasped a "little corner of the world", with *mens sive animus sive intellectus* and with it the transcendental with the psychological subject. But the ego, as psychological subject, as natural human ego, belongs to the "world" which has been subjected to phenomenological reduction. Only by means of the epoché do I reduce my psychological experience of self to my transcendental-phenomenological experience of self. The latter is called "transcendental" because it exhibits the rigorous correlate to the "transcendence of everything mundane" and, thereby, also of my mundane ego. This ego receives its sense and its validity of being only from me as the one who meditates philosophically in the reduction.

The field of transcendental experience, which was made accessible by the execution of the phenomenological reduction, can now be uncovered in its universal structures. The sphere of being of the cognizing ego, which was acquired in the epoché, does not only comprise the empty "I am" but also all real or merely possible cognitions as universal apodictic structure of experience. One can look at this flowing life of consciousness, in which the identical ego of the meditating person lives in his cognitions; this life can be interpreted and described according to its contents. However, such phenomenological description is essentially different from a psychology of consciousness. This is so regardless of the rigorous parallels between them. Psychology seeks "data" of outer or inner experiences which are related to the world which is presupposed as existing. Carried out under the strict observance of the phenomenological reduction, phenomenology always aims at the interpretation of my own experiences and their *intentionalities*.

This basic concept of phenomenology designates the unique structure of processes of consciousness; it signifies that every cogito *means* something and, in this sense, carries in itself the sense of what is meant: every experience of consciousness is consciousness *of something*. As far as my experiences of consciousness refer to the "world" they carry – in consequence of their intentional character – this relation "in themselves". This applies within the natural attitude as well as in the phenomenological reduction. However, only after execution of this reduction does it become visible that, for me, all that which naturally exists has validity only as cogitatum of my changing cogitationes which, in their changes, are linked to each other. Therefore, "objects" ["*Gegenstände*"] – in the reduced sphere as well as in the natural attitude – are nothing else than intentional correlates of their modes of consciousness.

This intentionality is the inexhaustible theme of phenomenology. Its phenomenological exploration must take place with that absolute lack of prejudice which distinguishes a phenomenologist – as "disinterested observer" after the epoché – from a person in the natural attitude who lives in straightforward naïveté and who naïvely believes in the world as existing. It is marked by a characteristic "duality" which may be designated as its *"noematic"* and *"noetic"* direction. The first aims at the *cogitatum qua cogitatum* (the sense of the object as object) that is meant by the *cogito* (the meaning-positing ego). It includes the determinations which are "attributed" to the corresponding modes of consciousness (for instance, the existential modes of being-certain, being-possible, being-presumed, and so forth). The second points to the modes of consciousness themselves (perceiving, remembering, retrotending to [*Retention*], and so forth).

Both belong inseparably together. This is based on the mode of the connection of consciousness with consciousness that is designated by the name, *"synthesis"*. The latter is characteristic of the region of consciousness. Its prototype is the synthesis of identification, that is, the intentional achievement of consciousness which executes the *"constituting"* of the processes of consciousness out of the manifold manners of the appearance of an object and into the consciousness of the "unity" of the intentional objectivity itself.

As further investigations show, the total life of consciousness is synthetically unified and this occurs in an all-embracing inner consciousness of time. The latter comprises not only the "actional" [*"aktuellen"*] processes of consciousness but also those potentialities to which actional consciousness points in the open horizons of "I can". All of this is accessible to *intentional analysis*. Its characteristic consists in uncovering the potentialities which are implied by the actualities of consciousness [*Bewusstseinsaktualitäten*], elucidating and clarifying in the first place in a *noematic* respect what is "also meant" in every intentional act. While every cogito, as consciousness, is in the widest sense the meaning of something meant, what is meant in every moment is, however, more than that which appears as *explicitly* meant in any given moment.

As I said, the intentional objectivity is "constituted" in the unity of synthesis. "Object", therefore, is nothing other than the "pole of identity" of the manifold of processes of consciousness synthetically tied together. Now, it is possible to describe as well the *noetic* intentionalities which achieve their synthesis in an essential and rigorously deducible typicality according to their characteristic mode of constitution. In this, the intentional object (placed on the side of the *cogitatum*) functions itself as "transcendental clue" to the cogitationes which constitute it. As a consequence objectivities are differentiated into sharply delimited structural types according to their formal-ontological and material-ontological particularizations. As a problem of a universal egology understood as the totality of all objects actionally or potentially conceivable for the transcendental ego, the world is not a chaos but is already ordered according to a predesignated typicality which can be investigated.

The typifications of ostensible objects of modes of consciousness which belong together synthetically also comprise those higher-level intentional syntheses which are correlates of *"reason"*. They are to be produced in essential acts by the transcendental ego. Therefore they themselves are universal structural forms of transcendental subjectivity and point to the problem of the "evidence" as givenness of "actual" objects themselves and their modifications. Here it is not possible to pursue this set of problems, although it will be provided in the context of the complex of ideas contained in Husserl's book, *Formal and Transcendental Logic*. Briefly I shall mention only the characteristic of these syntheses, called "evidence", which institute for me a "permanent possession"; consequently I can always again return to the actuality which I have recognized in them. Both habitual and potential evidence therefore function constitutively for the sense, "existing object". "World", as "actual" object, is nothing else than the correlate idea of a complete evidence of experience according to which the various kinds of objects [*Objektarten*] of the world – the regions – correspond to transcendental systems of particular evidences.

The content of the first three "meditations" has been indicated in the previous expositions. Were we to briefly summarize the result, we may say: *Every sense which anything existing has for me, is sense only by virtue of the achievement of the intentionalities of the flowing life of consciousness and their constitutive syntheses*. However, what about the constitution of this ego itself (even though it is inseparable from its experiences)? The ego exists as "object" being-for-itself and experiences its flowing cogitationes as "the same". Obviously, the identical ego places itself next to the one "pole of unity" of objects. As continuously constituting ego, it lives in all its processes of consciousness and, through them, relates itself to all object poles. But this centering ego is not at all an empty pole of identity; it is a substratum of habitualities, that is, of "acquisitions" of prior processes of consciousness. Remaining in them or "deleting" them, it constitutes itself in its own active genesis as "my personal ego".

Again, this personal ego is to be differentiated from the ego in the flowing many-sidedness of its intentional life and the objects which it constitutes as existing for itself. That is, the ego is taken in full concreteness which also comprises the total actual and potential life of consciousness. Deliberately recalling Leibniz, Husserl called it the *"monad"*.

The problem of the constitution of this monadic ego for itself has to comprise any and all constitutive problems; and the phenomenology of this self-constituting must be congruent with phenomenology as such. However, in order to approach this problem I have to transform my empirical factual transcendental ego into the universal eidos, "any transcendental ego whatever" – that is, into a universe of all forms of mental processes which are at all conceivable for my factual empirical transcendental ego by means of modification in in free variation.

This "free variation of possibilities" is the *eidetic method* of the inquiry into essences. The latter, next to the phenomenological reduction, is a fundamental form of all specifically transcendental methods. It has been described most precisely by Husserl in the first part of his *Ideas* [,First Book,] which stresses its basic significance for the founding of phenomenology. In the present work, the method is reintroduced at this late juncture only for pedagogical reasons. Roughly stated, it results from the following line of thought: In free variations I can phantasy everything factually given as a special case of mere conceivability, as a mere example of a pure possibility. The universal type, which is thereby established, can be questioned about what remains invariable in all of these variations. If I carry out this eidetic reduction of my empirical-factual transcendental ego, I discover the eidos thus acquired to be "any transcendental ego whatever". To it belongs a universal apriori which comprises the unending multiplicity of types of conceivable actualities and potentialities of life. This multiplicity regulates itself in co-existence and in succession, with the characteristic laws of motivation, within the unitary form of the consciousness of inner time – in short, in the formal regularity of "egological genesis" within which the two basic forms of *active [aktiven] and passive genesis* are to be distinguished.

The practically acting ego (in that broad sense which also embraces the judging and, in general, the "position-taking" ego) produces new objects on the basis of already pregiven objects. The latter – once produced – continue to be valid; they are "passively possessed" but can also be reproduced at any time. Parallel to this runs passive genesis, which also issues from intentionalities. Through it, those objects constitute themselves which, in the synthesis of passive experience [*Erfahrung*] in life, are encountered, so to speak, as "finished", as material for future acts. That passive genesis essentially participates <in the life of consciousness> is already demonstrated by the fact that everything which affects my ego as "object" can be apperceived.

The universal principle of this [passive] synthesis is association which, correctly understood, is a set of intentional-eidetic laws subsumed under the pure ego;[6] it is subject to one of the most universal forms of genesis, namely temporality. But the form of temporality itself is built up in passive genesis and thus acquires an "innate apriori" of the concrete constitution of the pure ego. Now, everything produced in active or passive genesis can be questioned and interpreted according to its "history", that is, according to the intentionalities which led to its production. This reduction of the whole set of problems to the static and genetic constituting of "objectivities" justifies the exclusive claim of phenomenology to be genuine *transcendental* theory of knowledge. It alone demonstrates in self-interpretation how the ego constitutes itself and everything which has existential status for itself. Likewise, it avoids the absurdity of which many theories are guilty when they claim to be transcendental philosophies: the presupposition of a universe of true being outside the universe of possible consciousness – and this usually expressed by their concept of transcendence.

Systematically and concretely carried out, phenomenology therefore is also "transcendental *idealism*" in a well-understood but novel sense which stands in the sharpest contrast to all psychological idealism. It does not depart from sense data or presuppose a world of "things in themselves". By way of the systematic uncovering of the constituting intentionalities, it demonstrates not only the absolute sense of existence of transcendental subjectivity, but also the sense of existence of the real "objective" world – a world whose reality is as unquestionable as its relativity with regard to transcendental subjectivity and the intersubjectivities which are constituted in it.

Here, however, there arises an extraordinarily difficult question: How is it possible to prove the "objectivity" [*"Objektivität"*] of the world within this egological cosmos? And because "world" is nothing else but "world" for everyone and thus also for "others", how is it possible to prove the existence of "others"? Did my transcendental ego not become a solitary self (*solus ipse*) in consequence of the execution of the epoché? How is it possible to derive the existence of others and moreover the intersubjectivity of the world from the intentionalities of my consciousness and its constitutive achievements?

In order to solve this task it is necessary to undertake a further reduction within the already phenomenologically reduced universal egological sphere. By means of this further reduction all constitutive achievements of those intentionalities which refer directly or indirectly to the subjectivity of others will be "screened off". Thus one initially abstracts from all "otherness". This means not only "others" as living beings but most of all "spiritual" objectivities of others (for instance, cultural objects) which determine or co-determine my phenomenal world. Finally, the characteristic of the world that "remains" now as the world for "everyone" itself is screened off. Husserl designated this epoché as the "second epoché" – in my opinion, not a very happy choice of words. After its execution what remains within the thematic field

[6]In Husserl's peculiar use of the phrase, "pure ego", that is, as a name for transcendental subjectivity uncovered by the transcendental, phenomenological reduction. [FK]

are exclusively those actional and potential intentionalities in which the ego is constituted in its "ownness" and in the synthetical unities which belong to this ownness.[7]

This is still a unitarily coherent stratum of the phenomenon, "world"; however, it is no longer the objective world for everyone but "reduced to Nature included in my ownness" (*nature qui m'appartient*).[8] Within this universe of what is peculiarly my own a "transcendental world" manifests itself, so to speak, as "immanent transcendence". This reduced world, the transcendence immanent to it, is still a determining piece of my own concrete being; in itself, in its constitution it is the first world "outside" (of course, not in the sense of external spatiality) of my own concrete ego. Therefore Husserl also called it the "primordial world" (or "primordial transcendence"). In contrast to this primordial transcendence, the transcendence of the objective world proves to be a world at a higher level in that it already presupposes the constitution of "others".

Among all bodies found in this actually reduced nature there stands out that one which I call "my body". It is privileged in that I impute to it "fields of sensations" and control it in immediate action. In the sphere of reduced to ownness, the "other human being" who appears in it is at first nothing but a "body": reduced to ownness. For Husserl's theory of the experience of someone else the following is of fundamental importance: Through an apperceptive transfer, based on [the perception of] my body, I impute to this other body the sense, "body", and that is from the outset the sense, "other body". This occurs in the mode of analogy. What is called here "'analogizing' apprehension"–or, using another term, "appresentation"–is a specific form of mediate intentionality. It is not at all limited to experience of others but comprises the whole vast realm of "pregivenness". Its character is the following: intertwined with the immediate givenness of an A itself is a co-givenness of B, which is appresented. This B itself never acquires real "presence", never becomes actual perception. However it is always intertwined with something perceived as it itself given – the A. For instance, with the directly perceived front of a thing its unseen back is always appresented.

The phenomenon of appresentation is only a special case of the universal phenomenon of "pairing". And the latter is nothing else but that primordial form of passive synthesis which can also be called "association" in a specific sense, that of "similarity" and "dissimilarity". When appresenting someone else, my own primordially reduced body is the always vividly present and primally instituting original. A "body" enters into my field of perception "similar" to my animate body; that means that it is of such a character that it has to enter into a phenomenal pairing with my own body. When this occurs, on the basis of perceiving my body

[7]For a discussion of Schutz's clearly long-standing criticism of Husserl's "second epoché" see Fred Kersten, *Phenomenological Method: Theory and Practice* (Dordrecht, 1989), pp. 58ff.

[8]The French phrase in parentheses is included by Schutz in his text, taken from the French translation; the equivalent German phrase used by Schutz is "*eigenheitlich reduzierte Natur*", that is, Husserl's phrase. The use of this phrase and others of Husserl's German text lends credence to the view that Schutz, like others at this time, had already seen the German text which circulated among the privileged few (Dorion Cairns was another who, at this time, also read the typescript of the German text). [FK]

I transfer the sense, "body", that is, "body of someone else". In order that an appresentation gain permanence and not immediately turn out to be an illusion, it must prove itself in further appresentations which are synthetically consistent. Thus, the sense, "body of someone else", must manifest itself continuously as "animate body" and therefore as "body of someone else" through its always consistent "behavior".

Appresented in analogizing modification, we also find with this experience of animate bodies of others everything which belongs to the concretization of this other ego as the other's primordial world in addition to the completely concrete ego of someone else. "The other therefore is appresentationally constituted as another monad in mine". Accordingly the other appears in my primordial world as an intentional modification of my self, even though appresented from the beginning with the sense, "self of someone else". I view the body of something else as *other* body, and not as a duplication of my own body. Among other things, this becomes clear in the following considerations: I myself am the bodily center of a primordial world oriented around me; my primordial characteristic as monad carries the index of "*hic*", of here. But the appearing body of someone else in my primordial sphere shows the index of "*illic*", of there, even though this index stands in the mode of the absolute "*hic*" for the other. While the "other body" there enters into a pairing association with my body here, the other is appresented as a now co-existing ego in the mode of there and thus of another ego. Both, however, belong to the functional communality of *one* and the same presenting-appresenting perception. Therefore that nature which appears in the primordial sphere of the other, and the animate body of the other which appears to me in the mode of *there*, are from the outset *the same* as the central body which appears to the other in the mode of here. Only: the *actual* perceptions are not the same. This is so because my changing perspectives are centered in my body here as zero-point (thus, "seen from there", "as if I were there"). But at the same time there is also constituted the objective nature of the phenomena of experience. This happens because my primordially constituted nature acquires a second level; it is appresentative, experienced and experienceable and issues from the experience of someone else: the same nature in the possible manners of givenness of someone else. This identifying synthesis of the same nature is simultaneously given and proven primordially and appresentatively. With it the co-existence of my ego and the other ego is primally instituted along with a common form of time.

In summary, it may be said that the intentionality of the experience of the someone else transcends my ownness, even though it takes place within the sphere of my ownness. Indeed, my primordial monad constitutes a monad of someone else which is extraneous and existing for itself, yet it is appresentatively demonstrable to me. However, thereby is founded only the first communality between ego and alter ego. Without difficulty all other intersubjective communalities can be derived from it: the human communality – I and others and everyone as human among other humans who have reciprocal experiences of one another and are experienced by me as such. From it also results the transcendental correlate of the communality of the monads in transcendental intersubjectivity. The latter, likewise, is constituted in me, the meditating ego, purely from sources of my intentionality. The specifically "social" communalizations follow and issue from "I-you-acts"; there correspond to them in the objective world the spiritual objectivities of social communalities, among them the "personalities of a higher order";[9] there is, furthermore, the "cultural world" which already presupposes primordial and secondary constitutions on different levels. Their constitution in itself is "oriented" around a "zero-point", a personality ("I and my culture").

It is in this way that the investigations reported on here realize their "Cartesian program", that is, the uncovering of the universal constitution of the world on the basis of the transcendental ego and comprehensible in its aprioristic-structural regularity. From this follows a whole set of new tasks for the continuation of the <investigations>, as Husserl indicates at the end. There is the problem of an *apriori* ontology of the real world, that is, the separation of the *apriori* which belongs to its universality; for it, every ontological conclusion which has been positively achieved is mere preparation. Furthermore, there results the problem of the concrete constitutive interpretation of primordial nature, most of all the genetic analysis of its space and its time, including the thing-phantoms which appear in it (corresponding to the questions of the origins of space, time, and perceptions of objects, often treated in psychology – although by disregarding their intentional genesis). In addition, there are certain metaphysical consequences, so for instance the generative problems of birth and death. Correctly understood – not in the sense of traditional, naïve metaphysics – they all recur to and can be constitutively demonstrated as constitutive problems in the monadic and intermonadic spheres. Finally, there is the problem of an *apriori* and pure intentional psychology, which is free from everything psychophysical. As eidetic science, it would have to execute the interpretation of the phenomena of intentional constitution in the natural conception of the world. Its fundamental structure has been already predesigned in the expositions of phenomenology.

To Husserl's list I would like to add a social science which, while limited to the social sphere, is of an eidetic character. The task <of such a social science> would be the intentional analysis of those manifold forms of higher-level social acts and social formations which are founded on the – already executed – constitution of the *alter ego*. This can be achieved in static and genetic analyses, and such an interpretation would accordingly have to demonstrate the aprioristic structures of the social sciences.

Of necessity the preceding expositions are rather incomplete and unfortunately often inexact. Nevertheless, they may have conveyed to the reader an idea of the fundamental significance of Husserl's investigations not only for pure philosophy but also for all human sciences [*Geisteswissenschaften*] and especially for the social sciences. But they will also have shown the extraordinary difficulties of the content of these investigations. Like all works of Husserl, the present one too will have to be conquered in painstaking studies. Anyone who does not shun them will be rewarded by the recognition that this book, with its classic expositions, will provide radically

[9]Wagner notes here that in his later work Alfred Schutz strongly objected to Husserl's idea of "personalities of a higher order".

new philosophical insights of the greatest consequences. This will be true even if one cannot agree with it all.

This book has appeared only in French. The skill of the translators merit praise. Unfortunately, this circumstance makes access to the book more difficult for the German reader. I wish to express the hope that its great author will not withhold any longer the original text from the German public.[10]

[10]See footnote 3 above.

CHAPTER 20

Husserl's *Formal and Transcendental Logic*

Editors' Preface

After reviewing Husserl's *Cartesian Meditations*, Schutz next reviewed Husserl's *Formale und transzendentale Logik. Versuch einer Kritik der logischen Vernunft* (Halle: Max Niemeyer, 1929), again for the *Deutsche Literaturzeitung* (1933, pp. 773–784). The English translation is a revision of one made by Helmut Wagner.

The review of Husserl's *Méditations Cartésiennes* (*Deutsche Literaturzeitung*, 1932, pp. 240ff.) recently published here reported on the most recent development of phenomenology. The present work under review offers an introduction to philosophy beginning with the elements of traditional formal logic. The *objective* constituents of the latter are subjected to a step-by-step critique by way of uncovering those hidden *subjective* forms which produce the theoretical formations, the objectivities of judgments and cognitions. Everything objectively logical has its correlate in its constituting intentionalities and the habitualities of thinking that emerge from them are systematically revealed by the thematizing logical activity directed to the subjective. As a result it is shown that all problems of logic directed to the subjective are not problems of a natural human subjectivity and thus not *psychological* problems, but instead problems of that *"transcendental subjectivity"* in the life of consciousness of which alone everything exists and acquires its meaning of being. This train of thought leads from formal to transcendental logic. It directly continues in the direction in which Husserl choose to move in his *Logical Investigations* (1900–1901).

For the purpose of clarifying the sense of traditional formal logic, Husserl turns first to objective themes. Like all positive sciences, traditional formal logic too investigates only these themes. <In contradistinction>, thematizing of the subjective is related to psychologism in its various forms. It is not even pursued with the innate means of logic when, as in the problem of "evidence", it becomes particularly conspicuous as the subjective correlate of the problem of truth. According to Husserl, the main reason for this is that formal logic emerged originally as formal *apophantics*, that is, as a theory of the forms of assertoric propositions ("judgments" in the strict logical sense).

This apophantic sphere has to be closely analyzed. It soon turns out that it is in no way uniform; rather it displays a characteristic triple stratum of its basic concepts. Each of its strata corresponds to a different logical discipline.

1. The first formal-logical discipline in itself is the pure theory of the forms of judgments as established by Aristotle: the theory of the division of judgments, of conclusions, and of the modalization of judgments, etc. If developed consistently, this discipline will be expanded to a "pure theory of the forms of significations", that is, to a grammar of pure logic. Its theme is the "mere possibility of judgments as judgments without posing the question of whether they are true or false or even whether, as mere judgments, they are compatible or contradictory".

2. The second stage of formal logic is reached when the question does not concern all possible forms of judgment but the *possible* forms *of true* judgments: the closed realm of consequence-logic (logic of non-contradiction). According to the essential laws of "judgment-consequence" the latter has to investigate the ("analytic") inclusion of judgments of specific forms in the corresponding premise-judgments. This thematic of formal logic could also be called *pure apophantic analytics*. Here one does not yet speak of the truths of individual judgments but only of their pure compatibility with one another. To the latter belongs also the compossibility of arbitrarily produced collections of judgments.

3. A third set of problems, comparatively higher than that of the consequence-logic, is reached when one poses the question of the essential conditions of possible truths. This had not as yet become thematic in the logic of non-contradiction. One – although only one – of these essential conditions is that of non-contradiction.

The separation of the two higher stages – consequence-logic and truth-logic – finds its correlate in specific modes of execution or, as one may also say, in specific differences in the evidences of judgments. According to very different manners of subjective givenness "the same" judgment may be evidentially "confused" or "distinct", "clear" or "obscure". The first pair of concepts corresponds to consequence-logic, the second to truth-logic. A vague judicative meaning can be made "distinct" simply by *explication* what is confusedly meant in it; and this by continuously filling with content the intentionalities which imply what is meant. Accordingly, what is explicated is made evident as the meaning "proper". Yet, to judge explicitly and thus distinctly is not yet equal to judging "in clarity". Rather clear judgments acquire their own evidences. In them is brought to self-givenness that to which the cognizing person aspires, namely, to clarify those affairs and affair-complexes which are objects of judgings.

For this reason every judgment which is impossible in distinctness is possible in confusion. And every judgment which is impossible in cognition with insight in clarity is possible in distinctness. Only judging in the fullness of clarity can be cognition and thus be *true* judging. However, in pure analytics thematizing is only the evidence of distinctness judging is made thematic; whether or not this judging can be made clear and become cognition directed upon truth remains unthematized. In pure analytics (consequence-logic) – aside from the "form" characteristic of all judging – judgings and judgment-members comprise as moments of their own essence merely the relations of inclusion (consistency), of exclusion (inconsistency), and of empty non-contradiction (compatibility of judging). Pure analytics deals only with analytic but not material countersense; and questions of "adequacy to the things themselves" do not belong to this realm. However for its part truth-logic presupposes pure analytics. In penetrating analyses which unfortunately cannot be discussed here, Husserl shows how the principles which explicate the concepts of truth and falsehood in traditional truth-logic find their analogies but also their justifications in the realm of pure analytics: so the principles of contradiction, excluded middle, of the *modus ponens*, and of the *modus tollens*.

The apophantic analytics, the strata of which were presented above, correspond to the closedness of traditional logic based on the Aristotelian concept of the form of judgment. It is not identical with the idea of formal logic universally. The latter also includes formal mathematical analysis as well as its unification with traditional syllogistics in a "*mathesis universalis*" in Leibniz's sense, i.e., in a logically fundamental science of mathematical form and rigor pertaining to a universal mathematics in the highest and most inclusive sense.

The thematic sense of formal mathematical analysis may be clarified first in juxtaposition with Aristotelian apophantic analytics. The definitionally fundamental concept of the latter is the assertoric proposition and thus the predicative judgment. It is easily expanded into an apophantic mathematics. It can be clearly seen that one can "calculate" as easily with propositions as with numbers. Now, opposed to this apophantic mathematics stands the traditional "formal analysis" of mathematicians, the mathematics of quantities, combinations, pluralities, multiplicities, etc. It has to be called non-apophantic mathematics because in it predicative propositions ("judgments" in the logical sense) do not appear at all as thematically fundamental concepts. Closer investigations show that the predicative "formal mathematical discipline" is adequate for them. Their fundamental concepts can be presented as deductive forms of the highest concept of form: "anything whatever", "any object whatever". Developed in its essence, this formal mathematics should be expandable to an "*apriori* theory of objects referring to the modes of 'anything whatever'". Or, using a term already introduced in the *Logical Investigations*, it can be expanded into a "formal ontology". Thus the clarification of the relationship between formal logic and formal mathematics can be achieved only by shedding light on the relationship between formal apophantics and formal ontology.

Regardless of the thematic differences <between formal apophantics and formal ontology>, Husserl demonstrated already in the *Logical Investigations* the material congruity of both. Now he demonstrates that a completely formal mathematics, expanded to *mathesis universalis*, is identical with complete logical analytics. At the beginning this occurs by defining the highest stratum of formal logic as a theory of deductive systems, that is, as a theory of the possible theoretical forms or a "theory of multiplicities" (in the modern mathematical sense). In the spirit of mathematical terminology, the concept of multiplicity is to be understood here as that of a realm of cognition as such, controlled by a theory which is *determined only in form*. Thus it designates a realm which is determined exclusively by the fact that it is subjected to a theory of this kind. Out of this concept grows the task, already sharply circumscribed in the *Prolegomena*, to attempt a theory that would deductively comprise all possible forms of the manifold (about the important concept of the *definite manifold*, cf. *Ideas*, pp. 135f.[1]

The duality of formal logic as formal apophantics and formal ontology is subjected to further phenomenological elucidation. In its course it is shown that the difference between the two consists in their thematic focus. The first aims essentially a *judgments* (and at the "syntactical" formations which are parts of judgments), and the second at *objects*. Finally, it is shown that the *mathesis universalis* too contains a differentiation in truth-logic and consequence-logic.

The result is the uncovering of the objective themes of analytical logic. Now the question of sense and justification can be raised with regard to the inititially postulated logical thematizing directed to subjectivity. By posing this question did we not fall prey to that psychologism which it is the great and unchallenged merit of Husserl to have opposed in the realm of logic in the first volume of his *Logical Investigations*? This is not all the case. Phenomenology, instead, demonstrates in careful analyses with intuition and evidence the ideality of logical formations in contrast to the psychologistic prejudice that formations of judgments display sense and existence only as phenomena of inner experience. Of course the *processes* of thinking are real happenings in real psychical life; but not so the *thoughts* which are produced in these processes of thinking. Such thoughts are "ideal (or, better, "irreal") objects; they are experienced with the same evidence as real objects. Here "evidence" is not to be taken as an appeal to an enigmatic and unmotivated apodicticity, as is done only too often. Rather it signifies the "intentional achievement of the giving of something-itself", the most universally distinctive formation of "consciousness of something" in which that of which there is consciousness is grasped as "it "itself". Thus evidence is "experience" in the widest sense; that is, "the primal instituting of the being-for-us of objects in their objective sense".

The form of the giving of something-itself, in which *logical formations* appear in their singularity, is that of the activity which produces it in the first place. In the forming activity of judging the ideal object, "judicative sense", is produced. This sense "is" not, as psychologism claims, merely "in" or "during" its production; it outlasts the acts of production. However, there is consciousness of ideal objects in their originary production in an intentionality of the form of spontaneous activity. And their manners of givenness in such originary activity is a form of perception which is their very own. One of the most significant tasks of phenomenology is the uncovering of the achievements of constituting subjectivity which are included in all theorizing.

This constituting subjectivity is not the psychophysical I who, tied to the given world, is itself part of this world. Rather it is transcendental subjectivity; it is that *ego cogito* existing prior to all positing of the world and in whose actions alone the world is itself constituted. This idea will be clear to everyone familiar with Husserl's earlier writings. When we execute the "phenomenological reduction" we abstain

[1]The page numbers are to the first edition, found in the margin of the English translation by Fred Kersten, Edmund Husserl, *Ideas Pertaining to a Pure Phenomenology and to a Phenomenological Philosophy. First Book. General Introduction to a Pure Phenomenology* (The Hague: Martinus Nijhoff, 1982).

from any experiential belief in the existence of the world as well as from any position about its objective existence. We "bracket" not only the transcendental objects [*Objekte*] but also the mundane psychological I, both of which belong to this world. Nevertheless what remains is the transcendental *ego cogito* and its cogitations and with them those unique achievements of intentionality which before I characterized as evidence. It is necessary now to explore such evidence closely in the phenomenological reduction, that is, in relation to the transcendental subject.

The author extensively treats this set of problems of transcendental logic in the second part of his book. Here I can indicate that treatment only in broad outline. Initially Husserl shows that every critique of analytical logic presupposes a subjectively oriented critique of its basic concepts and their subjective constitution. To carry it out, it is necessary above all to uncover and enter into the *constitution of the idealizing presuppositions* of analytical logic. First of all it turns out that the purely mathematical analytic (logic of consequence) does not relate to the intentionalities of judgings given in actual evidence which appear more or less "confused" or more or less "explicit" in experienced variations. It relates instead to the formations that are produced in the generating acts whose being-in-itself is established in identity. But traditional logic naïvely presupposes the living evidence of the transcending being of judgments instead of methodically investigating it as to its constitution. A further idealization as well is never explicitly brought out: the implicit presupposition of the reiterable infinity of "and so on" or, subjectively speaking, of "one can always again". Yet these idealizations silently underlie all essentially necessary reiterable sets of laws of the theory of analytic forms.

The emphasis on idealizing presuppositions which are contained in the basic principles becomes still more important in the transition from the consequence-logic to truth-logic. For instance, the proposition of excluded middle tacitly implies that in principle every judgment can be made adequate but further also that a judgment is true or false for everyone. Thus traditional logic assumes that all judgments can be decided in principle – if not for us so in themselves. Yet this logic does not recognize truth and falsehood as "constituting characteristics" of the judgment. But just the evidence for presupposing "truth" has to be investigated according to its characteristic sense and its consequences. Thus the question, "What is truth?" becomes the powerful problem of the possibility of reducing the critique of the evidence of logical principles to the critique of the evidence of experience.

This problem can be mastered only with the help of the analysis of the constituting sense. The judgment – like any other sense-formation – can be "investigated as to the history of this sense". This can be done by uncovering the intentional implications which are hidden in its "open and finished" sense. If we pursue this genesis of the sense of judgments we obtain a principle of genetic order or, subjectively speaking, a prefigured order of the process of making materially evident. For this analysis the first step must be the reduction of the judgment to its substrata, to the "objects about which" judgments are made. This means going back to the ultimate "core" basic to all syntaxes of judgment which are not themselves syntaxes.

For the consequence-logic, this signifies reduction to the final meanings of something, to the primal category of the "absolute something" and its variations. And this signifies for truth-logic the reduction to individual objects which, in their experiential existence, are therefore prior to all judging, to all "predicating". In its prime and pregnant sense, experience defines itself immediately as the direct relationship to that which is individual. But the genetic analysis of evidence cannot stop with simple judgments of experience. Rather it turns out that certainty, evident having of something itself, being identical, and identical sense are not exclusively characteristics of the predicative sphere. They already belong to the intentionality of the experience that is given prior to all judgments and are therefore "prepredicative". It follows that every theory of judgment has to be preceded by a theory of experience, of apperception, of passive "association". The genesis of these intentional achievements again points back to the time-form of intentional genesis and its constitution. On the other hand a fully developed theory of judgment has to describe unique higher evidences, moving upward from experience presentive of individual objects. These higher evidences become recognizable as soon as one executes eidetic universalizations in the sense of the material *apriori* (gained from the own essential content of what is materially individual, yet re-interpreted as example) but also of the formal *apriori* (resulting from emptying the content of what is individual, making it into anything-whatever).

The critique of the concept of truth is not at all concluded with this clarification of evidence and its achievements. Taken either as formal apophantics or as formal ontology, traditional logic has not raised the question of the possibility of anything existent whatever and thereby does not contain ultimate and absolute evidence. Traditional logic has instead naïvely postulated the world as being and as pregiven to everyone. Thus it places itself in the ranks of the *positive* sciences. All judgments, truths, all sciences to which this logic refers, concern actual existence within this naïvely presupposed world or else the latter itself. As envisioned by this logic, the *apriori* sciences are also mundane. This attitude has not been changed by the critique of experience by Descartes and his successors. When treating transcendental themes, they all operate with the naïve assumptions of ontological logical evidences.

The universal problem of transcendental philosophy reveals itself only if we return to the *ego cogito* in the pursuit of subjective logical themes. That which exists does so only in [acts of] evidence; that is, it exists if we execute the transcendental reduction to the *ego cogito* as subject of pure consciousness. Only on this ground is it possible to clarify the essence of "experience" and thereby of experiencing being, which is always "transcendent" being. But also the sense of "others", of consociates as well as of the "objective" world, which is world not just for me but also for others, [exist in acts of evidence]. It is the task of transcendental phenomenology to uncover the constitution of all that which exists in the subjectivity of consciousness.

The culmination of the whole presentation is reached in the present work in the chapters comprising pp. 197–235 which, for the most part, deal only with a sketch of the program of [transcendental phenomenology]. How the constitutive analysis departs from one's own subjectivity so as to develop the transcendental problems of intersubjectivity and of the intersubjective world, cannot, however, be further considered. Husserl dealt extensively with this problem in his *Méditations Cartésiennes of 1931*, which has already been extensively reviewed in this journal.

The basic idea of the transcendental-phenomenological constitutive analysis is the following: Everything which occurs in consciousness includes a *sedimented history* the intentional implications of which can be uncovered as constitutive achievements of consciousness. However, these analyses are not carried out as empirical investigations. They are instead investigations into essences and thus acquire an aprioristic character. By free variation of single factual cases, which may be seen as mere "examples", that which remains invariable in all these variations can be brought to light, that is to say we discover the essential ontic form, or the Eidos, exemplified by the examples. It then becomes clear that to every ontic *apriori* there corresponds a constitutive *apriori*. The former can be reduced to the latter so that the whole life of consciousness is dominated by an *apriori* which is universally constitutive, comprising all intentionalities which, because describable by way of the eidetic method and therefore in true universal validity.

It is here that we also find the final and radical separation of transcendental philosophy from psychology. As transcendental Ego, as constituting subjectivity, I am for myself in apodictic necessity. In contrast, the constituted world, along with my psychological and psycho-physical ego as human soul (person), has only presumptive existence (even though it is always again reaffirmed in the stream of my harmonious experience). All together, world, person, and the like, are "mundane concepts", transcendent apperceptions, and thus belong to the universal transcendental problem of the constitution of any objectivities whatever. Psychology is meaningful only as positive science, that is, only as a branch of anthropolgy. Its theme, then, is solely the psychological ego bound to the world.

If psychological analysis is executed in an eidetic-*apriori* way (which is always posssible) then it is constitutive analysis in the natural attitude (psychological phenomenology); that is, it maintains its relation to the corporeal and to the mundane. However, the results of the intentional analyses of transcendental phenomenology are also valid even in psychological apperception (although the transcendental attitude can be acquired from psychological apperception only by bracketing the world).

As shown, all problems of sense belonging to logic and science are not psychological ones but instead problems of transcendental intersubjectivity. It therefore follows that a genuine philosophical logic as theory of the eidetic possibilities of genuine science can originate only in connection with transcendental phenomenology. According to Husserl, traditional logic, thanks to its naïve reference to the world, is unable to help positive sciences out of their positivity which blocks the clarification of the meaning of the existence of their disciplines. Only transcendental phenomenology, because it has not succumbed to the world, is self-interpretation by the transcendental Ego as the sole absolute being. It alone can achieve the originary founding of all sciences as branches of constitutive achievements of one's own subjectivity. As a result, it eliminates both the bogeyman of an absolute being emptily presupposed and the illusion of an "absolute truth" which wants to be more than a regulative idea, namely more than the interpretation of the horizons of those intentional achievements which are called evidence. Husserl's book concludes with a short reference to the essential style of such a theory of evidence.

Obviously the preceding description of the course of these investigations can trace only the chief lines of thought. Important chapters have had to remain outside the purview of the reviewer. Thus, for instance, the three appended studies about syntactical forms and syntactical materials, about the phenomenological constitution of judgments, and about the idea of a logic of mere non-contradiction. These sections offer significant views of far-reaching investigations (the future publication of which Husserl announces).

This work is written in the most pregnant way and makes great demands upon the reader, It requires stamina, commitment, and strictest self-discipline. In its radicalism, this work eschews any compromise and offers access to the themes which comprise transcendental subjectivity by phenomenological research, that is, research into a depth the significance of which as yet cannot be fully appraised for philosophy. Anyone seriously concerned with the foundation of philosophy as a rigorous science will have to deal critically with this book and its circle of problems.

CHAPTER 21

Husserl's Notes Concerning the Constitution of Space

EDITORS' PREFACE

Schutz provided this "Editor's Preface" to a text of Husserl made available to the editors of *Philosophy and Phenomenological Research*, where it appeared in its original German version.[1] Husserl had written the text in 1934, and was one among several short pieces culled from Husserl's literary estate by Father H.L. Van Breda who had rescued it and transferred it to the University of Louvain.[2] As it appears here, Schutz's Preface appears substantially as it did in *Philosophy and Phenomenological Research*.

Among the reasons for including this brief preface here is that it shows the approach Schutz employed to Husserl's writings as well as how he regarded these unfinished works and the great importance he attached to them. But in addition Schutz is likewise mindful of the caution that must be exercised in reading them – a caution, it may be added, valid as much for Husserl's unfinished work as Schutz's own.

The following pages reproduce a manuscript of Edmund Husserl written in May 1934, and deal with the problem of the phenomenological constitution of space. It continues the manuscript composed at the same time and treating of the same topic published in *Philosophical Essays in Memory of Edmund Husserl* under the title, "Grundlegende Untersuchungen zum phänomenologischen Ursprung der Räumlichkeit der Natur".[3] This paper is only fully understandable as an attempt to approach some of the special analyses required by the basic problem considered in the first

[1]Edmund Husserl, "Notizen zur Raumkonstitution: Fortsetzung der Untersuchungen zur phänomenologischen Interpretation der kopernikanischen Lehre", *Philosophy and Phenomenological Research*, I (1940), pp. 23–37.

[2]See H. L. Van Breda, "Le sauvetage de l'héritage husserlien et la fondation des Archives-Husserl", *Husserl et la Pensée Moderne* (Den Haag: Martinus Nijhoff, 1959), pp. 1–77.

[3]*Philosophical Essays in Memory of Edmund Husserl*, edited by Marvin Farber (Cambridge, Mass.: Harvard University Press, 1940), pp. 305–326. (See also Edmund Husserl, *Shorter Works*, edited by Peter McCormick and Frederick Elliston, forward by Walter Biemel (Notre Dame: University of Notre Dame Press, 1981), "Foundational Investigations of the Phenomenological Origin of the Spatiality of Nature", translated by F. Kersten, pp. 222–233.)

essay. Both manuscripts are only first sketches for future studies. They are not worked out either from the point of view of style or of thought. They manifest all the merits and all the disadvantages of a first recording of a great inspiration. On the one hand, they reflect the ecstasy of discovery, the freshness and the originality of a first look into realms as yet unknown, the rapture of the creative spirit to which truth of a new kind reveals itself, the superabundance of ideas and the adventures of catching the thought in transition. On the other hand, the thought is not yet organized; the problems are intermingled; more or less relevant ideas are side by side on the same level; there are paradoxes and contradictions, repetitions and recommencements; the language is aphoristic and obscure with odds and ends of meaning substituted for detailed cross-references. These manuscripts of Husserl should not be considered as papers, not even as rough drafts of future literary works, but rather as a philosophical diary, a scrapbook of his thought.

There are more than forty thousand pages of posthumous manuscripts of Edmund Husserl. To understand this fact, we have to consider the manner of working of this extraordinary man who once said about himself that he had no merit other than to have tried to live a philosophical life to its fullest and most earnest strength. Since his retirement from academic lecturing, Husserl's typical day's work was as follows: In the forenoon, he took extended walks in the beautiful environs of Freiburg, accompanied by his assistants and by one or two of his closest disciples.[4] He liked to discuss with them those problems with which he occupied himself. Day after day and with exacting regularity, he spent three hours of the afternoon at his desk, writing what he had considered during the morning walk, rereading old manuscripts and working over them, a continual meditation, his pen in hand. Regardless of his physical or psychical disposition, regardless of disturbances by the external work, he continued his daily philosophical work with admirable self-discipline and conscientiousness. He liked to relate how, even if sometimes he found himself ill-disposed, he used all his energy "to set himself going". And each time, after having written for half an hour what came into his mind, the true buoyancy appeared and he worked in a satisfactory manner. The manuscripts so produced, therefore, contain the most important meditations of a passionate thinker as well as repetitions of ideas which the author himself had presented in a better and clearer manner elsewhere.

Whereas the manuscript published in the Husserl memorial volume seems to be written in a quiet state of mind and was reproduced without much reconstruction, unfortunately this is not the case with the present manuscript whose title page bears Husserl's note: "Zum Teil unter ganz argen Störungen zusammengeschrieben" ("Partially written under very great disturbances and difficulties").

Not without hesitation, therefore, have the editors of this journal decided to publish the following pages, brought into their hands by a happy chance, in an authorized, typewritten transcription of the original manuscript which, as do all the Husserlian manuscripts, uses symbols of a strange German shorthand known only by Husserl himself and by very few of this closest assistants. They recognized the danger that certain passages could provoke an enormous misunderstanding of Husserl's general

[4]See for example, Dorion Cairns, *Conversations with Husserl and Fink.* Edited by the Husserl-Archives in Louvain with a Foreword by Richard M. Zaner (The Hague: Martinus Nijhoff, 1976).

conception of philosophy among those who are beginners in phenomenological research or especially among those who never studied Husserl's chief works and who hope to gain a well-founded insight into his thoughts by reading this manuscript. These readers cannot be cautioned emphatically enough against forming precipitate conclusions. One of the most serious misinterpretations of Husserl's attempt at any analysis of space, for instance, would be the supposition that this philosopher ever had the intention of substituting constructions of a primitive speculation for the accomplishments of modern science and mathematics, which he knew as thoroughly as anyone. It must be reserved for another occasion to develop the motives for Husserl's set-up of this study and to circumscribe the place it has within the system of his philosophy.

This is essentially why the editors of this journal feel that the publication will be accessible only to those students who are familiar not only with Husserl's published work but also with the general structure of his style of philosophizing and with the peculiar character of his approach to problems and method of dealing with them. However, they believe that a glimpse of Husserl at work will definitely be a source of emotion and interest to those students in addition to the fundamental importance of the problem developed by the author in these notes. We are not presenting a finished work of Husserl but a fragment of work in progress – "quasi una fantasia", to use the words of Beethoven. But where is the friend of music who would not be delighted to have a true record of an improvisation of Beethoven, played by him, offhand, in the seclusion of his workshop?

The undersigned had the honor to be entrusted with the supervision of the manuscript by the board of editors of this journal. He accepted this task mindful that the men best qualified for this mission, i.e., Husserl's personal assistants in the last years of his life, would not be available during the European war. He made up his mind to refrain from all modifications of Husserl's text and to reproduce its wording unchanged, restricting himself, accordingly, to inserting such additions as seem advisable to him for logical or linguistic reasons, for the purpose of transforming aphoristic fragments into whole sentences and clearer grammatical constructions. The latter was done especially for readers whose mother tongue is not the German language. As the text of the original is extremely difficult, even for German-born people, and since the meaning of certain sentences and paragraphs is not clear, the additions made by the undersigned and marked with [brackets] frequently have the character of philological conjectures and often are open to criticism.[5] However, the reader always has the prerogative of checking and amending them because, by disregarding the terms within the brackets, he will find the original text of Husserl's manuscript.

Concerning the philosophical content of both studies – the present as well as the first one, published in the Husserl memorial volume – the writer looks forward to saying a few words in an early issue of this journal. He feels that Husserl could have added to both pages the same footnote which Leibniz, a philosopher whose manner of working was analogous to that of Husserl, bestowed upon one of his most important manuscripts: *Hic egregie progressus sum.*

[5]Note of Alfred Schutz: Valuable counsel has been received from Professor Felix Kaufmann, who has read the manuscript. I wish to express my sincere thanks to him.

CHAPTER 22

Husserl's *Crisis of Western Sciences*

EDITORS' PREFACE

This letter of Alfred Schutz to Eric Voegelin was written between 11 November and 13 December, 1943. It contains an extensive reply to a sweeping critique of Husserl's *Die Krisis der europäischen Wissenschaften und die transzendentale Phänomenologie*[1] which his friend Eric Voegelin had developed in a letter to him. Voegelin had found merit in some of Husserl's lines of thought but on the whole rejected them as much in their references to historical trends in European philosophy, which he showed to be arbitrarily selective and hence at variance with historiographical facts and objectivity, as in their philosophical inferiority because they were merely epistemological undertakings and as such did not reach the level of genuine philosophizing (i.e., they did not constitute a metaphysics). Schutz's defense of Husserl followed two lines of thought: First, that Voegelin misunderstood the whole philosophical intent of Husserl when he considered his interest in past philosophers as serving historiographical interests instead of interest in the problems they had posed; and, second, even if the whole philosophy of Husserl could be subsumed under the heading of epistemology, it would still maintain its high philosophical respectability.

At the very end of the letter Schutz spoke of the possibility of continuing this defense of Husserl's way of philosophizing in a further letter. However, no evidence has been found to indicate that he found the time to continue his attempt at vindicating Husserl's philosophical dignity.

The English translation of the letter is by Helmut Wagner.[2]

Your extensive and important remarks about Husserl's essay labelled by him *Krisis der europäischen Wissenschaften* deserve a careful and extensive response. Geographical distance forces us to written exchanges; at the least, this shall offer us the advantage of putting our ideas into the clearest possible and most orderly form.

Initially a personal word may be said about my relationship to the essay of Husserl

[1]Edmund Husserl, *Philosophia*, 1936.

[2]For the relationship between Eric Voegelin and Alfred Schutz, see Helmut Wagner, *Alfred Schutz. An Intellectual Biography*, Chapter 12 (the letter of Schutz to Voegelin translated here is discussed, pp. 191ff.).

which is the object of these considerations. I openly confess that I do not face it in a completely objective way. It is particularly close to my heart because during the years in which I was privileged to carry out many a serious dialogue with Husserl I have watched the essay originate and grow, and was fortunate to learn something about the over-all plan of the fragment. Thus I know that Husserl planned the work to encompass six to eight essays, each of which was to be as long as the one published. He expected it to become the summary and crowning of his philosophical life-work. So it is understandable that some of Husserl's enthusiasm was transferred to me. Indeed, it seems to me, as well as to you, that many things in this essay belong to the best of what we have inherited from Husserl. So most of all the chapter on Galileo.

Your main argument against the published part, but also against the whole of Husserl's work, is the following: you accept the achievements of Husserl in the area of epistemology but deny that they are a philosophically respectable undertaking. Epistemology may be a prologue to philosophy, but it is not a philosophical beginning. In none of his published writings did Husserl touch on any fundamental problem of philosophy, and it can hardly be expected that his literary estate would reveal new dimensions.

There are several things to be said to this point.

In the first place, it is a matter of personal evaluation whether one will refuse philosophical rank to an "epistemological achievement", as you call Husserl's work. I am convinced that the discovery of the prepredicative sphere, the uncovering of the problem of intersubjectivity, the retracing of logic, mathematics, the natural sciences back to the grounds of the life-world, contributions to the analysis of the consciousness of inner time and to the constitution of space: these are examples culled from the fullness of his work, do indeed touch upon philosophically fundamental problems.

I do not know whether one has to apply the ideal-typical academic concept of epistemology to this kind of investigations; in principle it makes no difference to me. If this should be the case, epistemology is a pursuit worthy of a philosopher. I would go even further and say that it is just these – and perhaps only these – problems that can be treated within Husserl's ideal framework of a "philosophy as a strict science". But I fully understand and even share the notion that beyond this ideal there exist philosophically fundamental problems that cannot be made accessible with the means of a rigorously scientific method; they demand the courage to do metaphysics. (As you know, I personally felt the need to supplement my phenomenological studies through Leibniz and Kierkegaard).

Perhaps you will rightly and justifiably respond that Husserl claimed to have laid out, if not constructed, a genuine and definite system of a universal philosophy in his transcendental phenomenology – and that in contrast to his phenomenological psychology under the title of which fall, with a few exceptions, almost all his published works. I openly confess that I cannot pose as a defender of transcendental phenomenology because I fear it collapsed at decisive places. For instance, it did not escape transcendental solipsism, nor did it overcome the rift in the conception of the "constitution of the world by the transcendental ego": it begins with the construction of the world of experience by consciousness and ends up with the creation of the world by the ego-become-god.

I ascribe much of the responsibility for these outcomes to Eugen Fink. What I have heard from him about so-called "constructive phenomenology" (dealing with birth and death, life and aging and other genuinely metaphysical questions) has not made me confident that the publication of the literary estate of Husserl will offer a solution to the metaphysical questions, and therefore to the fundamental problems in your terms. However, I expect many contributions to the solution of most important questions of the type of Husserl's posthumous essays about the "Origin of Geometry" and the "Analysis of the Constitution of Space" (essays you may know); they are for me contributions of this kind.

All this does not alter the circumstance that we can do justice to Husserl's last work even if we do not find in it the solution to philosophically fundamental problems. However, for this purpose we must make the problem posed in this essay into our own. Nothing is more fruitless than to reproach a writer for showing interest in problems not of interest to the reader and then accuse him of not having seen the world with the reader's eyes and deem other things more relevant than those close to the reader's concerns. And this is what I fear you are doing in part of your otherwise excellent critique. Here I arrive at a basic remark.

You treat Husserl's essay as though he intended to develop an image of the cultural history of mankind, and that from a speculative perspective. The characteristic problems of the Averroistic speculation, correctly characterized by you, arise only from the grounds of such an ideal of the philosophical contemplation of history.[3] Only from there may one explain the contradiction between the two possibilities of understanding the world which you characterize as the Christian Orthodoxy and the Heterodoxy of Siger of Brabant.

Certainly questions of the relationship between world soul and individual soul belong to a historically collectivist metaphysics. And in this general sphere there appear theological problems of the kind you describe as the Zenoistic, Averoistic and Kantian types. You accuse Husserl of having shifted the problem of humanity from this universality to history and of having narrowed the conception of "humanity", making "man" into the finite historical product of only certain periods of human history – of antiquity and the modern age.

Had it been Husserl's intention, in his essay, to carry out a philosophical speculation of the kind you specified, all three of your objections would be justified even though they do not agree well with one another. Namely 1), that Husserl did not occupy clearly a philosophically basic position with respect to the history of mankind, 2) that he shifted the problem from the universal sphere to that of history, 3) that his historical image of the world is insufficient because of the narrow selectiveness.

[3]Although not explicit, Schutz is clearly referring to Voegelin's essay on Siger of Brabant published in *Philosophy and Phenomenological Research*, Vol. IV, no. 4, 1944, pp. 508–525 – a copy of which Schutz had no doubt seen in manuscript. The reference is to the transformation of Aristotelianism in the commentaries of Averroes by the Faculty of Arts at the University of Paris, and according to which philosophy became a form of life, a "style of existence", for an intellectual elite in political society; see pp. 511ff. [FK]

Moreover, if Husserl had aspired to write a philosophy of history that was cosmopolitan in intent, and were his concepts of "originary foundation" and "final foundation" to be understood in the sense of a progressive ideal like that of Kant, then the omission of the Kantian "astonishment" about the attempt at interpreting all prehistory only as a step toward the final foundation would indeed be reason for concern. Were this so, the temptation would be great to view Husserl's essay as an example of a "demonic" historiography, his philosophy of history as that of a typical philosophy in the three phases [of history], and himself as a "messianic doomsday figure of our time". If Husserl had aimed at writing history, he certainly would not have ignored the self-witnessing of great thinkers. But, as I understand it, nothing of this was Husserl's intention.

Husserl himself poses the problem of the self-contemplation of the Western philosopher in his acting and doing. According to my opinion, unlike the Greek thinkers he does not stand at the beginning of philosophical wonderment about a world to be discovered and to be interpreted. The world of philosophical problems has already been discovered and interpreted. We are not "beginners" in philosophizing, we did learn to philosophize about philosophical problems from our teachers and their teachers. A great tradition of the philosophical interpretation of the world has come down to us; it is our motivation to philosophize and our directive for the formulation of our own problems. The typical forms of the problems and the typical possibilities of their solutions are not only assigned as traditional contents to our understanding, they are pre-interpretations of our own possibilities and tasks. Even though we partake in the happenings of philosophy only very moderately, in the chain of generations we are founders of new traditions in that we change what we inherited and in the optimal case augment it. Thus there results for *every* philosopher, not just for the phenomenologist and for Husserl, the dual problem of the originary and final foundation of the tradition in which he lives and in which he partakes receivingly and givingly.

Basically, this problem is not at all limited to the philosopher; it is a most common one. With certain significant modifications which I cannot discuss here, it is the problem of effecting a pre-given world that has its own whither and whence, and whose style is predesigned by the givenness of this world. In the introductory part [of the *Krisis* essay] Husserl refers to the self-reflection of the philosopher as an anthropologically basic category which, as far as I know, he wanted to pursue in many directions in his planned essays. His reference to "man" and to "mankind" are to be understood in this sense as is his declaration proclaiming the philosopher as a representative of mankind.

But let us stay with the philosopher. He has two possibilities: either he lives in the tradition, allows himself to be motivated by it, takes for granted and remains directed upon the objectives of his work without noticing how and to what degree they are determined by tradition. This attitude will be typical in the great school-bound philosophies and in periods of secure metaphysical or religious truths of salvation. Or the philosopher no longer feels himself secure in the inherited tradition; it remains his foundation but does not make it possible for him to adhere to the idealization of the "and so on". What has been taken for granted now becomes questionable and will be questioned about its origin and its history of interpretation. But it will not be questioned from the perspective of an objectivating onlooker who wants to know "how it actually was" but from that of a passionate participant who wishes to explicate the implications of the traditions in so far – but only in so far – as this is necessary for his self-understanding. This attitude is typical for thinking during periods of great spiritual crises in which the so-called "fundamental problems" are posed not merely in specific sciences but also in philosophy itself.

This is the attitude of Husserl in the whole analysis he planned which justifiably bears the title "The Crisis of European Sciences and Transcendental Phenomenology" and whose introductory chapter is called "The Crisis of the Sciences as Expression of the Radical Life-Crisis of the Life of Western Mankind". It is not Husserl's intention to ask about the meaning of this history of philosophy. Likewise, it is not his intention to write an *"apologia pro vita sua"* or to manufacture a construction according to which all prior thinking was only a preamble for his own achievement: the full execution and justification of the ultimate foundation [of the ultimate truth].

In my opinion the comparison you make of Husserl with <Otto von> Gierke is an absolute misunderstanding of Husserl's attitude; it does not spring from self-satisfaction but just from that Kantian "astonishment" which you correctly recognize as a genuinely philosophical idea and which you assert is missing by Husserl.

It is this astonishment about the failure of tradition to solve the present crisis of philosophy and of his own philosophizing that urges Husserl, from his deliberately tradition-bound point of view, to ask about the origin of these handed-down contents which had been *autobiographically* determinate *for him*, for his problems, for his style of philosophizing. However, himself a philosopher, he describes an essential element of the philosophical tradition when he justifies his selection by his autobiographical interest.[4] The word I just used, "essential element", is to be understood immediately in a technical-phenomenological sense. Although autobiographical, it is an eidetic analysis of the tradition that determines Husserl's and thereby our present philosophical situation and poses questions for it. Tasks arise here in a two-fold sense: first, to define one's own vantage point, and, second, to understand the meaning of his own plans. In the face of the crisis of our times, these two tasks can only be carried out when the philosophizing person retrospectively gets hold of the motives and urges which have, first, brought him to philosophizing as such, and, second, to philosophizing in one or the other philosophical style. This purpose is not served by a mere inventory of the self-documentation of great thinkers or even a study about the history of the problem of cognition in the manner of Cassirer.[5] To the contrary: a universal oversight over the eternal treasure of philosophical problems in the their contexts, a reaching-back to the specific subjective meanings which certain formulations of, and solutions to, problems had for prior thinkers – this would be directly

[4]The importance of Schutz's understanding and assessment of Husserl's way of philosophizing as expressed in the *Crisis* cannot be stressed enough. Nor is it a philosophizing that Husserl comes to at the end of his life; it is a style present from the very beginning. See Fred Kersten, *Phenomenological Method: Theory and Practice*, pp. 32ff. for an account of it in Husserl's early writings. [FK]

[5]Schutz is no doubt referring here to Cassirer's multi-volumed *Das Erkenntnisproblem in der Philosophie und Wissenschaft der neueren Zeit* (Berlin: Verlag Bruno Cassirer, 1922ff.) [FK]

incompatible with the specific formulations of problems for Husserl. Standing *in* the tradition which motivates him and defines his projects, Husserl selects only those elements from the historical treasure chest which he feels are alive in his own thinking. He does not judge the mode of their agreement according to the meaning-structures in which they stood for their producers but according to those in which they stand for himself. This may be so because they came down to him in many pieces and in differing reinterpretations; it may be because he gave them a specific sense within his own world of work.

This last-named case deserves particular attention because it is bisected by a new circle of problems, and in particular the problem of the unavoidable self-misunderstanding of the philosopher (in general, of the actor) with respect to his interests, goals and solutions. The basic thesis (not formulated by Husserl) may be expressed as follows: the philosopher understands his problem (more generally, the actor his objective) always incompletely. For him it stands in an essentially unfathomable context of meaning comprising unclarified implications, emptily anticipated. It has its open horizons which cannot be interpreted because they are unrealized: everything is in doubt. In retrospect, the philosopher can sometimes interpret empty horizons; the co-philosophizing contemporary can do this more frequently; and the successors who stand in his tradition can do this always because in the meantime the horizons show their specific features and their implications have become visible.

This is the vital function of [Husserl's] critique of all forms of the continuation of the philosophical tradition. (In the motivational chain of practical actions other categories of the reactions replace those of criticism. However, in the present framework I cannot deal with these contexts). Of course, the critique is unending and becomes a newly-set task for every new generation. It establishes the contexts of meanings between its subject-matters and their implications which, however, can be recognized only afterwards.

I am of the opinion that Husserl saw all of these connections clearly even though possibly he may not have formulated them clearly. He treated them under the labels of originary and final foundations. Pursuing his own motives back through historical tradition he arrived at the originary foundation of philosophy by the Greeks and at the originary foundation of the mathematizing natural sciences by Galileo. Thus he pursued just what you yourself have posed in the second and third parts of your manuscript, namely the biographical *anamnesis* of one's own effective motives. Only Husserl enclosed in his autobiographical medium all of the philosophical tradition in so far, but only in so far, as it was or is alive for this thinking. Truly, it is curious that the parallel between Husserl's intention and that of your own manuscript escaped your attention.

This much about originary foundation. The entelechistic character of the image of history established on this foundation results from the principle of turning back to tradition and of selecting and re-interpreting the pre-interpreted contents thus gained; the latter are interrelated with the former. [As a thinker standing in one of these traditions] I am questioning the tradition about its sedimentations in so far as they can be the foundations of my own philosophizing and the fields of my own work.

Connected with all this is the regulative principle [of the preservation] of its indefinite remoteness. (There is no narrowing of the gap between the answers established by successive generations and any metaphysically conceived ultimate goal.) The final foundation remains in the "same" remote "distance" [for all successive generations]. This holds for the entelechistic goal of my own design. Tradition as I transmit it enriched by my own activity will have to be interpreted by the world of my successors as traditional sedimentation. And others will come and will have to do the same thinking-back and [the results of] my philosophizing will be one of the sediments of the tradition they have to interpret – a tradition I co-created. But for these successors too will arise the problem of final foundation as it arose for me; [and as for me] this problem will loom in an indefinite future. Yet, when they will redraw the entelechistic course of the originary foundation of their tradition, the result of my philosophical doings will be included in their inherited sedimentations.

Dear friend: this is *my* interpretation of Husserl's basic idea. I cannot find any passage in the whole essay in which Husserl declares that the phenomenology created by him is the final foundation of the entelechistic movement. This would be in blatant contradiction to his spiritual and human stance. Husserl says merely that with transcendental phenomenology the "revelation of reason" – his view of the course of philosophy – has reached an *apodictic beginning* as human task with its horizon of an apodictic continuation. According to everything I have said about the self-misunderstanding of the philosopher, it is clear that only a later critique will be able to justify or correct this claim. But it is beyond doubt that the effort to reach an apodictic start in philosophizing was the determining motive of all of Husserl's philosophizing. Therefore, standing in the tradition, he interprets the *telos* of this tradition out of his own doing. Also, I do not believe that Husserl considered his own work – the piece of philosophical work he left behind – the executed foundation of an apodictic beginning ready for continuing execution. He does speak, with undeniable justification, as one "who lives through the fate of a philosophical existence in its complete sincerity"[6] and says of himself in another passage (*"Nachwort zu den 'Ideen'"*) that "practically" he had "to tone down the ideal" of his own "philosophical aspirations to that of a genuine beginner".[7] And he continued: "If the years of Methuselah were allotted to me, then I could almost hope that I might yet be able to become a philosopher". Is that the attitude of Gierke and the philosopher of Progress at the time of the establishment of the German Empire? Is that the Victorian image of history?

1. He who stands in the tradition (in this case, the "European") asks about the sediments that motivate him as to their origin, their entelechies, their becoming.

[6]Cf. Husserl, *Die Krisis der europäischen Wissenschaften und die transzendentale Phänomenologie* (Den Haag: Martinus Nijhoff, 1954), p. 15. In the text of this letter Schutz no doubt refers to the text published in *Philosophia* in 1936 – he refers to pp. 98f. (although his reference is more than likely to pp. 93f. Cf. the English translation by David Carr, *The Crisis of European Sciences and Transcendental Phenomenology* (Evanston: Northwestern University Press, 1970), p. 17.) [FK]

[7]Cf. Edmund Husserl, *Nachwort zu meinen "Ideen zu einer reinen Phänomenologie und phänomenologischen Philosophie"*, in *Jahrbuch für Philosophie und phänomenologische Forschung*, Vol 11, p. 569; cf. English translation by Richard Rojcewicz and André Schuwer in Edmund Husserl, *Collected Works*, vol. III (Dordrecht: Kluwer, 1989), p. 429.

(Historical tradition as autobiographical element is assigned to self–contemplation, "anamnesis" in your terminology.)

2. The contents thus gained can be examined in terms of their *Eidos* (by way of the searching for the invariant in phantasy-like transformation). From this follows the structure included in the essence of the teleological unfolding (in this case, the "self-revelation of Reason") with its originary and final foundation (always seen from the correlate situation of the interpreting person).

3. Starting here, a new interpretation of the tradition becomes possible in that it can be shown (a) that the "obvious" starting points of the great innovators (Galileo, for instance) were by no means obvious; (b) that and why they (standing themselves in a tradition) felt no need to make problematic what they posited as unquestionably given; (c) that they were not aware of the implications of their doing (for example, the indirect "co-mathematization of the filling" in the Galilean turn). And they could not have become cognizant of them (because "discovery" is always a mixture of instinct and method; these elements can only be taken apart in retrospect, p. 115, for instance[8]); (d) that the procedures of the re-interpretation – set in motion by the emerging tradition – and the (explicitly or implicitly) used fundamental hypotheses posited on the grounds of this discovery remain ununderstood even though they work (p. 117); their methods are devoid of meaning (p. 119), their operational functions technified (pp. 121ff.), their relations to the life-world as universal meaning-elements forgotten (pp. 130ff.). (Earlier I have summarized these problems under the heading of "self-misunderstanding of the philosophizing person").

4. <Further results have to be noted>: a typology of the positing of problems, of problem-solutions, of problem-enmeshing in the course of the tradition; likewise, the latter can be examined with respect to its style. (Compare Husserl's remarks about the problem of dualism and the difficulties which arise in the course of its continuing pursuit.)

5. From these analyses results the fixation of one's own point of view <in this case, phenomenology> in the tradition and with it the possibility and meaning-bestowal of further tasks. Most of all, however, this serves as an example of a dialectical difficulty: the interpretation of the tradition is possible only from one's own perspective while this perspective can only be clarified through the understanding of the tradition. The "methodological characteristic of our interpretation" follows from Husserl's clear circumscription at the end of the chapter on Galileo (pp. 132ff.) to which you have not given sufficient attention.

That much about the published essay. After all that I have heard from Husserl, I am sure that the analyses developed in the fragment were only meant as examples (eidetic examples) of further problems within the total context of his planned book:

A. The position of the philosophizing person in the tradition as an example of the position of human being in the pregiven world.

B. The place of phenomenology between originary foundation and entelechistic final foundation as example for relating all philosophizing back to the understood life-world. (Phenomenology will understand the life-world as the root of

[8]The page reference is to the text of the *Krisis* under discussion. [FK]

its existence); according to Husserl, this understanding shall establish the apodicticity of its beginning. It is not satisfied with universal theses which remain ununderstood even if they are operatively effective.

C. The set of problems mentioned under (A) and (B) together serve as examples of a possible (but not yet developed) philosophy of history. (The work *on hand* is by no means this, nor claims to be so. Your critique is based on the assumption that it is.)

D. The philosophy of history to be developed may become an example of the phenomenological analysis of the constitution of the "natural attitude" (compare this to the "*Nachwort*" p. 567.)[9]

I think that it would be an idle question to ask whether Husserl would have been capable of contributing an essential solution to these questions. But I believe that this thematic is worthy of a genuine philosopher.

I have spent a great deal of time on the analysis of Husserl's basic position; I believe that the exposition of his intentions refutes just about all of the objections which you, dear friend, offer in your critique. Of course, I presuppose that the interpretation of Husserl's essay, as presented by me, is correct. Should this be the case, there is no argument possible about the question why Husserl does not accept the Medieval, the Chinese, or the Indian philosophies as determining motifs of his thinking. Likewise, it is not a critical objection that he did not consider Hegel (who was ever foreign to him). (At one time I did ask him why he did not deal more extensively with Leibniz. He pointed out that he had planned to devote one of the essays of the planned series to the treatment of Leibniz's philosophy.)

Earlier I dealt with the role of philosophy in the wake of realized potentiality (*Entelechie*) against which you directed your critique. The concept of an unfolding world soul was completely foreign to Husserl. This, next to other sources, is manifested in his fifth Cartesian Meditation in full clarity. (As you know, I consider this meditation a failure.)

There remain your remarks about Husserl's interpretation of Descartes. You yourself have clearly established that and to what degree Husserl was entitled to begin with Descartes. Doubtlessly you are correct when saying that the course of the Descartes' Meditations grew out of a formulation of a problem distinct from that of Husserl, that the conception of the ego as *anima animie* (animated soul) has an important function which Husserl did not consider and that for Descartes the proof of God is only the occasion for an inquiry into a specific dialectical situation. I have no objections against any of this; on the contrary, I gained much from your important analysis. However, I am thoroughly convinced that Husserl too would have had no objections against your interpretation of Descartes. Likely, he would have willingly agreed that the elements you have laid bare are much more important *for Descartes* than for the foundation of transcendental philosophy. However, according to all the things I have said, Husserl's problem was not that of a historian. For him – Husserl – Descartes was and remained a step toward the apodictic foundation of transcendental philosophy: This was the living and effective motivating core of his thinking

[9]*Husserliana III*, pp. 158f.; translation, pp. 425ff. [FK]

as it had reached him in the tradition. For his specific formulation of the problem, the rest of the Cartesian philosophy was *irrelevant* – as relevant as it may be seen from different points of view, and as effectively as it may live on in other links in the chain of the tradition (which, by the way, is not the case). And thus for me Husserl's essay too is an important contribution to <the clarification> of the problem of relevance which is close to my heart and which is still very much unclarified.

I am very eager to hear from you what you think about the interpretation of the Husserl essay offered by me. The second and third parts of your manuscript deserve an analysis as detailed as this. It shall not remain missing. However, in the circumstances under which I presently live, it may take months before I will find the time to write out the continuation of my response.[10]

[10]Note of Helmut Wagner: No such continuation has been found in Schutz's literary estate. I doubt that he found the occasion to take time out from his quite hectic business pursuits at the time and thus had to refrain from carrying out the intentions he stated at the end of the letter.

CHAPTER 23

Farber's Foundation of Early Phenomenology

The title is by Helmut Wagner for Schutz's review of Marvin Farber's *The Foundation of Phenomenology: Edmund Husserl and the Quest for a Rigorous Science of Philosophy*, published in 1943 by Harvard University Press. The review was originally published in *Philosophical Abstracts*. Wagner noted that Farber's book appeared when the journal, *Philosophy and Phenomenological Research* had entered the fourth year of its publication, and when there was a period of close collaboration between Farber, its editor in chief, and his foremost Central-European consultants: Felix Kaufmann, Herbert Spiegelberg, and Alfred Schutz.[1] Schutz's review pays hommage to Farber's careful study of the early work of Husserl up to and including the *Logical Investigations*.

This book is not only by far the best study of Edmund Husserl's thought available in English, but also a standard work on the development of phenomenological philosophy up to and including the *Logical Investigations*. The author, a personal student of Husserl, president of the International Phenomenological Society, and editor of the quarterly journal, *Philosophy and Phenomenological Research* (published by the University of Buffalo), states in the Preface that it was his aim to combine freedom of presentation in rendering Husserl's ideas with exactness of meaning. It can be safely attested that he has fully succeeded in this endeavor. The present reviewer has compared paragraph by paragraph of Professor Farber's rendition of Husserl's *Logical Investigations* with the German original and was delighted to observe the author's skill in translating Husserl's difficult and sometimes rather cumbersome terminology as well as his acumen in selecting the material to be presented.

The book gives foremost place to an account of Husserl's contribution to logic. There are several reasons for this. On the one hand, the leading idea in Husserl's early development, as Prof. Farber shows with philosophical accuracy, was the attempt to separate the realm of pure logic from psychology and, consequently, to refute the psychologistic doctrine which prevailed in German philosophy when Husserl began his work. Moreover, it was logical problems, and above all the analysis of the elements

[1]For details on Schutz's friendship and collaboration with Farber, see Wagner, *Alfred Schutz. An Intellectual Biography*, pp. 78–84, 181–184.

of knowledge, which induced Husserl to perform the "break-through" to his later view of phenomenology. On the other hand, it is obviously Farber's opinion that Husserl's achievements in the field of logic are the most valuable part of his work and of special interest for English-speaking readers. Farber does not hesitate to turn away from the system of transcendental phenomenological idealism as developed in Husserl's later writings and criticizes sharply, using most striking arguments, certain features of the last phase of Husserl's philosophy as presented by Fink in an essay in *Kant-Studien* (1933).[2]

The first chapter of Farber's book gives the background of Husserl's thought by outlining the state of philosophy in Germany during Husserl's youth, and especially the theories of his teacher, Brentano. The next chapter is devoted to an account of Husserl's first publication, the *Philosophy of Arithmetic*. It is to the great merit of Farber that he reveals the rudimentary beginnings of later phenomenological analysis. Chapters III and IV render Husserl's discussion of contemporary German writings in Logic and Psychology, in which he makes interesting comments on symbolic logic, on the theories of Schroeder, Voigt, Stumpf, Ehrenfels, Wundt, Lipps, von Kries, Marty and others. Farber reproduces here material of highest importance for the understanding of Husserl's early thought which cannot easily be obtained since the writings referred to are scattered among various German scientific periodicals.[3]

The greater part of Farber's book (chapters IV, V, VII–XIV) consists of a free rendering of a major work by Husserl, the *Logical Investigations* (three volumes, first edition 1900–1901; second revised edition 1913 and 1921) which has never been translated into English.[4] Between both editions the "break-through" to phenomenology was accomplished in Husserl's book, *Ideas: General Introduction to Pure Phenomenology* (English translation by Boyce Gibson, 1931), and Farber carefully points out how this new stage of Husserl's philosophy is reflected in the revised edition of the earlier work.

The first volume of the *Logical Investigations*, entitled *Prolegomena to Pure Logic*, is devoted to a refutation of psychologism. According to Husserl, the psychologists confused the logical laws as "content of judgment" with acts of judgments themselves and the law as a causal element with the law as a rule of causation. Thus they were subject to the threefold prejudice 1) that normative laws of knowledge must be based upon the psychology of knowledge, 2) that ideas, judgments, inferences, truth, probability, necessity, and possibility refer to psychological phenomena and structures, and 3) that the locus of truth is in judgment, and evidence is a peculiar feeling which guarantees the truth of the judgment. In opposition to this point of view Husserl holds that pure logic is not a part of psychology but of the scientific system of ideal

[2]Schutz refers to Eugen Fink, "Die phänomenologische Philosophie Edmund Husserls in der gegenwärtigen Kritik. Mit einem Vorwort von Edmund Husserl", *Kant-Studien*, Vol. 38, 1933, pp. 319–383. (English translation in R.O. Elveton, *The Phenomenology of Husserl. Selected Critical Readings* [Chicago: Quadrangle Books, 1970], pp. 73–147.) [FK]

[3]Fortunately the articles of Husserl are now collected in *Husserliana* XXII: Edmund Husserl, *Aufsätze und Rezensionen (1890–1910)*, mit ergänzenden Texten herausgegeben von Bernhard Rang (Den Haag: Martinus Nijhoff, 1979). [FK]

[4]Since Schutz's 1944 review, Husserl's *Logical Investigations* has been translated into English by J.N. Findlay (London: Routledge & Kegan Paul, 1970). [FK]

laws and categories which are grounded purely in the ideal categories of meaning and therefore in concepts common to all sciences including psychology. This principle is worked out in the six logical investigations which constitute the second and third volumes of Husserl's work. They cover analyses of expression and meaning, of universals and abstraction, of wholes and parts, of the problem of pure grammar and the analyses of meaning, of intentional experiences and their contents, and of the elements of a phenomenological elucidation of knowledge. Step by step Farber's clear and condensed presentation of this work follows Husserl's argument, and the reader who earnestly studies the respective chapters can be assured that nothing of importance in the German original has been withheld from him.

Farber deliberately restricts the scope of the present volume to the foundation of phenomenology and reserves a detailed discussion of transcendental phenomenology for later publications. It can only be wished that he will soon fulfil this promise. In the last three chapters of his book, however, the author treats a few important topics selected from Husserl's later writings as samples of the technique of a presuppositionless method in philosophy. He gives a concise abstract of Husserl's theory of different levels of logical analysis as developed in his late book *Formal and Transcendental Logic*, of his analysis of time-consciousness, of his eidetic method, and of his investigations concerning the constitution of intersubjectivity.

For those familiar with Husserl's philosophy the last chapter of Farber's book is by far the most interesting. It criticizes frankly the exaggerated claim of the latest expressions of phenomenology to have achieved an absolute knowledge of the world and of the "phenomenological paradoxes" then arising. Farber's arguments will have to be either accepted or refuted by the thinkers connected with the phenomenological movement since they are directed against some of the principal theses of transcendental phenomenology as developed in the above-mentioned article by Fink. Those English readers, however, who, though not familiar with or not interested in phenomenological *philosophy* in the strict sense of this term, are eager to acquaint themselves with one of the major achievements of European logic in this century will be grateful to Farber for having made Husserl's *Logical Investigations* accessible to them, provided, of course, that they are willing to give to this book the study and attention which its difficult content requires and its importance deserves.

CHAPTER 24

The Paradox of the Transcendental Ego

The title of this untitled and undated manuscript is by Helmut Wagner. Because it would seem to be related in content to Schutz's article on "Multiple Realities" Wagner dates it around 1945 and suggested that it may even have been part of that article. Schutz would seem to accept, in this manuscript, Farber's critique of Eugen Fink's interpretation of phenomenology as an "idealism". This provided Schutz with a starting point for a discussion of the differences among the various finite provinces of meaning, re-enforcing his own interpretation of everyday life as "paramount reality". The paradox mentioned in the title is that concerning the possibility of communication among phenomenologists once they have performed – or co-performed – the phenomenological reduction.[1]

The aforementioned paradoxes, although on quite another level, are similar to the phenomenological paradox which Eugen Fink (backed by the endorsement of Husserl) has treated in his essay of 1933.[2] There he pointed to the difficulty of giving an account of the phenomenologically reduced sphere because communication is only possible after having left this reduced sphere, that is, after having re-assumed the natural attitude. Fink concludes that this phenomenological paradox remains unsolvable. The transcendental ego, whose experiences become merely visible after the performance of the phenomenological reduction, cannot use the common language without falling back into the natural attitude: however, it is then no longer the transcendental ego who gives account of his subjective experiences. It is the mundane ego who talks, and it talks in mundane language. Therefore, so Fink concludes, really transcendental experiences in the reduced sphere are not communicable. In other words, the transcendental ego is mute.

Marvin Farber has criticized Fink's arguments in a very convincing way. He shows that in the last development of phenomenology as presented in Fink's paper the

[1]See Eugen Fink, "Die phänomenologische Philosophie Edmund Husserls", *Kant-Studien*, Vol. 38, 1933, pp. 319–383; see especially pp. 381f. for the formulation of the paradox in question. For the record it should be noted that, in the specific context of Fink's essay, the paradox is a paradox only for a philosophy not effecting the transcendental phenomenological reduction; see p. 322, note 1 where Fink makes this point explicit. [FK]

[2]Schutz's text has "1937", which must be a mistake. It is the essay referred to in note 1 that discusses the paradoxes, and contains the endorsement by Husserl. [FK]

transcendental ego turned out to be the creator of the world and not only the originator of the activities of the mind and this is why experiences within the phenomenological reduction are not communicable in ordinary language.

The problem, we may add, is very much complicated by the assumption that in phenomenological theory there is not one single transcendental ego but a community of monads. However, the monads obviously cannot communicate directly and immediately but only by the mundane means of bodily gestures in the widest sense; this includes language of any kind. Elsewhere, the present writer did seriously ask the question whether the term, "transcendental ego", can be used in the plural form, that is whether there is conceivable only one single transcendental ego – so that fellowman and sociality themselves have to remain phenomena pertaining to the mundane sphere. It is his conviction that the idea of a transcendental community of monads requires additional metaphysical assumptions which cannot be warranted by a philosophy whose idea it is to be a rigorous science.

If we look at Leibniz's system of a community of monads we see that these monads too are unable to communicate directly. But Leibniz has shown the metaphysical assumption which nevertheless makes a communication of monads without windows possible: 1) there is no monad thinkable without a body; 2) each monad mirrors the whole universe; 3) body and mind are in pre-established harmony and so is the community of monads which is able to communicate. Of course, if we introduce the concept of a harmony pre-established by God, the phenomenological paradox easily disappears.

But both this paradox and the dialectic difficulties which we have pointed out before – concerned merely with the mundane sphere – can be overcome if we do not take the different provinces of meaning (or the reduced sphere) as ontological entities, as objectively existing outside the human mind who thinks them. They are not comparable to different countries with different coins which are of no use if we have crossed the border – unless we have exchanged them for domestic currency. They are not mental lives separated one from the other requiring a transmigration of the soul as the doctrine of *methempsychosis* assumes with the complete extinction of memory and consciousness through death. To be sure, they originate in different states of our consciousness, in different attentional attitudes toward life. But it is the one and same consciousness which shows different tensions and it is the one and same life, the mundane life unbroken from birth to death, which is attended to in different modifications. As we said before, during one single day or even hour our mind may pass through the whole gamut of tensions of consciousness; now living in the working acts in the natural attitude, now passing through a daydream, now plunging into the pictorial world of a photograph in a magazine, now indulging in a bit of theoretical contemplation.

All these experiences are experiences within my inner time; they belong to my stream of consciousness, they can be remembered and reproduced. This reproduction will be less and less inadequate the more remote the finite province of meaning is from the world of working. But even within the world of working I can remember or reproduce these experiences; I can communicate them in ordinary language to my fellowman through acts of working. However, what formerly seemed to be a reality while attended to may now be measured with the yardstick of the paramount reality of daily life and appear as non-real fiction, as fantasy or dream, etc. But if children play together in their make-believe world, if we discuss with a fellow the meaning of a work of art before us, if we philosophize with a friend, if we attend with a socius a performance in the theater, if we indulge in the same ritual with others, we are always with others within the working world and connected with them by communicative acts of working. And nevertheless both fellowman and I, we, have leaped together from this finite province of meaning called the world of everyday life into the finite province of art, of play, of religious symbols, etc.

We have shown before that working acts may be the "content" of fantasms, of dreams, of theoretical contemplation. Why should experiences originating in the finite province of dreams, etc., not become contents of my communicative working acts?

The paradoxical situation arises only if we assume that fellowman and sociality and communication can be realized within a finite province of meaning other than that of the world of everyday life, the world of working.

If that were true, why [should we] study the different finite provinces of meaning which obviously are merely embedded in the world of everyday life? Why not just turn to pragmatism or behaviorism? We hope that the preceding pages have answered this question. All the dimensions of our life which we have studied are meaningful only as long as we maintain the epoché in which they originate. Children start to play and stop to play; we turn to a work of art and turn away from it, we start a philosophical contemplation and end it. While we attend to a particular province of meaning we use the epoché peculiar to it. Here is our freedom of discretion: we may bestow upon each of these provinces the accent of reality and withdraw it again as we please.

CHAPTER 25

Husserl's *Paris Lectures* of 1929

This review of Husserl's *Cartesianische Meditationen und Pariser Vorträge*, edited by Stephan Strasser (The Hague: Martinus Nijhoff, 1950), was published in *Philosophy and Phenomenological Research*, XI (1951), pp. 421–423. Stylistic changes in the printed text were made by Helmut Wagner.

The present volume is the first publication of the "Archives-Husserl" at Louvain, guardian of 45,000 pages of manuscripts which the philosopher left behind unpublished and mostly unedited at the time of his death, April 27, 1938. Professor H. L. Van Breda of the *Institut Supérieur de Philosophie* at Louvain and director of the *Archives-Husserl* tells in a preface the history and the purpose of this institution, giving due credit to his helpers and assistants but hardly mentioning the fact that this outstanding center of phenomenological research in the first instance is his personal creation and that its achievements became possible only through his energy and self-denial. Any student of Husserl's philosophy who, like the present writer, had the privilege of enjoying the hospitality of the *Archives-Husserl* must have been deeply impressed by the tremendous work accomplished under most difficult circumstances with the help of a few competent scholars. He must have gained the conviction that the forthcoming publication of Husserl's writings will not only attain the highest standard of philological precision but also open new insights into the development of the philosopher's thought. The edition of the "Cartesian Meditations" now before the public fulfils the highest expectations in this respect.

Professor Dr. S. Strasser, for many years connected with the *Archives-Husserl* and now Professor of Philosophy at the University of Nimwegen, Holland, is the excellent editor of this volume. It contains the texts of four lectures, delivered by Husserl in the German language at the Sorbonne,[1] Paris, in February 1929, as well as a summary of these lectures prepared by the philosopher himself both in German and in French translation. In the same year these lectures, with the help of Husserl's assistant Eugen Fink, were elaborated into the first four "Cartesian Meditations" dealing with the approach to the transcendental ego, the field of transcendental experience and its structure, the problem of constitution (truth and reality); the constitutive problem of intersubjectivity was added later on. The manuscript of these five

[1]Husserl spoke before an audience at the Sorbonne in the amphithéâtre Descartes on the 23rd and 25th February, 1929.

Meditations, written in German, was translated by Dr. E. Levinas and Mlle. G. Peiffer into French and published in 1931 by A. Colin, Paris (republished in 1949 by Vrin). Until now this most important work was accessible only to students having full mastery of the French language since the translation, excellent as it is in its way, makes rather hard reading even to French-born philosophers. Husserl's plan to publish the German original never materialized because he found himself under the necessity of amending and enlarging the original text. In 1932 Dr. Fink prepared for Husserl a new (unpublished) version but the development of the political situation in Germany and other occupations barred Husserl from following up his plan. Therefore the present volume publishes for the first time the original German manuscripts underlying the French translation; a voluminous annex contains all the marginal notes, insertions, and amendments which were found in the manuscripts. Thus it makes available one of the outstanding works of Husserl to German-reading students. Professor Strasser wrote a carefully prepared introduction and an account of the gigantic philological tasks involved. The text is complemented by the very interesting comments to the first four meditations submitted by Professor Roman Ingarden of Cracow [and sent] to Husserl who highly appreciated them.

As Professor Strasser justly states in his introduction, the "Cartesian Meditations" are the second attempt of Husserl to sum up his thought in a systematic way. The first attempt was made in his "Ideas" of which only the first volume was published in 1913 (English translation by Boyce Gibson in 1931), whereas the second and third volumes exist merely in manuscripts. It is extremely gratifying to learn that these volumes will be published very soon by the *Archives-Husserl*.[2] The third attempt was made by Husserl at the end of his life and also remained unfinished because of Husserl's last illness. The first two parts appeared in the journal *Philosophia*, Beograd, 1936, under the title "The Crisis of European Sciences and Philosophy". Each of these three attempts follows a different avenue of approach: The "Ideas" start with an analysis of the problems of eidetic and of transcendental reductions in order to determine and to explore the transcendental field. This approach is a rather difficult one for the beginner; as a matter of fact starting with the eidetic problems of "*Wesensschau*" has proved for many to be a stumbling block rather than a vehicle for grasping the essential content of the phenomenological method; it has even created many serious misunderstandings of Husserl's philosophy. The "Crisis" makes the attempt to win access to the phenomenological method by way of a new interpretation of the history of Western philosophy. By reason of the fragmentary character of the finished parts of this work only those familiar beforehand with the aims and method of phenomenology can understand the systematic importance of this seemingly critical examination of the origin of modern occidental science since Galileo. The "Cartesian Meditations" try to unveil the field of transcendental phenomenology by starting from Descartes' method of radical doubt, which leads to a new concept of apodictic evidence and therewith to the transcendental foundation of the epoché; they are not only the most complete but in the opinion of this writer the easiest approach to the later phase of Husserl's philosophy.

[2]Schutz's reviews of these, the second and third volumes of *Ideas*, originally published in *Philosophy and Phenomenological Research*, have been reprinted in Alfred Schutz, *Collected Papers*, Vol. III.

It is impossible within the space at our disposal to offer a survey of the problems dealt with and the method followed in this outstanding masterwork of Husserl. Fortunately this is not necessary since the English reader will find in Professor Marvin Farber's *The Foundation of Phenomenology* (Cambridge, 1943, pp. 528–536) a brilliant although very condensed summary of the "*Méditations Cartésiennes*". Only a full translation of this work would be able to give a better understanding of this outstanding achievement of contemporary philosophy.

In spite of the gratitude the student of Husserl's work has to show to Professor Van Breda and Professor Strasser for their magnificent editorial job, it has to be regretted that the volume does not contain an index. To be sure, it is a highly difficult task to prepare an index to any of Husserl's writings. Yet it is unfortunate that, for instance, important statements of Husserl, such as those reproduced on pp. 238–241, disappear for the not too diligent reader in the bulk of text-critical remarks.

CHAPTER 26

On the Concept of Horizon

The title is by Helmut Wagner, substituting Schutz's original title: "*Hic egregie progressus sum*". The manuscript was dated by Schutz: 7 December, 1958. Wagner's editing consists chiefly of breaking up long sections into short ones.

I

We have to expand the concept of the structure of horizon to include the social as well. And this not only in the sense that each object of our consciousness displays the structure of the inner horizon, as exactly described by Husserl, but in the sense of its being externally-horizonally connected with other objects. Autobiographically it is also interlaced with other object-adequate modes of consciousness within the streaming, recognizing, feeling, and willing consciousness [of present experience]. All this corresponds to Husserl's inner horizon.

In this case too the autobiographical horizonal structure would be of indeterminate determination; it would display the character of being unquestionably given but at any time could be made problematic. This could become a possible explication of the relevance structure which is opaque, non-transparent; but potentially it can be made visible. Here all three types of relevance function together, although hidden, in their typical pre-givenness in the mode of familiarity. In this, so to speak, solipsistically perceived autobiographical situation "sociability" would be the tension between "I" and "Me" in the sense of James and Mead. (It is likely that this is the key to all possible self-interpretations on the basis of the becoming and passing-away of the relevance system which, in its manner, also functions as typically sense-bestowing – because it forms types and constitutes the problem-relevance of types – the "index", the "subscript".)

This "autobiographical sociality" can be laid bare in the reflective turn to my past states of consciousness, and this on two levels: as retention of the already past initial phases of an experience which continues, and as re-representation of that which has already faded into the past. Furthermore, [it can be pursued] in the direction toward the future, also on two levels: as potential and anticipatory representation of something having been accomplished at some point in the future (*modo futuri exacti*). This also would correspond to Husserl's inner horizon.

However, there exist here a series of complications which have to be considered. For instance, whether former but now co-represented relevance structures at the moment of reflectively looking-back are applied and can be applied to the given stock of experience (maybe merely as empty and possibly unquestionably given relevance structures): I change my opinion; this or that is still important to me under changed circumstances; I continue to think along established tracks and to act in traditional, habitual, affective ways, etc. (Weber). Or in reverse: Is it not possible that relevances which only now become effective can be turned upon that which I now re-present together with the corresponding stock of experience of being (autobiographical horizon of relevance)? (If I had known this before, I would have decided otherwise). Furthermore, there are typical ways in which the typicality of relevances is itself regulated: types of higher order, types of types. This also would lead to reiterated relevances: for instance, why is a motivational, a thematic, an interpretative relevance "relevant"? Is the question meaningful at all? Is "relevance" used here equivocally? Further: to what degree are actual and as such recognized relevances applicable to the future, and to what degree are they presently represented? More correctly: what is the basis of my confidence – my unquestioned and doubtlessly given "self-understood" confidence that these relevances can be applied to things in the future? And this in particular when things in the future are anticipated not protentionally but *modo futuri exacti*? Is this based on the idealization "I can again and again" (*Ich kann immer wieder*)?

[1][But – this is another problem altogether – this idealization (of "I can again and again") is questionable in two respects: a) autobiographical: can it be put in the grammatical past and future tenses ("*dekliniert* ", "*konjugiert*")? What happens if the statement "I always did do it again" turns out to be untrue, as it eventually must? We do *grow old* and that not only physiologically. Since this is neither an "assumption" nor a "conclusion", what entitles us to hope that "I will always be able to do it again" or "I will have been able to always do it again"? I will not be able to do it ever and ever again – if for no other reason than because I myself must come to an end. Death is merely a special case limiting the meaning of "I will always be able to do it again". Here, the problem is the "time structure of capability" (*Vermöglichkeit*). But aside from this time-structure, is the object of this "I can always again" not merely a typically ideal object? It cannot be "the same" already because it is recurrently "the same". Here lies a very serious problem. b) Socially: Why should there exist correlates to "I can always again" such as: "you can always again", "he can always again" and even "we can always again"? The time-elements mentioned under (a) would have to be included in all these variations: not mine but your, his and our time; and furthermore <we must include> the problematic of intersubjective capability mentioned under (a). c) The problematic of *intersubjective capability* becomes still more difficult: "I can what you can", "what we can", "what we, what they can", what "one", what "everybody" can. All this is subjected to the

[1]The brackets are those of Schutz.

temporal conjugation of the grammatically first person singular but also of every other person. (This again is problematic in itself: "I was able to do what he can, I will be able to do what he is able to do" and so on.)

But this is not all: the previous sentences cannot be reversed. "When I can (was able to, will be able to) to do what you can do" does not at all mean that the proposition, "you can (were able to, will be able to) do what I can (was able to, will be able to) do", is a valid proposition – and so through all grammatical persons with all the questionability of the implied sense of "the same" and its subjective and objective meanings (in Weber's terminology). Finally, "reciprocity" is already questionable here. But what about the "transitivity" of the capabilities of (a) social, (b) temporal? (Examples (a): if we assume the truth of the propositions "I can what you can" and "you can what he can", does this also mean that I can what he can? Example (b): I had been able to climb this mountain at the ages of forty and fifty and I still can do it today being sixty; but will I be able to do it when I am seventy?)]

As important as the bracketed problems of capability and its idealizations are, they belong into a different context. For the context of interest here (what may such a sentence mean in terms of my theory of relevance?) they are significant only in so far as it turns out that the "self-understood" confidence in the continuity of the relevance system can be traced back to the idealization of "I can always again". What, in this context, actually is hoped to be "constant"? The constancy of the situational elements of the "and so on"? The constancy of the system of motivational, thematic, and interpretative relevances (all or some of them?) or the constancy of both situational elements and relevance systems? [2][This brings up a new problem which belongs into the earlier brackets: Was Husserl correct when he took the idealization of "I can always again" as the subjective correlate of the idealization of "and so on"? Is it not necessary to make a sharp distinction here, a distinction of "basic importance"?] Be this as it may, perhaps it would be better to speak of *relevance horizon* instead of autobiographical horizon?

II

Everything said up to this point, be it called an autobiographical or a relevance horizon, would correspond socially to Husserl's inner horizon. By contrast the actual intersubjective social horizon would correspond to the outer horizon of Husserl. In this outer horizon objects in their relations to other objects will be "co-perceived" ("*mit*" *erfasst*); objects which, in their determinable indetermation of explicable implications, stand in the "background" (Husserl) or the "margin" (Gurwitsch). In the intersubjective social horizon (forthwith called social horizon for short) the character of the unquestionably given will be viewed as "founded" not only by me, the experiencing person. That which is unquestionably self-understood belongs also to you, to us, to everybody, to "anybody who belongs to 'us'" – self-understood in its givenness, accepted unquestionable until further notice. It is handed down to me as

[2]The brackets are those of Schutz.

such. It is that which is the socially derived, socially approved, and eventually socially imposed element of my available stock of knowledge together with the relevances belonging to it. It is recipe knowledge, knowledge of the opaque which is not understood but can be made understandable or at least transparent. Here occurs the separation of the available stock of knowledge according to clarity and into zones of distinctiveness, into expert's knowledge and layman's knowledge: *Origin of the distribution of knowledge and its structure of relevance within the implications of the social horizon*! (I can ask somebody who knows better!) And this again is only possible because the differentiation of the stock of knowledge originates at the point of the intersection of autobiographical, situation-rooted, and socially valid relevance systems! [3][The *legitimate* work of sociology of knowledge would have to start here the analysis of the relative-natural aspects of the world; it would find an immense field to explore.] *Origin of Ortega's theory of habit.*[4]

Again, a mass of implications occurs:

(a) Are the social horizons of the worlds of contemporaries and of consociates the same structure? Is not everybody dominated by different particular horizonal relevance structures? Is the social world of consociates ordered according to anonymity and fullness of the ideal types in which this world is perceived?

(b) New light is thrown on particular difficulties of the ideas of historicity, history, and social horizon. History, so to speak, exists in a dual sense (with regard to our problem): Retentional history in the sliding transition within larger environments and direct surroundings (*Umwelt und Mitwelt*). (Possibly) here is the key to the solution of two problems which have been sought for a long time: (a 1) The meaning of the succession of generations); (b 1) the persistence of the social group in the sense of Simmel (abcde – mbcde – mncde . . . mnopq); possibly also an important contribution (c 1) to the problem of *education* in general; and (d 1) to Piaget's genetic epistemology.

Next to this exists re-represented history of that which is no longer "kept in retentional grasp" but which had long since sunk below [the temporal horizon of the past]. What does this mean? All problems reappear here which had [already] been treated in section I: (a 2) The relevance scheme or, better, the continuity of its development, is broken off. (b 2) There is no situational constancy (both have their typical possibilities); (a 3) Culture of the Hykosos (conquerors of Egypt during the 17th century B.C.); (b 3) Eskimos (Toynbee).

But: In order to make history possible, the disappeared world of the predecessors has to be placed into a social horizon which is common to both this world of predecessors and our world of contemporaries.

Possibly, the writing and interpreting of history is the ongoing penetration of the undetermined determinabilities of this common social horizon (which are

[3]The brackets are those of Schutz.

[4]The reference is probably to José Ortega y Gasset, *El Hombre y la Gente* (Madrid: Revista de Occidente, 1957; English translation, *Man and People*, by Willard R. Trask, New York: W.W. Norton, 1957), Chapter X. Schutz was very interested in this book not just because of Ortega's references to his own work, but especially because of Ortega's notion of "social usage" (habit) and "linguistic usage". (FK)

typical and set as typical or as having to be typified). Not only has this horizon to be founded as common horizon, its *interpretation* is ever determined by the typical relevances which are valid for the interpreter. Therefore every generation will have to write anew the history of the glory of Caesar. Therefore here too exists a problem of education, namely the education of humanity in Lessing's sense. Therefore Ranke could say that all periods <of history> are close to God (however, only to God). *History as interpretation of the implications of the overlapping social horizons.*

(c) And the world of successors with its indeterminateness? What is open? Everything: systems of relevance, constancy of situations, social horizons. There is no historical pre-representation.[5]

[5]The manuscript breaks off here.

CHAPTER 27

Thou and I

EDITORS' PREFACE

The original title of this manuscript was *Du und Ich*; written between 1925 and 1927 it originated in connection with Schutz's drafts of his Bergsonian studies, although it was not included in the published texts of the latter.[1] Schutz wrote his manuscript notes in a very terse, abbreviated form. In translating them into English, Helmut Wagner expanded the notes into a coherent form consistent with his published translations of Schutz's writings from the same period.

If I pay attention in my memory to the "I" that I have been at some moment of the past, I view and posit this "I" as a kind of Thou which once had been me. Such positing of the I as a kind of Thou can only occur in the past tense. The Thou which I was once can be recaptured in imagination only after the fact (*ex eventu*) and therefore only in retrospect. Hindsight is possible for me: The Thou that I was once can be interpretatively recalled by me – up to the threshold of the very present, the now-here-thus of my experience.

In the Thou of an actual other person I encounter the center of indetermination: I have experienced only some discrete stretches of the enduring life of the Other. I know his past – up to the present moment – only intermittently and it is not likely that my encounters with him coincided with what were his truly "relevant moments", moments he considered and continues to consider to be of great relevance for him.

On the other hand, the future of any concrete Other is not at all determinable by me. This is so because I lack the knowledge both of the relevant factors of his past life and of the intrinsically personal effects they had on him and co-determine his present feelings and decisions. The *total* present of the Other, including memories of his that are co-determining influences on his present conduct, is not accessible to me.

In contrast, I am, in my own future, relatively determined by my actual present,

[1] Alfred Schutz, *Theorie der Lebensformen*, herausgegeben und eingeleitet von Ilja Srubar (Suhrkamp Verlag: Frankfurt am Main, 1981); *Life Forms and Meaning Structure*, translated, introduced and annotated by Helmut Wagner (Routledge & Kegan Paul: London, 1982). See also Helmut Wagner, *Alfred Schutz. An Intellectual Biography*, pp. 21ff.

respectively by my own past as it has elapsed up to the moment which has immediately preceded the moment of my actual Now-Here-Thus.

As past I, the self that I was is posited as the Thou-that-was-once-me. It is oriented to a Thou-index. However, this index is basically the same in which I see the course of the past of another person. The Now-Here-Thus of my present is related to a Now-Here-Thus index of the other Thou – an index that I evoke when dealing with other persons (in thought or interchange). The Thou is seen and experienced by me in its surrounding world in reference to my Now-Here-Thus.

The surrounding world, in relation to its reference to me, is strictly reversible.[2] However, in no way could I make similar determinations with regard to your apperceiving and interpreting your experiencing.

I am able to imagine my surrounding world in reference to my Now-Here-Thus by imagining the Thou being like me (an imagined Now-Here-Thus in reference to me): This imagining of the Thou in accord with the experienced Now-Here-Thus of my I, so I believe, can be imputed as intended, as expected, and as appertaining to surroundings of the Thou and its Now-Here-Thus. All this is posited by me for the Thou but is accessible to me only in reference to me and my surrounding world.

[2]In a note to this sentence, Wagner takes its sense to mean that, in retrospection, I am free to proceed from my I to my apperceptive experience of the surrounding world or else to concentrate on my surroundings into which I may but must not consciously place myself as a central hub. In so far as this decision comes about by my fiat, I am free to reverse myself at any time during my ongoing contemplation. [FK]

CHAPTER 28

The Foundations of the Theory of Social Organization

Editors' Preface

This chapter is a translation by Fred Kersten[1] of Schutz's review of Tomoo Otaka, *Grundlegung der Lehre vom sozialen Verband*, published in 1932 by Verlag von Julius Springer in Vienna. The review was originally published in the *Zeitschrift für öffentliches Recht*, Vol. 17, 1937, pp. 64–84.[2] As Schutz makes clear, Otaka developed a social theory which could be placed, roughly, between Kelsen's "pure theory of law", with its limited social implications, and Weber's sociology of understanding but without its emphasis on the individual. Schutz considered Otaka a close personal friend and a scholar who was his peer. Believing that he owed his honesty to each of such friends he criticized Otaka's book unsparingly, yet giving it the high praise it deserved at the end of the review.[3]

It is absolutely indispensable for the social sciences to continue to account for the logical features of their method and to strive for a sufficient philosophical grounding of their basic concepts. There is less clarity than ever in the controversies of social-scientific theories about the essence and being of social relations and social organizations, about the actuality and historicality of social objects, and about the bearing which sociology has on specific, individual social sciences.

[1]The translation was originally prepared as an introduction to a translation of Otaka's book under review by Schutz. The translation was revised by Helmut Wagner for inclusion here. [FK]

[2]For Tomoo Otaka, see Wagner, *Alfred Schutz. An Intellectual Biography*, pp. 36f., 332. Otaka was the son of a wealthy bookseller and a member of the faculty of law at Keijo University. After spending a year in Berlin he went to Vienna to study international law with Hans Kelsen, and it was in the latter's private seminar that he met Felix Kaufmann and Alfred Schutz. His intense scholarly discussions with Schutz led to a deep personal friendship. Otaka's humanist and democratic convictions landed him in political difficulties in Japan on his return, and after the defeat of Japan in World War II Otaka wrote the new constitution of his country. He renewed his contact with Schutz, and in 1956 died as a result of an allergic reaction to penicillin. [FK]

[3]Wagner noted that one is likely to misunderstand the tenor of the review unless one keeps in mind that Otaka's visit to Europe occurred over 50 years ago, that Otaka was one of the first Japanese scholars who went to Europe to study Husserl's philosophy, and that the linguistic difficulties in learning a European language were immense.

To have brought these problems into the foreground is the service performed by this book of Tomoo Otaka, Professor of Philosophy of Law at the University of Keijo. Otaka is an advocate of the "pure theory of law" and belongs to the group of students of Hans Kelsen. Of the representatives of the Vienna school it is Alfred Verdross who, with his idea of the essence of international legal organizations, has exercised a direct influence on Otaka. In philosophy he is a student of Edmund Husserl to whom he has dedicated the present work. Together, pure theory of law and phenomenological philosophy fashion the fundamentals of Otaka's investigations into the being and actuality of social organizations.

If it was the pure theory of law which made Otaka aware that social organization belongs to the domain of ideal formations produced by the mind, then it was his involvement with transcendental phenomenological philosophy that led him to investigate the problem of the actuality of ideal objects in general and, in particular, the ideal object, "Social Organization".

The importance of this problem posed by Otaka will be apparent to anyone minimally familiar with the sociological literature. In the Introduction to his investigations Otaka provides an overview of those theories to be taken seriously which are concerned with the ideal object, "Social Organization". He begins with Gierke's conception of social organization as a living unity of a whole composed of parts, and refers to Spann's ideas about social organization as a totality made up of mind and social action.

Rightly Otaka reproaches both views for avoiding the decisive problem of how far, namely, and in which way, the mental object, "Social Organization", comes to be actually existent in the historical-social world. Kelsen deserves credit for elucidating the ideal being of social organization. Although Otaka dismisses Kelsen's identification of state and legal order on the basis of considerations to be more precisely reported later, he recognizes that it was Kelsen who, above all, had emphatically pointed to the fact that the state – and, taken universally, social organization – is not a formation produced by Nature but rather produced by Mind and that, therefore, state and social organization taken universally acquire their own peculiar ontic mode, namely that of ideal objects.

Smend's well-known polemic against Kelsen's conception misses its mark, according to Otaka, because Kelsen had never denied the actuality of the state as an actuality of the Mind. In any case, Smend would have to concede that the task of seizing upon the historical being of the state by means of his theory of integration would have to be placed on a broader basis for discussion. This is so because the "actualization" of organization in social factuality would form the only foundation upon which the state could exist as an ideal formation produced by the mind. The conceptions of Kelsen and Smend thus aim at different levels of one and the same set of problems. Otaka guards himself against the expected objection that he renews, with this thesis, the dual theory of the state refuted by Kelsen and which would accordingly make him guilty of an inadmissible syncretism of method. According to Otaka, the concept of ideality is by no means incompatible with that of actuality; rather any mental actuality has the existential form of an ideal formation produced by the mind. As actually existing formation produced by mind, the ideal object, Social Organization, would now belong to historical-social actuality.

Nevertheless, in this connection, this historical-social actuality, which itself is a predicate of the ideal and objective formation produced by the mind, should not be confused with the continuously fluctuating *de facto* vital events of social life which, at best, are viewed as correlates of Social Organization. It is rather the case that between these factualities, which themselves do not acquire historicality, and the historical actuality of ideal formations produced by mind, there obtains a connection of founding: "The *de facto* social event therefore fashions the 'basis' upon which the Social Organization demonstrably shows its historical actuality. . . Actualization is the basis of actuality of the ideal object, but not of this object itself" (p. 13). We shall have to concern ourselves in still more detail with this characteristic notion of Otaka. Otaka himself emphasizes a certain kinship with Freyer's line of thought.

In the first chapter of his book (pp. 18–54) Otaka begins by critically establishing the sphere of ideal existence of Social Organization. He occupies himself with the breakdown of all attempts to view a social organization, for instance a State, as a real and factual object pure and simple.[4] <He ascribed this failure to> the circumstance that the factualities which become visible in empirical actuality – for instance, the social actions of human beings, especially those of the organs of the State – are comprehensible as the means of this mode of observation in which the State persists as "the same" in its supra-individual historical-temporal durations no matter how its factual "component parts" continually undergo change. The state "remains the *same* formation, even when all those who belong to the State sleep or are not involved in *de facto* acts and actions" (pp. 18f.).

This difficulty disappears as soon as we apprehend the state in its characteristic ontic mode, namely as an ideal object. "This is because an ideal object produced by the mind has in its innermost essence the self-sufficient determination of remaining identical in itself no matter how its differing 'ontic' properties continuously change" (p. 19). In the literature there is no lack of attempts to unify this identity of social organization with the change in its elements. Otaka subjects many such elements to examination. Against Simmel and von Wiese he objects that both include in their investigations only empirically pure psychological factualities, namely the ideas which the social actor has of social formations. This signifies nothing less than dissolution and elimination of the object itself under investigation. In Otaka's view, the same reproach may be leveled at Max Weber who indeed broke down social organization into interconnections of specific actions of individuals. But the case of Weber is incomparably more complicated: understanding sociology asks about the subjective meaning of the actor, which it tries to comprehend by the construction of ideal types. It must also work with ideal types of social organizations, for instance, with the ideal type, "the State".

[4]In this and several other contexts Wagner capitalizes "State" chiefly to emphasize the political organization of power of what, Wagner says, English writers call "Society" and writers in the German tradition, up to and including Schutz, called "State", reifying it into the predominate essence and ultimate principle of a nation's being in contrast to e.g., American writers who would emphasize citizenry as the foundation of the nation. Having grown up in an even more autocratic society, Wagner notes, Otaka adopted the German terminology as a matter of course.

In contrast, Otaka holds that neither a rational nor an irrational content of meaning is understandable "if it simply remains a subjectively meant content of meaning. On the contrary, a meaning is universally understandable in so far as we confront it as an objective sense. The objective sense, which is there not only for me but also for everyone, is a common good produced by the mind. Only by virtue of this objective understandableness, accessible to everyone, can the understanding of *de facto* subjective life of the mind be mediated by meaning." "If therefore the *ideal* type, 'the State', can mediate the meaningful understanding of a complex of *de facto* actions like those pertaining to the factual contents of the meaning, 'the State', this does not occur in the way Max Weber means. His ideal type is a one-sided and technically enhanced conceptual construction oriented toward the direction of rationality. Instead, taken fundamentally, it occurs because [the ideal type, 'State'] is a meaning-formation accessible and understandable in the same way for the actor as for the observer" (p. 31). "The type-forming methodology of sociological cognition thus leads necessarily to the recognition of the ideal existence of the State as an objective formation produced by the mind" (p. 32).

I have quoted directly here because in those words, there would seem to come to light a possible misconception of the essence of understanding sociology and the method of constructing ideal types. The achievement of the ideal-typical method is embodied precisely in finding an access to contexts of meaning by disclosing the subjective meanings of this or that actor – contexts of meaning to which the actor is oriented in the sense of "meanings for everyone", in short, as objective meanings. Weber expressly states that the so-called objective contents of meaning form sociologically relevant factual contexts in so far as actors orient themselves to the idea of their <socially pregiven> validity. Just in order to grasp these ideas it is necessary to form a personal ideal type of actor (for instance, that of the citizen or the ruler) oriented to the validity of a political order. Understanding sociology consistently focuses on the subjective interpretation of meanings. It never claimed that its assertions about the state or other social formations can or should comprehend the full content of these formations. To the degree to which such social organizations as idealities of the mind are relevant for understanding sociology, they are such only because of the circumstance that these contents of objective meaning enter into the contents of objective meaning of the actor or actors.

Otaka himself emphasizes (p. 35) that one should not confuse "the abstract-ideal formations of meaning constructed by science with technical-cognitive intentions" with the "concretely-ideal formations of the mind which are objectively fashioned in the course of historical developments" <as experienced and interpreted and typified in various social organizations)>.

This is wholly in line with the standpoint of understanding sociology. But then Otaka reproaches Weber – unjustly, in my opinion – of himself being a victim of this confusion: "Weber clearly realized that cognitively formed constructions (such as ideal types) cannot be the cognitive object (but rather only the cognitive means) of the social sciences. But he arrives at the false conclusion that every formation of mind would always *only* be an ideal type technically constructed as a means of cognition and that, as a consequence, the social sciences taken universally must refuse making the ideal-identical social organization into its object" (p. 35). Neither the social sciences in general nor indeed even understanding sociology have to make their work easy for themselves with such a refusal, at least not according to Weber's conception. However, understanding sociology has been given the task, first of all, of dissolving the so-called objective contents of meaning into subjective concatenations of meaning with the help of its own methods of forming ideal types. Further it also has to show how social organization (for instance, the state) constitutes itself in and on the basis of these concatenations of subjective meaning.

Otaka turns next to a critique of Kelsen's theory of "organization as normative ought". After reviewing the relevant doctrines of Kelsen, Otaka details his objections to two main points of Kelsen's conception, namely a) the identification of mental being with the normative ought, and b) the identification of the state with law.

Concerning the identification of mental being with the normative ought, Otaka objects – quite rightly, I believe – that "the normative theory denies from the outset conceiving the world of mind solely as the pure sphere of ideal meaning because the theory no longer regards the 'actualization' of the ideal formation of meaning in the sphere of factuality (in the factual course of life) as something mental but instead as part of the being of Nature" (p. 44). However, this limitation of the concept of mind [*Geist*] to the objective sphere of meaning would be untenable because the world of the mind also comprises mental factuality, which is neither the normative ought nor mere being of Nature. An example of such factuality of mind is any utensil that is, along with its materiality, also a "thing in order to" and which therefore points toward a specific behavior of the person who uses it.

In any case, this argument, as Otaka himself notes, has no bearing on the social organization which, according to Otaka's conception, is not a mental factuality but instead belongs from the beginning to the sphere of formations produced by mind at a higher level of ideality (p. 46). For it is certainly not correct to assert that any ideal being arises with a claim to normative validity. Instead it is the case that all normative attitudes, as practical attitudes of a higher order, presuppose a theoretical conception of the ideal object. An ought is subordinated, in the first place, to the theoretically conceived ideal object and, more particularly, "by means of the normative consciousness" the ought is so formed "that this idea [*Idee*] ought to be actualized or brought about" (p. 48).

These sorts of practical, normative attitudes can now be theoretically observed again, i.e., can be made an object of a theoretical science of norms. But the theoretical science of norms will never be identical with the theoretical cognition of the value idea grasped in its primitive form, nor will theoretical cognition itself be normative. In "its original form, an ideal formation of meaning, accordingly, need not be regarded as a normative ought; it is, first of all, discovered as pure being" (p. 50). If Kelsen repeatedly emphasizes that social organization could also be regarded as being, namely as being of the ought, then this being should not be confused with the being of the ideal object itself. The latter would be pure and original being, revealing no property of the normative ought, while the former would "only be knowable by means of transferring again the practical ought to the sphere of ideal objectivities and then regarding it as an object of the theoretical science of norms" (p. 50). From this assumption it follows for Otaka that the state must be conceived as sharply distinct from the legal order and that social organization must be understood as an idea and therefore non-normative formation produced by the mind which forms the object of a science of being directed to the ideal sphere of mind.

As an appendix to this polemic against the normative theory, it must be noted that the question of the object of being and the ought in itself needs clarification. The positing [*Thesis*] of the self-sufficiency of a domain of normative considerations can scarcely be justified on epistemological-theoretical grounds.[5]

Establishing the fact that Social Organization is an ideal objectivity leads to a series of complicated problems. "What is ideal can also be actual, but not every ideal being is an actual being." Even a fiction, e.g., a centaur, has ideal being although it is not actual. "Being in a universal sense which yet does not imply being actual" is what Otaka calls "existence" – although not without reservation and certainly in opposition to traditional terminology. The ideal being of social organization is now not mere existence, but actual being. "The state, which forms an object of the theory of social organization, is not identical with a 'utopian' state which is merely thought of. Social organization must, instead, still become established in its own kind of ideality by a 'positing of actuality' [*Wirklichkeitsthesis*]" (p. 52). However, as already mentioned, this actual being should not be confused with the mere "actualization" of its meaning in social factuality although, as can be directly shown, actuality accrues to social organization as an ideal formation produced by the mind in so far as its meaning is always again realized in the *de facto* course of social life. Extensive preparation is required, however, for the development of these interconnections which are not wholly clear at first.

The problem of actuality is correlative to the problem of truth. "If one frames a judgment with a positing of actuality, then the question arises if the object posited in the judgment as actual being is actually so 'given' as it is meant. In this case the problem is regarded from the side of the object of the judgment in question, and for that reason it exhibits itself as the problem of a being or an actual being. If, in contrast, one regards the same judgment from the side of the judgmental act and asks if the 'intention' of this act is correctly related to the relevant object, in which case the problem of the truth or correctness of the judgment arises. The concept of truth is related to the act of judgment, while that of actuality is directly related to the object itself. The problem of actuality must therefore be set and explained with that of truth" (p. 56).

The core of Otaka's formulation of the relationship of truth to actuality is correct, yet in many ways, unfortunately, defective. It is correct that a connection obtains between truth and actuality. If positing of actuality is extended to a real or an ideal object, then this can, obviously, be transformed into the proposition: the judgment, "this object is actual", is true. In contrast, it is incorrect that the concept of truth

[5]Note of Alfred Schutz: Cf. in this connection, Felix Kaufmann, "Juristischer und soziologischer Staatsbegriff", in a cooperative work edited by Verdross, *Gesellschaft, Staat und Recht*, Vienna, 1931, pp. 14–41; and more recently, Felix Kaufmann, *Methodenlehre der Sozialwissenschaft*, Vienna, 1936, pp. 169ff., especially pp. 175 and 293ff.

relates itself to the judgmental act. It relates itself rather to what is judged in the judging, thus to the judgmental *content* which is already set off from the intention of the judgmental act in which it is generated. This critical observation is indispensable because it is of significance for the further presentation of Otaka's theory.

It is the phenomenology worked out by Husserl which serves the goal of investigating the interrelationship between truth and actuality and for the clarification of both concepts. In this connection Otaka refers chiefly to places in Husserl's earliest major work, the *Logical Investigations* and especially to the Sixth Investigation; he also refers in part to Husserl's latest great work, the *Formal and Transcendental Logic*. Yet Otaka does not avail himself of the shift of phenomenology to constitutional analysis, which is carried out in the latter work, although just this constitutional analysis offers discoveries especially important for the problems set by Otaka – indeed, they are quite indispensable for dealing radically with those problems. Otaka takes his point of departure from one of the four concepts of truth posed in Husserl's *Logical Investigations*. There truth signifies complete agreement between what is meant and what is given, as given. According to Husserl, this *adequatio rei ac intellectus* is only present when an objectivational intention achieves its ultimate fulfilment by perfect perception, when what is objective is thus actually present or given precisely as that which it is intended to as being. Every meaning, thinking, judging, when accompanied by positing of actuality, aims as its objective correlate, "intends to" [*"intendiert"*] its objective correlate. This intending either achieves or does not achieve its fulfilment by what is immediately given. Only when the complete and total intending [*Intention*] achieves its concluding and final fulfilment in the immediately given is genuine adequation itself reached in the affair in question. "The object is, then, not merely meant, but given in the strictest sense just as it is meant and posited in the meaning".

In this case we may also speak of complete evidence, whereby we must keep in mind that, for Husserl, "evidence" is not a questionable feeling of evidence as in the traditional theory of truth, but instead an intentive product of consciousness by virtue of which the object is seized upon in the having of something itself. Here, as Otaka himself rightly emphasizes, there are degrees and levels of evidence. But how is the immediately given, how are "the things themselves", grasped? Husserl answers, and Otaka accepts his answer, that individual objects are given in the first and most pregnant sense through perception or experience, and that all truths must refer back to the primitive basis of experience. As a consequence, the necessary demand arises that the judgments about universals – and they comprise scientific cognition – be traced back to judgments about individuals and then must be verified by the having of something individual itself, thus in "possible experience".

In this context, "experience" is not to be understood in the superficial empiricistic sense, no more than "perception" should be restricted to sense experience. Rather, for Husserl, perception signifies sensuous as well as categorial intuition, and experience signifies the "primal instituting of the being-for-us of objects as having their objective sense".[6] But the world, which I experience, is not my private world. It is

[6]Husserl, *Formale und transzendentale Logik*, p. 147 [English translation by Dorion Cairns, p. 164.]

the world of all of us, everyone's world, and my experience of this world is therefore in advance community experience which is mutually legitimating and correcting. Otaka correctly comprehends this doctrine of Husserl when he says: "The being actual of an Objective object [*objektiven Gegenstand*] has its ultimate ontic and epistemic ground in immediate, transcendental-intersubjective experience of the world" (p. 65).

There now arises the difficult problem of how an ideal object is perceived and thus of how its actuality can be legitimately established. On the basis of, and in general agreement with Husserl, Otaka offers his solution in roughly the following way: Husserl has shown that just as there is a so-called categorial intuition along with sensuous intuition, so there is a perception of something ideal along with the perception of something real. It is peculiar to the categorial intuition that it yields an ideal object on the occasion of sensuous perception of real objects corresponding to <the ideal object>; in other words, all acts of categorial intuition are "founded" by acts of sensuous perception simpliciter. The sensuous, or real, objects are therefore objects of the lowest level of possible intuition, that is, perception simpliciter, while the categorial or ideal objects are objects of a higher order. To be sure, the ideal object is never itself given sensuously, but it can only be brought into view on the basis of a corresponding sensuous intuition. The real object thus founds the ideal object; it is the necessary occasion for the subsequent giving of the ideal object itself in the suprasensuous categorial act-level.

From the foregoing Otaka draws the conclusion "that, in the first place, an ideal object can only be conceived as something actually existent in a suprasensuous categorial intuition; secondly, that this conceiving of the ideal object must always be effected on the occasion of the sensuous perception of the corresponding reality. When, now, the social organization first of all, as an ideal formation produced by the mind, presents a self-sufficient object of scientific cognition; but when, at the same time, it is established as something actually existing rather than as something merely ideally existing: then, fundamentally, one must ask which is the real foundation on which the social organization ideally and, despite that, actually rests" (p. 72).

This review is not the place for a study of phenomenology or even for an explanation of the subtilities of this most difficult theory of ideal objects, of a theory which has undergone many modifications in the course of its development. Moreover, within the circle of phenomenological investigators there are those[7] – among whom the writer of these lines does *not* count himself as belonging – who reject categorial intuition or, better stated, the immediacy of experience of ideal objects. For this reason, let us consider Husserl himself. Otaka takes over his theory as set forth in the Sixth Logical Investigation. Otaka apparently does not appropriate the deepening and extending of the theory in the *Ideas Pertaining to a Pure Phenomenology and Phenomenological Philosophy, Book I* (1913) and in *Formal and Transcendental Logic* (1929). But it must now be emphasized that Husserl, in his earlier concept of the theory, only regards as ideal objects abstract categorial empty forms such as

[7]Footnote of Alfred Schutz: Cf. e.g., pp. 23ff., 175 of Felix Kaufmann's *Methodenlehre der Sozialwissenschaften* cited earlier.

"set", "plurality", "totality", "predicatively formed affair complex", "collectiva", and never material formations such as social organization in its socio-historical actuality. Otaka also explicitly emphasizes that (on p. 73), but finds, however, that Husserl's theory requires further elaboration, and this because "the real object itself, whose sensuous perceivability is outside of doubt beforehand, nonetheless ultimately contains something ideal in its ontic core without which it could not show itself as an 'identical' object in itself" (p. 74). The proof that even the real object contains an ideal moment, i.e., its identity in the variation of spatial and temporal perspectives in which it presents itself, is carried out by Otaka in a distinctive analysis (sec. 9, pp. 74–81) which continuously draws on the relevant passages in Husserl that give expression, *expressis verbis*, to this view and especially Husserl's later works,[8] which are not reviewed by Otaka, have subsequently referred to the fundamental importance of this insight. Above all, Otaka appeals to the theory of the "noematic core" developed by Husserl in his *Ideas Pertaining to a Pure Phenomenology and Phenomenological Philosophy, Book I* – the theory of the noematic core which remains unchanged in all noematic-noetic variations and, in this context, explicitly speaks of the opposition between constitutive and ontological ideality.

In the framework of this review it is not possible to enter more precisely into the consideration of the very difficult set of phenomenological problems justifying this distinction. Only by way of a note can we mention for those readers already prepared in phenomenology that the constitutive thematic of phenomenology, thus the question about the constitution of objects as objects of actual and possible consciousness, is deliberately neglected by Otaka even though it is indispensable for clarification of his problem that he deal with the constitution of the actuality of ideal objects. In any case, developing a proof for the correctness of this assertion would require an extended essay. To be sure, just the noetic set of problems selected by Otaka has proved to be quite insufficient for solving the question about the ideality of any object whatever – a set of problems which, in the development taken by phenomenology since the *Ideas* has, in contrast to the constitutive thematic, quite retreated into the background. The thesis that ideality accrues to all sorts of objectivities must be correctly understood in that connection as the thesis that all intentional unities exhibit a universal ideality in contrast to the multiplicities constituting them.

If it is therefore indubitably correct, within the limitations just made, that, as Otaka says, "every real object ultimately can subsist as a unitary and identical object, thus as an actual and Objectively existing object at all, by virtue of a certain ideality" (p, 81), then the questions arise as to whether there is any difference at all between real and ideal objects and, granting this, whether there are any criteria justifying the distinction. Now, it is Otaka's opinion that in all concrete, ideal (material) formations produced by the mind it is the physically real thing [*das Dinghafte reale*], the matter, which founds the mental or cultural sense of this formation.

As a paradigm for this material formation produced by the mind [*sachhaltige Geistesgebilde*], along with social organization in its socio-historical reality, Otaka

[8]Footnote of Alfred Schutz: Cf. especially *Formale und transzendentale Logik*, sec. 62, p. 148 [English translation, pp. 165f.]

refers to the "physical thing for the sake of", the work-utensil, the use-object, the "utensil" in the Heideggerian sense. The mental object, founded by real matter, already belongs to the ideal sphere of existence and in the cultural world reality simpliciter is applicable only as a limit concept. This lowest level of mental ideality, *immediately* founded by natural reality, but which still, because of its inherent "sense", must be sharply distinguished from merely external real Nature, Otaka calls "facticity" or "factuality". The identical existence of a determined factual object, however, is guaranteed by this ideal and senseful existential core, perceiveable in "senseful intuition" [*sinnhafte Anschauung*]. Senseful intuition is founded by sense perception, although effected at a higher level.

In place of the term, "senseful intuition", one may also say "understanding" [*"Verstehen"*]. According to Husserl's own usage, senseful intuition is nothing else than categorial intuition. Notwithstanding, Otaka reserves this term exclusively for designation of the most universal and abstract sphere of ideality. Not only is there a founding interconnectedness [*Fundierungszusammenhang*] between reality simpliciter and mental facticity but, analogously, between mental facticity and the reality superordinate to it. According to Otaka, this interconnectedness of founding can be of two kinds: it is homogeneous when the subordinated founding object, existing for itself, is not directed against the founded mental objectivity of a higher level; it is heterogeneous when the subordinated founding object, in the first place, in the structural concatenation with other co-ordinate objects, can serve as the basis of actuality of the founded object of a higher level.

As an example of homogeneous founding Otaka adduces the relationship of an original work of art (e.g., of a painting) to its imitations or reproductions; as an example of heterogeneous founding he adduces the work-utensil, always conceived in Heidegger's sense of a "utensil for the sake of" within a utensil-totality. Homogeneous and heterogeneous foundings can be effected in a hierarchical sequence of levels.

In the case of dealing with a Japanese woodcut by Utamaro I grasp, in the first place, the meaning of this specific work of art by Utamaro as what remains identical, e.g., in the homogeneous multiplicity of the factual; but I also then grasp, in general, the specific art of the woodcut, at a still higher level, the spirit of the Japanese woodcut of the Tokugawa period and, finally, of the Japanese woodcut as such. Something similar may be said about the heterogeneous founding. Thus it is to be emphasized that homogeneous and heterogeneous founding stand in the closest connection and, in common, construct both fundamental principles of the whole hierarchical structure of the concrete-ideal world of the mind. Homogeneous, or heterogeneous, founding constitutes the identity, or the unity, of the object. "The identical being of the ideal object is revealed once and for all at higher act-levels founded by the founding multiplicities. In the last analysis, a concrete-ideal mental formation is discovered as the unity and identical object only in the act of senseful intuition corresponding to it" (p. 91).

This result is of the greatest significance for Otaka's theory of social organization which, according to his conception, also proves to be an ideal object. As long as sociology only has its eye on the multiplicity of actualities founding the ideal object,

"Social Organization", it must as a consequence be led to deny the identically existing social organization. "The radical turn of the regard from the founding multiplicities to the founded unity and identity of the ideal object of a higher order creates the possibility of ascertaining and ultimately of confirming in the first place the true and self-sufficient actual being of the social organization" (p. 92).

According to the foregoing considerations, if it is now the case that the basis of actuality for idealities of a higher order lies in the sphere of founding multiplicities – the factualities themselves being meaningfully understood rather than being mere natural realities – then a circle would seem to be present in so far as the "sense" of the founding apparently presupposes the sense of what is founded by it, the result being a reversal of the founding-founded relationship. According to Otaka this objection does not hold. The appearance of this circle occurs, Otaka says, because of the fact that the actuality-founding and the meaning-founding are not carefully separated. "The reality, or the ideality closest to the reality founds once and for all the 'actual being' of the mental object of a higher ideality . . . If the sense of the founded ideal object existentially grounds in addition any factuality founding it, then it is indeed evident that one can never know further the actuality of this ideal object if no factual objectivity corresponding to it is at all present. An ideal art-formation, remaining in itself identical, is in fact no longer actual if not only the original as factual objectivity but also all copies and other sorts of reproductions become totally annihilated" (pp. 94f.).

It is quite different in the case of meaning or senseful founding. "What the peculiarity of mental factuality confers on mere physical thingness is nothing else but a determined '*sense*'. On the one hand, this sense or meaning can now be combined with physical thingness by virtue of the fact that the practically acting human being consciously effects a specific 'act of sense-fashioning' with respect to the physical thing in question. On the other hand, one can already find oneself in combination with physical thingness in the historical course of development of social existence" (p. 95). "The act of sense-formation . . . is, from the outset, an Objectively effecting act which, at the same time, is determined by a practically oriented 'goal' of which there is more or less clear consciousness" (p. 96). The sense or meaning, "in the last analysis, is created by a genuine act of objective-sense fashioning which is, accordingly, either consciously effected by an individual person or gradually and unconsciously accomplished in the supra-individual developmental course of history. Accordingly, every concrete-ideal object is, as to its essence, something 'formed' ['*Gebildetes*']; it is a 'mental formation' in the truest sense of the word" (p. 97). Otaka resolves the previously mentioned circle thus: "What is ideal founds . . . the factual object 'sensefully', but in its 'actual being' [what is ideal] is conversely founded by [the factual object]. The ideal sense of the concrete mental formation signifies what founds it in 'senseful founding;' it signifies in contrast what is founded in the 'actuality-founding'" (p. 97).[9]

[9]Note of Alfred Schutz: Instead of offering a critique of Otaka's levels here, I would like to refer to a completely different account of this problem in my book, *Der sinnhafte Aufbau der sozialen Welt*, Parts II and III.

What application do these insights acquired now have for a universal theory of actual being of ideal mental formations, and in particular for the object, "social organization"? With respect to mental factuality functioning as the actuality-being of the concrete-ideal mental formation, Otaka distinguishes two fundamental types. With respect to the first type – for example, a work-utensil or an artwork – according to Otaka factual objectivity is absorbed into a materially "determinate thing" [*materialen "Sachlichkeit"*], the concretely ideal mental formation, and he therefore gives this type the name, " *materially determinate* mental formation" ["*sachliches Geistesgebilde*"]. The other type of ideal mental formation of a higher order, e.g., a certain religion or a certain legal or economic system, in contrast finds its founding in meaningfully comprehensible actions of human beings; more precisely stated, in determined activities essentially related to the behavior of *others* or to *social* actions. Otaka therefore calls this kind of ideal mental formation *social* mental formation. Otaka himself has the feeling that this division is quite problematic, and that it is not correct to include a "work-utensil" or an "artwork" in the material mental formation or, perhaps, to subordinate science to this type on that account because it is referred to the work-utensil that is language.

The genuine philosophical problem which grounds Otaka's formulations is quite complex and can only be analyzed on the basis of extensive preparation. To that end one must not only thoroughly inquire into the problems connected with the essence of action, but one must also describe the modifications which the "sense" or "meaning" undergoes in the sphere of sociality. It would then be established that what Otaka calls "material" mental formation as well as "social mental formation" have their founding in actuality in previous social actions. In any case, however, no fundamental objections can be raised against the fact that Otaka sees the essence of social mental formations in their historicality and hence in their historical variability. Otaka distinguishes, now, from all other social mental formations (such as law, religion) the social organization by the fact that it alone is knowable "simply on account of the 'sociality' of its content of meaning, thus purely as a totality formed among human beings" (p. 115) – while law, religion, etc., refer back to materially oriented or, as Otaka says, material-social actions rather than to actions simpliciter.

The *pure* social formation *kat' exochén* is, in Otaka's view, the social organization and with this result it is, in his opinion, also sufficiently defined. Of course, other still more precise statements may be made about those social actions which alone can form the adequate actuality-basis of the social organization. The social actions must 1) be mutually related, thus be *social relations*; in addition, they must 2) bear the characteristic of *communalization*, and 3) be oriented or related back to the *Objective fashioning of sense or meaning* manifested in the historicality of the being-actual peculiar to social organization.

These three conditions of social actions constituting the basis of actuality of social organization are now subjected to a thorough analysis. The eidetic structure of the social relation is clarified in a critical discussion of Simmel's concept of reciprocal action. Otaka arrives at the conclusion that the social relation is a "concatenation of reciprocally directed social acts of many persons structurally joined by means of expression and understanding" (p. 121), although this holds for acts which normally have a material (and not simply a social) content of meaning. In the polemics with Simmel Otaka especially objects to the ambiguity of Simmel's concept of form and to the causal moment included in Simmel's concept of reciprocal action. Quite rightly Otaka emphasizes that the unity of the social relation is in its essence a structural and not a causal one (p. 135).

Which of the many social relations function, now, as the basis of actuality of the social organization? To answer this question, Otaka fashions, first of all, different types of social relations which, as he himself says, comprise only a few fundamental forms. "With respect to the content of the mental processes grounding the constitution of the relation in question, and providing it with a determined orientation" (p. 136), he sets up three opposing pairs of social relations: more particularly, a) harmonious and disharmonious relations, depending on whether the social experiences concatenated in the social relations by means of expression and understanding are focused on one another "affirmingly" (example: pure friendship) or "rejectingly" (example: war); b) rational and irrational relations, depending on whether the experiences of the persons standing in the social relation are related to each other by clear "consciousness of goal" or by "feeling"; c) relations of domination and equality, depending on whether the social experience of the subjects standing in the social relation includes a consciousness of a superordination or a subordination, or some sort of a coordination. With respect to the outward course of the social relation a further opposing pair can become fashioned: d) that of a direct or derived relation, depending on whether the persons *A and B* standing in the social relation simply express to the partner the content of their experience, or simply understand the expressed experiences as experiences of such a kind, or whether – purposefully or not – the content of experiences can be expressed in some transformed (diverted) way (lies, deceptions), or be understood in an inadequate way (misunderstanding) in an expression.

If one can already raise important observations against the appropriateness and even against the logical justification of this classification, perchance seeing as well a significant step backward over against Max Weber in the typology set up by Otaka, then one would withdraw even more from agreeing with Otaka when, by way of definition, he contrasts "socialization" ["*Vergesellschaftung*"] as a "rational-diverted-harmonious relation" to "communalization" [*"Vergemeinschaftung"*] as an "irrational (valuatively rational)-direct-harmonious relation" (p. 142). To justify this definition Otaka appeals not only to Tönnies and Weber, but also to Pfänder, Scheler and Vierkandt. When one sees, as Otaka does, the adequate basis of actuality precisely in communalization of the social organization, then it remains indispensable to prove whether the opposition in the social sciences between socialization and communalization – an opposition which has become a ruinous tradition – allows for critical reflection.

Unfortunately, Otaka has neglected to analyze this problem with the detailed precision otherwise customary for him. He satisfied himself with establishing the result that Social Organization can only be actual as social organization in so far as the communalization decisive for it fashions its basis of actuality. This is then the case when many persons, in the consciousness of their common membership in an organization stand with one another in an internally harmonious communalizing relation (pp. 145f.). Obviously there is present here a *petitio principii*, and Otaka does not realize this difficulty at all. However, he does see in this state of affairs that the communalization, as founding the social organization which, for its part, is itself founded by the co-given sense of the organization, is only a special case of the ambiguity, presented above, of the relations between founding of meaning or sense and founding of actuality. Previously the founding of actuality of the social organization was the topic of discussion, and in this setting of the problem of the factual communalization doubtlessly founds the social organization. In order to set aside the apparent circle, one must no longer, as in the previous investigation, remain with the question, under which conditions an organization as already objectively existing as *sense* in the communal-historical world acquires actual existence; instead, the problem of Objective formation of meaning of the social organization must be tackled.

Regretfully, what Otaka has to say about this is quite insufficient. He is satisfied with ascertaining that the act of formation of meaning of the social organization is an act which executes itself objectively when several persons undertake it more or less deliberately. This done, they then belong collectively to the organization originating in this way. As a rule, this act is also tied up with a more or less objectively recognized external formula (marriage contract, political constitution, and the like). Along with this there are also given in the concrete world of social existence numerous forms of organizations "the meaning-fashioning acts of which are unconsciously effected in the supra-individual developmental course of human history, whereby the sense of the organization in its imperturbable pregivenness is taken for granted and handed down in tradition". But what is of importance is that the objective fashioning of meaning of the social organization is a specific act, without entailing the actual being of the organization in question. As a consequence, if it is the case that this act of fashioning meaning is also capable of being performed on the basis of socialization, the natural right theory of the "social contract" then would be a presupposition of the sort which is increasingly hypothetical in the extreme. But should the social organization become actuality, then the socialization which serves as foundation of the act of objective fashioning of meaning must be replaced by a communalization in which those belonging to the organization are conscious of belonging to the communalization by virtue of their membership in the organization.

From the perspective of this theory a specific aspect of the problem of the historicality of the social organization also results. The actual being of the organization already has its historicality by virtue of the positive act of fashioning meaning whereby the organization is generated and over against which there are as well acts of cancelling or denying meaning. "The dissolved marriage or the annexed State are transformed into a 'merely ideal sense' and then exist as a mere sense-formation, as the sphere of pure ideality, free of actuality . . . [E]very social organization as an *actual* object, has its 'beginning' and its 'end' – it necessarily has its 'history'. The social organization, as a concrete-ideal object, can thus only be actual in the mode of historicality" (p. 154).

Otaka dedicates the fourth chapter of his book (pp. 155–196) to investigations of the internal structure of the social organization and, in this connection, begins by applying the relation of the social organization to its particular fellow members – a relation which, for Otaka, is presented as a relation between the universal and the particular. The social organization is a totality formed between human beings; it is neither a mere sum of the particular persons belonging to it, nor a complex of meaningfully understandable social actions of these particular persons. With this theory Otaka explicitly approaches Spann's universalistic conception of society. The *existential* core of social organization, according to Spann, is not found in the particular persons belonging to the organization but instead in the social totality itself. But in this ideal objectivity there is also to be found the ideality-core and the identity-pole of the social organization, as a result of which it remains the "same" organization in contrast to the coming and going of the particular persons belonging to it. The universal – the social organization – stands over against the particular in a relationship of domination. "Rulership" [*"Herrschschaft"*] is what is essential to the social organization. Where the particular rules, it does so in the name of the organization as the "organ" which "represents" the organization. Government and administration, coercion and enforcement have their origin here.

In contrast, however, the *actual being* of the social organization is a relative concept, that is, capable of having a number of levels. The social organization can find the center of its actual being in the "universal" or in the "particular", or, thirdly, its core of actuality lies precisely in the unitary connection of the universal to the particular. In this way three basic types can be distinguished according to total structure of the social organization. Otaka calls them community, society, and corporate body. It is only as corporate body, thus as synthesis of community and society, that the social organization can be actual in its totality (p. 163). The conceptual delimitation of community from society is made more precise by a critical discussion of the doctrines of Tönnies and Hegel. An example of a community (the center of actuality taken universally) is a totemistic tribal kinship; an example of society (the center of actuality taken in the particular) is the purely administrative organization [*Zweckverband*]; and an example of a corporate body (which is actual because the universal is actual by means of the particular, but the particular is actual by means of the universal) is, more precisely stated, a "cultural organization" (a group of artists, or a union of scientists). And each of these basic types is to be investigated with respect to its relation to economy, religion and law. In addition, many a wise word is said about the relation of the individual to these three types, about their "value-rational" [*"wertrational"*] attitudes toward the types, about the changes in the types throughout the course of history.

The fifth chapter (pp. 197–251) accomplishes the transition from the analysis of pure sociality, to which the first four chapters were dedicated, to the synthetical observation of the structural nexus pertaining to single material social formations and accordingly begins with an analysis of the structural nexus acquired by a criticism of the theories of Dilthey and Simmel. The concepts of the structural nexus and the causal nexus are taken over from Dilthey. In contrast to the world of Nature, the world of Mind fashions beforehand a necessary unity, the nexus (structure) of which is directly and originally "given" to our experience from the start and is accessible in the specific way of "understanding". If the causal nexus is the principle of the world of Nature, then the structural nexus is the principle of the world of Mind. The basic science which deals with this structural nexus, describing psychology in Dilthey's sense, is also for Otaka the science fundamental to the universal social sciences.

However, Mind, the object of analysis and description in the social sciences, is not only subjectively lived Mind, but also Mind objectivated in external materiality, by which Dilthey understands the multiple forms in which what subsists as common among individuals has been objectivated in the world of the senses. Even the objective cultural formations can be investigated with respect to their structural nexus; indeed, one may even say that something such as the social organization, as pure social organization, can only be grasped and intuitively described in its structural nexus in concretion with the "material" social formations such as relation, morals, legal and economic systems. Along with this structural nexus, which describes the world of the Mind in its contemporaneity, the causal nexus must, however, be established as the second basic concept of the cultural sciences, that is to say, that immanent-teleological nexus which conceives the totality of Mind as dynamic succession of historical development and change. Otaka assigns the analysis of the causal nexus to the historical cultural sciences, while the task of grasping the structural nexus is turned over to the systematic cultural sciences.

Consequently a basic theme of the systematic social sciences is the structural nexus of the purely social and the material or factual. The theme is demonstrable at two levels, i.e., at the level of the ideal sphere of existence of the social organization and at the level of the sphere of its mental facticity. Otaka limits himself to an analysis of a paradigm and, more particularly, to the clarification of the *social structure of law*.

After rejecting Stammler's theory, against whose thesis social life is explicitly ordered living-together of people, Otaka rightly objects that law is only a materially or factually partial region of social life, taking issue with Kelsen's conception of the normative character of law. Otaka arrives at the conclusion that the ordering function of law reveals distinct types in communalization and socialization. In communalization law has the task of establishing the "required harmonizing or the allowable disharmonizing" of the community. In communalization law is social ordering. The law peculiar to socialization, in which, according to Otaka, actual relations necessarily arise in a form characterized by the instrumental-rational and derivative harmony – : with respect to its essence, the law peculiar to socialization includes a highly developed coercive ordering by means of which the lost social ordering can be re-established. As social ordering, law is the normative law of the social behavior of the particular; as coercive ordering law is the behavioral rule of the social whole or its organs (punishment, execution, etc.).

Precisely here the peculiar dual structure of law is shown, but which also allows of being demonstrated on the basis of an analysis of legal judgments. Otaka blames Kelsen's theory of law for basically taking as "law" only the compulsory act as the legal sanction which includes the legal judgment, but not the social norm which prescribes directly and universally how the particular person should behave in a certain way. "The social norm", Otaka says (p. 232), "finds the immediate guarantee of its validity not in any sort of exercize of coercion but rather precisely in the more or less clearly conscious 'feeling of the law' peculiar to a people . . . Legal judgments as legal norms for the behavior of the social whole must, consequently, be clearly and distinctly contrasted to the social norm as legal norm for the behavior of particular persons."

This leads to the following conception of the State: "Ultimately, therefore, the State is nothing else than the complexly arranged organization which, as coercive ordering, stands with the systematically formulated law in the structural nexus and administers the enforcement of law through its own governmental and administrative apparatus. But since the set of laws as compulsory ordering is called 'statute' [*'Gesetz'*] one can also say that the State is an organization assembled by statute, and that, in contrast, the statute is law as coercive ordering systematized by the State" (p. 235). To be sure, to say this is not to fall back on the dual theory of the State criticized by Kelsen. This is because Otaka does not conceive the State as a thing of Nature but instead, just like the law, as an ideal object. Both objects, accordingly, belong to one and the same sphere, and both can therefore be the theme of one and the same science, that is, of systematic social science.

In a critical discussion of Verdross, Otaka applies his theory of the social structure of law to the idea of an international league of nations [*Weltverband*] and the positive international law [*Völkerrecht*]. He defends the opposition, established by Verdross, between the legal community of law and the legal ordering over against Hold-Ferneck's objections, whereby he interprets the legal community pertaining to the league of nations characterized by the international law as an ideal and yet actually existing formation produced by the mind which, however, reveals the structure not of communalization but only that of socialization. But the "essential feature of positive international law ultimately consists of the fact that, in spite of its peculiarity of being the 'law of socialization', it is still not expanded by a systematically developed 'law as coercive ordering'" (p. 249) and for these reasons still does not allow of any genuine construction in legal judgments in its present-day situation. The principle, "*pacta sunt servanda*", functions as the fundamental norm of the law of nations because, as "law of socialization", it is necessarily contract law.

In the final (sixth) chapter (pp. 252–279), Otaka seeks to determine the methodological place of his theory of social organization. He makes the claim that it is a phenomenologically justified ontological science of the actuality of social existence, the cognitive goal of which is the description and clarification of concrete organizations present in historical-social actuality. Otaka designates his theory as "ontological" because its object, in its genuine [*aktuellen*] actual being, already belongs to the sphere of ideal existence, while the empirical social sciences, such as the type-constructive, understanding sociology in Weber's sense, according to Otaka, finds its object only in the domain of factuality subordinate to the sphere of ideal existence. From the historical sciences, which observe actuality in its dynamic causal nexus, the theory of social organization is distinguished by the fact that it "conceives its object by means of the senseful intuitions peculiar to it, and is called upon to clarify its internal and external structural nexus" (p. 268).

However, as an ontological science of "pure" social existence as an ideal formation produced by the mind, according to Otaka, the theory of social organization is nothing else than the ontological constituent realm of sociology in so far as we understand "sociology" to mean not an empirical science of products fashioned by the mind [*Geisteswissenschaft*]. Along side it, as another constituent realm, is the theory of social relations which is a mental science of social existence in its factual sphere and hence investigates the basis of actuality pertaining to the concrete-ideal cultural formation. As theory of sociality, it falls to sociology to concern itself, however, with the structure of material social spheres and, moreover, always from the starting point of pure sociality. This is distinguished from the other social sciences which are concerned with the material domains of social life solely in relation to their material content of meaning. In so far as, e.g., the science of law is not the philosophy of law or the ontology of law, but instead the science of legal matters of fact [*Rechtstatsachenwissenschaft*], which undertakes the study of positive law as the concrete ideal legal formation in its historically actual being, it investigates the sphere of social-legal facticity with respect to the relevant legal content of meaning – while for the scientific sociology of legal matters of fact [*tatsachenwissenschaftliche Rechtssoziologie*] precisely this same sphere of objects is relevant only in so far as the legal sphere is socially determined and oriented.

This attempt to present the most important parts of Otaka's theory can provide only a fragmentary picture of the rich content of the book distinguished by many especially subtle analyses and by its logically closed structure. The form in which the occasionally extremely difficult lines of thought are presented is quite remarkable in view of the circumstance that here a Japanese has been able to appropriate all of the subtilities of German philosophical terminology. It seems to me of the greatest importance of all social sciences to critically examine the problems raised by Otaka. If his theory is also yet incomplete, as had to be repeatedly indicated in the preceding discussion, the thematic areas he reveals are undoubtedly of the greatest relevance. For a long time the attempt has been made to provide a philosophical grounding of the important concepts basic to the social sciences. Perhaps one can reject many of Otaka's theses, but one cannot refuse to recognize that his setting of the problems is genuine, novel, and extremely significant. And it seems to me that this is a praise in which only a few works in the social sciences can share. Let us hope that further investigations, especially by the author himself, will examine in more detail the disclosure of this new realm of problems and contribute to the indispensable clarification of the essence and being of social organization.

CHAPTER 29

Gnosticism and Orthodoxy: Contrasts in Fundamental Metaphysical and Theologial Positions

Editors' Preface

This is another letter to Eric Voegelin by Alfred Schutz, from November, 1952. The title is by Helmut Wagner, and the translation from German into English was made by Gregor Sebba,[1] which Wagner revised stylistically and terminologically for inclusion here. The apparent occasion for Schutz's letter is the arrival of a copy from the University of Chicago Press of Voegelin's just published *The New Science Politics*, and Schutz's reading of chapter drafts of the first volume Voegelin's *Order and History, Israel and Revelation* to be published by Louisiana State University Press in 1956.

As to my concern with establishing a general theory of relevance, I think that, basically, you understand me correctly. An ideally worked-out theory would include the various ethics and, in addition, the various relatively natural aspects of the world[2] found in prescientific experience. But it would also include other matters. For instance, it would elucidate the concept of so-called preferred action, and in the end it would have to provide a general theory of the motivation of human action. Perhaps one might say that a completely worked-out theory of relevance is nothing else than a phenomenology of motivation.

Not without irony, you refer to your limited imagination and say that, as long as this program remains unrealized, we must try to fill the gaps with examples drawn from the available stock of knowledge. As suitable examples you select certain typologies of Aristotle and Jaspers' psychology of basic types. I believe that we have progressed much farther and also that very substantial parts of the general

[1]Sebba's translation appeared in *The Philosophy of Order. Essays on History, Consciousness and Politics*, edited by Peter J. Opitz and Gregor Sebba (Stuttgart: Klett-Cotta, 1981), pp. 434–448. In a few cases, I have restored Sebba's translation which Wagner had altered, and some of Sebba's very helpful footnotes. For further discussion of the relationship between Schutz and Voegelin, see Wagner's article, "Agreement in Discord", in *The Philosophy of Order: Essays on History, Consciousness and Politics*, pp. 74–90.

[2]Footnote of Gregor Sebba: Schutz's term for Max Scheler's "relativ natürliche Weltanschauungen" as against "relativ künstliche Bildungen". Scheler, *Ges. Werke*, VIII (1960), pp. 63ff. and VI (1963), pp. 15ff.

phenomenology as I envisage it have already been worked out concretely. They can be found not only in Gestalt psychology, economic theory, and contemporary departures in sociological theory but also, within the strictly philosophical field, in certain writings of Husserl, Whitehead, George H. Mead, Gabriel Marcel, and other French philosophers, such as the *Philosophie de la Volonté* of Paul Ricoeur. I would even go one step farther. Although you will protest, I consider the theory you develop in *The New Science of Politics* (1951)[3] a constituent part of this general theory of motivation. Here I agree completely with our friend Aron Gurwitsch who wrote to me – among other things – in an immediate reaction to your book: 'a great work' – and one that is closer to us, that is to phenomenology, then he would admit. By and large, what is it if not phenomenology of historically active societies! The whole method is phenomenological, using the concept of motivation, only he does not call it by that name."[4]

Be that as it may, I do not believe that a general theory of relevance can limit itself to setting up a typological system or a catalogue of types, whether or not such a system or catalogue ultimately relates to a general theory of the good or of goods. To be sure, such a typology is part of the general theory of relevance, and I wholly agree with you when you say that such a typology must rest on a philosophical anthropology. But all of these problems comprise but one part of the scope of a general theory of relevance: the substantive problems in their static aspects. Obviously, a dynamic, that is, historical, elucidation of the forms of motivation in their theoretical problematic, should be equally possible: so for instance, to use your language, a theory of motivation from ritual via myth to symbol. The word, "historical", as just used by me, is to be understood in exactly your sense.

But here appears another quite different group of problems that interest me particularly; and they surely must be of great concern to you too since you are seeking a general theory of order. I am speaking of the formal problems of relevance, of what Gurwitsch in his letter to you (of which he sent me a copy) calls the analysis of the forms of self-understanding. No matter what types of categories of motivation we may accept as underlying prescientific everyday actions, no matter what hierarchies we use to organize these types, we shall always find certain formal structures common to all of them. How does it happen that something arouses my interest? That I concern myself with something? Take up something, set myself a task? What do we mean when we say both in practical and in theoretical life: "This interests me"? All questioning rests on the ground of that which is taken to be unquestionably given. And all answers presuppose the existence of a set of analyzable conditions under which, in a given case, the answer is acceptable as satisfactory and thus allows us to consider the problem solved. If the answer satisfies these conditions, the problem is no longer questionable; it has become unproblematic and is absorbed into the store of things taken-for-granted which in its entirety makes up the natural aspect structure of our view of the "world".

[3]Eric Voegelin, *The New Science of Politics* (Chicago: University of Chicago Press, 1952).

[4]Gurwitsch's letter referred to here is published in *Philosophers in Exile. The Correspondence of Alfred Schutz and Aron Gurwitsch 1939–1959*, edited by Richard Grathoff, translated by J. Claude Evans, foreword by Maurice Natanson (Bloomington and Indianapolis: Indiana University Press, 1989), p. 183. [FK]

A complete theory of relevance has to deal with another very important group of problems: "This and that interests me. *But in this connection* the following interests me too . . ." What does this mean? What do I mean when I say that something may interest me in connection with something else? And another thing: my interest changes. Not only does it change in the course of my biographical existence from youth to old age; it also changes within a working day or even a single hour. Here I sit putting my mind to a philosophical topic; later I shall play some music; then I shall spend some time with my little boy; then I'll read a short novel, and then I shall go to bed. Each of these occupations involves a system of relevances of its own, one that depends on the pertinent practical or theoretical problem on hand. What happens when I temporarily turn away from one problem and toward another? That is, what happens when I temporarily drop one relevance system and move into a different one? How is it possible for me to interrupt something I am working on and resume it the next day?

Two other very important groups of problems complicate the matter. If you still remember my paper on "Multiple Realities" you are familiar with my theory that we live simultaneously on different levels of reality, or can at least shift from one level to another. What is the mutual relationship between the systems of relevances of these different levels of reality? May not each level of reality show its own special structuring of the forms of relevance pertinent to it? Furthermore, all social relations, whether simple or complex, rest on the overlapping or sameness of the participants' systems of relevances. The whole function of "social roles", so important in contemporary theory in the social sciences, is grounded in this presupposition – which, of course, is still completely unclarified. What you call "*philia*" (liking) and "*amicitia*" (friendship) can be explained from the viewpoint of a theory of motivation as the overlapping of sameness of such social systems of relevance.

In my opinion, all of these questions are amenable to theoretical and philosophical treatment without recourse to a theory of the good, to a doctrine of goods, or to concrete problems of an empirical order. After all, in your book you proceed in a similar fashion. Your analysis of representation *per se*, of its elementary and its existential meaning, of its relation to social articulation, obviously is equally valid for all soteriological and all gnostic types of self-understanding. Of course I am quite aware that all these formal analyses can be carried out only on the basis of a philosophical anthropology in the widest sense; in fact, they themselves are part of such an anthropology. I hope you will agree on this point. We likely part company <on the following point>: I cannot see why a philosophical anthropology should be possible only if it is an "anthropodicy", to use Dempf's term.[5] But this touches upon a point of principle which I will raise in the second part of this letter.

I shall say only a few words about the problem of intersubjectivity with which you deal in the last paragraph of your letter. As you know, I wholly agree with you when you say that there is no solution for the problem as posed by Husserl. This problem came into being through (Husserl's) demand that the object should be constituted in the stream of consciousness. Quite justifiably, this demand appears to you

[5]Alois Dempf, *Theoretische Anthropologie* (Bern: A. Francke AG. Verlag, 1950), pp. 32, 51f.

unfulfillable. I agree with you when you state that the problem arose only with the Cartesian monadic isolation of consciousness. This isolation explains why there is no attempt at a solution by Plato or Aristotle or anybody else in the whole history of philosophy. But I cannot go along with you in concluding that there can be no knowledge of the *Sosein* (being-thus) of the other, except through the familiar methods of observing his actions and utterances. From them we develop images of this being-thus and learn that this frequently and perhaps necessarily leads to disappointments. Here we must make the distinction you propose rightly in your book: that between self-interpretation within social reality and the theoretical and philosophical treatment of the problem. Certainly, it cannot be claimed on the level of the self-interpretation of social reality that there can be no knowledge of the being-thus of the other person. It may be that such knowledge belongs to the realm of *doxa* and not that of *episteme*. Nonetheless the confidence in our knowledge of the other's being-thus is not blind but well-founded. It leads to many practical results, as the existence of every social acceptance [*Einbeziehung*] demonstrates. The basic belief that we understand the other person or at least can understand him as far as practical interests require it, is an axiom of the relative-natural aspect of the world. The open possibility of understanding the other is taken for granted as given notwithstanding the equally open possibility of misunderstanding. The latter also belongs to the relative-natural aspect of the world and to the realm of what is taken for granted. In principle, the analysis of the forms of understanding and misunderstanding can be executed within this framework of open possibilities; in itself it is part of a philosophical anthropology.

So much in response to your kind letter. You may think it strange that I deal in such detail with questions you touch on instead of addressing myself directly to the more important subject of this letter of mine: reporting my reactions to your book. I have answered your letter so extensively because it is extremely important for me to clarify my arguments in the hope that you will feel like I do: Here, no conflict of principles separates us. In addition, it seems to me that this beginning of my discussion is very closely related to what I have to say about your book. We would not understand each other properly if I would not have clarified my position to your letter as clearly as I can under the present circumstances. – Now finally to your book.

It is a marvellous book, over-rich and difficult because it is written in double counterpoint. Although I have been studying it continuously ever since it reached me, I am by no means certain that I have truly understood it in all its contents. Thus my comments are of a provisional nature. Yet, I have advantage of being familiar with a few finished chapters of your main manuscript; therefore I know that everything you say is supported by the literature in every detail.

Earlier you had mailed to me the introductory chapter and we exchanged letters about it. Rereading it, I find that I hardly need to change anything in my remarks made at the time. I hope that readers indeed will see this chapter as an introduction to the main chapters that follow. Knowing nothing but this introduction, it was something of a surprise for me to see the manifold and diverse turns your analysis takes as it proceeds.

The chapter on "Representation and Existence" [of <*The New Science of Politics*] is of fundamental importance. Your distinction between the self-interpretation of society through symbols and the interpretation of societal existence by the theorist (the Aristotelian method, as you call it) without doubt deals with the principal problem in the methodology of all social sciences. Again, you are completely correct in saying[6] that the classical distinction between *doxa* and the several *epistemes* has disappeared; in contemporary social science, it has been replaced by the concept of ideology.

After what I have said in the first part of this letter about the relatively natural world view, you will understand my conviction that the structure of *doxa* can (and must) be analyzed further without recourse to the concept of ideology. Of course, this must be done with the theoretical tools of *episteme*. This leads to the problem – paradoxical only at first sight – of how to elucidate structures of *doxa* by means of *episteme*. The matter is somewhat complicated by the fact that after some time and perhaps only to some extent the theoretical elements themselves can become elements of *doxa*. Eventually, this can lead to a theoretical insight becoming in its turn a symbol of the society's self-understanding – your book offers various instances of this. In such a case obviously the theoretical content has not been understood or had become ununderstandable. Thus, it can now again be taken for granted without questioning as a symbol of the society's self-understanding. The recent philosophical literature of the Soviet Union suggests to me that dialectical materialism may be headed in this direction just as in a different area in the West Freud's teachings are clearly undergoing similar formal and structural changes.

The second section of this chapter has given me much food for thought. It contains far more than a mere description of the elementary functions of representation. An expanding pursuit of this argument would elucidate the whole concept of institution; it would shed light on what Scheler was aiming at with this theory of real and ideal factors.

As you can see, my chief interest is concentrated on the theoretical and methodological threads which in your investigation interweave with all concrete analyses of the problem of representation and its theory. Thus I take everything you say about representation merely as examples of the quite general structures of every society. Now, in this effort I encounter some difficulties. It is true that you have pursued the very fundamental distinction between the elementary and the existential necessity of a society as far as this was required by your main problem, the problem of representation. <And in this context> the distinction has been made precise and was corrected. Nevertheless I am asking myself whether the concept of articulation, as developed on pp. 37 and 45, is an exclusively theoretical one – one the theorist must introduce because it is fundamental to the theory of existential necessities, or whether something approaching articulation may not already exist for those living in society.

But perhaps I misunderstood your concept of articulation. Perhaps articulation is nothing but an articulation of the political structure of society. My question then is this: is what we commonly call social stratification also articulation in your sense of the term? If so, does articulation as self-interpretation belong to the elementary sphere of society? And if this is the case, what distinguishes the actual structuring of society

[6]Note of Gregor Sebba: pp. 12f.

from the theoretical concept of articulation? I repeat, these questions have no bearing on the way you use the concept of articulation in your book, where it is fully justified and properly elucidated. My questions concern the problem of a general theory of society with which you do not deal.

I am raising this question mainly because on p. 49 you sum up your definitions by stating that a *politicial* society comes into existence when it articulates itself and produces a representative. However, this representative must be a representative in the existential sense, and he must realize the idea of the institution, as you say on the same page. If he does not do that, he is a representative only in the constitutional – rather than the institutional – sense. In this case a representative ruler in the existential sense will sooner or later finish him off, as you say quite rightly. For this reason you recommend that critical scholarship should employ the concept of representation only in the existential sense. Only then, you say, will social articulation come into clear focus as the existentially prevailing principle. If this recommendation is nothing more than a methodological principle, I am perfectly ready to accept it: Your book demonstrates how extraordinarily productive the application of such a principle can be. But if, as the next chapter on "Representation and Truth" suggests, only the idea of representation in the existential sense renders the attainment of theoretical truth possible, the following comes to my mind: In our most recent conversation in New York you expressed the view that all social forms find their explanation exclusively in the articulation of society in the existential sense under the symbol of the representative. Perhaps I misunderstood you at the time; I am very anxious to know your view on this point.

The second chapter on "Representation and Truth" evokes my admiration. The initial list of unquestioningly presupposed assumptions concerning the relations of the theorist to the social world, the truth of the theorist in contrast to the truth of the self-interpretation of society, the conflict between these truths, etc. – this touches the whole basis of the sociology of knowledge. I should like to remark here only that in my view it does not suffice to distinguish (as you do on p. 54) between the representation of society by its articulated representatives on the one hand, and the representation of transcendent reality by society on the other. Perhaps here we would add a third distinction outside of the theoretical sphere, namely the distinction between what society *A* sees as the truth of its representation in contrast to the way in which a concretely existing society *B (which may be contemporary with or later than A*) interprets this relation between representation and truth. This would be the relation between in-group and out-group interpretation or, if you prefer, between subjective and objective interpretation in Max Weber's sense. Your frequently mentioned example (e.g., pp. 34f.) of the differing interpretations of representation by the Soviet Constitution in Russia and by the Western World shows what I have in mind. It seems to me that the questions raised by you on p. 59 – whether all political societies are monadic entities expressing the universality of truth by their universal claim to domination – can be answered <only in terms of the in-group and out-group dichotomy>.

On p. 61 you discuss the ambiguity of Plato's anthropological principle; it has to do with this distinction. On the one hand this principle is general and serves the interpretation of society; on the other hand it is an instrument of social criticism.

I am quite aware that these considerations are relatively independent from the tremendous and lucidly developed main theme of the second lecture. Your concern is to show that it is not the task of theory to say something about human existence in societies; rather it must remain an attempt at making intelligible the meaning of existence by showing what is the content of certain classes of internal or external experiences. Likewise I know that it is far more important to point out that social and political existence has something to do with the order of the soul as well as that there exists next to the anthropological principle a theological one. Nonetheless I am asking myself whether it is not necessary for a philosophy of history as well as for a theoretical social science to take into account the self-interpretation of this existential order by the concrete society itself and in representations of this order given by other concrete societies. Would this too not be theory even if not in the sense intended by you? Such a theory may not be theory in the sense of Aristotle. In any case, I believe that this scientific task, regardless of what one may call it, can be carried out without recourse to concepts like *sophon*, *kalon*, *agathon*, and the like. I hope that these remarks contribute something to the clarification of the contradiction which I treated in the first part of this letter.

Your distinction between the two truths and the grounding of philosophical truth (let me call philosophical the truth you call theoretical) as distinct from the truth of self-interpretation. I find your reference to the relation between Greek political theory and Greek drama excellent and would like to see this relation worked out on a substantial scale – provided you have not done this already in your main work. After all, the experience of transcendence can also be captured by other means than philosophical speculation or soteriological religious experiences or representations in the existential sense. Art too is a medium for representing this experience, and so is myth. Here the question arises again on a higher level whether it is possible to design a general typology of all these procedures which aim at dealing with that which is transcendent. Further: is it possible to say something about their limits, about where they agree and disagree, what each of them obscures, where they overlap, and about the possibility of moving from one attitude to another. In short: Is an aporetic (analysis) possible of the experience of transcendence?

I have no comments on the third chapter; I have to thank you for the very deep insights it offered me. Your argumentation is excellent and very convincing to a layman like myself. Theoretically this chapter is particularly important for me because it demonstrates how one should and can do philosophy of history with the categories you developed theoretically and how they subject concrete historical situations to fresh illumination and interpretation.

However, the transition from this chapter to the next provides me with some difficulties. The third chapter concludes with the statement that the end of political theology was brought about by orthodox Christianity: The sphere of political power has become de-divinized and secular.[7] According to the definition on p. 107

[7]Footnote of Helmut Wagner: As Schutz stated correctly further below, only *total* immanentization without transcendental irruptions is called "secularization". Evidently he has difficulties in conceiving a radicalized profane society that understands itself to be a divinized sacred body. Already in 1938 Voegelin had spoken of totalitarian movements which mysticize and divinize the immanentist state; see Eric Voegelin, *Politische Religionen* (Vienna, 1938; Stockholm, 1939), Chapter 5, especially p. 53.

dedivinization means the historical process in which the polytheistic culture atrophies and dies and human existence is ordered anew through the experience of the determination of man's fate by the grace of a world-transcendent God granting eternal life. I find all this understandable and I have no objections to this concept of dedivinization. My difficulty is the claim that the specifically modern problem of representation is connected with the redivinization of society. Now, redivinization is <in your exposition> not to be taken as a resurrection of the polytheistic culture in the Greek-Roman sense. Of course, this assertion makes good sense provided its purpose is to establish that the modern political mass movements are not pagan in character but must be interpreted as a clear continuation of the inner Christian heretical branch, that is, as development out of components already present in the universal Church. The antithesis is that between eschatology within history and an eschatology of transhistorical and supernatural perfection. You show very clearly how the unified Christian society is articulated into a spiritual and a secular order. Historically, the secular order is realized by the Roman Empire. The medieval *imperium* must be understood as the continuation of the Roman Empire, and the struggle between pope and emperor[8] as a struggle between spiritual and secular order in the existential and transcendental sense. Now, you say on p. 116 that the specifically modern problems of modern representation grew out of this medieval society with its established system of symbols. This happens through the resurrection of the eschatology of the Kingdom of God. Later, on p. 119, this process simply becomes identical with the process of redivinization. I have great difficulties in seeing why this should be so. To me it seems that the processes of dedivinization and redivinization occur on fundamentally different levels. I think this point is not a detail but a point of decisive importance: from it stems your whole theory of Gnosticism and of any possible gnostic philosophy.

By way of illustration you cite Joachim of Flora's very interesting application of the trinity symbol to the course of history. From his theory emerge four typical symbols: 1) the Third Realm, 2) the Leader, 3) the Prophet or Forerunner, and 4) the Brotherhood of autonomous persons. Subsequently these four symbols are studied in their historical evolution with particular stress on National Socialism and Russia's political philosophy. At the beginning of the third section on p. 117 we find out that the new eschatology "decisively affects the structure of modern politics". This is convincingly demonstrated. Then follows the very interesting thought that "up to this point symbolism has been accepted only on the level of self-interpretation" and that it has been "described as an ahistorical phenomenon" (p. 118).[9] Now you begin to undertake a critical analysis of the principal aspects of this system of symbols and you establish correctly that Joachim's eschatology is speculation about the meaning of history which stands in opposition to that of Augustine. On p. 119 we read that Joachim's new idea is an attempt at "endowing the immanent course of history with a meaning". This is done by appealing to the sense of the transcendental course of history. However, Joachim's speculation still remains linked to the idea of Christianity.

[8]Note of Helmut Wagner: By mistake Schutz says "church" instead of "emperor".

[9]Note of Helmut Wagner: Schutz wrote "ein historisches" instead of "ein ahistorisches".

The radical development of the meaning-endowment of history as an inner-worldly process without transcendental irruptions occurs only in a subsequent movement <appearing only centuries later> which you say correctly leads "from Humanism to Enlightenment". Only in this movement is there gained what you call "secularization" in its final form.

I have summarized these trains of thought line by line so as to clarify them for myself. Unfortunately along the way I lost the concept of redivinization. Is secularization a process of redivinization in your sense? I am becoming confused because suddenly you raise the question here of whether there exists an *eidos* of history. I learn that this is not the case; for Plato and Aristotle the *polis* did have an *eidos* but in an entirely different sense: that of growth and decline. The soteriological truth of Christianity breaks asunder in the rhythm of existence to which these categories belong. Christianity does not know an *eidos* of history because the soteriological supernatural realm is not Nature in the immanent-philosophical sense. And then there is this (on p. 120): "Hence the problem of an eidos of history arises only when Christian transcendental fulfilment becomes immanentized. Such an immanentist hyposthasis of the eschaton, however, is a theoretical fallacy."

My dear friend, I have to confess that for me this statement is simply a *non sequitur*. I cannot grasp how an immanentist hypostasis of the *eschaton* should be a theoretical fallacy or why the conclusion follows from this that history can have no *eidos* because "the course of history extends into the unknown future". I cannot see why for the reasons given that the meaning of history has to turn out to be an illusion. Obviously, you believe that "this illusionary *eidos* is created by treating a symbol of faith as if it were a proposition concerning an object of immanent experience" (pp. 119f.). This sentence is the only one I can find in your whole book that could be regarded as proof of such a "fallacy". In the next paragraph on p. 120 and at the beginning of the fourth section on p. 121 you simply postulate as proven that every attempt at constructing an *eidos* of history must be considered a fallacy and has sinister consequences. In one word: all immanentization is evil; depending on the emphasis, it will lead either to the sinister consequences of the idea of progress, or to the utopian stance of a dream-world, or else to mysticism within Christianity itself.

Having read to this point, I assumed that you intended only to present the immanent development of the transformation of immanence within Christian philosophy as seen in a Christian perspective. But further reading showed me – perhaps mistakenly – that you stand completely on Christian doctrine. Every falling-away from Christian faith involves *gnosis* either in an intellectual, or emotional, or a voluntaristic form – as you subsequently discuss very instructively and skilfully. You say that gnostic experiences are at the core of all <attempts at> redivinization of society because the man who makes these experiences deifies himself by replacing faith in the Christian sense by other forms of participation in the Divine.

However, this interpretation is not in accord with your correct demonstration of gnosticism outside of Christianity: a Jewish, a Pagan, and an Islamic gnosis exist. In this context, you say that gnosis as such does not necessarily lead to that faulty construction of history which is characteristic of modernism since Joachim. I would appreciate your enlightening me about the circumstances under which gnosis must lead to an erroneous construction of history and under what circumstances it does not.

We also might ask: What are the meanings of the terms "fallacy" and "hypostasis" in theoretical and metaphysical speculations? Fallacy is only given when one pairs assumptions which contradict each other. Is the *eschaton* of Christian theology not also a hypostatization? Does not the fallacy you condemn arise only when this Christian hypostacy of the *eschaton* is accepted as axiomatic? Can there be no non-Christian experiences of transcendence in the sense of non-Euclidean geometries? Does the occurrence of the soteriological eschatology annul and prove as fallacious the metaphysical ideas of Plato and Aristotle? On p. 120, I read: "Things are not things, nor do they have essences, by arbitrary declaration". Does this mean that the eschatological supernatural exists while all immanent interpretations of the same transcendental experience is a mere hypostatization *per prescriptum philosophi*?

I foresee your rejoinder. You will reply that the very objection I raise proves how deeply I am myself entangled in gnostic thinking.[10] The very way in which I pose my questions will be proof for you that I think positivistic and pragmatically in terms of methodologies and procedures. Like another well-known gnostic I icily stare down the charge of being a gnostic. This, of course, under the condition that the term, "gnostic", can be really taken in such a broad sense as you do. Strictly speaking, I do not know one great metaphysician who would not have been a gnostic in your conceptual scheme. Types as different as Pascal, Leibniz, Hegel, Kierkegaard, in as much as they deviate from dogma, become guilty of the sin of gnosticism; I am not even sure whether Thomas Aquinas is wholly free from it. Perhaps what you call "gnosticism" is the fundamental category of all anthropology and every anthropodicy. Maybe I have misunderstood your argument here; but if so, it was not from ill will. To me your concept seems both too wide and too narrow. Let me explain this in somewhat greater detail.

If your study of the case of the Puritans in the fifth chapter of the book is a textbook example of the methods of political gnosticism – and everything you say is very convincing with one exception to be mentioned shortly – I cannot accept at the same time what you discuss in your sixth chapter as an example of gnostic philosophy and the evolution of gnosticism, if "gnosticism" is to mean the same in both instances. Looking back at the Introduction, I can still less consider Max Weber a gnostic case in the sense in which you demonstrated Puritan politics to be such a case. On pp. 138 and 140 you listed two technical features which in your view have become principal instruments of the gnostic revolution. These are, first the Koran character of the gnostic Holy Writ and second the taboo imposed upon all attempts at criticism. I maintain that these two technical features are general in nature, are common to all social spheres and all forms of society and have nothing to do with gnosticism. Both are expressions of social power, whether or not this power is in the service of Christian doctrine. The same thing is happening whether Socrates dies a

[10]Note of Helmut Wagner: To be sure, Voegelin responded emphatically that he does not consider his friend Schutz a gnostic. Without intending to insinuate that Voegelin was in any way insincere, I feel that this denial has a tinge of arbitrariness, not unlike the common American reservation, "present parties excluded".

martyr's death because he is accused of *asebeia* (blasphemy) or Christ because he did not respect the Koran character of the Torah; whether since earliest times heretics were killed because they did not respect the dogma of the Church Councils or whether betrayers of the doctrine of dialectical materialism suffer their deserved punishment. Power creates its Korans and its taboos, and the heretics always perish in this conflict.

In one of your earlier writings you have successfully worked out the concept of the counter-idea.[11] Every idea, once it comes to power (or, in your language, every idea, as soon as it has arrived at existential representation under a symbol) needs counter-symbols. In general, I am asking myself whether or not every symbolic system in your sense is not simultaneously a negative system and whether or not every theology does not simultaneously presuppose a negative theology. And hence whether there might not be – and must not be – a dialectic tension between the two poles, the positive and the negative, of the symbol systems and the theologies, and whether it is not here that the *eidos* of history has to be sought as Hegel tried to do.

In what follows I will base myself on the concept of "gnostic revolution" as you have developed it in exemplarily fashion in the first sections of the fifth chapter. Not only is there nothing to criticize on this presentation, but it is absolutely convincing. Above all, it has offered me totally new insights even though I had already learned a few things about this development from your German paper ("Gnostische Politik" in the Stuttgart journal, *Merkur* 4, 1932, pp. 301–317). However, something strange happens on page 156. In order to explain the attitude of Hobbes, who interprets Christianity in terms of its identity with the dictate of reason, and which derives its authority from its being sanctioned by government, you rightly consider it necessary to reopen the theological discussion of the fundamental concept of the soul. The opening of the soul is a historical event of the utmost importance, as you have already shown analytically in your chapter on Homer (Chapter 2).[12] The soul is the *sensorium* of transcendence. The critical and theoretical standards of human existence do not begin to emerge before the soul has been opened. Transcendental reality can be perceived only by the soul; through it, the truth thus opened up can be compared with the truth produced in the self-interpretation of society. Up to this point I am with you completely. It is my deep conviction, my faith if you like, that this experience of transcendentality is the fundamental prerequisite for all truth be it philosophical, metaphysical, or social. Also I am willing to follow you further and accept the idea of a universal God as the measure of the open soul, provided the universal God you mean (as you do here) is the Aristotelian *nous* or the Stoic or Christian *logos*. But this conception changes by a sleight of hand. On p. 160 Hobbes is charged with having tried to freeze history into an eternally existing finite empire on this earth. You go on to say that this would be possible only if the experiences of transcendence are simply ignored although they belong to the Nature of human being.

[11]Note of Helmut Wagner: Schutz referred to Voegelin's essay, "Die Juden als Gegenidee" contained in his book, *Rasse und Staat* (Tübingen, 1933), Part II, Chapter 7, pp. 181–183. The notion itself was not new, but apparently had never been seriously examined before.

[12]Schutz refers to the Chapter, "Homer and Mycene" in *The World of the Polis* (Louisiana State University Press, 1957), pp. 103ff. [FK].

You suggest that Hobbes would improve human being, a creature of God, by creating human being without transcendental experiences.

Of course, here I am not concerned with the interpretation of Hobbes; surely your interpretations apply to him. I am focusing on the principle, on gnosticism as such. As your opening considerations for the sixth lecture do show clearly, this is also your main concern. You state that the origin of the gnostic is to be explained by the vacuum which Christianity created in the course of devinization by the elimination of civil theology. As you say correctly, the problems of society in its historical existence are not exhausted by its historical existence and by waiting for the end of the world. Only the immanentization of the Christian *eschaton* made it possible to endow society in its natural existence with a meaning which had been denied it by Christianity. Continuing, you say that the gnostic experiment in civil theology is fraught with various dangers. The first is the tendency to replace rather than complement the truth of the soul. By becoming openly anti-Christian, gnosticism destroyed the truth of the open soul wherever gnostic movements appeared. You carry out this theme to its conclusion. On p. 165 you say that modern gnosticism is practically identical with the closure of the soul.

In this I cannot follow you at all. Why should a gnostic philosophy make impossible an open soul and access to the existential truth? If opening of the soul means nothing else than experiences of transcendence and search for truths made thereby accessible and graspable, it is impossible to see why the rejection of Christian eschatology should lead to the closing of the soul. <I would have to reject the assertion> that there can be and had been no metaphysics which preserved an open soul without a Christian eschatology. It would be most interesting to learn how you interpret Spinoza in this context. His political philosophy, so strongly influenced by Hobbes, is without doubt compatible with the opening of the soul to the divine *nous*, *logos*, or whatever you may wish to call it here. Or does Spinoza not fall under the category of gnostic politicians as you define them? Is not his idea of sovereignty or his doctrine of natural law a philosophy of immanence?

However you may reply to my question about Spinoza, I challenge your main thesis, as I have already done above, as you repeat it on p. 166: that the immanentization of the Christian *eschaton* leads to misrepresentation of the structure of immanent reality. There certainly are political philosophies that create counter principles to the principles of existence; <there are systems of> metaphysics that escape into a dream world for fear of looking existence in the eye. It is unquestionably true that such self-interpretations of society themselves become part of political reality. On pp. 168ff. you brilliantly analyze the reasons for this. What I cannot grasp is that this flight into the world of dreams, this replacement of reality by a counter-reality, is rooted in the immanentization of the Christian *eschaton*. What I cannot grasp is that opening of the soul for transcendent truth should not also make error possible. Here I see three components of your concept of the gnostic which I have great difficulties in reconciling.

Aside from this, everything you say in sections 2 and 3 is excellent and can be fully shared by anyone even if he does not accept your basic thesis about the origin of gnosticism. Here I have to ask only one question. If in Classical and Christian ethics *sophia* and *prudentia* are the first virtues, why should an ethics not be possible which is built upon the basic virtues of the *lumen naturale* or the *amor intellectualis dei*? Why is *ratio*, reason, not a basic virtue but the fall from Grace? After all, all pantheism rests on the assumption that Man and World are not regarded as creations of God but as being identical with God. Because he defended this view, Giordano Bruno died at the stake. Pantheism, called "acosmic" by Hegel, surely is an immanentization of the Christian *eschaton*. Is it therefore gnostic? Nonetheless, it is compatible with the highest discipline of the intellect. – By the way, I cannot make this type of immanentization fit any of the types you mention on p. 175, that is <the types of> theological, axiological, or activistic immanentizations.

While I purposively and repeatedly cited Spinoza and his political theory I am fully cognizant of the weighty difference between him and Hobbes. If this should be the case, your reply, I expect, will be to the effect that Spinoza is not a gnostic after all. But if this is so your concept of immanentization surely needs revision if it is to serve as the basis for the theory of gnosticism; or else, and this seems to me much more likely, one can maintain your basic thesis about gnosticism and yet forego to postulate the Christian *eschaton* as the only possible transcendental access to the truths of the soul. Obviously this objection is not directed against the historical fact you have demonstrated, namely that in the historical evolution of the last thousand years the turn to gnosticism has its *historical* beginning with the immanentization of the Christian *eschaton*.

But even if this is so and if one does accept your grandiose cyclical theory of historical evolution (p. 164)[13] there still remains the question whether this recourse to the *eschaton* is *theoretically* tenable, theoretically in the sense of a philosophical anthropology such as you have called for repeatedly. I do not believe that a philosophical anthropology can be developed on the basis of a metaphysics which is the sole road to salvation and which in effect makes the opening of the soul a very narrow one. Here I am much closer to Dempf's view <as developed in> his *Self-Criticism of Philosophy*.[14] In it he takes precisely as a fundamental axiom of his philosophical anthropology the collateral existence of the various self-interpretations in their historical evolution and of a list of types of metaphysics, even though his typology still falls considerably short of <comprehensiveness and> perfection . . .[15] It may be that I have misunderstood you in many respects and perhaps even in essentials. However, I believe that you have seen from what I have written that I have good reasons for admiring your book in spite of all our differences. . . .

[13]Footnote of Gregor Sebba: The "giant circle" represents the rise and decline of differentiated understanding. Pre-Christian civilizations ascended toward the appearance of Christ, toward the maximum of differentiation, and the peak of the cycle. Then the cycle turns down; the rise, blooming, and decline of Western civilization occurs within this downswing as the continuing growth of Gnosticism *reverses* the direction toward ever greater differentiation.

[14]Footnote of Helmut Wagner: See Alois Dempf, *Selbstkritik der Philosophie. Vergleichende Philosophiegeschichte im Umriss* (Vienna, 1947).

[15]Footnote of Helmut Wagner: The ellipses indicate an omission of four lines which contain mere technical matters and add nothing to the substantive content of the letter. The lines that follow complete the factual considerations. Another two lines have been omitted at the end for the same reason.

CHAPTER 30

Experience and Transcendence

Editors' Preface

The (revised) English translation of this manuscript is by Helmut Wagner. The title of the original was "Die Kontroverse mit Prof. Morris neuerlich durchdacht" ("Reconsideration of the Controversy with Prof. [Charles] Morris"). The occasion of writing the manuscript was the participation by Schutz in 1955 in the Fourteenth Symposium of the Conference on Science, Philosophy and Religion, concerned, this time, with signs and symbols. Together with the papers of other contributors, Schutz's lecture was published in Lyman Bryson, et al., *Symbols and Society* (New York: Harper, 1955). The lecture has been republished in *Collected Papers*, Vol. I, pp. 287–356. At the conference Schutz's lecture was discussed by Charles Morris, and both Morris' critique and Schutz's reply were published in the conference proceedings, but not reprinted in the *Collected Papers*. In 1958 Schutz reread his answer to Morris and found it "in part misleading and beside the point". He consequently wrote a new and detailed response in German, and the text was subsequently published by Thomas Luckmann in the documentary appendix to Alfred Schutz and Thomas Luckmann, *Strukturen der Lebenswelt*, Vol. II (Frankfurt am Main: Suhrkamp, 1984); the extended text begins on p. 337 and ends on p. 346. It should be noted that Schutz continued his discussion of the topic of experience and transcendence considerably beyond this point, although after p. 347 it can no longer be considered to have been occasioned by Morris's relatively short remarks. In the heading of the next section, Schutz dropped the reference to Morris and spoke instead of the "Continuation of the Analysis of the Symbol Essay".

What does Morris ask?

Is there a practical knowledge (*Erfahrung*) or experience [*Erlebnis*] of transcendence, or does one speak of the transcendence of practical knowledge, of the transcendence of experience?

What else could experience of transcendence or practical knowledge of transcendence mean if not that the content of experience, the content of practical knowledge, the *noema*, if you wish, always points beyond itself?

This is meant in the sense that the experienced noema includes its (inner and outer) horizons. Although they are experienced as horizons, are they only experienced as empty or non-sense-fulfilling horizons, as horizons always pointing forward and backward toward pre-experienced, retained, protended, anticipated further noematic contents which for their part include further horizons of the typically same experiential style? The noematic content is experienced, and that means just so and not experienced in any other fashion except as presented, as I already find it referring to what is not yet or no longer experienced whereby it remains open as to whether or not this is experienceable.

If this is correct, then what is not yet or no longer experienced, be it experienceable or not in principle, is transcendent over against the present [*aktuellen*] content of experience in so far as it reaches beyond it. But, on the other hand, this too belongs to the present content of experience in a typically pre-experienced manner: namely in the manner in which I always experience the content of experience as transcending itself when I experience it just so and not otherwise than as given. I can speak of this transcendence as of this empty and itself surmounting transcendence in the sense in which I say: The experience of the emptiness of horizonality belongs to the intentional content of the noema, just as it is given to me, in the manner of typical pre-experience. It is just this which makes every experiencing [*Erfahren*] of any content into an experience of transcendence – and that means here not merely into an experience of the transcendence of the content, in so far as the latter must move beyond a more or less empty horizonality, but experience of the necessarily transcendent character of any experiencing whatever, of the necessary incompleteness and imperfection of each isolated empirical act of experiencing.

In this sense the transcendence of experiencing as well as the experiencing of transcendence corresponds to the Leibnizian definition of consciousness as the ability to progress to ever new experiences. Spontaneity, after all, is only possible under two conditions: 1) the content of experience is experienced as transcending itself and this because it is experienced, just as it is, with all the relevant referrings beyond its present givenness; or 2) the act of experiencing is grasped as itself isolated but as pointing forwards or backwards to other perhaps performable, perhaps unperformable acts of experiencing. They all are founded in the unity of consciousness – be it the Kantian transcendental apperception or be it James' through-and-through-connectedness of consciousness.

This would mean: *Experience of the transcendence of the content of experience is intentionality of the horizon; transcendence of experience, that is, transcendence of the act of experience, is spontaneity*. All of this has to be thoroughly considered, given of course that the preceding considerations are correct.

How, then, is Prof. Morris' second question to be answered?

What about the transcendental implications of marks, indicators, signs, symbols?

In general, how, if at all, is the phenomenon of appresentation a phenomenon of transcendence?

In his second question Professor Morris formulates an alternative. He says: The experience of transcendence comes first and exists independently of appresentative relations. As far as I can see he does not discuss further this alternative. Indeed, it seems not to merit discussion as long as it has not been more precisely established what it means to "come first". Should it mean a temporal sequence in the life-world the thesis would likely have to be confirmed. The question becomes more difficult if "first" signified a foundational context established by eidetic law. It is by no means agreed upon that sense perception founds all appresentation. It would seem that at times this idea haunted Husserl, especially in the Cartesian trend of his thinking. In general, in this tendency Husserl was inclined to view perception and in particular visual perception as the basic model of all experiencing. Sometimes one has the feeling that his whole theory of perception is but a grandiose synecdoche for Husserl's significant thesis of "passive synthesis" which is the instituting of all pairing by way of analogy <and occurs> together with all phenomena of covering over and overlapping.[1] The "awakening", "calling up" of an appresented member of the pair by means of the appresenting [member], on the other hand, is sometimes conceived by Husserl as a "primordial fact of the life of consciousness" – but what might that mean?[2]

For the moment I tend toward the idea that this question, like the one about the experience of transcendence, can in fact only be clarified ontologically and not phenomenologically. The original experience of transcendence lies in my knowledge about my growing older (as continuous enriching or restocking of my horizonal intentionalities) and about my death (as the final stagnation of the enriching of the horizons, as the limit-situation at which, so to speak, the horizons end, or, better: beyond which no horizonal intentionalities can reach in so far as I remain trapped by subjectivity and do not include "horizonally" the intersubjective world of successors) – in other words, consciousness (a true primal fact) that the "world" will continue after my death just as it subsisted before my birth. But this is tantamount to saying that the finitude of my being, or, better, my knowing about it (can one still speak of experience?) founds all intentionality and, above all, its horizonal character. This may well be the case, but the line of thought may be owing more to Jaspers and Heidegger than to Husserl. As long as we adhere in the end to the transcendental ego, we must accept its immortality just as Husserl indeed did. But my own death is a matter of the *life-world*, and this – *certusan, incertus quando* – is certainly the first and originary experience of transcendence of the world beyond my own existence. <To realize the certainty of my own death> neither requires "pairing" nor "passive synthesis" and no appresentative references. On the contrary, one could insist that all of this is founded in the "originary experience" that all horizonal intentionality must come to a halt with my death, just as it is in all its emptiness and unfulfilledness.

There are correlates in the life-world for this originary experience which call for a precise phenomenological analysis and which Husserl possibly had in mind when he talked about "genetic phenomenology" in his last period. Such a correlate in the life-world would be sleep, the sentiment that "tomorrow I will wake up again", and that means that my horizonal intentionalities which come to a halt with my falling-

[1]Schutz's marginal note: *non sequitur!* Clearly a thought that got ahead of itself.

[2]For Schutz's line of thought here a personal recollection may be in order. At the time Schutz was writing his response to Morris he was reading a typescript given him by Dorion Cairns of Cairns' *Conversations with Husserl and Fink* (later edited by Richard Zaner and published by Martinus Nijhoff in 1976) and had heavily underscored Husserl's reported comments on pairing and passivity; see especially pp. 28f. and 84ff. [FK]

asleep – of course I know: only temporarily and <I am confident that they> will resume their work on just those empty intentionalities which are now coming to a halt.[3] Tomorrow I <Schutz while writing these considerations> will summarize this in passive synthesis by pairing what was actually presented at the time by me as an appresentatively grasped member with today's horizonal experience that tomorrow will be merely an *appresented* reference. Thereby I awaken what had been hidden during sleep. This is awakening in the truest sense of the term. It could be said that awakening from sleep or being awakened means nothing else but an awakening of horizonal intentionalities that existed prior to falling asleep (but at that time functioning appresentatively) to bring to awakening now in an appresentative mode. <If it would be tenable to assume> that the horizonal intentionalities continue their "dream-work" latently during sleep and that in true passive synthesis, it would <be possible to> clarify many a depth-psychological discovery – most of all the symbolism of dreaming that is "explained" both by Freud and Jung albeit completely insufficiently.

This phenomenological clarification of the disruptions of the activities of the life of consciousness, which constitutes the horizonal intentionalities by way of the process of falling asleep and by their resumption ("awakening"), is clarification of just *one* correlate in the life-world of the fundamental experience of that transcendence which is my death <at an undetermined time in the future>. Another I shall call "turning away" [*Abkehr*].

First of all let us take this term in its spatial meaning. According to it, the correlate in the life-world of the originary experience of transcendence (of my eventual death) is the gliding transition of the world of actual reach into a world having been in reach. I leave my room, I move myself away, I turn away from my world in actual reach. Walking down the street I remember a book which I left on my table. Before, the book had been in my reach; now it is no longer in my reach: it transcends my actual reach. But in this case it also belongs to my experience of this transcendence that it remains in my restorable reach. I have only to return to my room and thereby gain the great chance, for practical purposes, the certainty, that I will find again this room with table and book and in the order in which I left it. The house in which I live will still be standing (unless if destroyed by fire); the table will stand near the window (unless someone moved it); the book will lay on it (unless someone took it away). Clearly visible here are the connections that exist among typifications, the systems of relevance and interpretations of horizons, although their clarification is an entirely independent problem which must yet be carefully considered.[4]

Now I am "turned away" from all of this; and as long as this is so my possible "turning-toward" – its restorable reach – is an achievement of the horizonal intentionality of my present experience: Room, table, and book as I remember them now transcend the world in my actual reach. Remembering the book I left on the table

[3]Schutz's marginal note: This had been written before I saw the fine essay by Johannes Linschoten, "About Falling Asleep" in *Psychologische Beiträge* II, Heft 1 (1955/56). In part, Linschoten reaches similar conclusions.

[4]Schutz's marginal note: Namely, what in all of this is posited as "constant" in an unquestioning manner?

occurs in memory awakened by way of appresentative pairing (what is appresentative is a consciousness of a lack: "now I still do not have the book with me which I wanted to take to my friend"). <All of this is accompanied by the> anticipation that could, or can, bring back into restorable reach all that which now transcends my world in actual reach.

(This anticipation has been evoked as well by pairing. In it the appresentative member is the positing of the problem motivated by the feeling of lack: How could I make up this lack?) Both transcending elements, the remembrance of former and the anticipation of restorable reach, belong now to the actual content of the experience of my Now. But they "belong" to it in the unique mode of transcending it. Obviously the transcending elements are achievements of the horizonal intentionalities of the actual consciousness; the actual elements of it "awaken" the transcendental elements as appresentative members of the pairing.

One of the great problems G. E. Moore posed in his "Defense of Common Sense"[5] is that the world from which I turned away continues to exist and that in general in the manner in which we have experienced it. Kant too saw this problem and Scheler derided him for it by speaking of the transcendental fear of Kant and we would act otherwise and arbitrarily if we could escape the surveillance of our consciousness which dictates the rules of our behavior.

It is obvious that the described phenomena of turning-away are existentially connected with the transcendence of sleeping (which itself is a phenomenon of turning-away, turning away from the *attention à la vie*). On the other hand, compare: *Partir, c'est mourir un peu.*

There is still a third correlate in the life-world to be investigated: that of the originary experience of the transcendence of the other and of the world of the other. (In no way shall this mean that these three correlates exhaust the problem and there do not exist a series of other problems. It is very likely that ageing itself is such a correlate.) Concerning the transcendence of the other, the set of problems of the "here" and "there" is certain: world in his actual and *thus* in my potential reach of the first degree; world in his potential and *thus* world in my potential reach of the second degree, etc. I have treated this in detail in my Notebook I.[6] It is of eminent significance.

But do we not have to introduce a new idea which is immediately linked to the originary experience of transcendence – my death? From the outset: Is the other not experienced as that person who either will survive me *or* whom I will survive? Does this (essentially appresentative?) reference not contain a relation between the horizonal intentionality of my consciousness of the horizonal intentionality of the other's consciousness? And is the preceding "either-or" not a new transcendence of turning-away?[7]

[5]G. E. Moore, "A Defense of Common Sense", in *Contemporary British Philosophy*, Vol. II (1925).

[6]Note of Helmut Wagner: Schutz is referring to the first of the notebooks of which he made use while developing the reappraisal of this discussion with Morris.

[7]Note of Helmut Wagner: At this point Schutz began a new notebook, no. IV, which he opens with the following remark: The problem of the experience of transcendence; the turning-away, the other as survivor or person who is survived. All this still to Morris' second question, first alternative.

Turning away from my own actual situation with its uninterpreted but interpretable horizons: a phenomenological clarification of the problem of generations ought to be found in the problems of living-beyond (or dying-before) the other. What for me, in my situation, is an empty horizon is for those who are older already fulfilled in the situation they share with me. That which I anticipate, namely, that which is unquestioned and empty anticipation by me, is for the older person typically appresented by the passive awakening of this typically analogous pre-experience. He had already been in a similar situation and he appeals to his "experience of life" which under no circumstances could become mine. However, in spite of all autobiographical differences he is in command of the socially accepted typical recipes and the solutions to typical problems. At least he is capable of *diagnosing* the typicality of the given situation (which for him is a recurrent one while for me it may be radically new). He knows "what is typically the case in such a situation and how one deals with it typically". He himself has lived through such situations or he has "heard about" them; that means that he knows about them through socially derived knowledge. And now he is ready to make this knowledge accessible to me, to hand it on in the form of recipes, maxims, rules, proverbs, eventually mores and laws.[8]

Attention must be paid here to the following fact: From the transcendence of that which is typified emerge large numbers of variations of traditional pre-experiences appresenting (in the older person) or else merely implying empty horizonal intentionalities which, if need be, could be interpreted (by or for the younger person). One of the problems of the younger will always be: Which of these horizonal intentionalities can be interrogated? From this emerges a philosophy of educableness and education that to my knowledge has not yet been undertaken. The main goal of the education of the young is to learn how to typify "correctly"; to learn techniques of appresentative awakening; to learn how to diagnose that which is worthy of being questioned. However, what is really necessary is the determination of the connected motivational, thematic and interpretative systems of establishing what is worthy of investigation and of the conditions under which concrete problems are to be solved to a degree sufficient for the given purpose. In adult education there appears an important difference: teachers and students belonging to the same generation must share not only the definition of the situation but also both its empty and its interpreted horizonalities, and this in terms of the socially appropriated and derived schemes of relevance (including the typifying and rules of method) for problem-positing and problem-solving derived from this definition.

But all of this is a digression; it may be worth while to develop it.

In a nutshell, a first alternative of Morris' second question is to ask whether the experience of transcendence comes first and is independent of appresentative relations. About this question we may say:

1. The question can be answered meaningfully only if under "first" is meant that the experience of transcendence founds the transcendence of all appresentation.

[8]In what follows, Wagner's text differs in some details from that published by Luckmann in *Strukturen der Lebenswelt*, Band 2, p. 344. Because Wagner was obviously aware of the published German text, I assume that what he translated was what he preferred. I have thus edited his text according to his wishes. [FK]

2. The originary experience of transcendence can be clarified only ontologically but no longer phenomenologically.
3. This originary experience of transcendence is my aging in its finitude; this means the continuous enrichment of horizonal intentionalities with the limit of their ceasing completely – my death.
4. The originary experience (of the transcendence of the world) beyond the end of my life – transcendence of the world, a transcending that still belongs to my life-world) has immanent correlates in the life-world. The most important of these are:
   a) falling asleep, awakening
   b) "turning away";
   c) the other (as surviving me or survived by me) and his world, including the problem of generations.

The phenomena of appresentative awakening in the style typical for them <that is, for each generation> are demonstrable in terms of these correlates.

Concerning the Second Alternative of the Second Question of Professor Morris

Relationship between transcendence and marks, indications, signs, and symbols: Is the experience of transcendence simply the experience of these appresentative relations?

In my answer to Professor Morris[9] I have answered this question with an emphatic "No", perhaps too emphatically but in any case not clearly enough. However, I have admitted that experiences of the transcendent can only be "mastered" with the help of appresentative references (in order to come to terms with them). What does this mean?

"To come to terms" could mean, at first sight: Integration into the stock of experiences and therefore <evoking their> understanding (at least analogically); gaining knowledge of *what* transcends, *how* it essentially transcends, *where* the empty places are.

Further: How that which is not knowable [*Unwissbare*] can be appresentatively interpreted through that which is knowable. <That is, it can be shown> how it can be understood as an ontological condition of all capabilities [*Vermöglichkeiten*] and as an open frame for the intentionalities which constitute the former. In this sense <it leads to> the establishing of its being-valid-for-me.

However, appresentation goes along its own peculiar paths here: every transcendence acquires its particular typical style of "ability to be mastered" [*Bewältigbarkeit*] by analogous appresentation. Yet the starting point of analogous appresentation is the correlate in the life-world always arising through passive awakening, through the transcendence of experience [*Transzendenzerlebnis*] (through the experience of transcendence [*Erfahrung der Transzendenz*]. See the examples a) to c) above for such correlates (for example, the analogy of sleep and death awakened through the experience of transcendence of the latter). Conversely: Sleep taken as starting member

[9]Note of Helmut Wagner: At the conference of 1955.

– as appresenting member of the once instituted pairing through which death – as appresented member – appears as the ultimate limit of sleep without the horizonal references to wakening which, in and by itself, belongs to the life-world, as a "pause" upon which nothing follows, so to speak, as an unceasing pause and thereby as transcending the life-world itself.

(Something similar may be demonstrated as well for the phenomenon of "turning away" – turning away without any implication that a later turning-toward-something would ever recur <either for myself or> for the other in his world.

All of this is only tentatively established and requires very precise, further consideration.

APPENDIX

Fragments Toward a Phenomenology of Music

Editor's Preface

This appendix takes the place of what would have been the fourth part of the *Collected Papers*, Volume IV. At the time of his death, Wagner apparently had not yet decided on the contents of this fourth part other than to suggest the inclusion of the present manuscript. "Fragments Toward a Phenomenology of Music" was originally edited by Fred Kersten, with an Introduction and Notes, and published in *In Search of Musical Method*, edited by F.J. Smith (London, New York, Paris: Gordon and Breach Science Publishers, 1976), pp. 5–72.

Schutz wrote the manuscript in 1944 during the week of 16 July to 23 July in Lake Placid. Unfinished in the elaboration of its content, containing but few revisions, the manuscript is clearly a first draft. Some sections, announced in the text, are missing (such as the section on rhythm); other very short sections would seem to be incomplete. The title of the manuscript and its division into sections are by Schutz. I have added some section titles, made some changes (minor) in terminology, in punctuation, grammar and style for the sake of a more readable text. Unless otherwise noted, the footnotes are mine and refer principally to further development of similar ideas in Schutz's published writings. The footnotes clearly indicated as by Schutz, with one exception (noted), are parentheses or paragraphs which did not seem to be appropriate parts of the text had it been completed.

In addition to Schutz's hand-written text, I used a typescript of the manuscript prepared by Lester Embree and carefully corrected by Ilse Schutz. The Introduction to Schutz's text has been omitted here.

§1. Music and Language

A piece of music is a meaningful context. It is meaningful to the composer; it can be understood as meaningful by the listener; and it is the task of the interpreter to bring about the correct meaning. Applied to music, the terms, "meaning" and "context", "understanding" and "interpretation", are used, however, in a specific way which is different from other meaningful systems such as languages. To be sure, language is also a meaningful context. Each term within the system of a particular language has its specific semantic functions. Each term is a symbol of the concept which it conveys, and the concept itself refers to the real or ideal objects of our thoughts, to the qualities of these objects, to what happens to them with or without our interference. Thus the three main elements of any language – nouns, adjectives, verbs – refer to a conceptual scheme by which we interpret the world in which we live, including ourselves, men among fellowmen who live in the world with our minds and bodies, our thoughts and emotions. These three classes of terms are completed by the important groups of relational or operational terms and by a set of rules – called grammar or syntax – indicating the operational functions of each of the meaningful terms within the meaningful unit of a sentence or a proposition.

The propositions themselves are either true or false, compatible or incompatible with other propositions; as a unity, propositions either have or have not a specific meaning which can be verified or falsified. An additional meaning supervenes from the context in which a proposition stands and from the occasion on which a proposition is used. Thus, a universe of discourse has been organized, each unit of which refers, if it is meaningful, to the conceptual scheme of references by which we interpret the world. The structures described here very roughly and imprecisely, have been studied by modern logic, especially symbolic logic. However, the science of logic, even when applied to meaningful systems, has always been merely a science of concepts; meaning became the object of the science of logic only when it dealt with the representative function of the symbol.

Music is an instance of a meaningful context without reference to a conceptual scheme and, strictly speaking, without immediate reference to the objects of the world in which we live, without reference to the properties and functions of those objects. Music does not have a representative function. (Musical notation, of course, does have a representative function.)[1] Neither a piece of music, nor a single theme, has a semantic character. There is no analogue in music to propositions which are either true or false; and there is no analogue in the meaning of music to verification or falsification. But there is, nevertheless, an analogue in music to the syntax of language, namely, the set of rules governing the musical form. However, this syntax of the musical form does not have the character of operational rules.

§2. Art and Language

But is it not true that any work of art is a meaningful context of the same kind as that of music? All works of art based upon language – poetry, the novel, drama – use a semantic system as their basic material; it is a semantic system which shares with all other language the character of relating to a conceptual scheme and to grammar. To be sure, the language of the poet confers upon each unit of language, even upon each term, a meaning in addition to that which a unit or term would have if it were used in colloquial conversation or in scientific discourse. There are even additional syntactical functions in the language of poetry which are supervenient to the syntactical functions of ordinary language. Yet the reference to a conceptual scheme and the

[1]For further discussion of this idea, with critical reference to the contrary theory of Halbwachs, see "Making Music Together", *Collected Papers*, Vol. II, pp. 163, 165f.

reference to the objects of the world subsist; this conceptual scheme and these objects merely receive a particular interpretation, a particular symbolic character or, as we may say, a specific representational value.

For example, the paradox – meaningless or false in terms of a logic of propositions – may become a means of conveying the highest truth in poetical language. To be sure, the elements of the paradox itself are conceptualized, the words which are used are defined in the dictionary, and the reference to the world of objects subsists. Only the meaning of these words, concepts, or objects has changed in so far as they are interpreted as merely indicating something else rather than as standing for themselves. This, however, is instead a definition of what is called "representation". Since language itself is representational in character, language receives additional representational values in the arts as means of expression. The representational functions of poetry are functions of a higher degree.

§3. Abstract Painting and Music

The art of the painter, the art of the sculptor and, to a certain degree, the art of the architect, do not have, of necessity, a reference to a conceptual scheme. Nevertheless, those arts do refer immediately to objects of the outer world, bestowing on the objects representative values which they would not have in their natural settings. For instance, it is not the physical aspect alone of the model or the landscape which is reproduced upon the canvas; the canvas stands for many other things of which it is merely a symbol. But what that which is reproduced on the canvas stands for is brought out by the significative functions of a sector of the world, a sector chosen in such a way that it suggests its hidden relationship to what is represented and, in the last resort, to the universe. This does not hold good for so-called "abstract" paintings. But abstract painting admittedly tries to transplant the technique of music to the dimension of spatial expression. The counterpart of abstract painting is so-called "program music" which tries to transplant the technique of painting into the dimension of inner time.

§4. Music and the Ornament

Perhaps the closest analogy to the meaning-context of music is offered by the ornament, the pattern, for instance, of a Persian carpet. But the ornament suggests either geometric forms or the shape of plants or animals, or religious or cultic symbols. As a rule, the ornament is not entirely free of conceptual schemes. However, in the repetitions and interlacements of the pattern the ornament does offer a structure similar to that of music – a structure which is meaningful and, nevertheless, without representative value.[2]

[2]In this connection, see Schutz's discussion of Rousseau's ideas about music in "Mozart and the Philosophers", *Collected Papers*, Vol. II, pp. 182f.

§5. Music and Dance

The art of the dance and of the mime certainly have to be considered separately. In so far as they are abstract, that is, without any relation to a religious or social ritual, or represent occurrences in daily life, they constitute meaningful patterns without reference to a conceptual scheme. This partially explains the close connection between music and dance. The rhythm is the connecting link.

§6. The Phenomenological Approach to Music

A phenomenological approach to music may safely disregard the physical qualities of the sound as well as the rationalization of these sounds which leads to the musical scale. As Scheler had already correctly pointed out, in listening to music we do not perceive sound waves emanating from the oscillation of the sound producing matter. Two different schemes of reference may be confused. The physicist may say that sound waves emanate from the oscillating matter; the sound waves affect the tympanum of the human ear. The physiologist, as far as his abilities go and as far as his science permits, may explain what parts of the inner ear, what nerves and brain cells, respond to the stimulus which the tympanum receives. All this is immaterial to the experience of the listener. He responds neither to sound waves, nor does he perceive sounds; he just listens to music.

It is customary that nearly all books on the theory of music go back to the mathematical foundation of music, back to the simple proportions in which the scale is built up, back to the sequel of harmonic tones,[3] and so on. Interesting and even miraculous as this relationship is when compared to other points of view, it has little to do with the experiencing of music, just as the frequency of amplitudes of colors and their place in the spectrum has little to do with the experience of the beholder of a painting, or just as the anatomic structure of the human pelvis has little to do with what the art of the dancer conveys.

The relations between sounds and mathematical proportions cannot even contribute anything to the questionable problem of consonance or dissonance, which are historical categories of the aesthetics of music prevailing during certain periods in certain cultures. The ideal of musical beauty prevailing in ancient Greece considered the musical interval of the third as a dissonance, while the culture of the "faux-bourdon" period recognized sequences of empty fifths as consonant. The solution of the so-called "Pythagorean comma" employed to build up the scale of medieval music brought about a rationalization and middle-of-the-road solution incompatible with the simple mathematical proportions of the interval. And our system of "temperament" is just a further step in this direction. Scales in use in other cultures (China, Arabia, primitive tribes) are incommensurable with ours and with the simple proportions of the mathematically pure intervals. And even the development of modern Western music shows that what is considered to be dissonant or consonant changes with the generation and education of the listener's ear. There has not

[3]The manuscript has the German term, "Obertonreihe".

been a composer from Bach to Schönberg who has not been criticized by his contemporaries because of his cacophonies. What one generation blames as dissonant is accepted by the following one as aesthetically consonant and becomes an element of the prevailing ideal of perfection.

§7. The Phenomenological Approach, Continued

The many vehicles and means of performing music and of preserving and reproducing it may equally be disregarded. Musical instruments in the broad sense, including the human voice, the technical possibilities and limits of musical instruments, the way to use them. Musical notation, mechanical devices such as records, ensemble playing of all kinds – from accompaniment of a song to the modern orchestra – all of these are merely means for the production, the reproduction and conservation of the work of music, and they have only a mediate impact on the experience of the listener as well as of the composer. As will presently be shown, they do not even have a direct connection to the form of existence peculiar to the work of music.

§8. Music as an Ideal Object

It is erroneous to think that a symphony exists only in the score or in its performance by an orchestra. Both the score and the performance have the same relation to the work of music as the printed book or lecture has to the existence of a philosophical thought or a mathematical theory. To be sure, the score, the performance, the book, the lecture, are indispensable means for communicating the musical or scientific thought. They are not, however, this thought itself. A work of music, or a mathematical theorem, has the character of an ideal object.

The communicability of a work of music or a mathematical theorem is bound to real objects – visible or audible objects – but the musical or scientific thought itself exists independently of all these means of communication. The overture to *Don Giovanni* which, according to legend, Mozart wrote down the night before the first performance, existed in his mind long before, although it was inaccessible to anyone else. If Beethoven filled his notebooks with sketches for his compositions, he did so for his own convenience. The themes noted down did not enter into existence by his writing them down; they existed in his mind long before. On the other hand, he who knows a piece of music "by heart" does not need any reference to print, to any musical instrument or to performances heard or previously made, in order to reproduce the piece of music from beginning to end for his inner ear.[4]

§9. The Ideality and Mode of Existence of a Musical Work

There is, however, a peculiarity of the way in which the ideal object, "Work of Music", constitutes itself. For instance, if I am studying the Pythagorean Theorem, I learn how to derive it step by step from certain assumed premises, each of the steps

[4]See the similar discussion in "Making Music Together", p. 164.

following the rules of arriving at a correct conclusion. The ideal object, "Pythagorean Theorem", has, therefore, been built up in our mind in a series of interconnected mental operations, or, to use a technical phenomenological term, it has been built up *polythetically*. After having performed this procedure, in one single glance I may look back at the whole process of polythetic steps and, by doing so, I can grasp the meaning of the resulting proposition, "$a^2 + b^2 = c^2$". And I can do this without recurring to, or starting over again, the performance of the single mental operations whose outcome is the proposition and its meaning. I can, thus, grasp the meaning of the ideal object, "Pythagorean Theorem", once constituted, "monothetically" – that is, in a single ray without any recourse to the polythetic steps in which it was built up.

It is not possible, at least not possible for the ordinary human mind, monothetically to look at the ideal object, "Work of Music".[5] In one single ray we cannot grasp the constituted meaning of a work of music. At best, we can grasp in one single ray the content which the work of music conveys, the particular mood or emotion it evokes in us, or its inner form, as when we say: "These were variations with a finale in the form of a passacaglia". The work of music itself, however, can only be recollected and grasped by reconstituting the polythetic steps in which it has been built up, by reproducing mentally or actually its development from the first to the last bar as it goes on in time. By necessity, this process will be a process in time (the nature of which will have to be studied carefully). And it will take "as much time" to reconstitute the work of music in recollection as it will to experience it originally in its unfolding, polythetic constitution while listening to it for the first time.. In other words, the specific existence of the ideal object, "Work of Music", is its extension in time; its specific way of constitution is a polythetic one.

§10. Monothetic and Polythetic Constitution

The specific mode of constitution of the work of music requires, however, further analysis. First, it is not the ideal object, "Work of Music", which alone has the peculiar form of existence described so far. A poem, for instance, can equally be reconstituted only in polythetic steps, and exists merely in such a reconstitution. The poem may have a conceptual content, and this conceptual content, of course, may be looked at in one single ray. In one or two sentences, I may tell the story of Enoch Arden, but I can bring Tennyson's poem before my mind only by reciting or reading it from

[5]To this passage Schutz appended the following note: To the best of my knowledge, there is one single instance to the contrary. In a letter to his father, Mozart describes his experience, while composing, of hearing the whole composition from beginning to end simultaneously, and he describes this experience as curious as well as wonderful. It would seem that Mozart's genius had the capacity to grasp monothetically the whole composition. But it must be admitted that the passage just referred to is not quite clear and that, at any rate, experiences such as described by Mozart are only accessible to a genius of his kind." Schutz does not give any source for this letter of Mozart, which can be found in Vol. IV of *Mozart. Briefe und Aufzeichnungen (Gesamtausgabe)*, edited by W.A. Bauer and O.E. Deutsch (Basel: Bärenreiter, 1963), pp. 529f., where it is listed as of doubtful authenticity and dated 1790. Schutz's source for this letter may well be William James, *Principles of Psychology*, Vol. I, p. 255, footnote, where James translates the part of the letter to which Schutz refers.

beginning to end. Therefore, it can be stated that the dichotomy between polythetic and monothetic constitution refers to an underlying conceptual scheme of reference, and the statement that music cannot be caught monothetically is merely a corollary of the thesis that the meaning-content of music is not related to a conceptual scheme.

§11. The Existence of Ideal Objects and Time

We may even find an analogue to the existence of ideal objects, such as a Work of Music, in the dimension of time in a phenomenon of the outer world, namely in movement as an ongoing occurrence. Bergson's philosophy has taught us, in full clarity, the double aspect of movement: On the one hand, movement means the ongoing motion, the perceptual change of place of an object, an event which happens in time and which can only be grasped as a unit by our sense of inner time – the *durée*. On the other hand, for the movement as an ongoing occurrence our mind substitutes the spatial path traversed by the moving object. This is a conceptual scheme, incompatible with the pure *durée*. It requires the exteriorization of *durée* into space, the transformation of the inner sense of time into spatial time, into the time of our clocks, of our life with others – the time in which earth turns around its axis and completes its course around the sun.

Consider the flying arrow of Zeno. Regard its flight as an ongoing movement. It is a unit from the instant it was shot from the bow until it reaches its goal. Following this movement with your eyes, you experienced one single event in inner time. Afterwards, in hindsight, when this movement will have been completed, when the arrow has traversed its path, you may consider the movement – once performed and accomplished – as identical with the trajectory traversed by the arrow. Then you may break down into pieces the unity of the ongoing motion. In this dimension of spatial time, you may even designate the spot occupied by the arrow at any chosen instant during the flight. But then you have dropped entirely the idea of an ongoing motion. It is no longer a question of the motion of the flying arrow held still or passed at any instant, at a point of the parabolic trajectory: only the arrow which you imagine as having been arrested at such a point remained for an instant at the spot designated. But, then, the arrow does not fly any longer. By intermingling these two aspects of the same event – ongoing movement as a unity, accomplished movement as divisible into parts – the Eleatic paradox arises that the flying arrow does not move at all. As an ongoing motion it is a unit and participates in the stream of your consciousness in inner time.

§12. The Problems of a Phenomenology of Music

Returning to our problem, namely the problem of the existence of the ideal object, "Work of Music", in the extension of time, we find that the way in which we described its constitution as a polythetic one requires a certain restriction. There is no doubt that the dimension of time in which the work of music exists in the inner time of our stream of consciousness – in Bergson's terminology, the *durée*. This statement will be corroborated by the analyses which follow.

But are we entitled to speak of a polythetic constitution in inner time? Did not our analysis of motion prove that as a development, as an ongoing motion, the whole event shows all the criteria of an indivisible unit? Did we not come to the conclusion that it is only the movement once accomplished which seemingly breaks down into pieces? Do we not have exactly the same situation in the work of music itself? Is not what we call a polythetic constitution in reality only a polythetic reconstitution of the music once accomplished? As long as a piece of music lasts, and as long as we are listening, we participate in its flux; or, more precisely: the flux of music and the flux of the stream of our consciousness are interrelated, are simultaneous; there is a unity between them; we swim, so to speak, in this stream. And music goes on as a unit which is indivisible. Only if we stop this ongoing development, only if we bring the flux to a standstill, only if, so to speak, we step out of the stream and look back: then it seems that what we experience as a unit while it lasted, has been constituted in polythetic steps.

But how? Was not the ongoing flux of music structurized? Did we not have the feeling that a certain configuration, which afterwards we will call a musical theme, started, developed, ended, recurred? And while listening to this theme: did the theme not have a special structurization too? Was it not articulated in several ways, first showing what we usually call a rhythm, then a specific relation to its starting point – a relation which music theory will teach us to interpret as its melodic or harmonic structures? And, in a more complicated composition, could we not distinguish, when first listening, the theme, its accompaniment, subordinate voices, counterpoints, and so on? Again, do we not run into an Eleatic paradox? Does music move at all? Is it not a sequel of static situations? Where is the unit? What dimension of time is there in question? Or is the whole analogy not misplaced, and are we not merely victims of a fallacy? Is, perhaps, the antithesis, "polythetic-monothetic", only applicable to operational processes of the mind within a conceptual scheme of reference? And is the antithesis, "flowing-arrow" – "trajectory", applicable only to movements in space or in the spatial-temporal dimension in which the outer world exists? Is there a spatial element in music? And, again, in either case: What gives us the right to speak of music as a meaningful context? How is this meaning constituted?

All of these questions have to be investigated. But this tentative approach shows that we cannot use a current philosophical doctrine without careful investigation if we want to describe the musical experience in a phenomenologically correct way. Even the phenomenological method itself, as far as it has been developed up to now, may prove to be insufficient. On the contrary, it may be hoped that a careful analysis of the musical experience may contribute one or another detail to phenomenological theory.

§13. The Spatial Element in Art in General and in Music in Particular

As a convenient first approach to the problems outlined in §12, let us analyze the spatial element in music. There is no difficulty in constituting the experience of space by visual or tactile elements, especially if, with Husserl, the movements of the entire body in walking are reduced to experiences of the haptic sphere.[6] Starting from oculomotoric and haptic kinaesthesias, we may build up isolated optic and haptic spatial fields, each of them centered around a kernel of optimal accessibility. This kernel of optimal accessibility is the sphere of nearness with my own body in the center, constituted as the origin of the whole coordinate system which I apply to the spatial field. The remote things are, then, either those which I may approach by performing certain kinaesthesias, especially the kinaesthesias of walking, or they are the things which may, if they are self-moving, approach my sphere of nearness, or they are the things which, by resemblance to things within my sphere of nearness, are interpreted as having structures, shapes, qualities, and so on, analogous to things within my sphere of nearness.

The whole spatial field, thus constituted, is structurized in perspectives; it has its distances, its horizons and its observational optimum. The latter, in the optical sphere, is the optimal standpoint, permitting us to choose a focus which brings the selected sector of the field into optimal *sharpness*; in the haptic sphere the observational optimum is the possibility of touching the thing, of following its surface with tactile organs of my body, my hands, my limbs, etc. These experiences may be corroborated if they reappear after an interruption. I close my eyes and reopen them again, I withdraw my hands from the surface of the thing and then touch it again. The previous experiences recur, the thing is still there, and so are its experienced parts and portions. There is, furthermore, the synthesis between these different fields, the mutual control of visual by tactile impressions and vice versa, the anticipation of approaching the remote thing, the reference back to previous experiences of successful approaches, and so on. In this way, although it would seem insufficiently, G.H. Mead has studied this structurization under the title of the "manipulatory sphere",[7] a term which suggests, roughly, what Husserl calls, much more precisely, the optimal sphere. Thus, the constitution of space refers back to our kinaesthetic experiences of our bodily organs of sight and touch and our actual or virtual ability to perform the kinaesthesia of locomotion.

The arts using spatial elements as a medium take into account these ways of constituting the dimension of space. The frame of the picture delimits the sector of the visual field selected. There is one standpoint assigned to the beholder, from which the painted space appears optimally centered and from which all the painted

[6]In this connection, see the two essays of Edmund Husserl edited by Schutz: "Grundlegende Untersuchungen zum phänomenologischen Ursprung der Räumlichkeit der Natur", published in *Philosophical Essays in Memory of Edmund Husserl*, edited by Marvin Farber (Cambridge: Harvard University Press, 1940), pp. 305–326 (English translation by Fred Kersten, in Edmund Husserl, *Shorter Works*, edited by Peter McCormick and Frederick A. Elliston (Notre Dame: University of Notre Dame Press, 1981), pp. 213–233); and its continuation, "Notizen zur Raumkonstitution", in *Philosophy and Phenomenological Research*, I (1940), pp. 21–37 and 217–226. It is worth noting here that Schutz uses the idea of kinaesthesia in Husserl's meaning of the term, "kinaesthesia". See Fred Kersten, *Phenomenological Method: Theory and Practice*, pp. 79ff., 159f.

[7]Schutz refers to G.H. Mead, *The Philosophy of the Present* (Chicago: University of Chicago Press, 1932), pp. 124ff., and *The Philosophy of the Act* (Chicago: University of Chicago Press, 1938), pp. 103–106, 121ff. Schutz's discussion of this idea may be found in "On Multiple Realities", *Collected Papers*, Vol. I, pp. 223f.

perspectives gain their correct proportions. Within this field the art of the painter, by specific devices, guides the oculomotoric kinaesthesias of the beholder required to appropriately organize this field. The eye has to follow certain contour lines; it is guided by the distribution of colors, lights and shadows, etc. Although the painting represents a set of coexistent and immovable images, these images are not perceived by the beholder in simultaneity but in succession. His eye is incited to wander around within the limits of the frame. He is invited to shift the center of his visual field from one of the painted objects to the other, pushing to the horizon what formerly was in the center, and so on. If his oculomotoric movements return to the starting point, he will find the same aspect as before.

Thus the art of the painter frequently creates in the beholder the impression of rhythmic recurrences, and suggests in some cases even the experience of a movement as an element of inner time. It is the reversal of the Eleatic problem mentioned before: the flying arrow depicted in its place of rest on the trajectory produces in the beholder the experience of its flight by provoking oculomotoric kinaestheias which refer to previous experiences of motion in inner time. Thus, it is the special problem of the painter to refer the beholder to the experience of his inner time by using as means elements exclusively pertaining to the dimension of space. By the specific way in which he distributes coexistent, unchangeable elements in space, the painter incites the beholder to transform the coexistence into succession, to modify the unchangeable by recurrent experience, to translate spatial experiences into those belonging to the flux of his stream of consciousness. All this is possible only because the beholding of the painting requires the performance of oculomotoric kinaestheais which are, as such, experienced exclusively in inner time, but which, in succession, permit the building up of a coexistent spatial field of vision.

The works of architecture require the beholder to perform locomotion and the adherent kinaesthesias. A work of architecture is based upon the idea that there is not one single optimal sphere of looking at it, but that any of its aspects can be brought into nearness by walking around it, the successive images of the same structure organizing themselves in a planned way regardless of whether the object appears as a remote one in the horizon of the visual field, or as a near one – whether I walk around it or enter it. The architect takes into account that the shape of the exterior suggests its interior, the frontside the back, the roof the structurization of its foundation. The plan of the architect anticipates all possible perspectives in which his work may appear to a beholder who is not only free to choose his standpoint, but to change his standpoint at random.

However, it is not only the kinaesthesia of walking around which is required for an appropriate approach to the work of architecture. The devices applied by the artist suggest that each of these aspects and perspectives be structurized in itself in a particular way. The planned arrangements of pillars or windows lead the eye to follow a certain pattern. The eye has to accept the features selected by the architect as the elements relevant for such a structurization. The roving eye has to start from them and return to them. This again leads to oculomotoric movements, to departures and returns, experienced in inner time, and thus the impression of a recurrent rhythm is created again in the beholder. Architecture, therefore, refers to both: the visual and the locomotive kinaesthesias and their mutual control and verification.

As to the work of sculpture, it seems that we have to distinguish between large statues which in gross outline require the same attitude of the beholder as do works of architecture with the important difference, however, that they do not have an inside which can be entered and that their outer shape does not suggest a corresponding structurization of the interior. But they, too, leave open to the observer the standpoint from which the perspectives offered structurize themselves, and prescribe certain relevant aspects as guidance for the beholder's oculomotoric kinaesthesias. Like a painting, they may provoke rhythmic recurrence of such kinaesthesias and even create the impression of motion in inner time. As to smaller objects of the plastic arts, which can be held in the hand, the dimension of haptic kinaestheia supervenes, experiences in one field always checking, verifying, amending or annihilating those originating in the others.

In all the cases considered so far, we found that the experiences of the observer referred to his possible kinaesthesias, the visual, the tactile, the locomotive ones. Yet, the organ by which we experience music, the ear, does not have any kinaesthesia. There is no center of nearness and no horizon of the acoustical field, nor is there a structurization analogous to that of perspective. Of course, I hear approaching steps, I hear the distant thunder. But in analyzing these cases we find that the experiences meant by the terms "approaching" or "distant" are not those of the mere acoustic field. They are based upon preconstituted spatial experiences which were not purely auditive ones. There are, for instance, in the case of approaching steps, recurrent acoustic impressions – starting low and becoming louder and louder; and we know from other experiences, such as visual ones, that the steps of the approaching walker sound the louder the nearer he comes. Thus, the ear is not able to build up the dimension of space. The only references to it is the capacity of the ear to give a certain orientation as to the directions where the sound comes from. In order to listen better to the sound, I have to turn my head or my body; however, this is not a kinaesthetic movement peculiar to the auditive sphere. At any rate, the art of music does not make any use of the ear's capacity to localize the origin of the sound. Music does not require any kinaesthesia on the part of the listener.

Another peculiarity of the sense of hearing is that the impressions transmitted by the ear cannot be interrupted voluntarily. I may withdraw from the visual field by closing my eyes, from the haptic field by removing my hands. If I open my eyes again, or touch the object again, I find that my previous experiences still subsist, or I find that they have changed. The ear is always open to acoustic impressions. I cannot interrupt my hearing of them, I may only stop listening to them. I permanently apperceive all the events in the acoustical world even if I discontinue perceiving them. Analyzing the peculiar devices that the arts of the spatial dimension use in order to induce the beholder to bring forth a rhythmical pattern, we find the importance of the departure and the return of the same experience originating in the recurrence of the same visual, tactile, and locomotive kinaesthesias. The ear is not capable of creating such a recurrence, and therewith it is incapable of creating a rhythmical pattern and an anamnesis of pre-experienced impressions. The art of music knows, of course, rhythm and pattern, but they do not originate in our experience of space. In this sense we may say that the art of music and the means it uses are independent of our spatial experience. Or, as we put it in the beginning, music is without a specific reference to the objects of the world in which we live. Further investigations will modify this statement to a certain extent. It will be shown that the time dimension in music refers back to our spatial experience. But this can only be done after examination of the nature of this time dimension itself.

§14. The Temporal Element in Music[8]

I have here a box of different kinds of 78 rpm records. If you look at your watch, you will find that it takes about three minutes to play one side of a twelve-inch record. This is an important fact for the person in charge of making up a radio program. It is entirely immaterial to the listener. To the listener, it is not true that the time he lived through while listening to the slow movement of a symphony was of equal length to the time he lived through while listening to its finale, although each movement needed the playing of two sides of a twelve-inch record. The listener lived, while listening, in another dimension of time which cannot be measured by our clocks or other mechanical devices. In the measurable time there are pieces of equal length, there are minutes and hours. There is no such yardstick for the dimension of time the listener lives through; there is no equality between its pieces, if there are pieces at all.

We need not have the specific experience of listening to music in order to learn the incommensurability of the time we are living through by the dials of our clocks. The hand of our watch runs equally through half the circle of the dial, whether we waited before the door of the surgeon who operated on a person dear to us, or whether we had a conversation with a friend on a topic in which we are vitally interested. But we will be astonished in the first case that the waiting period which seemed without end lasted only half an hour, and, in the second case, that we spent so much time, although we had intended to see our friend only for five minutes. The time of our waiting, the time within which we grow old, the inner time of our stream of consciousness, is entirely free from elements of space. It is the same dimension of time in which we experience movement as an unbroken ongoing occurrence, first of all as the movement of our own body. Considered as an event in space, as a trajectory or path run through by the moved thing, movement (and, first of all, our bodily movement) becomes spatial in character. Inner time projected into space becomes the dimension in which our actions take place, the dimension which we share with our fellowmen, and which, by a supervening idealization, may be conceived as the cosmic time or the time of the physicists. This spatialized time may be measured and divided into equal parts. But all measurement of time is done by measurement of spatial distances, be it the way traversed by the earth when revolving around its axis or circling around the sun, be it the way made by the hands of our clocks around the dial. In a last formalization, this concept of outer time leads to Riemann's Continuum of four dimensions in which time takes on the mathematical function of a fourth dimension which is supervenient to the three dimensions of space.

[8]For a similar discussion of the idea developed in this section that music is a "meaningful arrangement of tones in inner time", see "Making Music Together", *Collected Papers*, Vol. II, pp. 170ff.

Philosophers from Augustine to Husserl, James and Bergson have studied the nature of immanent time, or *durée*, as Bergson calls it, and of our stream of consciousness (under which title James deals with the problem). Without entering into a thorough discussion of the teachings of these philosophers, we have to point out certain other basic concepts relevant to our problem in order to show that music is experienced as an occurrence in inner time.[9]

Our mental life has been described by the metaphor of an ongoing stream of our thoughts. Experience follows experience in an unbroken and interconnected way. Every Now emergent within this stream turns into a Just-Now if I try to catch it, and becomes a more and more remote past, whereas other experiences emerge, forming other Nows which, in their turn, can only be caught when having become a past. We may take a double attitude toward this ongoing stream of consciousness. Sticking to the metaphor of a stream, we may say that we can swim with the stream. Then we are living in our thoughts, in our acts, and we are directed toward the objects of our thoughts or acts; or, we may stop swimming with the stream, we may step out of its current, bring it to standstill, and look back in what is called an attitude of reflection, toward the past phases of the stream of our thought. Then we are no longer living in our acts directed toward their objects; we make our acts themselves objects of our reflective thinking.

This attitude of reflecting is made possible by that peculiar feature of our mind which is generally called the faculty of memory. The Now which turned into a past does not entirely disappear; it may be recollected; it is then no longer an actual vivid experience, but it subsists as remembrance of things past. It is this faculty of memory which makes the stream of our consciousness an unbroken and interrelated sequel of our thoughts in inner time. At any moment of our stream of thought the actually experienced Now sinks down into a recollection of this Now, which thus became a past Now, and which can be recollected as such by a reflective attitude which we are assuming in another Now, the actual Now of our reflection. But it belongs to our state of mind in this second Now that we are turning back to a past Now, the past, which we are, reflectingly, bringing before our mind as a past, which formerly was a Now. Thus, the past elements of our inner life continue in our actual Now in the form of recollections.

It is clear that the images of our recollected past experiences will change because they depend upon the Now in which we assume the reflective attitude. The same object of our thoughts has another aspect (1) if actually experienced; (2) if looked at as an object actually experienced in a past, but now recollected; (3) if looked at later on in a third Now – as an object, actually experienced in a past and previously already recollected; the remembrance of the past actuality must also include in this case a reference to the past Now in which it was recollected, a reference to a past Now which was such a Now only because it included this recollection: such is the third Now, which is only such a peculiar Now because it includes both the recollection of the object and the recollection of having previously recollected it. In all three cases, it is the same object, but the same object as modified, as having changed, as

[9]This passage is marked for deletion in the manuscript.

offering new aspects, new features, new structures of relevance. Thus a specific style, a type of object of recollection and of its peculiar modifications is built up which, too, becomes an element of our stock of experiences at hand.

We now have to distinguish two different types of remembrance within what we called recollection. First there are reflective attitudes towards an experience which was actual in a Now *just* past. The remembrance, then, attaches itself immediately and without interruption to the actual experience. Although it sinks into the past, the actual experience is still retained, and, therefore, the term *retention* has been used for this special type of remembrance. A border line case of such a retention – very important for the experience of music – is the experience of a lasting object which, therefore, participates in several Nows of our stream of thought; for example, a sound which lasts for a certain period of time. We have, then, in any Now in which we perceive this lasting sound both the actual experience of this sound and the retention of its initial phases, which belong to past Nows. The second type of remembrance – called *reproduction* – does not attach itself immediately to actual experiences. It refers to more remote Pasts which are reproduced in these recollections of other experiences having emerged between the past Now, in which the recollected object of our thought was actually experienced, and the actual Now, in which it is recollected. Retention and reproduction are, thus, the two outstanding types of memory. Both are equally important for the constitution of musical experience.

But our analysis of the stream of thought has so far dealt only with the actual Now and the past, and with the phenomenon of remembrance. We now have to examine the dimension of time which is called the future. By living in our experiences, by being directed towards the objects of our acts and thoughts we are always oriented towards the future, we are always expecting certain occurrences and events. What we are foreseeing is suggested by the general style or type of our past experiences or by the assumption that things will continue to be what they have been so far, and that what has proved to be typical in the past will also be typical in the future. These expectations, of course, are uncertain, they are empty, they may or may not be fulfilled by the anticipated event when it materializes in actuality. Remembered objects of facts are no longer empty. They were what they were; my memory might deceive me, but the remembered objects are definite and definitive. Future objects, however, may turn out to be quite otherwise than we anticipated, and there is no warranty whatever that they will even be of that general type or style which we ascribed to them in foresight.

Closer analysis shows that we may distinguish between two types of expectations in a manner analogous to the way in which we distinguished two types of recollection: on the one hand, there are those which immediately attach themselves to the actual experience; they may be compared to retentions and, therefore, the term *protention* has been used for them; and, on the other hand, there are those which refer to events and experiences of the more distant future; they correspond to the reproductions, and are called *anticipations* in the strict sense. It is quite clear that although both protentions and anticipations are empty, the former are more likely to be fulfilled by actuality than the latter, especially if a protention attaches itself to an actual experience which itself contains a retention of the same object. To come back to the example just used: if I have been perceiving an enduring sound of a specific, unchanged pitch, I may assume that this sound will have the same pitch in the following fraction of time. Retentions and reproductions, protentions and anticipations are constitutive for the interconnectedness of the stream of consciousness. They are equally constitutive for the experience of music.

But, by necessity, this analysis gives a wrong impression because the terms used like "now", "just now", "past" experiences, have an atomistic connotation. The reason for this is that language, designed to establish a universe of discourse with our fellow human beings and to describe acts and events pertaining to the spatio-temporal world, is itself atomistic. It dissects the continuity into pieces; it creates the impression of parts and pieces, where a single indivisible unit should be depicted. The thought expressed may be a unit but it is expressed by, reconstructed from, the fragments of words which compose the sentence rendering the thought. When Bergson tries to convey the image of the onrolling *durée*, he gives the example of a melody, a melody, however, not structurized as to rhythm, harmony or difference in pitch or loudness.[10] The insight that the inner time cannot be broken down into units (in contrast to the spatialized time within which the spatial elements of points and distance can be assumed and even measured) shows that the notion of the present deserves further consideration.

The present of our vivid experiences is never a mathematical point, a mere instant, an ideal limit between past and future. The assumption of such a mere instant would be an abstraction borrowed from the geometry of space or its analogue, the spatialized time. The vivid present encompasses everything that is actually lived through; it includes elements of the past retained or recollected in the Now and elements of the future entering the Now by way of protention or anticipation. The present we are living in is always a specious present, as James calls it, having in itself is structurization, having a before and an after. It may include very unequal elements of the past and the future. Its shape will depend upon what Bergson calls the tension of our consciousness, and this tension itself is merely a function of our attention toward life. Life requires acting within the outer world, dealing with its objects, mastering the outer world, and performing all these activities in collaboration with others, making fellow human beings objects of our acts and being motivated by theirs. This everyday life is life within the outer world, amidst its objects and fellow human beings; it is life in space and the spatio-temporal dimension.

To master this everyday life requires a degree of high tension in our consciousness, called full awakeness. Living in such a state means being directed towards the objects of the outer world, including our fellow human beings, and to live in the activities which these acts have as object. The spatialized time of our daily life corresponds to the attitude of full attention to it, to the state of full awakeness. This tension hides our experiences of our inner life which become visible only if we return from full attention to life, only if we diminish the tension correlated to full awakeness necessary for our dealing with the outer world. Thus, a gradual withdrawal from the spatio-temporal dimension is performed together with the transgression to other levels of our conscious life, that is, to levels which are more intimate

[10]The manuscript has the German term, "Tonstärke".

and nearer to the experience of the stream of our *durée* but unfit for performing in them our activities gearing into the outer world.

§15. The Experience of Music

If we abstract from the special use of music to accompany certain events in the outer world – music for dancing, music for marching, music in combination with the drama (a use which will have to be analyzed separately) – we find that the decision to listen to pure music involves a peculiar attitude on the part of the listener. He stops living in his acts of daily life, stops being directed toward their objects. His attention toward life has been diverted from its original realm; in Bergson's terminology, his tension of consciousness has changed. He lives now on another plane of consciousness. This, of course, has nothing to do with the intensity of his listening. He may be engaged and, for the most part, he will be engaged, with greater intensity in listening to music than in the performance of his daily routine work. But when the conductor raises his baton, the audience has performed a leap (in the sense of Kierkegaard) from one level of consciousness to another. They are no longer engaged in the dimension of space and spatial time, they are no longer involved in the maze of activities necessary to deal with human beings and their things. They accept the guidance of music in order to relax their tension and to surrender to its flux, a flux which is that of their stream of consciousness in inner time.

§16. Elements Common to Music at Large

In order to attempt a truly phenomenological analysis of the listener's experience of music, we must try to establish those elements which are common to all kinds of music and we must disregard – temporarily at least – all the features characteristic of particular musical culture only.[11] The way in which the listener educated in the Western civilization of our times looks at music is determined by a certain education, by habits of listening, by habits of interpretation, by general concepts of the function of music, by certain assumptions as to the typical style prevailing in the musical works of past periods, and by a peculiar attitude toward contemporary music. On the average, he knows only a very small sector of music, the Western music of the last 250 years, from Bach and Handel up to our times. This kind of music has formed an ideal of his education which involves, among other things, rhythmicality, tonality, a peculiar concept of harmony, a peculiar kind of counterpoint, a peculiar kind of possible modifications of a theme, and of a standard of musical forms, and so on.

Furthermore, the listener has a specific idea of the faculty of music to express certain feelings or moods, to depict occurrences in the outer world; he cannot forget the standard set up by the Viennese classics for symphonic forms, and by Richard Wagner or Verdi for the opera; he not only looks at contemporary music as a derivation from, or a modification of, these standards; he even reads the works of Bach or

[11]For an account very similar to what is found here in §§16 and 17, see "Making Music Together", pp. 167ff.

Mozart with other eyes than did his fathers and grandfathers. The reason for this is merely that for the latter the standard of music set up by Wagner and his school had an importance which differs from its importance for us. But all the Gregorian antiphons, the Gothic music, the music of the Masters of the Flemish school, the Arabian, Chinese and primitive music must show certain features which are essential for the experience of music *as a phenomenon of our conscious life*, and it is exactly these elements which have to be investigated by a phenomenological description. Having secured a few results by this endeavor we may investigate some features peculiar to the kind of music regarded as a valid ideal within our musical culture.

§17. The Frame of Reference of the Experience of Music

That does not mean that such a phenomenological analysis would disregard the existence of specific standards for music prevailing in certain periods. Of course, we have to take into account that the listener – any listener – has a certain set of experiences as to the general style or type of music he is listening to. Unless he has such a previous knowledge, the music he hears does not make any sense to him. He may understand that the sounds he perceives are meant as a meaningful context, but he cannot grasp them as such. If I, who have no knowledge of the Hungarian language, am hearing somebody recite a poem in this language, I understand that this man is reciting a poem; it has rhythm, rhymes, and a certain arrangement of vowels and consonants which are similar to the general idea of a poem I have experienced within the frame of reference of languages which I understand. And by the expressional values, which he who recites this poem bestows upon what he recites, I become convinced that he understands what this poem means. Even more, I may receive a vague impression of the meaning, the general mood, for instance, which the poem wants to confer – that it is sad or gay, and so on.

On the other hand, I may even understand that the language of the poem is the Hungarian language because, by virtue of previous experiences, I have formed a certain typical idea of how the Hungarian language sounds, of the inflection and the treatment of vowels and consonants in such a language. Briefly, I may refer what I am hearing to a series of frames of reference which are derived from previous experiences and which are now at hand as typical features of the unknown. But I am lacking that peculiar frame of reference, called the Hungarian language, which would enable me to grasp the recited poem as a meaningful context. The average musician of our times and civilization will have a similar experience if confronted for the first time with Gothic music or a modern composition written in the twelve-tone system.

Our analysis will, therefore, have to take into account the fact that, while listening, the listener uses previous experiences of the kind of music he is listening to. He has a certain knowledge of its general type and style. This knowledge functions as a frame of reference to which he refers his actual experiences. The knowledge of this type or style enables him to follow the flux of the music he is listening to, to be directed at any Now toward the experience which the next Now will actualize: By this general knowledge of the typical, he foresees what will follow, he anticipates it;

it is clear that these anticipations (or protentions) are empty and will or will not be fulfilled by the actual event when it materializes itself in another Now. But in order to perform such anticipatory functions it is sufficient *that* the listener *has* knowledge of *some* type or style which he uses as a frame of reference, whether it is a type or style derived from a general knowledge of the musical culture to which the work of art he listens to belongs, or whether it is of the style of the individual composer, or even of the peculiar work itself.

Consequently, a phenomenological analysis of the experience of music has to take into account only the existence of *some* frame of reference at the disposal of the listener. *What* the *peculiar* features of this frame of reference are is immaterial for a general theory of musical experience. It is the task of a history of music, a history surpassing the biographies of musicians and their adherent anecdotal materials, to describe the peculiar styles and types or frames of references used at different times in different musical cultures. On the other hand, it is quite possible for theoretical analysis to apply its results at the level of concrete analysis of a given musical culture, its typical forms, structurizations, etc.

§18. Summary of the Elements Common to the Musical Experience

There are relatively few elements common to any kind of musical experience. They can be summed up in the following propositions:

1. All musical experience originates in the flux of inner time, in the stream of consciousness. It does not necessarily refer to objects of the outer world. If musical experience does refer to objects of the outer world, it uses specific devices for coordinating the events within the spatio-temporal dimension with those within inner time. These specific devices originate in the suggestions of movements and, first of all, in the movements of the human body, which occur simultaneously in both dimensions – the inner *durée* as well as the spatialized time.
2. Musical experience is based upon the faculty of the mind to recollect the past by retentions and reproductions and to foretaste the future by protentions and anticipations. The musical experience takes place in a specious present which, by means of recollection and expectation, includes elements of the past and the future. As an ongoing flux it shares the flux of the stream of consciousness in simultaneity. The listener may partake in the flux or "bring it to a standstill". He may assume a "Dionysian" or "Apollonian" attitude toward it (Nietzsche).
3. The basic element of all music is a unique configuration called the theme. It is itself extended in inner time. It is apperceived as a unit (*Gestalt*), or as a combination of those units. It may be itself structurized, it may have parts and "moments", these parts or "moments" may be dissected afterwards. But it is experienced as a whole.
4. A theme may recur. It may be repeated immediately or recur after other themes have intervened.
5. A theme may be modified and then, nevertheless, be recognized as the same but modified – it may be inverted, reversed, enlarged, diminished, transposed, varied, embellished, and so on. It is, then, experienced as the same theme, but inverted, etc.

6. A theme may be combined with other themes or with itself or its parts or "moments" or its modifications. This combination may take place either in succession or in simultaneity.

As will be seen, rhythmical structurization is not included in this list; the problem of rhythm will have to be dealt with later on. It is not at all certain that rhythm is essential to musical experience itself. Rhythm is only peculiar to certain musical cultures. The Ambrosian or Gregorian music, even Palestrina's music, is not rhythmical in the same sense as our modern music. Add to this that the concept of rhythm is an equivocal one, referring, on the one hand, to physiological occurrences (beating of the heart, breathing), on the other hand to occurrences in the outer world (marching, walking, dancing), and, finally, to specific structurizations of our modern musical ideas (rhythm as a function of harmony). That is the reason why rhythm is not included in the catalogue of elements of our musical experiences. The aforementioned aspects of rhythm will be considered at the appropriate places.[12]

§19. Phenomenological Analysis of a Sequence of Tones

A piece of music starts. We are perceiving the first tone, c, in the actual vivid experience of a Now.[13] The tone lasts, it has a certain extension in time. We have the actual perceiving of this tone and, at the same time, a retention of its initial phrases. Both coincide. It is the same tone, c, that we are perceiving now as before; it is an enduring tone. A second tone, d, follows, experienced in the vivid present. When perceiving it we have a vivid retention of the first one (c), although it has now ceased to be actually perceived. We are hearing the interval (c-d) between both, we are referring the second one to the first and say: That is an interval of the second upwards. The second note (d) is followed by a third one (e): we perceive it actually, retaining the second one (d), and in this retention we retain the interval (c-d) between the first (c) and the second (d), and retain, therefore indirectly, the first one (c).

We have, then: (1) the third tone (e) in actual experience; (2) the second one (d) retained; (3) the interval (d-e) between the second and the third; (4) the first one (c) as a retentional element of (2) (d); the interval (c-e) between the actually experienced third (e) and the first one (c). The fourth (c) will be acknowledged by a synthesis of passive recognition as having identical pitch with the first (c), the fifth (d) as having identical pitch with the second (d), all of them retained directly or indirectly by retentions of retentions, etc. Since we recognized the fourth (c) and the fifth (d) as being identical with the first (c), and the second (d), we may expect by

[12]The discussion of rhythm is lacking in the present manuscript. See the brief comments on rhythm in "Making Music Together", p. 164.

[13]The following diagram was written on the reverse side of the preceding manuscript page, and may be presumed to have been used as a guide by Schutz as he wrote this section:

way of protention that the sixth one will be of the same pitch as the third (e). We consider, then, the sequence of the first three tones c-d-e as "theme", as a unit which is expected to recur by way of immediate repetition. But this expectation – if we have it at all – would be deceived by the actual experience of the sixth tone which is not, as the (assumed) protention might have indicated, an e, but a d. The non-fulfillment of the (assumed) protention makes us understand that what has to be considered a unit or a theme is not the thematic sequel c-d-e, which repeats itself, but the whole sequel of six notes: c-d-e-c-d-d.

§20. Three Basic Categories of Musical Experience

Let us open a parenthesis and consider the relationship between the fifth and the sixth tone (both d), and compare it with the mechanism of retention studied in the light of the example of the first tone while it lasted. When the first note was experienced as an enduring one, there was a coincidence between the actual experience of the actually perceived note, c, and the retention of its initial phases – also c – and there was no intermittence between the two. We not only experienced the pitch of the retained sound as identical with the pitch of the actually perceived one. But we also experienced the same sound as enduring. The case is different in the relationship between the fifth and the sixth note. While listening to the sixth note, we know by way of retaining the fifth note that both have identical pitch and timbre. It is the same sound; but, nevertheless, we are convinced that the fifth note did not last; it ceased to be perceived actually and started again; in intermittence of the actual experiencing, there as this d, although the retention of it was not discontinued. When listening to the sixth note we do not say: "This is the fifth one which still lasts". We say: "The sixth tone is a repetition of the fifth one; it is a tone, having the same pitch as the previous one, but it is not the same one which still lasts; the fifth one came to an end, it had its final phase, which is not identical with the initial phase of the fifth, but followed the end-phase of the fifth. There is no continuance, but repetition of the 'same'."

This observation is important in a two-fold respect for the phenomenology of musical experience. (a) It shows three basic categories of all musical experience, namely continuance and intermittence (repetition) in the equivocal use of this term; (b) it gives an interesting aspect of the difficulties involved in the ascertainment of the sameness; (c) it shows the differences of the style of experiences related to space (by kinaesthetic movements) and those related to inner time.[14]

§21. The Category of Continuance and Repetition

Ad (a). I. The terms, *continuance* and *repetition*, are opposites merely if applied to the experience of one single tone which either lasts or finds its final phase succeeded by an initial phase of the same tone. But even this statement is not precise enough.

[14]This paragraph is somewhat garbled, but it is left essentially as it is in the manuscript because Schutz constructs the following sections around it. From what follows it is clear that there is a three-fold respect, namely, the three categories of continuance and intermittence, sameness, and movement.

As an example, take a repeated bass tone in a composition. It will have the same function as a continuous base tone. In both cases, we speak of a "pedal point". The reason is that by way of retention the intermittent repetitions of the same tone are brought to coincidence and apperceived as a specious continuance, although actually repetition of the same occurs.

This phenomenon is of great importance for the theory of music. It is not merely restricted to the repetition of the same tone. As used here, *repetition* is merely a special case of the intermittence of a continuance. It is intermittence of a sameness. (This statement will be qualified by the following paragraph.) However, by way of retention a virtual unity may be established even between intermittent notes of different pitch. This unity should be better called a *coherence*, the term "continuance" being reserved for the same enduring tone. Terminologically, we have, then, the antithesis, coherence-intermittence, of which continuance-repetition, as used above, are merely special cases. Now, we said that a virtual coherence may be established by retention even between intermittent sounds. Within the flux of a composition a specious coherence might be established by the listener, for instance, between the top notes of an inverted melody. Actually, only this one melody – the real voice – materializes. But by retaining the intermittent notes a second and, eventually, a third and fourth specious voice are experienced as present. A monodic composition may, therefore, be experienced as a polyphonic one, consisting of one real voice in counterpoint to one or more specious voices. Ernst Kurth has seen this problem and dealt with it in his book, *The Linear Counterpoint*.[15]

II. Continuance and repetition have, however, another meaning if referred to functional units themselves, to themes or groups of themes, or, finally, to independent parts of the musical forms. Then they do not originate in pure retention. They are based upon the other forms of memory; the repetition originates in a synthesis of recognition between the reproduced past experience of the theme with its actually experienced recurrence, and the continuance originates in a fulfillment of the previously anticipated development by the actual experience.[16] These relations can, however, only be studied after further investigations as to the constitution of the units of musical experience, such as the theme. We must mention this problem here in order to show its origin.

§22. The Category of Sameness

Ad (b). The question of "sameness" is one of the most difficult problems of phenomenology. According to Husserl, there is a passive synthesis of recognition or identification which brings the recollection of a past experience of the same object of thought by "superposition" into congruence with a renewed originary experience of the same (or, at a secondary level, produces such a congruence between recollections or even recollections of recollections of the same). But, on the other hand, Husserl has shown that we may recognize an object as the same, but modified, and

[15]Ernst Kurth, *Grundlagen des linearen Kontrapunkts: Bachs melodische Polyphonie* (Berlin, 1922, 3rd).

[16]This sentence is marked "unclear" in the manuscript.

that we have, furthermore, to distingish between sameness and likeness. We may find likeness between two different and distinguishable objects; we may find sameness of the object, although the object has changed meanwhile. Here, again, we will have to distinguish sameness and likeness of a single tone, and we will have to make that distinction of a functional unit, such as a theme, is in question. For the time being, we restrict our investigation to the first problem.

In our example in §20, the tone, d, is repeated as the "same". Certainly it is the "same" – only interrupted – if we merely consider the pitch of both; it is, in our example, furthermore of the same length as its predecessor; it may be assumed that it has the same timbre. However, it is different from it in several respects. First of all, it is a repeated tone. Its initial phase started after the end-phase of the "same" preceding tone ended. The retention of the actual experience of the first tone in its complete development – initial phase, enduring phases, end-phase – has been retained when the second tone was actually experienced. Secondly, the entry of the second tone certainly adds something new to our previous experience. But it is not entirely new, there is no contrast between this experience and the previous one, as it was the case when the first d followed a c. The mere interplay of retentions, described earlier, gives a d which follows a d a character different from a d which follows a c. The singer and the player of an instrument know this difference very well. They will give the second (repeated) d a slightly different accent, dynamically and even agogically. Imagine that the six notes used as an example had to be sung to the word, "Amen", or "Kyrie eleison", and it will be clear that the last note in our example will have quite another character than the note before last – no difference having been made as to pitch, timbre, or length. It could be argued that this difference results from the deception that the anticipated reduplication of the first three notes, c-d-e, by the last three notes did not materialize; or that an anticipation occurred, that the last note will be a c instead of a d, thus returning to the beginning of the melody.

But such an argument would be void. If we had played only the first five notes and had stopped inviting the listener to continue, we would have had a certain knowledge of his anticipations. In our example, these anticipations would be different for different individuals; it is not at all excluded that a repeated d# was anticipated. This is especially true in our case where nothing has been stated as to the closing character of the sixth tone, nothing as to the "tonality" of the composition, and the principle of the leading tone has not been established by previous knowledge of the type of musical culture to which the composition in question belongs. The previously mentioned difference merely originates in the structure of the *durée* as a permanent flux or stream. The same occurrence, if repeated, is not experienced as strictly the same, it is not even experienced as being a like experience. Our mind has changed, infinitesimally, but, nevertheless, changed by already having once pre-experienced the tone, d, in the same context. This is important because, we will presently see, this is one of the several origins of musical rhythm.

§23. The Category of Movement

Ad (c). So far, phenomenological investigations have dealt mainly with experiences of the outer world. since the world of rigid objects is of the greatest importance for dominating our environment, all philosophical speculation has considered the rigid visible and tangible object as the paradigm of the notion of "thing". This thing endures, it has its own dimension of time, it lasts, and even if moved or deformed or changed. The synthesis of recognition – based upon passive identification – can be verified by congruent kinaesthetic experiences. I see an object. I close my eyes and reopen them. The object is still here, and it is the same object as seen before. The same holds true if by some kinaesthetic performance I change my field of vision, turning away from the object and then turning back to it. It still is the same and recognized as such. It is clear that for the object of my haptic experiences a similar situation prevails if I release the object from my touching fingers and grasp it again. In the case of visible or tangible objects, the synthesis of identification can be verified by releasing it from my field of experiencing through the performance of an appropriate kinaesthesia and by re-establishing the previous field through the performance of an opposite kinaesthesia which undoes the first one. These kinaesthesias interrupted my experience of the enduring sameness of the object. But this holds good only for the spatial dimension. The ear does not know kinaestheias of this kind.

Of course, approaching the cascade I may perceive its distant murmur. If I withdraw, the murmur is no longer audible; it reappears when I approach it again. But in this case my knowledge that this is the same murmur is based on my knowledge that the object, "cascade", exists and that it has lasted while my experiencing of it was interrupted. It is the knowledge of a lasting quality of an external object which is in question. If the wind blows intermittently through the trees before my window, it is the same tree which is pushed by different and successive waves of the storm.

In the purely auditive field, however, in the realm of music, intermittence can never be ascribed to a kinaesthetic change which re-establishes or even verifies sameness. Intermittence has not a subjective, but an objective character. The sound, the tone itself, has ceased to exist, and another one has started to appear. This other one may be one like the first but it is, strictly speaking, never the same one. In the dimension of inner time, sameness has to be understood in another way than when tangible or visible objects are in question. The synthesis of identification works differently in the former dimension than it does in the latter dimension. Sameness does not mean that the same object survived while my experiences of this object were interrupted. It means that the identification is experienced in the form of a recurrence of a like object. Likeness, however, presupposes comparison, the possibility of "superimposing" one object upon the other, the possibility of bringing both to congruence. This, in its turn, presupposes the coexistence of both objects and, therewith, the categories of space within which alone two objects may coexist as distinct and separate unities. In the sphere of inner time, in the sphere of purely auditory experiences, there is no coexistence. Likeness or sameness refers to succeeding objects; there is not the possibility of looking from one object to the other in order to perform the synthesis of identification or of recognition. And, nevertheless, we identify the recurrent tone as a tone like the first, or we even say that the same tone has been repeated. If I define sameness as numerical uniqueness, it is, of course, not the same tone but just a like tone, following the first one, which has now disappeared. But I experience it in a way which identifies it with the first one as to pitch, timbre, length and still as another one, by the mere reason that a like tone preceded it.

We conclude, therefore, that in the dimension of inner time, or in the purely auditory sphere of music, the form of sameness is not that of a numerical unity but of recurrent likeness; and after this explanation we will use the term, "sameness", exclusively for conveying recurrent likeness, keeping in mind what has been stated in this and the preceding paragraph.

§24. Passive Synthesis and the Experience of Music

But another problem still remains unsettled. According to the teachings of phenomenology, the synthesis of recognition or of identification is a passive synthesis which does not require any activity of our mind. There has always been something mysterious about this passive synthesis even when experiences of visible or tangible objects are exclusively under scrutiny. But if we try to explain such an identification or recognition within the purely audible sphere, in which there is no coexistence of objects but merely succession of our experiences of them, we have to examine more closely the mechanism of the so-called passive synthesis.

For this purpose we have to consider the irreversibility of the stream of consciousness. Within the spatial field I have the possibility of changing my standpoint freely and, therewith, of changing my perspectives: I may walk away and I may return: there is the same aspect in the same perspective, the same object in the center, the same field of vision and the same horizon. If so, I say, nothing has changed. Or, if something has changed, it stands out as a strange thing over against the unchanged, which remains in its familiarity. On investigation it may prove to be the pre-experienced Same, but changed. At any rate, I have the possibility of undoing all the changes originating in my different kinaestheais – kinaesthesias belonging to the optic or haptic field, kinaesthesias of walking, and so on – by re-establishing the former position through opposite kinaesthesias. I am skipping them, so to speak; I am skipping the interval of my non-perceiving of the same, I am disregarding my absence from my "home-position" in which everything had its character of familiarity, and I always have it in my power to return to his home-position and to reassume the contact with the familiar surroundings. This creates the impression as though a passive synthesis of "superimposition" had been performed, but such an impression prevails only in hindsight. It prevails because in space nothing hinders me from returning to where I started. But, and this is the decisive point, in such a case I am looking in a single glance, in a single ray of thought, at the field and its objects as ready-made, as having been constituted in a process of successive experience now sedimented. I do not necessarily have to run through the process of constitution again. What I am comparing is the recollection of the outcome of this previous process, once performed, the recollection of the ready-made picture I had in mind when leaving my home-position, with the actual ready-made experience I have when returning to it. What we called "familiarity" is the striking experience of the familiar things, that they were somehow pre-experienced in successive activities of our mind. In looking at them again I do not start again to re-perform all of the polythetic steps by which I built them up at the first time; I grasp the field monothetically by one single ray, and I find that there is a coincidence between the actual monothetic experience and the recollection – and the monothetically recollected, previous one. What gives the illusion of a "passive" synthesis is merely the superfluousness of starting over again the polythetic activities of our mind in which the monothetic experience of the field has been built up.

This illusion of a passive synthesis disappears if I do not look monothetically at the spatial field from my regained home-position. I may start again to run through the polythetic steps in which the visual field constitutes itself and these steps are the "same" as those which I had to perform when I first experienced this particular sector of the visual field with its particular objects. Then, if any step actually performed corresponds to *like* steps previously performed and not recollected, and if the actually performed step had a sedimentation *like* the recollected ones, I say that the field re-perceived, or the objects re-experienced, are the *same* or the same, although modified.

The first way, that of monothetic recognition, is restricted to the spatial field because it presupposes the freedom to return to the home-position, and the undoing of the changing aspects arises while I was absent from the home-position. The second way, that of polythetic recognition, may be performed within the spatial dimension, and will be performed if what was anticipated to be familiar turns out to be strange. Objects existing merely within the dimension of inner time, merely audible objects and, especially, musical objects, can only be recognized polythetically.

The irreversibility of the stream of consciousness does not permit another attitude toward the object existing merely within the dimension of inner time *as long as* we follow the stream, *as long as* we have not stepped out of the flux and established, thus, so to speak, a kind of home-position. Having heard many times the First Symphony by Brahms I may look forward to hearing the theme of the French horns in the introduction to the finale. I may not only recognize this theme if somebody whistles its initial four notes – it is the fourth note only which makes it that specific, unique theme, and makes it recognizable (the first three notes alone may and do occur in an indefinite number of other compositions) – I may even immediately know how the fifth, sixth, and seventh note continues. I may not only identify this theme and the work of music to which it belongs. I may immediately present the role of this theme within the finale, the modifications in which it will appear later on, the reference involved back to other themes of previous movements of the same symphony, the similarity of this theme to others typical for Brahms.

To me personally, and probably to many others, this peculiar theme is the key to the understanding of Brahms' First Symphony. That is what I know by previous experiences. If the first notes of the beginning of the first movement start, I am directed by my anticipations toward the French horn theme which will appear later on at the end of the introduction of the fourth movement. All the preceding occurrences in the symphony receive, to me, their peculiar meaning and significance because I know that they will lead to this theme, all the events that follow derive their meaning from it. (This is, of course, an account of my personal experience and even, as it cannot be otherwise, of an experience which does not always prevail in my listening to this Symphony. Neither is it pretended that this peculiar theme has or has not a key position to any [other] listener, nor that [the theme] has [such a position] from the point of view of objective analysis of musical form, nor that such a functional röle was intended by the composer.) Thus, to me, this peculiar theme functions as a kind of home-position which may be reassumed any time if I am listening to this symphony or reproducing it before my inner ear.

But in order to think of this theme it is, nevertheless, necessary to reproduce in my mind the succession of the seven, or, at least, the first four notes, by which it is built up; and, furthermore, its functional importance for the symphony refers to my acquaintance with the whole work – from previous listenings, from playing it on the piano, from studying the score with all kinds of concomitant recollections not immediately related to the work of music itself supervening. However, in such a case I am no longer guided by the experiences of the ongoing musical events as when I listen to the work in question for the first time, recollecting by retention or repoduction what the onrolling music itself suggests that I recollect, anticipating to what the past Now of the actually experienced part of the work points. If I remain within this flux, I recognize emergent themes as recurrences of themes previously experienced. But I do not perform, then, a merely passive synthesis. It is identification, step by step, of the building up of the theme in actual experience with *like* steps, previously experienced in actuality, and now retained or recollected and leading to the same configuration of a unit. But, this again is done within the flux of the ongoing stream of consciousness, living in the direction from the first note to the last one; but so living we are, by retention and recollection, mindful of the past phases. Presently, this will be investigated further.

Here we have only to draw the following conclusions from what has preceded:

a) Sameness and likeness having meanings in the spatial world of visible and touchable objects different from those in the world of pure music which has its existence merely in the dimension of inner time.
b) Within the experience of pure music the synthesis of recognition is another one if referred merely to recurrent times or to recurrent thematical units.
c) It is quite another kind of synthesis at work if I recognize musical recurrences when listening to a work of music for the first time living within the ongoing flux (or if I re-establish such a situation), or if I recognize a piece of music or its thematical elements, not being immersed in the ongoing flux but reproducing in my mind music with which I am familiar.

It is to be hoped that this will become clearer if we close now the all too long parenthesis and resume the investigations where we interrupted them at the end of §19.

§25. Reflection and the Experience of Music

In §19 we studied the mechanism of retention which enables us to apperceive the six-tone sequence c-d-e-c-d-d as a theme. But what we really described was the experience of a person *having* listened to this sequence of tones, *having* apperceived it as a unit (called a theme), having stopped to listen to what follows, or even to expect that anything will follow, but having turned back to what he experienced and having asked himself what happened in this consciousness while he was listening. That means that the analysis offered is an analysis in hindsight. The mechanism of interlaced retentions only becomes visible for an attitude of reflection. In performing such an analysis, we are no longer dedicated to the listening to music as an ongoing flux. We are, as it is frequently said, no longer living *in* our acts of listening directed toward the object of such listening, namely the music as it goes on to build itself up within the stream of our consciousness. We have brought this flux to a seeming standstill. We turned back, living now in our acts of reflection, and made objects of these reflective acts not the music itself, but rather the acts of listening we have just perceived. We make objects of the acts of listening guided by a theoretical interest in that phenomenon of consciousness which is called "listening to music". We are not induced to do so because we hope to improve our understanding of music, and it is by no means contended that any listener or even some listeners are aware of the interplay of retentions described. It is very important to make it perfectly clear that the experience of listening itself has quite another structure. The listener lives in his acts of listening, he is directed toward the ongoing flux of music as it flows. The stream of his inner time (of his consciousness) and the stream of music are simultaneous within the precise meaning given by Bergson to this term. He calls two fluxes simultaneous if, at my discretion, I am able to look at both of them as a unit or at either of them distinctly.

Within this attitude, however, I am experiencing the sequence of the six tones under scrutiny as a unit which does not have any pieces and which cannot be broken down into its elements. It is an attitude similar to that in which we experience movement not as an event in space, but as an occurrence within our inner time. While I write the word, "time", on this sheet of paper, I am performing a movement of my fingers and of my hand which is an indivisible unit from the inception of writing the letter *t until the end of the letter e*. If I am reaching for this box of cigarettes, I have performed a single impulse of grasping this object. If I am following the arrow shot from the string of the bow it is one single kinaesthetic motion which accompanied its flight up to the bull's eye, and I grasp this movement as an indivisible unit. It is the Eleatic problem mentioned before applied to the realm of music.

To give another example: A trained pianist playing a piece of music at sight grasps in one single glance the passage his left hand has to perform in the E-major scale and, being trained to play such a scale, he performs the required movements of his fingers and hand in one single impetus without hestitation. Now, as a physiologist to explain to you what happens in the human body if you move merely the fifth finger of the left hand. You will be surprised to learn from him how many muscles, nerves, etc., have to be put in action for this single movement. And, then, remember the difficulties for the learning child in grasping the correct fingering of the E-major scale. There is no doubt that the pianist in our example performs in one single indivisible impulse a movement which is enormously complicated in itself. Nor is it a sufficient explanation to reduce this capacity to the categories of acquired skill and training. If this were an explanation at all, it would refer merely to the skill acquired by the practising child in learning the correct fingering. It would not explain the physiological occurrences enabling the player to innervate the many muscles and joints involved. I may be an excellent piano player and musician, even an excellent piano teacher, without being interested in the physiology of piano playing. But there is no doubt that all the events the physiologists explain are by necessity involved in what the player performs in one single impulse of his conscious life and in what he experiences as such.

Thus there is no incompatibility between both of our propositions: 1) The listener experiences the theme as an indivisible unity, as a single impulse, as long as he lives within the flux of the ongoing music; 2) what enables him to experience the theme as a unit is the interplay of retentional and protentional mechanism of his conscious life, described before, but this mechanism only becomes visible to him if he ceases to participate in the ongoing flux, and turns back to his past experiences in an attitude of reflection – making the acts of his listening the object of his reflection.

If we said that the listener experiences the theme as a unit we tried to circumscribe the meaning of the term, "Gestalt", as used by modern psychologists. As a matter of fact, it would be the most adequate way for describing the units of musical experiences in terms of Gestalt-psychology if the latter would not operate with unclarified concepts of the whole and parts.

For our problem, that of the musical theme, it is important to study certain constitutional elements which render a sequence of tones a theme. When talking parenthetically of the French horn theme of the final movement of Brahms' First Symphony (§24), we observed that this theme, consisting of seven notes, can only be identified by at least its first four notes. As a matter of fact, it is articulated in such a way that the first four notes form a sub-unit of the theme, as do the last three notes. Indeed, in the subsequent development of this theme, Brahms makes separate use of these sub-units. Any other combination does not give the impression of a unit. Neither do the first three notes represent the theme, nor are, for instance, combinations of the second-third-fourth notes or even of the second-third-fourth-fifth notes felt as a unit, a Gestalt. Or, take the well-known four-note theme with which Beethoven's Fifth Symphony starts. Leave out the fourth or any of the preceding notes and you do not have another unit but, instead, no unit at all. (This clearly shows why the terms of Gestalt-psychology cannot be applied uncritically to musical experiences. Each of the themes of our examples, modified as suggested, would still represent an individual "Gestalt", but it would not be considered as a musical theme.) We have, therefore, to ask again: Why is it that we experience some sequences of notes as a thematical unit, other sequences of notes, however, not as such a unit? We just used the term, "articulation", in order to refer to units and sub-units. We have to find out what this term implies.

It implies, certainly, a feeling of virtual finality. If the musical flux stopped here and nothing would happen thereafter, the original impulse has its peculiar meaning, a meaning which might be incomplete, which makes us expect by protention or anticipation an additive which would complete this meaning but which, as a fragment of the whole, has its clear, fragmentary meaning. What we called "virtual" initially corresponds to what James called the "resting places" of thought. According to him, the movements of our stream of consciousness may be compared with the movements of a flying bird.[17] There are phases of flight changing with phases of rest. There is a continuous change between these two types of movement of our thought. The resting places articulate the totality of the bird's movement, they bring the initial phases to an end and a new phase starts thereafter. Compare this Jamesian image with the outcome of Husserl's Fifth Logical Investigation on the theory of pure grammar.[18]

We have to distinguish, Husserl says, between a collection of words which does not give any meaning (although each of these words means something), and the fragments of sentences which convey meaning – although incomplete ones which require a supplement for full precision. The kind of meaning Husserl has in mind refers, of course, to the standarized intersubjective meaning of language as a universe of discourse. But his statements are also applicable to subjective meaning constituted within the stream of insulated consciousness, such as the meaning of a theme. What does meaning in this latter use signify? Meaning is certainly nothing else but the aspect in which past experiences are conceived by the mind which performs in the actual or virtual reflective attitude toward its own experiences. An experience while occurring, that is, while we are living in it, does not have any meaning; only the past experiences toward which we may turn back, are meaningful. However, a certain caution is necessary here.

The use of expressions like "an experience *has* meaning", or "an experience *is* meaningful", suggests that meaning is a predicate or a quality of something called "experience". This is not the case; by internal reason of its grammar, the nature of language suggests a relationship which does not exist. "Meaning" is nothing else but the attitude of the experiencing mind toward its past experiences. Only the past, therefore, is meaningful; the future is only conceived as meaningful if it is conceived in terms of that which will have happened, so to speak, in the past-future tense. All purposes or projects preceding our actions are events fancied to have happened in the future. That past experiences are meaningful for the reflective attitude means that they are felt as belonging to the Now in which this attitude is assumed; it is the insight that these past experiences lead to the Now which would be quite another one if these and those peculiar experiences had not preceded them, and preceded them in this peculiar sequel – each of them having this and that peculiar extension in time and having affected our mind with this peculiar intensity. We now have to ask two questions: 1) What are these experiences which are selected by the

[17]A marginal note to this passage in the manuscript reads, in part, and in translation, "All of this has to be made (formulated), of course, much more precise, and [more] thoroughly elaborated in the places indicated."

[18]I am uncertain about the reference to the Fifth Investigation; the problem is treated in the Fourth Investigation, §§9ff. See also Schutz, *Reflections on the Problem of Relevance*, pp. 110ff.

reflective glance, and what is the principle of selection then prevailing? 2) How is the reflective attitude possible? What are its prerequisites and conditions?

1) The past experiences grasped by a reflective attitude among all other experiences are, of course, either retained or reproduced experiences. But not all experiences which may be retained or reproduced are really retained or reproduced. In other words, it is not our whole past which is made an element of our specious present by the act of reflection. Not all of the past experiences seem to stay in a context with our present, not all of our past experiences seem to have led to this present and have made it what it is. We say that some of the recollected or recollectable experiences may be brought into a unit-context with the actual Now, others may not. Or, to put it otherwise, some are relevant, others are not. The first consequence is that what is relevant depends on the Now in which the reflective turning back is to be performed and that it will change from Now to Now. Therefore, the aspect of the past experiences for the reflective glance, in other words, their meaning, will also change from Now to Now if for no other reason than because other experiences of the past are always brought into the unifying glance of the reflective attitude. Not only the sector of the past selected by this reflective ray changes, but within this sector other configurations or contour lines stand out as relevant, others are in the center, others are brought into the horizon, others enter the field, others disappear from it. Let us compare this reflective attitude with the cone of a moving searchlight which continuously changes the perimeter of its cone as well as the intensity of the source of light. This searchlight moves on, changing the direction, the reach, the intensity of its rays, while other objects and always other objects become visible or fall back into darkness.

But is the comparison correct? Is there any steering in the selecting mechanism of the reflection? Or is the appearance or disappearance of the past quite independent of such a mechanism? Are recollection and that which is recollected imposed upon us, or are they searched for, look for? And, in either case: is this process of a random [pressing][19] haphazardly once this, once that happens, or is relevance itself organized, and if the latter is the case, according to what principles does all this happen?

Only a complete theory of relevance could answer all these questions. Tentatively, the following answer could be given: in selecting what is relevant both principles cooperate. On the one hand, there are recollections imposed upon us; there are the phenomena called "association" by older psychologists, the same phenomena which have to be analyzed under the captions of Sameness, Likeness, Similarity, Types, and phenomena of that kind of contiguity which makes an event simultaneous in time, or coexistent in space with the recollected experience, which comes into our mind quite involuntarily if we try to grasp by reflection this single experience with respect to which the others are quite accidental. It may be that these accidental experiences themselves prove to be relevant with respect to which the others are quite accidental. It may be that these accidental experiences themselves prove to be relevant either with respect to the Now in which the reflection is performed, or secondary to the experience at which the reflective ray is directed. If so, they enter into

[19]The bracketed gloss is a guess at the word in the manuscript, which is badly blurred at this place.

the relevance unity, established or to be established, by the reflective ray. Or, they prove entirely irrelevant for the purpose at hand; they cannot, as in the first case, give the context of meaning another fringe. Then they are rejected as entirely immaterial, and we may even become angry that such unimportant things come to our mind which tries to concentrate upon vital problems.

On the other hand, there is definitely a kind of steering mechanism at work in building up the relevant meaning context of the past experiences grasped by the reflective ray. These phenomena have to be considered under the captions of Attention and Interest. Attention is a function of the interest dominating the Now in which the reflective attitude is performed. This interest itself is constituted by the stock of my previous experiences, my knowledge at hand, by the protentions and anticipations prevailing at this time – not only those related immediately to our activities, such as plans for work, for leisure, for life, and not only related to our prevailing attention for life (the tension of our consciousness if we are dealing with the outer world in full awakeness, or in day-dreaming, or in theoretical or religious contemplation), but also those related to our emotional sphere, such as hopes, fears, remorse. Furthermore, most of the unconscious and subconscious experiences with which psychoanalysis deals legitimately enter here: they are integral determinants for our interest and, therefore, indirectly for our attentional selections of the relevant elements of the past. All this would have to be dealt with by a complete theory of relevance.[20]

2) As to the prerequisites of the reflective attitude, we mentioned before that recollection (and, therefore, retention or reproduction) is essential for performing the reflection. For terminological reasons, we shall distinguish this kind of reproduction, which requires us to stop the flux of consciousness and to turn back to our past experiences, and which we called "recollection", from remembrance; remembrance shall include the stock of our past experiences, itself organized, which we have permanently at hand in the form of knowledge. I know, that is, I remember, that $2 \times 2 = 4$, that forty-eight states form the United States, that the sun rises in the East. Of course, I once had to learn all this; now I know it by having kept in mind what I learned. I remember it, but it is not necessary for me to turn back to the process of my learning by a special act of reflection. I just have my stock of experienced, remembered knowledge at hand. This remembered knowledge is important to the extent that it determines my interest, that it, therefore, determines the selection of the relevant in my past. (To give an example from music, my knowledge of the typical style of a certain musical culture such as the Viennese classics, and within it of an individual composer such as Haydn, governs my anticipation of the further occurrences. If I am listening, say, to a minuet in a Haydn symphony, I am sure that there will be two parts, in some manner affiliated one with the other, that each of these parts will be repeated, that a trio will follow, that, then, the two parts of the minuet will be played again, and so on.) Remembrances of this kind function like a manual of reference which I can open and close at my discretion; they have, as such, nothing to do with what we called recollections.

[20]This task of developing a complete theory of relevance is laid out in detail in *Reflections on the Problem of Relevance*, a manuscript begun just a few years later; see Zaner's Introduction, pp. xiiiff.

We have frequently said that the reflective attitude can only be performed if we stop the flux of our consciousness, and turn to our past. It is now the question whether we can do so at any time, at random, at our discretion, and, nevertheless, still bring the relevant sector of our past into a meaningful context by virtue of the unifying power of our reflective ray. It seems that the answer is in the negative. If we conceive the stream of our consciousness as a series of impulses, as a continuous change between flight and resting places, we can perform such a turning back only at a resting place, at the end of the phase of such an impulse in order to bestow meaning upon our past experiences. If we look at the events of our inner life, we find that we do not at any time "stop and think". We are doing so only if we feel ourselves stopping before the beginning of a new phase, whereas the previous one had ended. By a considerable effort we may, of course, interrupt this natural flux and, so to speak, turn back in the mind to the onrolling wave. But, then, we will try in vain to look at the past experience which led to the Now, as a unit of which this Now is an element. I shall not find a unit, but just pieces, not a Gestalt but incompatible parts. It seems that the reason for this is the following: We have no power to define the limits of our specious present, to draw its border lines over against the past or the future. Our stream of consciousness is itself articulated. Impulses and resting places, periods of tensions and relaxation alternate. Wave follows wave, each wave having its crest and valley. Each of these impulses is experienced as a unit, a movement in inner time which tends to fulfil its final phase as soon as it starts. If we interrupt this development before the impulse comes to an end, if we make this impulse abortive, we cannot grasp our specious present and the relevant sector of our past adherent to it.

All of this will have to be worked out in elaborate analyses which are not immediately connected with the problem of musical experience. However, we had to make these preliminary remarks in order to clear up the problem of the musical theme. Let us now draw some conclusions from what has preceded.

First of all, we have to consider what we called the articulation of the musical flux into unit and sub-units. Any musician knows this problem very well. It has for him the name of musical phrasing. The art of musical phrasing consists in making each unit and sub-unit discernible by bringing together into one single phrase what belongs together, and to separate it from the next phrase by a very short interruption of the flux of music – so short, sometimes, that even no sign of notation is required in order to mark the short pause between the end of the first and the beginning of the next phrase. It is these small fractions of time, incommensurable in our current notation, which the singer or wind instrument player needs for breathing, or the string instrument player needs for changing the stroke of his bow. The composer of our times orders the player by the use of ties or [rubato],[21] or even in special cases by the use of rests, to observe these thematical units and sub-units.

These very short intermittences are the resting places during which the flux of music comes to a standstill. The listener is invited and incited by them to look from

[21]In the manuscript, Schutz has the German word, "Akzentzeichen". It seems to me, however, that "accent" makes little sense here because what he is talking about is more likely a matter of stress than of "time". Thus "rubato" might be closer to what he has in mind. See also "Making Music Together", pp. 166f.

this end-phase back to the initial phase, to return to the beginning still accessible to him by reason of the interplay of retentions analyzed before. Looking back to the initial phase, the listener becomes aware that there was a single impulse going on, that each element of the unit was connected with its predecessors and attracted or, better, brought about its successor; he will conceive, then, the unit or sub-unit as a meaningful context, meaningful within the precise definition given before. The meaning may be incomplete and require a supplementary fulfilment: this will, then, especially be the case if the musical culture of the period to which the listener belongs, or his knowledge of the period to which the composition in question belongs, induces him to make certain anticipations in order to obtain typical completeness not granted by what he actually hears. In such a case, the listener will be in the same situation as the reader of a fragment of a sentence: the words he read make a meaning, but an incomplete one; they may be followed by a comma but not by a period. That is exactly what we understand under a sub-unit. The six-note theme used in §19 as an example is, for our modern ears, at least, such an incomplete sub-unit requiring a conclusion in order to be complete.

This the way in which a theme constitutes itself. Once constituted, it becomes a Gestalt within the meaning of the Gestaltists. As a unity, it can now be recollected as an entity with particular meaning. But his recollection will no longer take place in the form of a retention or a retention of a second degree. It can be, however, recollected by a "reproduction" and recognized when it recurs by immediate or mediate repetition. It will be recognized as the same, or as the same but modified (inverted, enlarged, in another key, etc.). It has become a Gestalt with a specific configuration. As such its sequel will be anticipated as soon as the initial phases have been suggested. Finally, it may become entirely familiar, it will be known in such a way that no recollection will be necessary. It has been remembered and is now at hand.

Just one word in concluding as to the mechanism of this special kind of reflection. The attitude of the listener, his decision to follow the flux of music, involved his preparedness to perform the reflective attitude as soon as the flux of music itself invites him to do so. He does not, therefore, have to change permanently the state of tension of his consciousness. He starts his listening in the expectation that the music he listens to will turn out to be a meaningful context, and this interest determines his attention toward the ongoing music and steers the selective activity of his scheme of relevancies. However, what is relevant is also indicated by the musical structure itself, by the devices applied by the composer in order to evoke the appropriate reactions of the beholder.

One of the most important of these devices, rhythm, we can study later on.[22]

[22]At this point, the manuscript breaks off. See above, note 12.

Index of Names

Index of Subjects

Phaenomenologica

66. D. Cairns: *Conversations with Husserl and Fink.* Edited by the Husserl-Archives in Louvain. With a foreword by R.M. Zaner. 1975 ISBN 90-247-1793-0
67. G. Hoyos Vásquez: *Intentionalität als Verantwortung.* Geschichtsteleologie und Teleologie der Intentionalität bei Husserl. 1976 ISBN 90-247-1794-9
68. J. Patočka: *Le Monde naturel comme problème philosophique.* 1976 ISBN 90-247-1795-7
69. W.W. Fuchs: *Phenomenology and the Metaphysics of Presence.* An Essay in the Philosophy of Edmund Husserl. 1976 ISBN 90-247-1822-8
70. S. Cunningham: *Language and the Phenomenological Reductions of Edmund Husserl.* 1976 ISBN 90-247-1823-6
71. G.C. Moneta: *On Identity.* A Study in Genetic Phenomenology. 1976 ISBN 90-247-1860-0
72. W. Biemel und das Husserl-Archiv zu Löwen (eds.): *Die Welt des Menschen - Die Welt der Philosophie.* Festschrift für Jan Patočka. 1976 ISBN 90-247-1899-6
73. M. Richir: *Au-delà du renversement copernicien.* La question de la phénoménologie et son fondement. 1976 ISBN 90-247-1903-8
74. H. Mongis: *Heidegger et la critique de la notion de valeur.* La destruction de la fondation métaphysique. Lettre-préface de Martin Heidegger. 1976 ISBN 90-247-1904-6
75. J. Taminiaux: *Le regard et l'excédent.* 1977 ISBN 90-247-2028-1
76. Th. de Boer: *The Development of Husserl's Thought.* 1978 ISBN Hb: 90-247-2039-7; Pb: 90-247-2124-5
77. R.R. Cox: *Schutz's Theory of Relevance.* A Phenomenological Critique. 1978 ISBN 90-247-2041-9
78. S. Strasser: *Jenseits von Sein und Zeit.* Eine Einführung in Emmanuel Levinas' Philosophie. 1978 ISBN 90-247-2068-0
79. R.T. Murphy: *Hume and Husserl.* Towards Radical Subjectivism. 1980 ISBN 90-247-2172-5
80. H. Spiegelberg: *The Context of the Phenomenological Movement.* 1981 ISBN 90-247-2392-2
81. J.R. Mensch: *The Question of Being in Husserl's* Logical Investigations. 1981 ISBN 90-247-2413-9
82. J. Loscerbo: *Being and Technology.* A Study in the Philsophy of Martin Heidegger. 1981 ISBN 90-247-2411-2
83. R. Boehm: *Vom Gesichtspunkt der Phänomenologie II.* Studien zur Phänomenologie der Epoché. 1981 ISBN 90-247-2415-5
84. H. Spiegelberg and E. Avé-Lallemant (eds.): *Pfänder-Studien.* 1982 ISBN 90-247-2490-2
85. S. Valdinoci: *Les fondements de la phénoménologie husserlienne.* 1982 ISBN 90-247-2504-6
86. I. Yamaguchi: *Passive Synthesis und Intersubjektivität bei Edmund Husserl.* 1982 ISBN 90-247-2505-4
87. J. Libertson: *Proximity.* Levinas, Blanchot, Bataille and Communication. 1982 ISBN 90-247-2506-2

Phaenomenologica

88. D. Welton: *The Origins of Meaning.* A Critical Study of the Thresholds of Husserlian Phenomenology. 1983 ISBN 90-247-2618-2
89. W.R. McKenna: *Husserl's 'Introductions to Phenomenology'.* Interpretation and Critique. 1982 ISBN 90-247-2665-4
90. J.P. Miller: *Numbers in Presence and Absence.* A Study of Husserl's Philosophy of Mathematics. 1982 ISBN 90-247-2709-X
91. U. Melle: *Das Wahrnehmungsproblem und seine Verwandlung in phänomenologischer Einstellung.* Untersuchungen zu den phänomenologischen Wahrnehmungstheorien von Husserl, Gurwitsch und Merleau-Ponty. 1983 ISBN 90-247-2761-8
92. W.S. Hamrick (ed.): *Phenomenology in Practice and Theory.* Essays for Herbert Spiegelberg. 1984 ISBN 90-247-2926-2
93. H. Reiner: *Duty and Inclination.* The Fundamentals of Morality Discussed and Redefined with Special Regard to Kant and Schiller. 1983 ISBN 90-247-2818-6
94. M. J. Harney: *Intentionality, Sense and the Mind.* 1984 ISBN 90-247-2891-6
95. Kah Kyung Cho (ed.): *Philosophy and Science in Phenomenological Perspective.* 1984 ISBN 90-247-2922-X
96. A. Lingis: *Phenomenological Explanations.* 1986 ISBN Hb: 90-247-3332-4; Pb: 90-247-3333-2
97. N. Rotenstreich: *Reflection and Action.* 1985 ISBN Hb: 90-247-2969-6; Pb: 90-247-3128-3
98. J.N. Mohanty: *The Possibility of Transcendental Philosophy.* 1985 ISBN Hb: 90-247-2991-2; Pb: 90-247-3146-1
99. J.J. Kockelmans: *Heidegger on Art and Art Works.* 1985 ISBN 90-247-3102-X
100. E. Lévinas: *Collected Philosophical Papers.* 1987 ISBN Hb: 90-247-3272-7; Pb: 90-247-3395-2
101. R. Regvald: *Heidegger et le Problème du Néant.* 1986 ISBN 90-247-3388-X
102. J.A. Barash: *Martin Heidegger and the Problem of Historical Meaning.* 1987 ISBN 90-247-3493-2
103 J.J. Kockelmans (ed.): *Phenomenological Psychology.* The Dutch School. 1987 ISBN 90-247-3501-7
104. W.S. Hamrick: *An Existential Phenomenology of Law: Maurice Merleau-Ponty.* 1987 ISBN 90-247-3520-3
105. J.C. Sallis, G. Moneta and J. Taminiaux (eds.): *The Collegium Phaenomenologium. The First Ten Years.* 1988 ISBN 90-247-3709-5
106. D. Carr: *Interpreting Husserl.* Critical and Comparative Studies. 1987. ISBN 90-247-3505-X
107. G. Heffernan: *Isagoge in die phänomenologische Apophantik.* Eine Einführung in die phänomenologische Urteilslogik durch die Auslegung des Textes der *Formalen und transzendenten Logik* von Edmund Husserl. 1989 ISBN 90-247-3710-9
108. F. Volpi, J.-F. Mattéi, Th. Sheenan, J.-F. Courtine, J. Taminiaux, J. Sallis, D. Janicaud, A.L. Kelkel, R. Bernet, R. Brisart, K. Held, M. Haar et S. IJsseling: *Heidegger et l'Idée de la Phénoménologie.* 1988 ISBN 90-247-3586-6
109. C. Singevin: *Dramaturgie de l'Esprit.* 1988 ISBN 90-247-3557-2

Phaenomenologica

110. J. Patočka: *Le monde naturel et le mouvement de l'existence humaine*. 1988 ISBN 90-247-3577-7
111. K.-H. Lembeck: *Gegenstand Geschichte*. Geschichtswissenschaft in Husserls Phänomenologie. 1988 ISBN 90-247-3635-8
112. J.K. Cooper-Wiele: *The Totalizing Act*. Key to Husserl's Early Philosophy. 1989 ISBN 0-7923-0077-7
113. S. Valdinoci: *Le principe d'existence*. Un devenir psychiatrique de la phénoménologie. 1989 ISBN 0-7923-0125-0
114. D. Lohmar: *Phänomenologie der Mathematik*. 1989 ISBN 0-7923-0187-0
115. S. IJsseling (Hrsgb.): *Husserl-Ausgabe und Husserl-Forschung*. 1990 ISBN 0-7923-0372-5
116. R. Cobb-Stevens: *Husserl and Analytic Philosophy*. 1990 ISBN 0-7923-0467-5
117. R. Klockenbusch: *Husserl und Cohn*. Widerspruch, Reflexion und Telos in Phänomenologie und Dialektik. 1989 ISBN 0-7923-0515-9
118. S. Vaitkus: *How is Society Possible?* Intersubjectivity and the Fiduciary Attitude as Problems of the Social Group in Mead, Gurwitsch, and Schutz. 1991 ISBN 0-7923-0820-4
119. C. Macann: *Presence and Coincidence*. The Transformation of Transcendental into Ontological Phenomenology. 1991 ISBN 0-7923-0923-5
120. G. Shpet: *Appearance and Sense*. Phenomenology as the Fundamental Science and Its Problems. Translated from Russian by Th. Nemeth. 1991 ISBN 0-7923-1098-5
121. B. Stevens: *L'Apprentissage des Signes*. Lecture de Paul Ricœur. 1991 ISBN 0-7923-1244-9
122. G. Soffer: *Husserl and the Question of Relativism*. 1991 ISBN 0-7923-1291-0
123. G. Römpp: *Husserls Phänomenologie der Intersubjektivität*. Und Ihre Bedeutung für eine Theorie intersubjektiver Objektivität und die Konzeption einer phänomenologischen. 1991 ISBN 0-7923-1361-5
124. S. Strasser: *Welt im Widerspruch*. Gedanken zu einer Phänomenologie als ethischer Fundamentalphilosophie. 1991 ISBN Hb: 0-7923-1404-2; Pb: 0-7923-1551-0
125. R. P. Buckley: *Husserl, Heidegger and the Crisis of Philosophical Responsibility*. 1992 ISBN 0-7923-1633-9
126. J. G. Hart: *The Person and the Common Life*. Studies in a Husserlian Social Ethics. 1992 ISBN 0-7923-1724-6
127. P. van Tongeren, P. Sars, C. Bremmers and K. Boey (eds.): *Eros and Eris*. Contributions to a Hermeneutical Phenomenology. Liber Amicorum for Adriaan Peperzak. 1992 ISBN 0-7923-1917-6
128. Nam-In Lee: *Edmund Husserls Phänomenologie der Instinkte*. 1993 ISBN 0-7923-2041-7
129. P. Burke and J. Van der Veken (eds.): *Merleau-Ponty in Contemporary Perspective*. 1993 ISBN 0-7923-2142-1
130. G. Haefliger: *Über Existenz: Die Ontologie Roman Ingardens*. 1994 ISBN 0-7923-2227-4
131. J. Lampert: *Synthesis and Backward Reference in Husserl's* Logical Investigations. 1995 ISBN 0-7923-3105-2
132. J.M. DuBois: *Judgment and Sachverhalt*. An Introduction to Adolf Reinach's Phenomenological Realism. 1995 ISBN 0-7923-3519-8

Phaenomenologica

133. B.E. Babich (ed.): *From Phenomenology to Thought, Errancy, and Desire.* Essays in Honor of William J. Richardson, S.J. 1995 ISBN 0-7923-3567-8; Pb 0-7923-3568-6
134. M. Dupuis: *Pronoms et Visages Lecture D'Emmanuel Levinas.* 1996 ISBN 0-7923-3655-0
135. D. Zahavi: *Husserl und die transzendentale Intersubjektivität.* Eine Antwort auf die sprachpragmatische Kritik. 1996 ISBN 0-7923-3713-1
136. A. Schutz: edited with preface and notes by H. Wagner and G. Psathas. In collaboration with F. Kersten: *Collected Papers.* Volume IV. 1996 ISBN 0-7923-3760-3
137. P. Kontos: *D'une Phénoménologie de la Perception chez Heidegger.* 1996 ISBN 0-7923-3776-X
138. F. Kuster: *Wege der Verantwortung.* Husserl Phänomenologie als Gang durch die Faktizität. 1996 ISBN 0-7923-3916-9

Previous volumes are still available

Further information about *Phenomenology* publications are available on request.

Kluwer Academic Publishers – Dordrecht / Boston / London